Making Adjustments

Making Adjustments:
Change and Continuity in Planter Nova Scotia, 1759-1800

Edited by
Margaret Conrad

Acadiensis Press
Fredericton, New Brunswick

1991

Canadian Cataloguing in Publication Data

Making adjustments

Proceedings of the Planter Studies Conference sponsored by the Planter Studies Committee and held at Acadia University in October 1990.
Includes bibliographical references.
ISBN 0-919107-33-8

1. New Englanders — Nova Scotia — History — Congresses.
2. Nova Scotia — History — To 1784 — Congresses.*
I. Conrad, Margaret.
II. Acadia University. Planter Studies Committee.
III. Planter Studies Conference (1990: Acadia University)

FC2321.25.M35 1990   971.6'00413   C91-097629-5
F1038.M35 1990

COVER: Illustrations from "Mary Miller Her Book," Courtesy of the Colchester Historical Museum, Truro, Nova Scotia. Design by Julie Scriver.

MAKING ADJUSTMENTS:
CHANGE AND CONTINUITY IN PLANTER NOVA SCOTIA, 1759-1800
Edited by Margaret Conrad

EXPLORATIONS

FUTURE DIRECTIONS

ACKNOWLEDGEMENTS

As is usually the case when publishing conference proceedings, the editor is indebted to many people for their assistance. Marjorie Baird and Brenda Naugler (the latter funded by one of those invaluable SEED grants) spent many hours entering and correcting manuscripts. They undoubtedly know more about footnote formats than most lucky mortals. Barry Moody offered editorial advice on a number of manuscripts, and tolerated my advice on his own. Doug Baldwin cheerfully pitched in when heavily leaned upon, and Pat Townsend in the Acadia University Archives pursued obscure references. Contributors to this volume were more capable of sticking to deadlines than I proved to be. When I insisted on delaying publication so that I could secure ''the right'' illustration for the cover, our publisher, Phillip Buckner, demonstrated remarkable patience. Nan Harvey at the Colchester Historical Museum was wonderfully efficient in getting copies of illustrations from Mary Miller's singing book and I am very grateful to her. Ultimately, this book was made possible by those who helped to fund the Planter Nova Scotia Conference, including the Occasional Conference Jury of the Social Sciences and Humanities Research Council, the Canadian Parks Service, the Government of Nova Scotia and Acadia University.

As for the errors in spelling and inconsistencies in footnote format, I blame them all on WordPerfect's spell check and the authors. Where was Esther Clark Wright — she of the saying ''Hang on to your spelling'' — when I needed her?

Margaret Conrad

Introduction

In October 1990 the Second Planter Studies Conference, sponsored by the Planter Studies Centre of Acadia University, was held in Wolfville. The registration of over 150 people was even larger than that for the first Planter conference held three years earlier, and the programme was equally interesting and varied. *Making Adjustments* is a selection of the papers from the 1990 conference which focused on New England Planters in the wider Nova Scotia and international contexts of the second half of the eighteenth century. I hasten to add that the title of the conference — "Planter Nova Scotia, 1759-1800" — was meant to be an inclusive one and not an imperialist attempt by conference organizers to lay exclusive claim to this period for the Planters.

As the articles in this collection indicate, the topic was a fruitful one. The range of papers presented at the three-day conference left most participants with a daunting sense of the complexity of Nova Scotia society in the eighteenth century and an appreciation for the fact that the Planters and other Nova Scotians, not unlike ourselves today, were faced with what John Reid in this volume describes as "a profound societal realignment." "What was taking place continuously," Professor Reid maintains, "was the devising of collective strategies by peoples who had seen their lives profoundly changed by the geopolitical events of the 1750s and early 1760s and who now had to adapt as best they could to the political and environmental contexts that were unfamiliar to them." In short, everyone, whether Native or newcomer, slave or free, was forced to make adjustments to the new realities shaking the foundations of the late eighteenth-century North Atlantic world.

The first section of this volume, "Contexts," includes articles by four intrepid individuals who tackle some of the big questions facing eighteenth-century scholars. On the opening evening of the conference, Dr. E. Jennifer Monaghan, Department of Educational Services, Brooklyn College, City University of New York, inaugurated the Esther Clark Wright Lecture Series on Eighteenth-Century North Atlantic Culture and Society with a discussion of historiographical developments in the history of literacy. Dr. Monaghan opens a whole new field for Planter scholars, and her postscript in the article published here even offers hypotheses on Planter literacy rates based on New England findings. John Reid's article allows us to stand back from particular events to survey the general trends of the period. His call for a more comparative approach — taking into account contemporary developments in Florida and Louisiana as well as New England and Nova Scotia, and looking at the experiences of Natives, Blacks and Acadians, as well as British Americans — set the tone for the conference and offers a rationale for many of the papers published here. Julian Gwyn's study brings insights from recent research in economic history to bear on Nova Scotia, while Donald Desserud explores in some detail the ideological framework that informed Nova Scotians in the age of the American Revolution. Both papers break new ground in our understanding of eighteenth-century Nova Scotia.

The next five articles focus on the diversity of cultural experiences in Planter Nova Scotia. As Bill Wicken and Gary Hartlen reveal, making adjustments had different meanings for Mi'kmaq and slave than it did for white settlers in the British colony. Whites with minority cultures also found their moorings shifting. The Quakers, Allen Robertson tells us, failed to maintain their distinctive religious customs beyond the mid-nineteenth century, whereas first generation Germans in Nova Scotia, according to Deborah Trask, left few distinctive gravestone markers as a document to their unique language and culture. Carol Campbell suggests that the Scots-Irish seem to have been successful, at least for a time, in maintaining their community identity, but they, too, gradually became less obvious in the Nova Scotia cultural mosaic.

Several case studies offer new insights into the Planter period of Nova Scotia history. By looking at land transactions and inheritance patterns in Granville Township, Barry Moody raises questions about how land was used by the Planters. Richard Field challenges previously-held assumptions about Planter housing styles by analyzing the probate records of first generation Planters. The peregrinations of John Seccombe, described by Gwendolyn Davies, suggests that there is much to be learned by looking at the lives of Planters before and after they came to Nova Scotia. If John Bubar's family is any indication, mobility and occupational continuity are themes that warrant further scrutiny. All four of these papers attest to the value of family history and genealogical research in adding flesh to the bare bones of historical analysis.

The final section of this volume explores a variety of topics that offer exciting avenues for further research. By focusing on government activities relating to mapping the Planter townships, Joan Dawson highlights the traditional assumptions underlying official settlement plans and suggests how these may have been undermined at the local level. Marc Lavoie reminds us of the value of archaeology in helping us to understand Planter material culture, a field only beginning to be cultivated. In exploring the image and function of women in early Maritime poetry, Thomas Vincent opens a window on the emotional and imaginative world inhabited by the Planters, a fascinating world that needs further exploration. Nancy Vogan's discovery of Mary Miller's singing book in the Colchester Historical Museum's holdings enables her to provide a tantalizing glimpse into the musical culture of Planter Nova Scotia. Although readers of this volume cannot hear the voices of the choir that demonstrated Mary Miller's music at the conference, Professor Vogan's article conveys some of the exciting possibilities of eighteenth-century cultural studies. Finally, Brian Cuthbertson brings the Planters into the nineteenth century — a development strongly urged by many Planter Studiers — by exploring voting patterns in Planter townships. His conclusion suggests that Planters did not have a homogeneous political identity, thereby underscoring the diversity which seems to be a central feature of the Planter legacy to Nova Scotia.

On Sunday morning six conference participants from a variety of interests and disciplines reflected on the conference and suggested future directions for Planter

Studies. Their presentations are published here, as is the spontaneous response of George Rawlyk, Professor of History at Queen's University, who was proclaimed a Planter Scholar at the banquet on Saturday night. As Professor Rawlyk indicates, there was not always as much interest in the history of eighteenth-century Nova Scotia as there is today. Of course, much of the credit for this new enthusiasm must go to Professor Rawlyk.

Interest in eighteenth-century Nova Scotia in general, and in the New England Planters in particular, has grown remarkably over the past decade, guaranteeing an ever larger constituency for the work of Acadia University's Planter Studies Centre. As the comments in ''Future Directions'' suggest, there is still no consensus on our immediate task — do we need more spade work or is it time for a new synthesis? should we focus on the eighteenth century or move on to the nineteenth? can the Planters be best understood by looking at them in a Maritime-New England context or do we need a broader comparative base? The more we learn about Planter Nova Scotia the more questions are raised. Controversies abound. For instance, Richard Field asserts in this volume that the claim that Planters constructed their houses on Acadian cellars, is ''a romantic notion, based more on speculation and wishful thinking than on fact.'' Marc Lavoie, using archaeological evidence, suggests that, at least in certain areas of the old province of Nova Scotia, Acadian sites were indeed used by their successors. Some scholars see the Planters as relatively affluent and highly fortunate immigrants; others point to their poverty and lack of material possessions. While some research is conducted on the assumption that the Planters were a reasonably cohesive settlement group, other research has highlighted the Planter diversity.

Despite such differences, there are issues upon which we all seem to agree. It is widely conceded that the multidisciplinary approach to Planter Studies advances us in our individual disciplines and may eventually lead to exciting interdisciplinary endeavours. Similarly, the larger cultural and comparative context seems to be a more rewarding avenue for research than one that focuses narrowly on the Planters themselves. Finally, the participation of the general public, drawn largely from interested Planter descendants, brings an especially vital thrust to all that we do.

In the near future Planter Studies research will be aided by *A Bibliography of Primary Sources: New England Planters in the Maritime Provinces, 1759-1800* compiled by Judith A. Norton for the Planter Studies Centre. It contains over 3000 entries gleaned from archives, museums and libraries in the Maritimes and New England. A computerized version is up and running at the Centre and will also be available to scholars in 1992.

MARGARET CONRAD
July 1991

Literacy in Eighteenth-Century New England: Some Historiographical Reflections on Issues of Gender

E. Jennifer Monaghan[1]
Department of Educational Services
Brooklyn College, City University of New York

Excerpt from Dixon's *The Youth's Instructor in the English Tongue* (1767):

> A Boy that once to School was sent,
> On Play and Toys was so much bent,
> That all the Art of Man, they say,
> Could not once make him say great A.
> His friends that saw him in these Fits,
> Cry'd out, for shame, leave off thy Tricks;
> Be not so dull; make it thy Play
> To Learn thy Book; come say great A.
> The Dunce then gap'd, but did no more.
> Great A was yet a great Eye Sore.
> The next Boys jog him; sure say they
> 'Tis not so hard to cry great A.
> No, no, but here's the Case, says he,
> If I cry A, I must cry B,
> And so go on to C, and D,
> And that won't do, but still there's Jod
> Lurks in the Way with X, Y, Zod.
> And so no End I find there'll be,
> If I once learn A, B, C.
> But as Things stand I will not do it,
> Tho' Sure I am one Day to Rue it.[2]

Excerpt from Thomas Tickell, *A Poem in Praise of the Horn-Book* (1728):

> *Thy Heavenly Notes* like Angels musick cheer
> Departing Souls, and sooth the dying Ear.
> An Aged Peasant, on his latest Bed,

---

1   For the bibliographical notes that follow, I wish to acknowledge the assistance of an unpublished paper by R.P. McDermott, ''A Bibliography of Literacies (with special attention to scripts not based on the Roman alphabet and to their use in traditional societies),'' Teachers College, Columbia University, 1987. I would also like to thank Leila F. Monaghan for anthropological references.

2   *The Youth's Instructor in the English Tongue: Or, The Art of Spelling Improved ... Collected from Dixon, Bailey, Watts, Owen, and Strong* (Boston, 1767), 20-21. The schoolmaster ponders on a cure: there is a tree that grows in a wood ..., Of course it's the birch, and the moral (in the prose version) runs: ''He that will not learn by fair Means, must be whipt.''

Wish'd for a Friend some godly Book to read.
The pious Grandson, *thy* known *Handle* takes,
And (Eyes lift up,) this sav'ry Lecture makes.
Great A, he gravely roar'd, th' important Sound
The empty Walls and hollow Roof rebound:
Th' expiring Ancient rear'd his drooping Head,
And thank'd his Stars that *Hodge* had learn'd to read;
Great B, the Yonker bawls: O heavenly Breath!
What Ghostly Comforts in the Hour of Death!
What Hopes I feel! *Great C,* pronounc'd the Boy;
The Grandsire dyes with Ecstacy of Joy.[3]

Literacy — the focus of much attention in the eighteenth century, as these poems suggest — is a very popular topic today. In the last five or six years alone, we have been treated to books on literacy in ancient Greece and Rome, on the relationship between identity and literacy in Scotland in the seventeenth and eighteenth centuries; between books and the common man in eighteenth- and nineteenth-century Ulster; and between literacy and popular literature in prerevolutionary Russia.[4] Works on literacy span the whole chronological range, from ancient writing in the third millennium B.C. through literacy in the late Middle Ages to discussions about the legacies of literacy and to — often gloomy — speculations about the future of literacy in a changing world. Technological inventions like the printing press and the computer all fall within the purview of the student of literacy.[5]

---

3   Thomas Tickell, *A Poem in Praise of the Horn-Book* (Dublin, 1728), reproduced in Andrew W. Tuer, *History of the Horn Book* (1897; rpt. New York, 1979), 228. This mock-heroic poem is supposedly written during an attack of gout, and the hornbook is apostrophized throughout for its healing powers. One of its many virtues is said to be its ability to offer the spiritual solace of literature at life's last moments. Here, the role of the hornbook as the cradle of learning is pushed to absurd limits, as is the equation of oral spelling with reading.

4   William V. Harris, *Ancient Literacy* (Cambridge, Mass., 1989) and Tony M. Lentz, *Orality and Literacy in Hellenic Greece* (Carbondale, 1989); R.A. Houston, *Scottish Literacy and the Scottish Identity: Illiteracy and Society in Scotland and Northern England, 1600-1800* (New York, 1985); J.R.R. Adams, *The Printed Word and the Common Man: Popular Culture in Ulster, 1700-1900* (Belfast, 1987); Jeffrey Brooks, *When Russia Learned to Read: Literacy and Popular Literature, 1861-1917* (Princeton, N.J., 1985).

5   J.T. Hooker, introd., *Reading the Past: Ancient Writing from Cuneiform to the Alphabet* (Berkeley, Cal., 1990); Jo Ann Hoeppner Moran, *The Growth of English Schooling, 1340-1548: Learning, Literacy, and Laicization in Pre-Reformation York Diocese* (Princeton, N.J., 1985); Harvey J. Graff, *The Legacies of Literacy: Continuities and Contradictions in Western Culture and Society* (Bloomington, 1987); Daniel A. Wagner, ed., *The Future of Literacy in a Changing World* (New York, 1987); Elisabeth Eisenstein, *The Printing Press as Agent of Change*, 2 Vols. (New York, 1979); Peg Griffen and Michael Cole, "New Technologies, Basic Skills, and the Underside of Education: What's To Be Done?" in Judith A. Langer, ed., *Language, Literacy and Culture: Issues of Society and Schooling* (Norwood, N.J., 1987).

Ideology and Literacy

There are good reasons why literacy is in the spotlight today: literacy is an article of faith in a democratic society. We take it for granted that being illiterate means more than just suffering from some personal disadvantage or diminished employment opportunities: illiterates threaten the stability of the Republic because an enlightened citizenry is believed to be the backbone of a democracy. No one is going to convince us that the citizenry can obtain its enlightenment solely from television: it must come from newspapers, magazines and books as well.

The United States has been particularly concerned about illiteracy. The low literacy levels of young American adults have been called "The Subtle Danger," while poor performances on literacy measures are among those features that are said to have made the United States "A Nation at Risk." In an effort to come to terms with this impending national disaster, the United States National Academy of Education established a commission, whose report was published in 1984 under the title *Becoming a Nation of Readers*. Clearly, Americans are not assumed to be a nation of readers already. Moreover, even if we do read, we are susceptible to the charge that we are culturally illiterate.[6]

Nor is the concept that literacy matters on a national scale peculiar to one country or one time period, nor indeed is it unique to democracies; on the contrary, as a volume edited by Robert Arnove and Harvey Graff has documented, there has been a host of national campaigns, over a period of some four hundred years, to raise literacy levels in countries as diverse in time and place as Scotland in the sixteenth century and Nicaragua in 1980.[7] The emphasis on literacy as a national jewel, and illiteracy as a national peril, is a reflection of societal needs. Arnove and Graff have argued that nationwide efforts are not a function of urbanization, industrialization or democratization, but rather are related to the desire of some centralizing authority to "establish a moral or political consensus" or, over the past two centuries, to foster nation-building.[8]

In this context, of the two sides of the literacy coin, it is reading, not writing — in the United States and elsewhere — that has born the brunt of nations' eagerness to improve their literacy performance. At the national level, the United States has sponsored a Right to Read Program. At the international level, there has been the Year of the Reader, and recently the United Nations declared that we were having the Year of the Young Reader. None of this enthusiasm for reading has

---

6   Richard L. Venezky, Carl F. Kaestle, Andrew M. Sum, *The Subtle Danger: Reflections on the Literacy Abilities of America's Young Adults* (Princeton, N.J., 1987); National Commission on Excellence in Education, *A Nation at Risk: The Imperative for Educational Reform* (Washington, D.C., 1983); Richard C. Anderson, Elfrieda H. Hiebert, Judith A. Scott, Ian A.G. Wilkinson, *Becoming a Nation of Readers: The Report of the Commission on Reading* (Washington, D.C., 1984); E. D. Hirsch, Jr., *Cultural Literacy: What Every American Needs to Know* (Boston, 1987).

7   Robert F. Arnove and Harvey J. Graff, eds., *National Literacy Campaigns: Historical and Comparative Perspectives* (New York, 1987).

8   *Ibid.*, 2; cf. Graff, *Legacies of Literacy*.

been matched by a comparable enthusiasm for writing. There has never, to my knowledge, been a Right to Write Program, a Year of the Writer, or a Year of the Young Writer, let alone a United States Commission on Writing. The closest we have come to acknowledging the importance of writing is the United Nations' declaration of an International Literacy Year.

Of the many reasons why reading acquisition has, historically, received more attention than writing acquisition, the most potent has been that reading instruction is the better vehicle of the two for transmitting societal values.[9] Historically, we have been much more interested in having children listen to what we say (by insisting that they read certain books) than in listening to what children have to say (by reading what they have written).

Textbooks designed to teach reading, in particular, have been used by successive cultures to convey important messages to learners, whether they be children or adults. One of the first words taught in the primer created for the 1980 Nicaraguan literacy campaign was *la revolución* — a brilliant choice at every level, pedagogical as well as political, as *la revolución* contains all the five vowels of the Spanish alphabet. In early New England, as David Watters has shown, the alphabet verses of the *New England Primer* (a colonial American bestseller) moved a child through every step of Christian belief. The verse for the letter *A* portrays the original act of disobedience in which all shared: "In Adam's Fall/ We Sinned all"; but the very next letter immediately introduced the child to reading as a means of salvation: alongside a picture of an open Bible is the verse, "Thy Life to Mend/ This Book Attend."[10] The crucial connection between reading, religion and salvation in New England had been established for children by the time they reached the letter *B*.

Whether or not we agree with Arnove and Graff that cultures have, over the centuries, been using reading instruction for their own controlling ends, the individual has remained keenly aware of the potentially liberating possibilities of being able to read and write. The classic example is the slave Frederick Douglass, who learned from his master (outraged by his discovery that his wife had been teaching Douglass) that to teach a slave to read "would forever unfit him to be a slave." Deprived of his mistress's instruction, Douglass successfully continued his quest for liberation through literacy on his own. Paulo Freire, while castigating conventional education as an exercise in domination, has also argued that literacy, when taught as a dialogue between teacher and student, can analyze a

---

9   E. Jennifer Monaghan and E. Wendy Saul, "The Reader, the Scribe, the Thinker: A Critical Look at the History of American Reading and Writing Instruction," in Thomas S. Popkewitz, ed., *The Formation of School Subjects: The Struggle for Creating an American Institution* (Philadelphia, 1987), 91-92.

10   Robert F. Arnove, "The 1980 Nicaraguan National Literacy Crusade," in Arnove and Graff, *National Literacy Campaigns*, 275; David H. Watters, " 'I Spake as a Child': Authority, Metaphor and *The New-England Primer*," *Early American Literature*, 20 (1985-86), 193-213, ill. 198. See also Richard L. Venezky, "A History of the American Reading Textbook," *Elementary School Journal*, 87 (1987), 247-65.

"dehumanizing reality" in order to transform it, "in the name of the liberation of man."[11]

The "liberating versus controlling" aspect of literacy is only one of the topics on which scholars have been unable to agree. They agree least of all on who "owns" literacy as a professional subject. Although few historians would venture opinions on aspects of quantum physics, or a quantum physicist on the Seven Years' War, a large number of scholars from a wide variety of disciplines have felt free to opine on the topic of literacy — presumably banking cn the fact that they can plausibly offer an opinion because they are so literate themselves.

Four groups of professionals in particular have regarded literacy as part of their bailiwick. The first in numbers, if in no other way, is, of course, the reading profession, represented by the International Reading Association (IRA) with a membership of over 90,000, most of whom are elementary classroom teachers. For writing, the National Council of Teachers of English (NCTE) is the professional counterpart to the IRA; significantly, in terms of our earlier discussion, the NCTE does not include the term "writing" in its title, but merely subsumes writing under the larger rubric of English literature. Another group with plenty of excuse to put in their tuppence-worth are the linguists. They have focused on such features as the structure of the orthographic system or the uses to which literacy is put as viewed from a sociolinguistic perspective.[12] A third group are the anthropologists, who have talked, like Shirley Brice Heath, about the different meanings that literacy holds for different groups, or discussed, as does Judith Langer, literacy as a "culturally-based *way of thinking*," or have reminded us, as does Brian Street, that literacy skills are "encapsulated within cultural wholes and within structures of power." In general, anthropologists have focused upon the nuances of social context — upon how literacy functions in different milieux in our own and other cultures.[13] Fourth and last (if we ignore folks like the psychologists and literary theorists, both of whom have some excuse for voicing their

---

11   Frederick Douglass, *Narrative of the Life of Frederick Douglass* (New York, 1968), 49; Paulo Freire, *Pedagogy of the Oppressed* (New York, 1970); Paulo Freire, "The Adult Literacy Process as Cultural Action for Freedom," *Harvard Educational Review*, 40 (1970), 205-23.

12   See, for example, Richard L. Venezky, *The Structure of English Orthography* (The Hague, 1970); Michael Stubbs, *Language and Literacy: The Sociolinguistics of Reading and Writing* (Boston, 1980).

13   Shirley Brice Heath, "The Functions and Uses of Literacy," in Suzanne de Castell, Allan Luke, Kieran Egan, eds., *Literacy, Society and Schooling: A Reader* (Cambridge, 1986), 25; Shirley Brice Heath, "What No Bedtime Story Means: Narrative Skills at Home and School," in Bambi Schieffelin and Elinor Ochs, eds., *Language Socialization Across Cultures* (Cambridge, 1986); Judith A. Langer, "A Sociocognitive Perspective on Literacy," in Langer, *Language, Literacy and Culture*, 17; Brian V. Street, "Literacy and Social Change: The Significance of Social Context in the Development of Literacy Programmes," in Wagner, *Future of Literacy*, 50; Alessandro Duranti and Elinor Ochs, "Literacy Instruction in a Samoan Village," in Bambi B. Schieffelin and Elinor Ochs eds., *Acquisition of Literacy: Ethnographic Perspectives* (Norwood, N.J., 1985).

opinions), there are the historians, the subject of this paper.[14]

Opinions of scholars from all these disciplines have not been slow in being proffered. The central debate is over how much literacy matters. The conventional view (held, for instance, as an official opinion by the International Reading Association) is that literacy is a Good Thing. This conventional view is in essence supported by scholars like Jack Goody, who believes that the development of writing has been the key to both organizational and cognitive change. He claims that writing has had a major influence on social organization and has also led to new forms of more "objective" knowledge because it encourages abstraction and logical thinking. An opposing view (if I may greatly oversimplify) is held by several scholars. Among anthropologists, Sylvia Scribner and Michael Cole found, in a much-cited study, that for the Vai people of Liberia literacy was not associated with higher-order intellectual skills. For historians, the revisionists have been led by Harvey Graff, who attacks "the ideological interpretation of literacy's intimate connection with North American enlightenment, modernization, politicization, and mobilization." The view of Graff and other scholars is that literacy was and is not a determining factor in effecting social change, and we should, accordingly, reduce our expectations about its significance. Graff, in fact, titled his study of literacy and illiteracy in nineteenth-century Toronto *The Literacy Myth*.[15]

There are lesser debates. One is over whether or not there is a great gulf between literacy and orality. Walter Ong has argued that there is, while others point to the central role of oral reading in early cultures, including that of New England, and insist that print penetrated deeply even among the illiterate. Even for our own times, several scholars castigate the notion of a "great divide" between orality and literacy and suggest an oral/literate continuum.[16]

14   For an example of a multidisciplinary look at literacy which includes the perspectives of psychologists and literary theorists, see Langer, *Language, Literacy and Culture*.

15   Jack Goody, *The Logic of Writing and the Organization of Society* Cambridge, 1986; Jack Goody, *The Domestication of the Savage Mind* (Cambridge, 1977); Sylvia Scribner and Michael Cole, *The Psychology of Literacy* (Cambridge, Mass., 1981); Harvey J. Graff, "Literacy and Social Development in North America: On Ideology and History," in W.B. Stephens, ed., *Studies in the History of Literacy: England and North America* (Leeds, 1983), 89; Harvey J. Graff, *The Literacy Myth: Literacy and Social Structure in the Nineteenth-Century City* (New York, 1979). In a similar vein to Graff's, see R.A. Houston, *Literacy in Early Modern Europe: Culture and Education, 1500-1800* (New York, 1988), vii, 232-33; Shirley Brice Heath, forward to Harvey J. Graff, *The Labyrinths of Literacy: Reflections on Literacy Past and Present* (New York, 1987), ix. Heath cites others supporting this revisionist view: Scribner and Cole, *Psychology of Literacy*, and Brian Street, *Literacy, Theory and Practice* (Cambridge, 1984).

16   Walter J. Ong, *Orality and Literacy: The Technologizing of the Word* (New York, 1982); Ruth Finnegan, "Literacy versus Non-literacy: The Great Divide," in Robin Finnegan and Robin Horton, eds., *Modes of Thought: Essays on Thinking in Western and Non-Western Societies* (London, 1973); Deborah Tannen, "The Myth of Orality and Literacy," in William Frawley, ed., *Linguistics and Literacy* (New York, 1982); and Deborah Tannen, "The Oral/Literature Continuum in Discourse," in Deborah Tannen, ed., *Spoken and Written Language: Exploring Orality and Literacy* (Norwood, N.J., 1982).

The ever-growing number of studies on literacy, historically considered, is not without its guidebooks. Harvey Graff's work on the history of literacy is the most extensive, and the bibliography in his *Literacy in History: An Interdisciplinary Research Bibliography* (1981) can be supplemented by the citations in his 1986 *Legacies of Literacy: Continuities and Contradictions in Western Culture and Society*. For a briefer introduction to the historians' view of literacy, I recommend Carl Kaestle's ''The History of Literacy and the History of Readers,'' Richard Venezky's ''The Development of Literacy in the Industrialized Nations of the West,'' and the special issue on literacy published at the end of 1990 in the *History of Education Quarterly*.[17]

Given the wide-ranging international debate on the meaning of literacy, it will come as no surprise to learn that historians have disagreed with one another about literacy in eighteenth-century New England. They have argued over how many people were literate, particularly women. Kenneth Lockridge, using the evidence of signatures and marks on wills as measures of, respectively, literacy and illiteracy, has contended that while men reached 84 per cent literacy by the 1760s, women never attained an average of more than 45 per cent literacy as late as the 1790s. In contrast, David Hall has maintained that when literacy is defined as the skill of *reading* English, then literacy was ''almost universal'' in seventeenth-century New England, because of the religious emphasis on the importance of reading.[18] There have been debates, as we shall see, about the meaning of a signature as an indication of literacy, and about the value of book ownership as a clue to the *mentalité* of bookowners. Once again, the most heated debate has revolved around the effects of literacy. Some scholars, like Kenneth Lockridge, have contended that literacy had a conservative effect on New Englanders in the conservation of piety; others, like Lawrence Cremin, have maintained that literacy, as a key component of popular education in general, was ultimately profoundly liberating.[19]

In the midst of these sandstorms of involvement, contention and bibliography, there is one surprise: except for the studies on New England just mentioned, along with a handful of others, little attention has been paid to literacy in colonial New England, and not much to anywhere else in colonial America. Even the magisterial summary of New England scholarship by my illustrious predecessor at the

---

17 Harvey J. Graff, *Literacy in History: An Interdisciplinary Research Bibliography* (New York, 1981); Graff, *Legacies of Literacy*; Carl F. Kaestle, ''The History of Literacy and the History of Readers,'' in Edmund W. Gordon, ed., *Review of Research in Education*, Vol. 12 (Washington, 1985); Richard L. Venezky, ''The Development of Literacy in the Industrialized Nations of the West,'' in Rebecca Barr, *et.al.*, eds., *Handbook of Reading Research*, Vol. 2 (New York, 1991); ''Special Issue on the History of Literacy,'' *History of Education Quarterly*, 30 (1990), 483-682.

18 Kenneth A. Lockridge, *Literacy in Colonial New England: An Enquiry into the Social Context of Literacy in the Early Modern West* (New York, 1974), 17, 38-39; David D. Hall, *Worlds of Wonder, Days of Judgment: Popular Religious Belief in Early New England* (New York, 1989), 32.

19 Lockridge, *Literacy in Colonial New England*, 100-101; Lawrence A. Cremin, *American Education, the Colonial Experience, 1607-1783* (New York, 1970).

first Planters Conference, Jack Greene, does not include any references to literacy. Lawrence Cremin of course discussed the topic in his *American Education: The Colonial Experience* (1970), but the best known study of literacy in colonial New England remains that by Kenneth Lockridge, mentioned earlier, which was published in 1974. Subsequently, there have been three other key studies specifically devoted to the topic — those by Ross Beales, Linda Auwers, and William Gilmore — while some attention has been paid to book ownership by the husband and wife team of Gloria and Jackson Turner Main, for whom the topic was only of incidental interest in their larger exploration of colonial New Englanders' standards of living.[20] The organizers of this conference have, therefore, shown special insight and perception in inviting comment on a topic that is curiously underrepresented in the historiography of colonial New England, yet considered worthy of serious thought in almost every other quarter.

Studies of Early New England Literacy
Historians of literacy in colonial New England have addressed three questions, but have chosen not to ask two others which I consider important. The first and most widely explored question is, who were literate? The second, to what extent were the literate literate? I myself am professionally interested in a third question, one of the two that are less often asked, namely, how did a child or adult acquire his or her literacy?[21] A fourth question relates to the first, but is nonetheless rarely asked: if women were indeed less literate than men, why was this so? The fifth question is one that every one asks, and properly so — what difference did literacy make to its possessor? This last query is the great "so what" of historical enquiry, and one that relates directly to the controlling/liberating debate.

Quantitative Evaluations of Literacy
The first question, "Who were literate?" is at heart a matter of measurement. Researchers who have asked this question have therefore had to confront the problem of how they could reasonably evaluate bygone literacy — the reading and writing of the past. It is easy to see that the reading ability of the past cannot be measured directly. Reading is oral, and the sounds of the past are lost; or it is silent, and may be detected even today only by observing the fixation of eyes on a page, the turning of pages of a book, or perhaps a few lip movements. Nor can we discern from these meager hints whether or not reading with understanding (which,

---

20 Cremin, *American Education: The Colonial Experience*; Jack Greene, "Recent Developments in the Historiography of Colonial New England," in Margaret Conrad, ed., *They Planted Well: New England Planters in Maritime Canada* (Fredericton, 1988); Lockridge, *Literacy in Colonial New England*. See below for the other references.

21 Both David Cressy and William J. Gilmore, however, have included discussions of literacy acquisition in their accounts: David Cressy, *Literacy and the Social Order: Reading and Writing in Tudor and Stuart England* (Cambridge, 1980), ch. 2; William J. Gilmore, *Elementary Literacy on the Eve of the Industrial Revolution: Trends in Rural New England, 1760-1830* (Worcester, Mass., 1982), 98-102, 104-114.

at least where I come from, is taken to be the goal of reading) has actually occurred. Those tests of comprehension with which we badger the modern child (''read this passage and mark your answer to a multiple-choice question'') are a twentieth-century invention. It is impossible, therefore, to directly measure the reading ability of the past.

Writing, in contrast and indeed by definition, leaves visible traces. In fact, apart from archaeological evidence, the vast majority of sources for our study of New England's past are written ones or derive directly from written ones: for all colonial imprints imply an earlier manuscript. Writing, therefore, is amenable to direct measurement, whether it is the evidence of authorship or the simple fact that some people signed their own names.

A mere signature has carried a weighty freight: indeed, many scholars have settled on the signature as the hallmark of literacy. (The beginning of this discussion is usually dated to a chapter by Roger Schofield, ''The Measurement of Literacy in Pre-Industrial England,'' in a 1968 book, while Cipolla's 1969 book was the starting point for a survey of literacy rates in Europe.)[22] That anyone could equate a signature with the possession of literacy is based on the well-documented fact that reading instruction was conducted prior to, and independently of, writing instruction. We have ample evidence of this fact from both European countries and the American colonies. Because a child learned to read first, the argument goes, and because writing required more advanced instruction, anybody who could write, could also read. A signature has therefore, given this view, been taken as a ''universal, standard and direct'' measure of both reading and writing ability.[23]

There are two complementary notions. One is that a signature may be regarded as a valid indicator of literacy, from at least the sixteenth up to and including the nineteenth centuries. The other is that a mark on a document (whether this was a crudely scratched X, a personal mark or a person's initials) is a valid indicator of illiteracy. These convictions have become so widely accepted that counting signatures versus marks is still the most popular method today, among literacy historians, of ascertaining how many people were literate. Those who have tabulated marks and signatures within the last fifteen years or so, to ascertain the literacy of past English speakers, include David Cressy and Rab Houston, using English and Scottish documents respectively for their sources. In Canada, the best known practitioner remains Harvey Graff, for his study of Toronto. The names

---

22 R[oger] S. Schofield, ''The Measurement of Literacy in Pre-Industrial England,'' in Jack P. Goody, ed., *Literacy in Traditional Societies* (Cambridge, 1968). Cf. Lawrence Stone, ''Literacy and Education in England, 1640-1900,'' *Past and Present*, 42 (1969), 61-139; Carlo M. Cipolla, *Literacy and Development in the West* (Baltimore, 1969). For examples of earlier uses of signatures to measure literacy in colonial New England, see those cited in Bernard Bailyn, *Education in the Forming of American Society* (Chapel Hill, 1960), 84.

23 For the sequence of reading and writing instruction, see ''The Acquisition of Literacy,'' below; Schofield, ''Measurement of Literacy,'' in Goody, *Literacy in Traditional Societies*, 319; Cressy, *Literacy and the Social Order*, 42.

of those who have counted early American signatures and marks may be conveniently found in a recent article by R.W. Grubb. For New England, the two major quantitative studies of literacy are those by Kenneth Lockridge (once again) for the colonial period and William Gilmore for the early Republic.[24]

An important question for signature-counters revolves around the documents upon which the signatures appear. There is nothing in colonial America to match, for sheer national coverage, the English marriage registers that have been kept by the Church of England since 1754. As all Britons who wed — perhaps 90 per cent of the population — had to sign them, these registers have been used as evidence for the literacy or illiteracy of the brides and grooms (and their two witnesses) who had to subscribe to them. As those involved would have been in their early twenties or thirties when they signed or marked, marriage registers provide what I call an "up-to-date" look at signing behavior. As we shall see, the age at which a person signed a document is important.

In the absence of any comparable source on this side of the Atlantic, Kenneth Lockridge used 3,126 wills as the data base for his study of literacy in colonial New England; they represented a ninth of all New England wills. (Lockridge, by the way, equates a signature with "fluent" reading.) He found that the proportion of males able to sign their own wills rose from 61 per cent in the 1660s to 69 per cent around 1710; the rate of progress then virtually doubled, and male signing rose to 84 per cent by 1760, and nearly 90 per cent by 1790 (this last figure being based on a smaller sample). Female signing rates, however, were much lower throughout the same period: only a third of the female testators signed their own wills before 1670, and although this proportion increased, it reached only about 40 per cent at the turn of the eighteenth century, and rose very slowly to a mere 45 per cent by the 1790s. When rural women were disentangled from Boston women, the rates for the latter were higher, but never more than about 66 per cent, and then only in the 1760s, while rural women, in the 1760s as in the 1700s, signed at only about a 35 per cent rate. In the 1790s, Boston women's signing slumped to a 60 per cent rate, while rural women averaged about 42 per cent.[25]

Wills, however, are in some ways a misleading source of information. Lockridge has discussed some of their biases. Wealth is obviously one of these: rich

24 For Tudor and Stuart England: Cressy, *Literacy and the Social Order*; for seventeenth- and eighteenth-century Scotland: Houston, *Scottish Literacy and the Scottish Identity*; for nineteenth-century England, W.B. Stephens, *Education, Literacy and Society, 1830-1870: The Geography of Diversity in Provincial England* (Manchester, 1987); in Canada, Harvey Graff explored the literacy of nineteenth-century Toronto, in Graff, *Literacy Myth*. For colonial America, see F.W. Grubb, "Growth of Literacy in Colonial America: Longitudinal Patterns, Economic Models, and the Direction of Future Research," *Social Science History*, 14 (1990), 451-82. In New England, the chief tabulators are Lockridge, *Literacy in Colonial New England* and Gilmore, *Elementary Literacy on the Eve of the Industrial Revolution*. For a roundup of female literacy in New England, see Joel Perlmann and Dennis Shirley, "When Did New England Women Acquire Literacy?" *William and Mary Quarterly*, 3rd ser., 48 (1991), 50-67, esp. 58-63.

25 Lockridge, *Literacy in Colonial New England*, number of wills sampled, 128 n.4; "fluent reading," 7; 17, 19 (Graph 1); women, 38-42; Boston v. rural women, 41 (Graph 8).

people make more wills than poor people. Gender is another: out of Lockridge's 3,126 will makers, fewer than 15 per cent were women, and they represented less than five per cent of the adult females who died during the period he studied. Age, of course, is the biggest bias, and not all of us may agree with Lockridge that upward biases of wealth were neatly offset by the downward biases of feebleness or forgetfulness.[26] Yet another problem with wills is that they are (unlike marriage registers) in a sense "out-of-date" relative to the time when a person signed the will. If wills were indeed made late in life by most people, a signature or mark made in the 1750s may represent the acquisition of, or failure to acquire, penmanship as much as 50 years earlier. Lockridge's figures, therefore, may really be misleading us both as to the pace of the rise in male signing over the eighteenth century (for it is clear that there was indeed a rise) and perhaps on the proportion of female signers.

Four years after Lockridge's study, Ross Beales, recognizing the biases in wills, took a new approach to evaluating literacy. He used deeds and probate records in an ingenious piece of research that was based on a 1747 assessment list for just one town: Grafton, of Worcester County, Massachusetts, a township only extensively settled in the late 1720s. This assessment list provided Beales with the names of 102 males and 81 females resident in Grafton in 1747. (All but one of the women were wives of the assessed men; the remaining woman was a widow.) Beales then looked at nearly 2,000 deeds and probate documents to see if he could find the signatures or marks made by these residents, and succeeded in tracking down 95 of the men and 56 of the women. All but two of the men signed their documents; 26 of the women signed (about 46 per cent) while 30 marked. While women were still underrepresented, as the assessment list did not reveal, for example, adult single sisters or female servants, they were more fairly represented by this Grafton study than in Lockridge's study. In this rural community, Beales therefore found a nearly 98 per cent male signing rate and a female signing rate that was equal to Lockridge's figures for women overall and better than his figures for rural women.[27]

A study published in 1980 by Linda Auwers is illuminating, because it focuses only on female signing. By using deeds as her source, Auwers found 941 landowners and their witnesses who had signed or marked their names (over 500 more female marker/signers than Lockridge had), as she examined female signing over time in the town of Windsor, Connecticut. The innovative aspect of Auwers' study is that she was able to ascertain the dates of birth of the 623 markers and signers who were born in Windsor, and allocate them to what she called "birth cohorts." Her results contrast strikingly with those of Lockridge and Beales. She found that there was a clear increase in female signing as time progressed, and that it occurred earlier than, and rose higher than, the rates in Lockridge's study. The proportion

26   *Ibid.*, 7-13, 128 n.4.
27   Ross W. Beales, Jr., "Studying Literacy at the Community Level: A Research Note," *Journal of Interdisciplinary History,* 9 (1978), 93-102.

of women who could sign their names to documents rose steadily from 48 per cent (for the cohort born between 1690 and 1709), to 76 per cent for the 1710-29 cohort, to 81 per cent for the 1730-49 cohort. When this last figure was further subdivided into decades, 76 per cent of the 1730-39 cohort and an astounding 90 per cent of the 1740-49 cohort signed. Significantly, of 31 women who subscribed their names to both wills and deeds, eight (26 per cent) signed their deeds but marked their wills — implying either, as Auwers suggests, the marginality of female signing, or perhaps the negative impact of aging.[28]

Although Auwers found more female signing behavior than Lockridge did, her study, like Beales', focused on just one area. So an exploration by William Gilmore is of particular interest, as far as signature counts are concerned, for Gilmore covers a vast territory. His research revolves around another Windsor, but this time far north up the Connecticut River, in what was to become Vermont. Like Auwers, Gilmore used deeds and wills, but he also used account books and township petitions as his data base. His search of sources (which required, *inter alia,* eliminating duplicate signatures/marks from 21,000 deeds) netted no fewer than 10,467 signatures/marks on documents dated between 1760 and 1830 in the Upper Connecticut Valley. (The bulk of the evidence, however, dates from the 1770s rather than the 1760s.) Using this ''multiple moment'' approach, as he likes to call it, Gilmore found that (apart from the bottom twenty per cent of the population whose literacy remained inaccessible) ''adult male elementary literacy … reached near-universal levels throughout Windsor County as early as the 1760s and surely by the mid-1770s.'' Despite Gilmore's broader use of sources, women are inevitably still underrepresented (only 839 of his signers/markers were women), but he found that female signing began at about two-thirds in the late 1770s and rose thereafter to nearly four-fifths by the late 1780s. Thereafter it fluctuated, but stabilized at about 85 per cent after 1812.[29]

There are two points that we should note here. First, because the bulk of Gilmore's evidence came from account books or deeds, and wills generated fewer than ten per cent of his data, his findings, just like those of Beales and Auwers, have a much more current ring to them, as it were, than do Lockridge's, which were based on wills alone. Second, Gilmore rejects the equation of signing with fluent reading, and regards a signature as an indicator of only ''elementary'' literacy. We shall defer our own analysis of the meaning of a signature for later.

It is time to summarize the evidence up to this point. Lockridge's will-based data reveal that the ability of New England men to sign their own names increased dramatically throughout the eighteenth century. His figures indicate that on average nearly 80 per cent of all males were signature literate by the 1760s. But given

28   Linda Auwers, ''Reading the Marks of the Past: Exploring Female Literacy in Colonial Windsor, Connecticut,'' *Historical Methods*, 13 (1980), 204-14.

29   Gilmore, *Elementary Literacy*, 127 n., 98, ''multiple moment,'' 95-98, quot. 114. The total number of women (N = 839) is as follows: account books, N = 21; deeds, N = 658; wills and witnesses, N = 151; petitions, N = 9: *ibid.*, 116, 127n, 148, 139. (For the signatures/marks of an additional 38 women obtained from ''loose deeds,'' see *ibid.*, 127.)

the age biases of wills that we have discussed, this is likely to be an underestimate. Gilmore's figures for the 1760s for Windsor district (in what would later become Vermont), based on more ''up-to-date'' evidence such as deeds, put male signature literacy at over 90 per cent. So do Ross's data, which found a 98 per cent male signing rate in one small rural Massachusetts community in the mid-eighteenth century.

While all this research suggests that men were signature literate earlier in the eighteenth century than Lockridge's study indicated, there is no comparable agreement where women are concerned. In fact, there is a downright discrepancy. Lockridge's data show that women always signed at a lower rate than men, and this imbalance is supported by both Gilmore's and Beales' study (and, indeed, by every literacy study of colonial America). Whereas Lockridge, however, documented a female rate that averaged 45 per cent in the 1760s, Auwers, with a larger sample and disentangling women by age, found, at least for the small community of Windsor, Connecticut, that women in their thirties by the 1760s (that is, the 1730-39 cohort) had a 76 per cent signing ability. (Gilmore's figures for women do not begin until the 1770s.)

The Extent of Literacy

Our second question was ''How literate were the literate?'' One of the great weaknesses of counting signatures is that the activity really presumes that literacy is a dichotomous variable — that one either is or is not literate. It has taken historians of literacy a long time to appreciate what reading teachers have always known: that there is a huge range in the literacy continuum, from the barely literate at one end to the intensely literate at the other.

One attempt, therefore, to answer the question of how literate was literate has focused, not unreasonably, on finding out what people read. One way to find that out has been to use inventories — those lists made by probate officials of the belongings of the deceased — to ascertain book ownership. Jackson Turner Main has investigated this source for colonial Connecticut. For the seventeenth century, he found that the proportion of Connecticut inventories that revealed the possession of at least one book rose from 59 to 66 per cent. (These overall numbers, however, mask several disparities: rich men were more likely to own books than poor men, older men than younger men, and men in well-established towns than in newly established ones.)[30]

Disappointingly, from our point of view, Main's study is not able to provide a comparable look at eighteenth-century book holdings. Instead, Main summarizes book ownership over time, for the whole colonial period in Connecticut, as a function of occupation. The proportion of male householders who owned at least one book at the time of their death was as follows: 43 per cent of the free laborers,

---

30 Jackson Turner Main, *Society and Economy in Colonial Connecticut* (Princeton, N.J., 1985), 104 (I have reversed Main's figures of ''% none'' on appendix 3D to percentage ownership, rounded), 75-76, 105.

75 per cent of both the farmers and the artisans, 86 per cent of the traders (a rather catch-all group that included anyone who had anything to do with commerce, from peddlars to merchants), and virtually all the professionals.[31]

Main discusses the implications that a monetarily more valuable library had for a wider range of reading. A library worth '2, for example (as assessed by the probate evaluators), represented perhaps two dozen books or else an unusually valuable Bible along with, say, a few sermons. Like book ownership itself, the estimated value of a library also varied by occupation over the entire colonial period. A library valued at '2 or over was owned by only 8 per cent of the farmers and 30 per cent of the traders, but by 70 per cent of the professionals. Few of the traders, in other words, despite often considerable wealth, had used that wealth to improve their libraries. In the last 15 years before the American Revolution, for instance, 21 of the traders enjoyed the large sum of '1,000 in personal wealth — yet seven of these rich men owned books valued at less than '2, while only three of them had books valued at over '10.[32] The group that could most afford books, in short, seems not to have been enthusiastic readers.

Gloria Main has done similar inventory probing in Massachusetts. She looked at colonial inventories (apparently for both men and women) taken in some five counties extending west of Boston to the Connecticut River Valley to examine a rise in rural standards of living. She divided her decendents into three groups: the "poor," with property valued at from £1-£49; the "middling," from £50-£224; and the "rich," whose estates were worth £225 and up. Main found that 59 per cent of even the poorest households (those whose property was valued at under £50) had at least one religious book between 1644 and 1674, and that this proportion rose to 65 per cent in the last quarter of the seventeenth century. From then up to 1764, when Main's figures stop, the proportion of households who owned religious books, no matter what their wealth was, never fell below two-thirds. An even higher proportion of the middling and wealthy households owned a religious book throughout both centuries — in fact, from 1725 on, well over 80 per cent.[33]

These figures on religious book possession are even more striking when we consider what the same rural Massachusetts households did not own. With the exception of household linens and, after 1700, coarse earthenware, a far larger proportion of households owned religious books than they did fine earthenware, knives or forks, mirrors or clocks, wigs or pictures. This holds true for all time periods up to 1764, when Main's figures end, and for each of the three wealth groupings.[34] When we look at Main's figures for secular books, however, the

---

31   *Ibid.*, 313.

32   *Ibid.*, 313, 301; traders defined, 278.

33   Gloria L. Main, "The Standard of Living in Southern New England, 1640-1773," *William and Mary Quarterly*, 3rd ser., 45 (1988), 124-34, esp. 133. See also "A Note on Book Ownership in Seventeenth-Century New England," in Hall, *Worlds of Wonder*, 247-49.

34   Main, "Standard of Living," Table VII, 133-34. Bibles were always identified as such in inventories.

contrast could not be more striking. Over the whole period that she studied, from 1640 to 1764, secular book ownership by poor families averaged 1 per cent, that by middling 4 per cent, and by rich only 15 per cent.[35] What does all this information mean? Is it evidence of piety rather than literacy? Why did the third of the wealthy Connecticut merchants who could most afford to purchase books buy such a miserably small number? I suggest that our view of these figures is once again influenced by our preference for reading as a literacy skill over writing. The traders all wrote voluminously — you could not manage a business without writing or supervising some clerk who wrote for you. That was the direction their literacy took. Gloria Main's book figures tell us that religious book ownership in the eighteenth century mattered to at least two-thirds of the poorer members of the community, and to three-quarters of the middling and wealthy members. They too had bought into the prevailing view of the importance of reading, and afford a striking example of the close relationship between reading and religion.

The History of the Book

What is missing in numbers produced by inventories is, of course, information on how many persons had access to books or reading material other than the ones that were in their possession at death. In some respects, we know very well that certain kinds of materials — newspapers and almanacs in particular — were often in households, as judged by publication figures, yet never appear in inventories. Both were considered disposable kinds of print. Nor do there appear to be schoolbooks in these inventories, despite the fact that both colonial publication and importation of spelling books, increasingly a key reading instructional text, rose during the eighteenth century.[36] A branch of scholarly enquiry generally known as the "History of the Book" addresses all these issues.[37] (Incidentally, this particular scholarly pursuit once again implies the importance of reading over writing for the ordinary person.) Briefly, historians of the book aim to integrate books into social history. They view books both as windows into cultural experiences and as products of the marketplace. They envision a "communications circuit" — a system in which the author, publisher, printer, shipper, bookseller and reader each affect one another in sequence. Nor is this an enclosed or autonymous system: for it is influenced by larg-

---

35   *Ibid.*, 134.

36   Schoolbooks do appear in Gilmore's post-revolutionary inventories, so it is quite possible that their absence from a given colonial inventory indicates an absence from the home. See note 38.

37   In its present form, "History of the Book" scholarship dates from the two volumes, published in 1965 and 1970, of François Furet and Jules Ozouf's *Livre et Société*, while its best known American exponent is probably Robert Darnton, whose 1982 essay, "What Is the History of Books?" is considered one of the classic statements of the field: François Furet *et al.*, *Livre et Société dans la France du xviii Siecle*, 2 Vols. (Paris, 1965, 1970); Robert Darnton, "What Is the History of Books?" *Daedalus*, 111 (1982), 65-83; reprinted in Cathy N. Davidson, ed., *Reading in America: Literature and Social History* (Baltimore, 1989), 27-52.

er factors such as economic and social forces, intellectual and political ones. Or, to put it more poetically, as William Gilmore says of his own book, the premise of book history is that "cultural and material strands of life are part of the same tapestry."[38] Entrance into this system or tapestry at virtually any point, of course, presupposes literacy.

Once again, that assiduous counter William Gilmore has given us an example of the history of the book scholarship. The post-revolutionary dates are a little late for this audience, but I want to review his work briefly. For his new book, titled *Reading Becomes a Necessity of Life: Material and Cultural Life in Rural New England, 1780-1835* (1989), but actually focused on Windsor District, Vermont, Gilmore identified the inventories of 396 families whose heads of household had died between 1780 and 1835, and whose inventories revealed the possession of a library — a "library" being defined as at least one book. These libraries contained 5,630 print items in all, or about 1,250 different titles. He was able to identify the full titles of nearly all of these books by good detective work on the appraisers' notations of the "spine title."[39]

Gilmore also ascertained the communication routes of this deep rural area, and as a result posited five kinds of "human habitats." These ranged from "hard-scrabble" at the low end of the scale — dwellings where life was hard and communication was difficult in the extreme — to the "fortunate village" at the other end of the scale, which enjoyed a happy combination of easy access to roads, good educational facilities and the ready availability of print. (In support of these categories, Gilmore delineates such factors as increases in newspaper publication, local printing and membership in subscription libraries.) He compares the libraries of each habitat, finding that library holdings, from the least to the most favored habitat, rise from 50 to 85 per cent of the total population, and their content correspondingly shifts from what he calls "intensive" to "extensive" reading. Two of Gilmore's overall conclusions are that between 1760 and 1830 Vermont witnessed the rise of "a wholly new kind of rural mass literacy," and that the years from 1780 to 1835 saw the dawn of a new and modern age of reading.[40]

Despite the advances that Gilmore's study has made in so many areas, I think we should treat certain of his conclusions with caution. The notion implicit in

---

38 Darnton, "What Is the History of Books?" in Davidson, *Reading in America,* esp. 29-31; William J. Gilmore, *Reading Becomes a Necessity of Life: Material and Cultural Life in Rural New England, 1780-1835* (Knoxville, 1989), 9. For useful overviews of the topic, see the editorial introductions to two volumes of collected essays: David D. Hall, "The Uses of Literacy in New England, 1600-1850," in William L. Joyce *et al.,* eds., *Printing and Society in Early America* (Worcester, Mass., 1983); and Cathy N. Davidson, "Toward a History of Books and Readers," in Davidson, *Reading in America.* The American Antiquarian Society, Worcester, Mass., has a program in the history of the book in America, for which it publishes a newsletter titled *The Book: Newsletter of the Program in the History of the Book in American Culture;* and there is a Center for the Book at the University of Iowa.

39 Gilmore, *Reading Becomes a Necessity of Life,* 142, 415 n. 5.

40 *Ibid.*, ch. 4, 150-51, 346-52 (esp. 347), quot. 133, ch. 10.

Reading Becomes a Necessity of Life is that we are what we read. The book is therefore full of statements on the cultural and intellectual values held by families as inferred from their book holdings. The "self-sufficient hamlet" habitat, for instance — a grouping that stands plumb in the center of the hardscrabble and fortunate village continuum — had a mix of book holdings, and so is said to have evinced an intellectual split: "Some families adhered to an eighteenth-century mentality.... A majority participated in the gradual transformation of belief and values that characterized nineteenth-century thought."[41] But this and similar statements throughout the book embody a large inferential leap that not all of us may wish to make.

Similarly, Gilmore's claims that this was the first rural society to be so literate may have to be reevaluated in the light of the Mains' evidence on colonial book ownership. After all, by the 1760s two-thirds of the poorest families in those portions of rural Massachusetts examined by Gloria Main were owners of at least one (religious) book, whereas only half the hardscrabble families of Vermont owned a library in the 1780s or later.[42]

Historians of the book, including Gilmore, have correctly advanced the notion that there were different ways of approaching text. David Hall has sketched a picture of "traditional" literacy (termed "intensive" by Gilmore): a deliberate and reverential approach to reading; much oral reading in the family; learning to read by memorizing certain texts; a limited contact with books, but the use of the Bible, psalmbook, primers and other "steady sellers" that were the staples of this kind of literacy. "Extensive" reading, in contrast, is represented by a greater quantity of books, chiefly secular ones, which were read through rather than read and reread.[43]

Cathy Davidson has warned us, however, against taking these categories as mutually exclusive. She has argued that readers of novels in post-revolutionary America — who would be categorized as reading in the "extensive" mode — scrutinized their texts with just as much rapt attention as when they were reading the Bible. Marginal comments of "Impious!" or "Just vengeance!" on one copy of a 1797 novel eloquently betray the level of involvement that could be inspired by "extensive" reading.[44] The same person could clearly do both.

---

41 *Ibid.*, 320.

42 *Ibid.*, Table 4-3, 151.

43 David D. Hall, "The Uses of Literacy in New England, 1600-1850," in Joyce *et al.*, *Printing and Society in Early America*, 20-38, esp. 20-24; Gilmore, *Reading Becomes a Necessity of Life*, 265-68 and *passim*. Gilmore goes further and identifies specific *texts* as intensive or extensive.

44 Cathy N. Davidson, *Revolution and the Word: The Rise of the Novel in America* (New York, 1986), 72-73, 77. For a critical review of the "intensive/extensive" dichotomy, see Richard L. Venezky, "Books, Readers, and Society," *History of Education Quarterly*, 30 (1990), 652-53. Cotton Mather is an early example of someone who read both "intensively" (the Bible and devotional works) and "extensively" (he was skilled at skimming): E. Jennifer Monaghan, "Family Literacy in Early Eighteenth-Century Boston: Cotton Mather and His Children," *Reading Research Quarterly*, 26 (in press).

The Acquisition of Literacy

What then of our third question, how did the literate become literate? Elsewhere, in an article (also a book chapter) titled "Literacy Instruction and Gender in Colonial New England," I have drawn upon evidence from a variety of sources in order to explore the literacy curriculum of colonial New England, and shall restate only my main conclusions here.[45]

1. Reading was considered easy to teach, and reading instruction unaccompanied by writing instruction was the province of women, both at home and at school (private or town-sponsored). Texts for reading instruction were cheap and easy to obtain. They ranged from hornbooks, which were imported into colonial America as late as 1760, through primers (usually the famous *New England Primer*), psalters, the New Testament and the Bible.[46]

2. Writing, in sharp contrast to reading, was considered difficult to teach and taught by men who had often undergone an apprenticeship to a writing master in order to qualify as writing masters themselves. Texts for writing instruction were comparatively expensive and difficult to obtain, and imported from London rather than printed on local presses. One of the most popular texts, used by all the writing masters of the three eighteenth-century writing schools of Boston, was *The Universal Penman* (1743), engraved by George Bickham.[47]

The separation of literacy instruction by gender is nicely illustrated by a poem from Philadelphia, written around the end of the seventeenth century.

> Here are schools of divers sorts,
> To which our youth daily resorts,
> Good women, who do very well
> Bring little ones to read and spell,
> Which fits them for writing, and then,
> Here's men to bring them to their pen,
> And to instruct and make them quick
> In all sorts of Arithmetick.[48]

3. As we already know, reading instruction preceded, and was independent of,

---

45   E. Jennifer Monaghan, "Literacy Instruction and Gender in Colonial New England," *American Quarterly*, 40 (1988), 18-41, esp. 33-34; or "Literacy Instruction and Gender in Colonial New England," in Davidson, *Reading in America*, 53-80, esp. 70-71.

46   For the almost mythical role that the hornbook was believed to play in the acquisition of literacy in eighteenth-century England, see Thomas Tickell's poem quoted at the beginning of this essay.

47   George Bickham, *The Universal Penman, Engraved by George Bickham, London 1743*, rpt. with an introductory essay by Philip Hofer (New York, 1968). For its use in the Boston writing schools, see E. Jennifer Monaghan, "Readers Writing: The Curriculum of the Writing Schools of Eighteenth-Century Boston," *Visible Language*, 21 (1987), 167-213.

48   Quoted in Carl Bridenbaugh, *Cities in the Wilderness: The First Century of Urban Life in America, 1625-1742* (1938; rpt. Oxford, England, 1971), 283-84.

writing instruction. That this could be so was a function of pedagogy: instruction in reading was conducted orally, by means of the alphabet method, and involved no writing at all.

Both poems cited at the beginning of this essay suggest the crucial importance of the alphabet in learning to read. New Englanders might well have read the first poem, for it appeared in *The Youth's Instructor in the English Tongue*, a spelling book compendium published on Boston presses from 1761 on and imported from England before that.[49] It depicts a stouthearted little boy who is so well aware that learning his ABCs will start him off on the long hard road of literacy that he utterly refuses to take the first step: he balks at "saying Great A" — that is, of pronouncing the capital letter *A*.

It is difficult for the modern literate to believe that the two pedagogies of imparting reading and writing could have been conducted so independently of each other. Let me, therefore, cite just one piece of evidence among many in support of this contention. It is an advertisement that appeared in the *Boston Weekly Newsletter* in 1755. In it, Mr. William Elphinstone promised to teach "Persons of both Sexes from 12 Years of Age to 50, who never wrote before ... to write a good legible Hand, in Five Weeks, at one Hour per Day."[50] Mr. Elphinstone obviously assumed that there were some *Newsletter* readers who could make good use of his services.

4. New Englanders, particularly the intensely Puritan immigrants who settled Massachusetts Bay, New Haven (which was initially a separate colony) and Connecticut, considered reading to be vitally important. The religious reasons were paramount, but there were also political and economic ones.[51] The governments of these colonies therefore early passed legislation that required reading of all children. The first of these was, in essence, the first Poor Law. Passed in 1642 by the Bay Colony, it empowered the selectmen to examine parents to make sure they had taught their children to read (writing is not mentioned) and legislated a series of penalties against parents who had failed to do so which ranged from fines to the removal of the child from the parent to be apprenticed.[52]

5. Writing, in contrast to reading, was considered a job-related skill that society only required of boys. The later history of the Poor Laws, just mentioned, is instructive. A 1703 supplement to the earlier acts reaffirmed the need to provide apprentices with an education by stipulating that the masters should "provide for the instructing of children so bound out [apprenticed], to read and write, if they

49 Roger P. Bristol, *Supplement to Charles Evans' American Bibliography* (Charlottesville, 1970), No. B2262.

50 Quoted in Robert F. Seybolt, *The Private Schools of Colonial Boston* (Cambridge, Mass., 1935), 39.

51 For a discussion of the symbiotic relationship between reading and religion, see Hall, *Worlds of Wonder*, 22-43.

52 Nathaniel B. Shurtleff, ed., *Records of the Governor and Company of the Massachusetts Bay in New England*, Vol. 2, *1642-1649* (Boston, 1853), 6-7.

be capable.'' Clearly, as children of either gender could be apprenticed, both sexes were to be taught reading and writing. It turned out, however, that the legislators had not intended this: in 1710, an amendment was passed that altered the order to: ''males to read and write, females to read.'' The act was repeated in the same form once a decade until 1741, when the requirement of ''cyphering'' (arithmetic) was added to the regulations for males. Finally, in 1771, the legislation was changed once again, and it now stipulated, ''males, reading, writing, cyphering; females, reading, writing.''[53]

The job-related skill that corresponded, for girls, to what writing was for boys, was needlework. (Girls in fact formed their letters in thread in their samplers.)[54] This is well exemplified by Anne Bradstreet, whose first book of poetry appeared in London in 1650. She clearly felt that she was incurring odium by stepping outside the role prescribed by society for women, in exchanging her needle for a pen:

> I am obnoxious to each carping tongue
> Who says my hand a needle better fits,
> A Poets pen all scorn I should thus wrong,
> For such despite they cast on female wits.[55]

6. Writing was one of the key components of the curriculum of the town schools, which were taught by men and in many cases restricted to boys. Girls won access to some, but by no means all, of the masters' schools from the 1690s on. As one New Englander put it, reminiscing about his school days in Lynn, Massachusetts, ''In all my school days which ended in 1801, I never saw but three females in public schools, and they were there only in the afternoon to learn to write.''[56]

7. Towns began to employ women (known as ''school dames'') to teach reading to small children of both sexes from the 1680s on. If these conclusions are correct, then we must draw two further ones:

8. Because reading was required to be taught, and because people could and did learn to read without also learning to write, we cannot assume that all those — particularly women — who only marked documents were totally illiterate. Some, or even many, of them may have been able to read to a certain extent, even though they could not write.

9. However, because educational standards in New England were raised over time, marks have to be interpreted in context.

The import of all this, in relation to our present discussion, has three thrusts.

---

53   Robert F. Seybolt, *Apprenticeship and Apprenticeship Education in Colonial New England and New York* (New York, 1917), 46-47.

54   As members of my audience at the Planters Conference reminded me.

55   Quoted in Thomas Woody, *A History of Women's Education in the United States* (1929; rpt. New York, 1966), 1: 132.

56   Walter H. Small, ''Girls in Colonial Schools,'' *Education*, 22 (1902), 534.

First, I agree with Gilmore that a signature should probably be assessed conservatively as an indicator of a *minimal* amount of reading ability, as Carl Kaestle has also suggested, rather than equivalent to fluent reading.[57] This does not, of course, preclude the possibility that someone who signed could read fluently.

Second, as I have just suggested, because reading was taught prior to, and independently of, writing, a mark cannot be automatically used as an indicator of total illiteracy: a person who marked a document may have been able to read, at least to some extent. Evidence from other, but contemporary, cultures amply supports this point. For instance, a number of the Wampanoag Indians of Martha's Vineyard, an island off the coast of Massachusetts, acquired literacy in their own language from 1643 on. Many more of them were able to read the books that were published in the Massachuset tongue as part of the "Indian Library" than were able to write.[58] Further evidence has come, either for the seventeenth or eighteenth centuries, or both, from England, Scotland, Sweden, Norway and colonial New Mexico, of children and adults who were taught to read — all of them for religious reasons — but much more rarely to write.[59]

But finally, as I have also suggested, the mark must be interpreted in context. Educational standards rose over time. Given the expectations by the 1770s that every male, white New Englander should be taught both to read and write, and that even female white children should learn to write as well as read (if we can generalize from the example of the Poor Laws of Massachusetts), the later we get in the eighteenth century, the greater the likelihood that, in New England, a person who made a mark was genuinely illiterate.

Why the Inequity?

This brings us to our fourth question, which we can now frame in a different manner. The question is not the one usually asked — why were women less literate than men in colonial New England? — but the question we can now ask — why did it take so long for New England society to believe that girls should be taught to write?

---

57 Gilmore, *Elementary Literacy*, 92 and *passim*; Kaestle, "History of Literacy and the History of Readers," 21.

58 E. Jennifer Monaghan, " 'She loved to read in good Books': Literacy and the Indians of Martha's Vineyard, 1643-1725," *History of Education Quarterly*, 30 (1990), 493-521.

59 For England see Margaret Spufford, *Small Books and Pleasant Histories: Popular Fiction and Its Readership in Seventeenth-Century England* (Cambridge, 1981), 22, 27, 29, 34-35; Victor E. Neuburg, *Popular Education in Eighteenth Century England* (London, 1971), 55, 93. For a review of David Cressy's *Literacy and the Social Order*, suggesting that Cressy's own evidence supports the contention that people could read who could not write, contrary to his premise, see June R. Gilstad, rev. of Cressy, *Literacy and the Social Order*, in *History of Reading News*, 7, 1 (1983-84), 3. For Scotland see T.C. Smout, "Born Again at Cambuslang: New Evidence on Popular Religion and Literacy in Eighteenth-Century Scotland," *Past and Present*, 97 (1982), 114-27. For Sweden see Egil Johansson, "Literacy Campaigns in Sweden," in Arnove and Graff, *National Literacy Campaigns*. For Norway see Knut Tveit, "Elementary School in Rural South-

The answer given by many in the sixteenth and seventeenth centuries was that women were naturally the intellectual inferiors of men. Ann Hopkins, who was the wife of Edward Hopkins, governor of Connecticut in the 1640s (and better known for being the aunt of Elihu Yale for whom Yale College was named), was considered an intellectual. She gave "herself wholly to reading and writing," according to Governor John Winthrop in his journal, "and had written many books." It drove her mad — that, at least, was Winthrop's interpretation: "For if she had attended her household affairs, and not gone out of her way and calling to meddle in such things as are proper for men, whose minds are stronger, etc., she had kept her wits, and might have improved them usefully and honorably in the place God had set her."[60]

A more plausible reason, never voiced overtly, was that women who could write would accede to a power that men wished to deny them. Writing was closely related to the commercial world, just as arithmetic was, which most girls were not taught until after the American Revolution. The assumption was that women would not, and ought not to, be involved in commerce in any way. In fact, this was simply not the case. There is evidence of female shopkeepers from very early on — there is a splendid court case in New Haven in the 1640s where a woman is accused of price-gouging in her sale of primers — and there is plenty of indication from eighteenth-century newspaper advertisements of female entrepreneurship.[61] The discrimination against women in regards to writing, therefore, was likely based on an unconscious wish to keep the tools of power out of the hands of women. Women, it was thought, should be receiving messages from their superior males, from the Almighty on down, not transmitting them.

Women, however, had one great ally: the writing masters. It was eminently to the advantage of the private writing master to encourage penmanship among the gentler sex. In fact, writing masters were so successful at attracting clients of both genders that "facility with the pen" had become one of the female accomplishments like embroidery, playing a musical instrument, painting and perhaps learning French. At one point there had even been a special female script that was appropriate for women but not men. Middle-class parents on both sides of the Atlantic, therefore, had long paid private instructors to teach their daughters to

---

East Norway, 1730-1830" (paper presented at the University of Oslo, August 1989), 6, 7: "Every child was taught reading and religion. ... Less than 10% of the pupils in ambulant schools had writing as a school subject around the year 1800. ... Few, even among well-to-do people, were able to make their own signature as late as 1830." For colonial New Mexico see Bernardo P. Gallegos, "Literacy, Schooling, and Society in Colonial New Mexico: 1692-1821" PhD thesis, University of New Mexico, 1988, 50, 63-64, Appendix 1.

60   James K. Hosmer, *Winthrop's Journal, "History of New England," 1630-1649* (New York, 1908), 2:225. For learned women (and opinions of them) in seventeenth-century England, see Antonia Fraser, *The Weaker Vessel* (New York, 1984), 4, ch. 7.

61   Charles J. Hoadly, ed., *Records of the Colony and Plantation of New Haven, from 1638 to 1649* (Hartford, Conn., 1857), 176; e.g., an advertisement by Elizabeth Decoster for seeds, *Boston Weekly Newsletter*, 19 April 1744.

write. Cotton Mather, in early eighteenth-century Boston, set great store on his daughters' writing.[62]

Girls often also had an ally in their own families, just as Cotton Mather's daughters did. There was unquestionably a shift in opinion in the eighteenth century about teaching girls to write that long antedated the shift in the Poor Law legislation relating to apprentices. In the eighteenth century, there was a confluence of a range of factors that had the net effect of creating a better climate for education in general, and for girls' education in particular. These cannot be detailed here, but they include a tougher attitude by New England colonies on townships' maintaining schools; an increased flow of printed material, imported and domestic, that included chapbooks and, at the end of century, novels; the introduction of the spelling book as an improved instructional textbook for teaching reading; the beginnings of publications designed to amuse children rather than instruct them — real children's books; and a decided shift, probably before the beginning of the eighteenth century, of the locus of literacy instruction from the home to the school.

The crucial question then becomes, when and where were girls admitted to the schoolmasters' winter district schools where writing was taught? Many girls had been given private writing instruction, but widespread literacy in writing could only have occurred if they were allowed to attend the town school throughout the year, and not just in the summer.

I would like, at this point, to offer a couple of hypotheses. First, I posit an inverse relationship between female access to town-funded literacy education and schooling pretentiousness: the fancier a town's educational ambitions, the fewer the opportunities available to girls for town-funded schooling. Boston provides an extreme example of this relationship. By 1720 it had opened, for its sons, two Latin grammar schools and three writing schools, all of which were free; but it offered nothing to its daughters. It was not until 1789 that primary schools were opened up in Boston for both sexes.

Second, I believe that the newer and, by definition, more frontier settlements after, say, about 1740, took it for granted that they should not only open an ''English'' school (rather than a ''Latin'' one), but admit girls to it year round. This would have been the background, therefore, of the great majority of the rural New Englanders who migrated to Nova Scotia from 1759 on.

There is no doubt in my mind that girls became part of a town's elementary schooling in many places in New England in the eighteenth century, perhaps particularly in Connecticut, which prided itself on its elementary schooling. We already know that they did so in Windsor, Connecticut. Newer townships valued education highly. Kent, for instance, was founded in 1738 in one of the most western parts of Connecticut. Its school was mentioned in the minutes of May of the following year, five months before it was even officially incorporated as a town by act of assembly, and two years before its inhabitants formed a covenanted

---

62 Monaghan, ''Family Literacy in Early Eighteenth-Century Boston.''

church. Apparently no inhabitant of Kent, male or female, ever had to mark a document.[63]

The Effects of Literacy

We are now in a position to answer the last of my questions, what were the effects of literacy? As suggested already, Kenneth Lockridge has argued that they were conservative, while Lawrence Cremin has claimed they were liberating. I myself believe that we can only achieve a reasonable answer by looking at the literacy experiences of individuals. I shall close this paper with four examples, in chronological order, of literates in New England. They are one male and three females: Hannah Heaton, John Thomas, Phillis Wheatley and Anna Green Winslow. These literate New England individuals shall serve as our witnesses to the difference that literacy made in the lives of ordinary people, young and old, urban and rural, white and black, in eighteenth-century New England. Among them, they invite three conclusions: that even a modest library can bear witness to an avid reader; that to many people writing could be even more important than reading; and that by the 1770s even children could be both intensive and extensive readers.

The first witness is a farm wife named Hannah Heaton (1721-94), whose diary provides evidence on all the topics, except for literacy education, that we have looked at so far. Heaton had presumably been taught to read and write in Long Island, where she grew up, but she moved to North Haven, Connecticut, upon her marriage in 1743 and lived there until her death in 1794. She kept her diary intermittently — she called it a ''spiritual history'' — from some time in the 1750s to a few months before her death. There were some of her books, we must presume, that were included in the inventory made after her husband's death in 1791 as ''1 Old watts Psalm Book/Dead Faith Anatomized/1 old Bible/Spiritual Logick/11 small books.''(Their value was given as only six shillings and three pence.)[64]

Hannah read devotional works avidly. (''i read constantly and find it teaching,'' as she put it.) The books she read, however, far exceed those listed in the inventory: her diary mentions her reading more than two dozen books, all of them related by her to her own spiritual pilgrim's progress. Among them were those staples of the colonial publishing industry, John Bunyan's *Pilgrim's Progress* and Michael Wigglesworth's *Day of Doom*, but they also included at least one comparatively contemporary publication, Jonathan Edwards' *An Account of the Life of the Late Reverend David Brainerd* (1749).[65] Hannah's experience suggests

---

63 Cremin, *American Education: The Colonial Experience*, 541-42; Charles S. Grant, *Democracy in the Connecticut Frontier Town of Kent* (New York, 1961), 1, 23, 25, 157, 158.

64 Barbara E. Lacey, ''The World of Hannah Heaton: The Autobiography of an Eighteenth-Century Farm Woman,'' *William and Mary Quarterly*, 3rd ser., 45 (1988), 280-304; quotations, 282, 288; Barbara E. Lacey, personal communication 17 June 1991.

65 *Ibid.*, 288-89, esp. 288 n.10.

that even a relatively small library valued at under a pound, may seriously underestimate (as Jackson Turner Main and William Gilmore have already suggested) the extent of reading undertaken by the library owner. In Hannah's case, she had access, through borrowing, to many books other than those in her family library. Book sharing could be, as David Hall has suggested, part of a mutual ritual of caring.[66] Hannah's case also illustrates the blurred line between the so-called intensive and extensive reader. True, her reading diet was largely devotional (intensive), but she also read widely (extensive).

Important as Hannah's reading was to her, her writing was more so. As Barbara Lacey has put it in her analysis, "the composition of the autobiography was as important to Heaton as any of the experiences she set down." Like other spiritual autobiographers, Hannah did not merely record; she explained, codified and integrated her experiences into her interpretation of them as way stations along a spiritual journey. Her diary provided her with strength and solace for her inner life amid an often turbulent outer life.[67]

Our second diarist is John Thomas. John's diary, which he kept during the Seven Years' War, has been reproduced in the *Nova Scotia Historical Society Collections* and is one of many such diaries used by Fred Anderson for his marvelous book, *A People's Army*. The so-called Seven Years' War was waged between the French and the English, with Indian and American assistance, from the years 1754 to 1762. Anderson analyzes the social effects of this war upon its Massachusetts participants.[68] Anderson early decided that he would have to modernize the spelling of his sources, for the simple reason that otherwise no one would have been able to understand them. Thomas was a surgeon who joined in the British expedition of 1755 against the Acadians — he records performing several amputations. As a surgeon, he was presumably a man of some education, and his spelling is less bizarre than those in some of the other soldiers' diaries but slightly more unorthodox than Hannah Heaton's. It is certainly far from standard.

The sample I have provided below is excerpted from John Thomas' entry of 4 June 1755, where he was describing his regiment's first major attack against a French position. The attacking forces consisted of some 2,100 New Englanders joined by 250 Regulars. They had set off at 6 a.m. and by 11 that morning could clearly see the French defense.

> ... about 11 Clock we Came on Large Salt mash whare we ware in Plain vew of a French Blockhouse & Fausines thrown up Sufficient to Screen a Large No of men whare thay could Secure themselvs from our Fire & yet have all the advantage on us but we marched on Direct for the enemy this being

66 Hall, *Worlds of Wonder*, 237.

67 Lacey, "The World of Hannah Heaton," 282. See *ibid.*, n.6 and 8 for references to spiritual autobiographies.

68 Fred Anderson, *A People's Army: Massachusetts Soldiers and Society in the Seven Years' War* (Chapel Hill, 1984).

the only Pass we Could have over to the main Fort that we ware Designed for Now we hear the Indians begin to make thare most Hideous yells & Large Numbers of the Enemy Appearing Redy to Ingage us our troop keep on thare march & when we have Got within musket Shot we Recived The Fire of thare Swivel Guns with Partrige Shot which seemd to Come very thick wounded Several of our men but None killed we Returned the Comple[men]t with one of our Field Peases upon which they Gave us a voley of Small arms I beleve not Less than Six Hundred upon which our troop Fired Briskly Capt Brooms who Comanded the arteliery Plied the Field Peases Clostly & the Fire from the Enemy was very warm for they Had two Carage Guns & Four Swivels Beside thare Small Arms but our Fire was So warm upon them & thay See our troops So Resolute that thay Found we would Force them from thare Ground thay sot all thare Buildings on Fire & Fled[69]

This rout resulted in victory for the British and Americans.

While this entry would not pass any college freshman composition test today, I suggest, at the risk of being thought permissive, that John's literacy did what he wanted it to do — it enabled him to record events that held deep personal meaning for him. Elsewhere he mentions writing letters home: literacy, even at this non-standard level, enhanced both his ability to record events and his possibilities for communication. Nowhere in his diary does he mention reading a book.

Our third witness is Phillis Wheatley. Phillis was a phenomenon by any standards. She had been brought on the schooner *Phillis* as a slave from west Africa to Boston in 1761, at the age of perhaps eight, and sold into the household of John Wheatley (a prominent Boston merchant), his wife Susanna, their eighteen-year-old twins and several slaves. Mary, one of the twins, taught Phillis language and literacy, and Phillis became one of the best educated women in America, and certainly the single best educated African American. She read the Bible, contemporary poets like Pope, was learning Latin, and read, presumably with the aid of translations, Roman poets such as Vergil and Ovid. She wrote her first poems only four years after her arrival in Boston; one of them first appeared in print in 1767. A book of her poetry was published in London in 1773, after Boston publishers had failed to take an interest in her manuscript.[70]

If it took time for the notion to be accepted that all free girls should be taught to write, we can readily predict what the official position would be on teaching slaves literacy: if taught at all — and there was plenty of dispute about that — they would be taught to read, whether male or female, as part of their conversion to Christianity, but not to write. Sure enough, when Cotton Mather set up an even-

69 ''Diary of John Thomas,'' *Nova Scotia Historical Society Collections*, 1 (1878), 119-40; quotation 123.

70 Julian D. Mason, Jr., ed. and introd., *The Poems of Phillis Wheatley*, rev. and enl. ed. (1966; Chapel Hill, 1989), 2-5, 8.

ing charity school for slaves around 1717, they were to be taught reading and religion only.[71] In the case of slaves, there were most practical reasons for not teaching them to write: the first thing any self-respecting slave would do was forge his or her own pass.

While Phillis was treated much more like a family member than a slave, the attitude in the family towards her literacy is revealing. In a letter to her London publisher, her master John Wheatley remarked that only sixteen months after arriving in America, and without any formal schooling, "only what she was taught in the Family," she was able to read "the most difficult Parts of the Sacred Writings, to the great Astonishment of all who heard her." Once again, the emphasis within the family had initially been on the oral reading of the Scriptures. The Wheatleys were not the only ones to think that Bible reading was the most appropriate literacy activity Phillis could undertake: in one of her letters, written in 1772, Phillis thanked a London correspondent "for recommending the Bible to be my cheif study [.]" "I find and Acknowledge it," she said, "the best of Books."[72]

It was Phillis herself, however, who had insisted on learning to write. "As to her WRITING," said John, "her own Curiosity led her to it." One of her poems, written in 1767, is addressed, rather wistfully, to the students of Harvard College: "TO THE UNIVERSITY OF CAMBRIDGE, WROTE IN 1767 — While an intrinsic ardor bids me write/ The muse doth promise to assist my pen." No woman ever claimed to write without some kind of help from someone other than herself, just as no woman claimed she had really written for publication — the work was only published because of the "Importunity of many of her best, and most generous Friends," as Phillis put it in her preface.[73]

Our last witness is Anna Green Winslow. Although her father traced his ancestry back to a brother of Edward Winslow, a founder and one of the governors of Plymouth Colony, Anna herself was brought up in Cumberland, Nova Scotia, where her father had been Commissary-General of the British Forces in the 1740s.[74] Anna had been sent to Boston to live with her Aunt Deming (her father's sister) and complete her education at private Boston schools. Her journal, begun in 1771 while she was still only eleven, reflects the new eighteenth-century child: one who was just as deeply religious as her forebears, but also one who had access to a greatly enlarged range of texts.

Anna's journal itself is a paradox: here she was attending Master Samuel Holbrook at the South Writing School (as a private pupil when the boys were not in school), yet she could write — in the sense of both penmanship and composition

---

71 Cotton Mather, *Diary of Cotton Mather*, Vol. 2, 1709-1724 (New York, 1957), 379, 442, 500, 663.

72 Mason, *Poems of Phillis Wheatley*, 47, 188.

73 *Ibid.*, 47, 116, 45.

74 Alice Morse Earle, ed., *Diary of Anna Green Winslow, A Boston School Girl of 1771* (1894; rpt. Williamstown, Mass., 1974), ix, xi.

— perfectly well already. Her letters, in her version of round hand, are legible and even, and her spelling much more conventional than that of John Thomas, and always intelligible even when unconventional. (One charmingly Puritan misspelling is her description of being given a handsome book "In nice Guilt and flowers covers.") Punctuation, by modern standards, could use some help, but eighteenth-century punctuation in general differed from our own.[75]

The emphasis of writing schools upon penmanship (which became, for the most advanced pupils, lessons in calligraphy) is evident from Anna's comments. She shows a healthy contempt for the focus of the writing school upon form, and articulates her own preference for writing as the communication of content: "I have just now been writing four lines in my Book almost as well as the copy. But all the intreaties in the world will not prevail upon me to do always as well as I can, which is not the least trouble to me, tho' its a great grief to Aunt Deming. And she says by writing so frightfully above." Almost at the end of her diary, after two years of Boston education, she says that she has been attending all her schools regularly, but the writing school without much benefit: "I have paid my compliments to messrs Holbrook & Turner (to the former you see to very little purpose) & mrs Smith as usual." (Mr. Turner was her dancing master and Mrs. Smith was her sewing instructer.)[76]

Anna's penmanship, so good by our standards for a twelve-year-old, may have caused Aunt Deming "great grief," but her powers of communication through writing were marvelous. Not only did she keep her journal (itself a sort of open letter to her parents), but she composed "Billets" (formal little notes, written in the third person) for friends, wrote letters, and recorded such chunks of theological discussions from ministers' sermons and lectures that her aunt urged her to desist because the "perticulars ... she finds lie ... somewhat confused in my young mind."[77]

Anna's diary reveals what she read as well as what she wrote. Far from keeping her journal private, she read it aloud to her aunt and even to company, at the risk of being laughed at. She borrowed children's books from her younger cousins, and so read imported works (published by the Newbery firm in London) like *The Puzzling Cap*, *Goody Two-shoes* and the *Mother's Gift*, that were actually designed for younger children. She herself was at the level of reading *Pilgrim's Progress* and abbreviated versions of *Gulliver's Travels* and *The History of Joseph Andrews*. She and a female cousin at one point "read out" (i.e., aloud) the *Generous Inconstant* and began to read aloud Richardson's *Sir Charles Grandison* (no doubt also in an abbreviated version). But none of this so-called "extensive" reading interfered with her "intensive" biblical reading. She regularly read aloud from

75 *Ibid.*, Samuel Holbrook: 92-94; the condition of the manuscript: vi; quotation, 13. The book was "the History of Joseph Andrews abreviated."

76 *Ibid.*, 39, 70. For the curriculum of the Boston writing schools, see Monaghan, "Readers Writing."

77 *Ibid.*, billets: 41-43; letters: 66; sermons, e.g. 1-3, 24-25, 53-54; quotation, 56.

I hope aunt wont let one wear the black hatt with the red Dominie— for the people will ask one what I have got to sell as I go along street if I do. or, how the folk at Newguinie do? Dear mamma, you dont know the fation here— I beg to look like other folk. You dont kno what a stir would be made in sudbury street were I to make ony appearance there in my red Dominue & black Hatt. But the old cloak & bonnett together will make me a decent Bonnet for common ocation (I like that aunt says, its a pritty some of the ribbin you sent wont do for the Bonnet— I must now close up this Journal. With Duty, Love, & Complements as due, perticularly to my Dear little brother, (I long to se him) & M.ʳ Law, I will write to her soon I am Honᵈ. Poppa & mama,

Y.ʳ everDutiful Daughter

N. B. my aunt Deming, Anna Green Winslow. dont approve of my English. It has not the fear that you will thenk her concern'd in the Dittion

A page from Anna Green Winslow's diary, Alice Morse Earl, ed., *Diary of Anna Green Winslow, A Boston School Girl of 1771* (Boston, 1894).

the Bible — or sometimes another book — to Aunt Deming each morning, and often by candlelight at night. She knew the Scriptures so well that, like Hannah Heaton, she easily integrated biblical quotations and references into her journal.[78]

An entry for 9 March 1772 indicates how hard she worked at her literacy. It was what she dubbed a piecemeal day: she sewed on the "bosom" of her uncle's shirt; mended two pairs of gloves and two handkerchiefs, sewed on half of a border onto her aunt's apron, "read part of the xxist chapter of Exodous, & a story in the Mother's gift," and, of course, wrote all these efforts down in her diary.[79]

In short, although Anna spoke as if she regarded reading and writing, along with sewing, as work, she clearly also used her literacy as a recreational skill. It was, however, a recreational skill only up to a certain point. When she had a gift of money from her father, it all went on "a very beautiful white feather hat" that she had long coveted, "with the feathers sew'd on in a most curious manner white & unsullied as the falling snow"; nowhere does she record purchasing a book.[80]

Conclusion

If we are to answer the five questions that have (and should) be asked about literacy in New England or anywhere else, we need to look not just at how many people could or could not sign their names, or what books they did or did not own at death, but at what literacy meant to those who possessed it. For this, an interdisciplinary approach is necessary — one that capitalizes upon the skills of the quantifier yet shares in the insights of those who approach literacy qualitatively. We need the tools of the anthropologist, in particular, as well as those of the historian and social scientist, and of the educator as well as those of the bibliographer and the literary analyst. Here I concur with Carl Kaestle, who has called for a "new history of literacy" that would move away from studies of crude literacy rates towards examining how literacy functioned in the lives of the literate.[81]

Our four examples of diary keepers show us literacy at work in the eighteenth-century context. The four cases are not equivalent, of course, quite apart from the fact that they span four decades: Anna Green Winslow was an urban child (at least when we meet her through her diary), as was Phillis Wheatley, while Han-

---

78 *Ibid.*, reading journal: to aunt, 51; to company, 72. The Newbery books appear in the diary as "The puzzeling cap, the female Oraters & the history of Gaffer too-shoes" [sic], 64; (*The Puzzling Cap* was a collection of riddles), 64; *The Mother's Gift*, 40; *Pilgrim's Progress*, 34; other books: 60, 13, 70 (bis); reading to Aunt Deming: 21, 41; Biblical references, e.g. 15, 42. These were in addition to her regular recording of texts discussed in sermons and lectures.

79 *Ibid.*, 40.

80 *Ibid.*, 31.

81 Kaestle, "History of Literacy and the History of Readers." For a good example of a mixed quantitative/qualitative approach see Ross W. Beales, Jr., "Literacy and Reading in Eighteenth Century Westborogh, Massachusetts," in Peter Benes, ed., *Annual Proceedings of the Dublin Seminar for New England Folklife*, Vol. 12, *Early American Probate Inventories* (Boston, 1989), 41-50.

nah Heaton and probably John Thomas lived in rural areas. Anna had no house-
work to do, as the Demings owned servants, and she was of a higher social class
than any of the others. Nonetheless, we can make a few generalizations. Books
were still fewer, and read more intently, than would be the case in the early Republic and thereafter, but the door to recreational reading had been opened wide by
the 1770s — and indeed earlier — for anyone who had access to imported English
books. The secularization of reading was now in place, and it was permissible
to read books designed primarily to amuse rather than instruct.

It is writing, however, not reading, that emerges as the more important of the
two literacy skills for all our four users. In each case, they codified as well as
recorded their experiences, seeking to understand them better as they wrote them
down. In a reevaluation of eighteenth-century literacy, we shall need to avoid the
biases in favor of reading that are so plain in our own times — as I suggested at
the beginning of this paper — and appreciate the role played by writing in the lives
of the literate, despite the lack of any formal instruction in composition. To come
to grips with the effects of literacy, then, we should look, not to modernization
theory, but to a theory of the "expansion of personal space" that has been for-
mulated by Richard Venezky.[82] It is not only the public but the private and personal dimension that will, I predict, be found to be one of literacy's chief contributions to the lives of its eighteenth-century possessors.[83]

Postscript

In the time intervening between my delivery of this paper and its publication,
scholarly interest in literacy has shown no signs of abating. In fact, some of my
strictures on a lack of interest in New England literacy must be toned down: two
articles have appeared that relate directly to this very topic. I have incorporated
a few post-conference references into the text of this essay, for the reader's con-
venience, but deal here with these two articles.

The first, by Joel Perlmann and Dennis Shirley, explores the question of when
New England women acquired literacy. It is a refinement of the first of our five
questions, asking not only who was literate but when they became so. The authors
dodge the thorny problem of women who could read but not write (and for whom
a mark is therefore not a valid measure of illiteracy) by defining "full literacy"
as the ability to both read and write. Just as there is a discrepancy between Linda
Auwers' findings and Lockridge's, there is also a conflict, the authors suggest,
between Lockridge's findings and those they obtained from the United States census of 1850. This census was the first to ask questions about the respondents' literacy: according to their self-report, literacy was almost universal. The authors ask
how women could have leaped from such a low to such a high literacy level within

---

82   Venezky, ''The Development of Literacy in the Industrialized Nations of the West,'' 48.

83   For an example of the role played by literacy in the lives of the members of the (Wampanaog)
     Indian community of Colonial Martha's Vineyard, see Monaghan, '' 'She loved to read in good
     Books.' ''

half a century. They conclude from a review of earlier studies on New England literacy (including all those discussed above) that female literacy was already high by 1765 and rose thereafter, and that female literacy was ''prevalent'' as early as 1780 rather than 1830.[84]

There are difficulties with comparing such different data as signature evidence and census self-reports, as the authors of course realize. In any case, the census evidence is too late to be of interest to us. One piece of new research, however, is relevant. The authors investigated *all* Suffolk wills made by women from 1787 to 1795 (Lockridge had only sampled these for this time period). They found a 78 per cent signing rate among Boston women and a 53 per cent rate among rural women, compared with Lockridge's figures of 60 and 42 respectively. When the ''out-of-date'' nature of wills is taken into account, as discussed above — these women were perhaps 40 years old and up when they made their wills — this supports the position that women, especially urban women, were able to sign their names (and by implication read) earlier in New England than Lockridge's figures suggested.[85] The Perlman and Shirley study therefore lends some support to my own hunches about female literacy, discussed above.

In the second study (also quantitative and again equating signing with literacy), F.W. Grubb investigated the growth of literacy in colonial America overall by reexamining the results of all earlier studies to see if he could find patterns in male literacy growth. He draws several major conclusions. First, there was a significant difference between rural and urban signing, in favor of the latter, in both Europe and colonial America. Second, the level of literacy in colonial America was superior to that in Europe. Third, while levels of literacy did vary among the colonies, the highest levels were fairly evenly distributed among the different colonies. Urban literacy in one colony, for instance, was comparable to urban literacy in another.[86]

Another major finding was that growth throughout colonial America was non-linear: there were temporary declines in male literacy after the initial settlement throughout America, followed by a renewed upward surge over time. Grubb's ''creolean degeneracy'' hypothesis, as he dubs it, posits that immigrant Americans failed to transfer their literacy successfully to American-born colonists, but that subsequent generations made up for lost ground. (He also discusses literacy as an economic factor within a supply/demand framework.)[87]

Implications for Planters Studies
All the research, to sum up, suggests that the great majority, perhaps nearly all, of the male New Englanders who left their native farms and villages for the lure of Nova Scotia would have been what today we would call functionally literate.

---

84   Perlmann and Shirley, ''When Did New England Women Acquire Literacy?''

85   *Ibid.*; Lockridge, *Literacy in Colonial New England*, 128 n.4.

86   Grubb, ''Growth of Literacy in Colonial America,'' 452-59.

87   *Ibid.*, 461-72.

By modern standards their literacy, like John Thomas', was far from flawless, yet it was perfectly adequate for their needs. The majority of women would also have been able to write, and virtually all of them to read.

Grubb's study, in particular, has useful implications for the Nova Scotia Planters. There is a general impression, not yet substantiated by research, that the literacy skills of the Planters degenerated over the next generation — an example of Grubb's "creolean degeneracy." While Grubb does not venture a reason for this backsliding, it is possible to make a few suggestions. In the stress and backbreaking work of wresting new farms, either from those that the Acadians had been forced to abandon or from land never previously tilled, the new settlers in Nova Scotia presumably had more pressing matters on their minds than attending to the literacy of their young. The schooling context is crucial here, too. Because schooling was in the hands of Anglican clergy in Nova Scotia, transplanted New Englanders were unable to create institutions parallel to the district schools they had left behind them. By and large, schools were sadly absent from initial settlements. Parents who wanted their children to be literate would often have had to teach them themselves. If these two disadvantages were further buttressed by a lack of piety — the engine that had driven New England reading acquisition for so long — the value to the Planters of imparting their literacy to their young would have faded. Investigations into Planter literacy could also profit from examinations of book holdings in estate inventories. In homes of the deceased where there was no Bible, the literacy outlook was grim indeed!

A final word about the mark in the Planter context. Given the expectations by the 1770s that every white male child should learn both to read and write, and even that every white female child (if we can generalize from the example of the Massachusetts Poor Laws) should be taught to write as well as read, the mark in this context does indeed seem to stand (as it did not earlier in the history of literacy) for illiteracy. In New England, because most girls at the end of the century had access to schools in the winter, where writing was taught, and because of the improved literacy standards of the eighteenth century overall, anyone born after about 1765 who did not learn to sign his or her name can indeed be considered genuinely illiterate. In the Nova Scotia context, only if there were a resurgence (in the absence of schools) of parents who taught their children to read at home but not to write (which seems unlikely) would this observation not also hold true of the next generation of Planters.

Change and Continuity in Nova Scotia, 1758-1775

Dr. John G. Reid
Department of History
St. Mary's University

In 1956, a prominent historian from Lehigh University in Pennsylvania made the following published statement: "the year 1759 may . . . be taken as the beginning of the great New England migration that was to transform Nova Scotia . . . , even before the inundation that came with the mass movement of Loyalists into the province as a result of the War for American Independence."[1] The author was Lawrence Henry Gipson, and the quotation comes from the ninth volume of his monumental history of *The British Empire Before the American Revolution*. Gipson's treatment of the Planters is interesting in the context of the widely-held and generally but not entirely accurate assumption that, apart from J.B. Brebner and a handful of Maritime-based historians (D.C. Harvey, R.S. Longley, W. Stewart MacNutt, J.S. Martell, and Esther Clark Wright being the major examples), serious scholarly interest in the era of the Planter migration did not predate the late 1960s.[2] Although Gipson's account, influenced as it was by Brebner, was not outstandingly original in its interpretation, it was based on primary source research in London, Ottawa and Halifax. It also showed that Gipson believed the Nova Scotia experience to be worth a 29-page chapter in his treatment of the British Empire in the early 1760s, longer by eight pages than the one devoted to the province of Quebec. As would be expected in a member of the so-called "imperial school" of American colonial history — Gipson's mentor for his Yale doctoral thesis on the Connecticut Loyalist Jared Ingersoll had been the *doyen* of that school, Charles McLean Andrews — Gipson concentrated on the institutional development of Nova Scotia in the period, though also giving attention to the Planters and, at some length, to the enterprises of Alexander McNutt.

The historiographical fortunes of the approach taken by Andrews and his disciples waned in the 1950s in the face of criticism from historians — such as Ber-

---

1   Lawrence Henry Gipson, *The Triumphant Empire: New Responsibilities Within the Enlarged Empire, 1763-1766* (New York, 1956; Volume 9 of *The British Empire Before the American Revolution*), 135.

2   See, among the other works of these authors, John Bartlet Brebner, *The Neutral Yankees of Nova Scotia: A Marginal Colony During the Revolutionary Years* (New York, 1937); D.C. Harvey, "The Struggle for the New England Form of Township Government in Nova Scotia," *Canadian Historical Association Report*, 1933, 15-22; R.S. Longley, "The Coming of the New England Planters to the Annapolis Valley," *Nova Scotia Historical Society Collections*, 33 (1961), 81-101; W.S. MacNutt, "The Beginnings of Nova Scotia Politics, 1758-1766," *Canadian Historical Review*, 16 (1935), 41-53; J.S. Martell, "Pre-Loyalist Settlements Around Minas Basin: A History of the Townships of Cornwallis, Horton, Falmouth, Newport, Windsor, Truro, Onslow, and Londonderry, 1755-1783, With a Survey of the French Period," MA thesis, Dalhousie University, 1933; Esther Clark Wright, "Cumberland Township: A Focal Point of Early Settlement on the Bay of Fundy," *Canadian Historical Review*, 27 (1946), 27-32.

nard Bailyn and Perry Miller — who emphasized the distinctness of the American experience from that of Great Britain and thus questioned the political and cultural ascendancy of the parent country. The turn in the 1960s to detailed social analysis of the North American colonies removed the centre of gravity of colonial scholarship even further away from the "imperial" approach. The importance in its day of the work of Andrews and his students has continued to be recognized in historiographical studies — one recent appraisal credited Andrews with having "more than any other historian..., invented the colonial period of American history" — but Andrews's magisterial volumes on *The Colonial Period of American History* continue in the 1990s to adorn the shelves of virtually all North American university libraries without ever reaching the circulation desks on any but the rarest occasions.[3] As for Gipson, the sheer weight of his 15-volume study of *The British Empire Before the American Revolution* continued to be impressive, and his 1954 volume on *The Coming of the American Revolution, 1763-1775*, published in *The New American Nation Series*, assured him of an even wider audience for many years thereafter.[4] Nevertheless, Gipson's unabashed celebration of the British Empire and his institutional approach tend to be sceptically received by modern readers. In British North American history, and that of Nova Scotia in particular, it is the work of another of Andrews's principal legatees, Viola Florence Barnes, that continues deservedly to be attributed historiographical significance for Barnes's pioneering observations on the refusal of Nova Scotia to join the American Revolution.[5] It might be added in parentheses that at the time of Andrews's retirement in 1931, more than 40 per cent of his students were women, and it has recently been suggested that the lack of academic opportunities open to women at major universities may have been one reason for the rapid faltering of the influence of the "imperial school."[6] Be that as it may, there can be few scholars of early Nova Scotia who at present would place a high priority on examining the work either of Barnes — except for historiographical purposes — or of Lawrence Henry Gipson.

It will not be my purpose here to attempt in any full sense to rehabilitate the work of Gipson or of other scholars of similar approach and vintage. Nevertheless, I

---

3   Richard R. Johnson, "Charles McLean Andrews and the Invention of American Colonial History," *William and Mary Quarterly*, 3rd ser., 43 (1986), 528; Charles McLean Andrews, *The Colonial Period of American History*, 4 Vols. (New Haven, 1934-38).

4   Lawrence Henry Gipson, *The British Empire Before the American Revolution*, Vols. 1-3 (Caldwell, Idaho, 1936) Vols. 4-15 (New York, 1939-70); Gipson, *The Coming of the Revolution, 1763-1775* (New York, 1954).

5   Viola F. Barnes, "Francis Legge, Governor of Loyalist Nova Scotia, 1773-1776," *New England Quarterly*, 4 (1931), 420-47. See also the extracts and commentary in George A. Rawlyk, ed., *Revolution Rejected, 1775-1776* (Scarborough, Ont, 1968), 30-33; and [George A. Rawlyk, ed.,], "Revolution Rejected: Why Did Nova Scotia Fail to Join the American Revolution?," in Paul W. Bennett and Cornelius Jaenen, eds., with Jacques Monet, George A. Rawlyk, and Richard A. Jones, *Emerging Identities: Selected Problems and Interpretations in Canadian History* (Scarborough, Ont., 1986), 146-47.

6   Johnson, "Charles McLean Andrews," 532, citing Ian K. Steele.

shall argue that their work should not be ignored as determinedly as it has been in recent years, and further that when their approach is put in juxtaposition with an important comment made by a thoroughly modern scholar at the 1987 Planter Studies conference, some interesting conclusions may suggest themselves. An effort should be made, argued Graeme Wynn at that time, to "abandon the blinkers of traditional historical scholarship to seek a fuller knowledge of the past interrelations of people with their environments, and heighten our understanding of the evolving character of societies *and* places."[7] Environmental history in this sense, and political history in the manner of Andrews, Barnes and Gipson may seem at first sight to represent an unlikely partnership. Unlikely or not, I suggest that it is one that is worth exploring both in the immediate context of Planter Studies, and in the study of other areas of North America in the same era.

First of all, however, it is necessary to review what I would take to be one of the central dynamics of the Planter experience, and the one that is embodied in my title for this paper: the question of change and continuity. It does not demand any great departure from our present understanding of the era of the Planter migration to argue that the relationship between change and continuity was a complex one. In one sense, the Planter migration was the result of a dramatic series of changes that had taken place in Nova Scotia between 1755 and 1758. The expulsion of the Acadians belonged chiefly to those years, though of course it continued sporadically until 1762. The British conquest of Ile Royale and Ile Saint-Jean brought to an effective end in 1758 the French imperial presence in the territory that had constituted the old French colony of Acadia. For potential New England migrants, however, these changes were significant chiefly for the way in which they appeared to promise a kind of continuity. The removal of the French military capability and of most of the Acadians eliminated the perceived threat that in the past had tended to deter New Englanders from settling in Nova Scotia. Furthermore, if the longstanding Micmac resistance to British rule were taken to depend on the incitement of the French, it was reasonable to expect that this pressure would also now relax. No doubt there were some who, like the young Henry Alline, continued in 1760 to nourish "the fear of the Indians in that country," but the apparent submission of "the several Districts of the general Mickmack Nation of Indians" in 1761 at the governor's farm in Halifax provided reassurance.[8] Now, there was reason to believe, the experience of settling in Nova Scotia would be no more alien to New Englanders than that of migrating within New England itself. This expectation was further strengthened by the efforts of the government

7   Graeme Wynn, "The Geography of the Maritime Colonies in 1800: Patterns and Questions," in Margaret Conrad, ed., *They Planted Well: New England Planters in Maritime Canada* (Fredericton, 1988), 150.

8   James Beverley and Barry Moody, eds., *The Life and Journal of the Rev. Mr. Henry Alline* (Hantsport, N.S., 1982), 33; Treaty Ceremony, 25 June 1761, Great Britain, Public Record Office, CO 217/18, f.276. On Micmac hostility to the settlement of the Foreign Protestants during the 1750s, see Winthrop P. Bell, *The "Foreign Protestants" and the Settlement of Nova Scotia* (2nd ed., Sackville, N.B., 1990), 502-18.

of Nova Scotia to portray a political environment that would be essentially familiar. ''The Government of Nova Scotia is constituted like those of the Neighbouring Colonies,'' declared Governor Charles Lawrence's proclamation of 11 January 1759.[9] Following on the calling of the first elected assembly in October 1758, and the issuing shortly thereafter of a proclamation that had extended a formal invitation to New England settlers, the proclamation of January 1759 was enough to give the strong impression to prospective migrants that virtually complete conformity with New England practices — extending even to town government — would be found in Nova Scotia. Thus, the land hunger or alternatively the desire for immediate access to productive fishing grounds and harbours — in either case, the acquisitiveness that has been described by one scholar as ''the motor of colonization'' among the Planters — could be unleashed with the assurance that a fundamental continuity of experience could be maintained.[10]

Comforting as such a prospect might be, it was misleading in a number of important aspects. It was true, of course, that the formal French presence was gone. It was not true either that the Acadians had been extirpated even by the extremities of the expulsion or that the removal of the French had destroyed the capacity of native peoples for independent thought and action. While the Acadian, Micmac and Maliseet responses to the Planter migration deserve much more detailed research, it is clear enough that these peoples impinged significantly on the consciousness of Planter Nova Scotia. The direct relationship of Planters and Acadians was a limited one, with Acadians at times supplying wage labour for the care of the dyke systems on which depended the marshlands now used by Planters. At a political level, the Acadian return — whether from exile or simply from hiding, as the deportation finally ground to a halt in the early 1760s — was a matter of urgent concern. Lieutenant-Governor Montagu Wilmot responded vehemently to a suggestion of 1763 that a group of Acadians be settled on the Miramichi river: the Acadians, wrote Wilmot, ''are most inflexibly devoted to France, and the Romish Religion, and being much connected with the Indians . . . , their power and disposition to be mischevious is more to be dreaded . . . .''[11] To be sure, Wilmot's statement was that of a professional military officer who may well have been mentally refighting the battles of the 1750s, but it did reflect the remarkably persistent belief — all contrary evidence notwithstanding — in Acadian treachery and militancy that may also have owed something to the perceptions that had been nourished by the New England folkloric memory of such incidents as the battle of Grand Pré in 1747.

More substantial was the challenge posed at times by native inhabitants. The siting of the Planter community at Maugerville was prompted by the armed

9 Minutes of Nova Scotia Council, 11 January 1759, Public Archives of Nova Scotia (hereafter PANS), RG 1, Vol. 188, 42.

10 Debra McNabb, ''The Role of the Land in the Development of Horton Township, 1760-1775,'' in Conrad, *They Planted Well*, 160.

11 Montagu Wilmot to the Earl of Halifax, 22 March 1764, PANS, RG 1, Vol. 41, No. 5.

intervention of the Maliseet to forbid settlement on the originally-chosen site at St. Ann's.[12] In Falmouth, recalled Henry Alline of his early years in Nova Scotia, "it was frequently reported, that the Indians were about rising to destroy us; and many came out among us with their faces painted, and declared that the English should not settle this country."[13] For Alline, this threat bulked large in the spiritual struggles that preceded his personal religious awakening. How far, and in what ways, it affected other members of Planter communities remains to be investigated. What seems clear is that, despite what had taken place at the governor's farm in 1761 — and it would certainly be imprudent at best to accept at face value either the British texts of the agreements signed there or the role as intermediary of Nova Scotia's official Indian agent at the time, the Abbé Pierre Maillard — native people retained an active sense of the limitations that should legitimately be placed on non-native settlement and a continuing determination to devise strategies towards this end. If, moreover, the Planters soon found that the native treaties were not quite what they seemed, the same discovery awaited them with respect to the proclamation of January 1759. That document had implied more than would ever be delivered in terms of New England forms of town government, and the resulting political struggles have been well documented.[14] Far from moving to a colony that closely resembled Massachusetts, Connecticut or other New England provinces, the Planters found that the quasi-military flavour of government in Nova Scotia was a clear legacy of the struggles of the 1750s, and was further entrenched by the importance of Halifax as a military and strategic centre. Along with the more predictable problems of settling in what was for them a new land, the removal to Nova Scotia had demanded of the Planters adjustments that belied any notion of ready continuity of experience.

Furthermore, the experience of the non-British inhabitants of Nova Scotia offers evidence of the changes which Planter settlement in turn exacted from others. It was true that Nova Scotia was not yet crowded with human beings, or at least not by the standards of earlier and later times. Even by the eve of the American Revolution, the combined population of Nova Scotia and the Island of St. John — perhaps a little over 20,000 — was probably substantially less than in the era prior to first European contact with native people in 1500 or thereabouts, and also much less than would soon come about in the wake of the Loyalist migration. Human inter-relationships, however, and the relationship of human beings to their natural environment, are not simply tied to numbers. Although it might be true in a limited sense that there was room for all in Nova Scotia, the Planter migrations combined with others of the era from 1758 to 1775 to impose environmentally-related changes on both Acadian and native inhabitants. For Acadians, whether those who

---

12 L.F.S. Upton, *Micmacs and Colonists: Indian-White Relations in the Maritimes, 1713-1867* (Vancouver, 1979), 69.

13 Beverley and Moody, *Life and Journal of Alline*, 33.

14 See Harvey, "The Struggle for the New England Form of Township Government in Nova Scotia," 20-22.

had avoided deportation or those who subsequently returned, the direct impact was clearest in the covering of the three principal areas of former Acadian settlement by Planter townships. Henceforward, despite some isolated survivals of Acadian marshland agriculture in places such as Minudie and Memramcook, the Acadian relationship with both land and sea would be radically changed. The English traveller Gamaliel Smethurst described a meeting with some Acadian refugees on the Mirimachi in late 1761 and their departure for Miscou to hunt walrus.[15] Hunting of sea mammals, fisheries, small-scale agriculture and, in later years, wage labour in the woods, would now form the basis of the necessary strategies by which the new Acadian communities would subsist around the Maritime coastline, while Planters continued to farm the marshlands until it became economically unprofitable to do so. For native inhabitants, and especially the Micmac of peninsular Nova Scotia, British settlement — including that of the Planters — introduced environmental encroachments that had not proceeded from the former Acadian communities. Clearing of uplands, the grazing there of cattle, and the progressive occupation of harbours and transportation routes that had been important to native fisheries and communications: these changes, as William Cronon has shown with respect to the early phases of colonization in New England, undermined the foundation of native economies and produced changes that were irreversible.[16] By the very process of devising strategies to deal with the increasing threat, native inhabitants took irrevocable steps towards redefining their relation to their environment, whether through strengthening connections with Newfoundland, seeking presents from the government of Nova Scotia, or experimenting with agriculture or fish curing. It was true that resistance could still be contemplated, and occasionally put into practice, but an increasingly unfavourable numerical and military balance of power meant that accommodations were difficult to avoid.

Historiographically, these struggles of non-British inhabitants have not generally been well portrayed in accounts of the Nova Scotia of the Planter era. In part, this neglect reflects biases in most of the available evidence. It was a rare piece of introspection when Captain John MacDonald reflected in 1795 on the criticisms often levelled by non-Acadians at the farming abilities of Acadians at Minudie. "We are a Saucy nation," wrote MacDonald to J.F.W. DesBarres, "too ready to despise others — because we have happened to be the Conquerors — we are of a different origin, Religion, &c. &c. Having taken them [the Acadians] in an early stage, we have destroyed them and the course of their prospective Improvement in their own way. . . . Sure I am we are not more virtuous or happy than

---

15 Gamaliel Smethurst, "A Narrative of an Extraordinary Escape out of the Hands of the Indians in the Gulph of St. Lawrence . . . ," *New Brunswick Historical Society Collections*, 2, 6 (1905), 377.

16 See William Cronon, *Changes in the Land: Indians, Colonists, and the Ecology of New England* (New York, 1983). See also the more general approach taken in Alfred W. Crosby, *Ecological Imperialism: The Biological Expansion of Europe, 900-1900* (Cambridge, 1986).

they are and I fear we have made them worse men and less happy than they have been.''[17] More generally, it is only with the relatively recent development of techniques in history and historical geography to do justice to native and environmental history that it has become possible to gauge the complexity of the changes that were taking place between 1758 and 1775. When the experience of the non-British peoples is juxtaposed with that of the Planters, a picture develops that differs somewhat from the more conventional impression of an era of orderly migration during which new communities peaceably emerged in a way that was easily overshadowed by the hurry and scurry of the Loyalist invasion some years later. Nova Scotia in the Planter era was in the throes of a profound societal realignment. It was true that there was surprising lack of outright violence. What was taking place continuously, however, was the devising of collective strategies by peoples who had seen their lives profoundly changed by the geopolitical events of the 1750s and early 1760s and who now had to adapt as best they could to political and environmental contexts that were unfamiliar to them.

This phenomenon was not peculiar to Nova Scotia. North America during the 1760s was in the grip of a more widespread realignment of human societies, again related to the military developments of the Seven Years' War and to the political démarches that were embodied in the Treaty of Paris in 1763. In some respects, the results of these processes have been thoroughly examined by historians. In Canada, the adjustments that followed in the province of Quebec, along with the immigration of Scottish and other merchants to Montreal and the creation of a new business elite, have been subjected to exhaustive historiographical discussion in both the French and English languages.[18] In the United States, the western migrations that resulted from the elimination of the French from the valley of the Ohio river and from those of other tributaries of the Mississippi has likewise attracted sustained scrutiny from historians, notably in the context of the Royal Proclamation of 1763 and of the role of its controversial and ultimately unsuccessful restrictions on settlement in the causation of the American Revolution.[19] To these historiographical exercises, however, there has been a certain teleological quality. It is no accident that in both cases — the forming of the province of Quebec, and the trans-Appalachian migrations — national mythologies have been involved. In the one case, prominence was assumed by the related notions that Canada was essentially the product of events taking place in the St. Lawrence valley and that French-English relationships formed a crucial dynamic of that process. In the other, the myth of the frontier joined with the question of the genesis of the Revolution to make the Proclamation line and its ineffectiveness a mat-

---

17 John MacDonald to J.F.W. DesBarres, 1795, quoted in Mason Wade, ''After the *Grand Dérangement*: The Acadians' Return to the Gulf of St. Lawrence and to Nova Scotia,'' *American Review of Canadian Studies*, 5 (1975), 62.

18 See Fernand Quellet, ''Quebec, 1760-1867,'' in D.A. Muise, ed., *A Reader's Guide to Canadian History, 1: Beginnings to Confederation* (Toronto, 1982), 45-77.

19 See Frank Freidel, ed., with Richard K. Showman, *Harvard Guide to American History: Revised Edition*, 2 Vols. (Cambridge, Mass., 1974), I, 324-44; II, 656-65.

ter of repeated enquiry. Other areas of significant migration in the same era —
Nova Scotia, the Floridas, Louisiana, to name the major ones in continental North
America — have traditionally received much less attention. In these cases, consciously or unconsciously, the teleological preoccupations of historians tended
to discourage interest rather than attract it. All exponents of Planter Studies are
familiar with the peculiar notion that population movements in Nova Scotia prior
to 1783 have limited importance because it was only with the arrival of the
Loyalists that permanent patterns of settlement emerged. Why expend energy in
examining East and West Florida after 1763 when we know perfectly well that
they are going to be handed back to Spain just twenty years later? And Louisiana
stands as the perennial historical anomaly of colonial North America, passed back
and forth between empires before attaining what some would see as its real destiny in 1803. Not much grist for the historical mill in any of these fringe areas,
or so it might seem.

Furthermore, certain important perspectives were largely missing from the
traditional scholarship. First, in all of the areas that were affected by population
movements stimulated by geopolitical changes, what was the relationship between
the larger geopolitical forces and the human agency of the settling populations?
Governments and private colonial promoters operating on various scales, ranging from the relatively modest endeavors of, say, Alexander McNutt to the gran-
deur of John Perceval, 2nd Earl of Egmont, played prominent roles. Colonists,
however, had their own agendas, and in the eighteenth century as in the seventeenth the resulting conflicts of interest could be among the crucial — if sometimes obscure — determinants of social and economic formation. Secondly, what
relationships emerged between new populations and existing ones, native or non-
native, and how did all of the peoples involved form or change their relationship
with the natural environment? It is in posing this question that we really come to
grips with the question of permanence and impermanence. Eighteenth-century
geopolitical changes in North America came in several instalments, each of which
can be conveniently associated with a major treaty date. It is easy enough when
dealing with — to put it crudely — those of 1763 and those of 1783 to assign priority to the later and thus seemingly the more lasting patterns. But changes in the
way people relate to their environment have a habit of being, as we are finding
out in the 1990s, irreversible. To be sure, changes in direction can still take place,
but a realignment of human societies as thoroughgoing as that in North America
in the 1760s could not be erased or undone by any later developments. Thirdly,
what does all of this reveal of the multicultural realities of eighteenth-century
North America? The processes of change that were taking place in the 1760s and
1770s were widespread, and deserve a continental — though not a continentalist
— perspective.

There are a number of significant studies that offer a wide perspective. One of
them, of course, is the work of Gipson, though as with all the historians of his
"imperial" inclination he took a particular approach. "We have been especially
interested," wrote Gipson in the conclusion of his volume dealing with the years

from 1763 to 1766, ''in certain problems confronting Great Britain and the Empire that arose directly from the peace settlement of 1763.''[20] Max Savelle, in his 1974 study of *Empire of Nations: Expansion in America, 1713-1824*, took a comparative approach that distinguished in a sophisticated way between the European empires throughout the Americas, while also insisting that ''the experiences of the Americans in America itself had also created 'unities' within the hemisphere that defied imperial boundaries,'' notably in regard to trading relationships.[21] By studying all of the Americas over a period of more than a century, however, Savelle virtually excluded the possibility of finely-grained discussions of particular colonial societies or of doing more than hinting at the active roles of native people. The works of two more recent authors, those of Bernard Bailyn and Donald Meinig published in 1986, have already been thoroughly discussed in their relation to Planter Studies by George A. Rawlyk at the 1987 Planter Studies conference.[22] Bailyn's study — or studies, as his 1985 Curti Lectures delivered at the University of Wisconsin are complementary to the larger volume, *Voyagers to the West* — has a variety of merits which have been recognized in the deservedly favourable critical reception of his work. Among them can be counted the sheer depth of the treatment of the movements and motivations of British emigrants to North America between 1773 and 1776, and Bailyn's recognition of a degree of unity in the experience of those in ''the peripheral lands,'' which he further subdivides into ''the great inland arc'' (North Carolina, Georgia and New York) and ''the extremities'' (the Maritime northeast, and East and West Florida).[23] Again, however, the native role is sketchily portrayed, despite some interesting reflections on the violence of frontier wars between native and non-native. The importance of native peoples finds greater recognition in Meinig's remarkable and successful synthesis of five hundred years of human geography of Atlantic America, including the period of ''reorganization'' that followed 1763.[24] Here, the relationships between geopolitics and the settler experience, and between new and old populations are explored, though it is a function of the scale of the enterprise that few pages or paragraphs can be devoted to the experience of any particular place and time.

To Bailyn's identification of ''the extremities'' can be added Louisiana. Although not part of the British sphere of influence in North America, that colony was also profoundly affected by the societal changes associated with the events

---

20 Gipson, *The Triumphant Empire*, 336.

21 Max Savelle, *Empires to Nations: Expansion in America, 1713-1824* (Minneapolis, 1974).

22 Bernard Bailyn, *The Peopling of British North America: An Introduction* (New York, 1986); Bailyn, *Voyagers to the West: A Passage in the Peopling of America on the Eve of the Revolution* (New York, 1986); D.W. Meinig, *The Shaping of America: A Geographical Perspective on 500 Years of History, Volume 1, Atlantic America, 1492-1800* (New Haven, 1986); G.A. Rawlyk, ''J.B. Brebner and Some Recent Trends in Eighteenth-Century Maritime Historiography,'' in Conrad, *They Planted Well*, 106-12.

23 Bailyn, *Voyagers to the West, passim.*

24 Meinig, *The Shaping of America*, 267-95, *passim.*

of the 1750s and the treaty of 1763. From the standpoint of Planter Studies, it is the southern experience that most aptly illustrates the overall North American context of these changes by offering certain parallels. Specific parallels, in themselves, are not essential to the task of showing that the societal realignment of the 1760s and 1770s was a North American phenomenon. The interactions between human beings and environments that followed from geopolitical changes in that era were necessarily diverse, in a way that implies that no parallels are likely to be exact in any detailed sense. Nevertheless, the experience of Planter Nova Scotia and, in particular, the lower Mississippi valley have affinities that make their comparison especially useful in demonstrating that Planter Studies have a profound North American as well as Nova Scotian significance. To focus on the lower Mississippi is not to deny that other aspects of southern history in this era can be regarded as significant in the same context. A strong case might be made for examining East Florida, where the list of those who became land speculators and would-be colonial promoters on a grand scale includes the Earl of Egmont and a number of other names familiar in Nova Scotia.[25] The increasingly urgent public and private efforts to recruit settlers, to a province that had been virtually evacuated by the previous non-native — that is, Spanish — inhabitants, yielded a more spectacular example of the potential conflict of interest between promoters and settlers than any in Nova Scotia. The 1400 predominantly Italian and Greek settlers brought in 1768 by the Scottish promoter Andrew Turnbull to ''New Smyrna,'' some 100 kilometres south of St. Augustine, endured a high enough mortality rate that only a small proportion were able in later years to reveal in formal testimony the oppressive conditions of their indentured servitude.[26] For the native inhabitants of East Florida, the transfer of 1763 was important for offering the opportunity to develop trade-based economic strategies. Creek eastward migration into Florida had already been influenced by the demand for deer and cattle skins among Georgia and Carolina traders. The inauguration of the British regime in East Florida prompted the arrival of British traders in St. Augustine and the establishment of trading posts in economically strategic locations. The results were lasting, even though East Florida itself was not; a trading economy so thoroughly established that even the Spanish authorities after 1783 continued to tolerate the presence of British traders, and an important stimulus to the distinct identity of the native communities that now evolved away from the Creek Confederacy and became known as the Seminole.[27]

If the study of East Florida raises some comparable questions to those that are relevant to Planter Nova Scotia — relationships between colonists and those who

---

25   Bailyn, *Voyagers to the West*, 438.

26   Charles Loch Mowat, *East Florida as a British Province, 1763-1784* (Berkeley and Los Angeles, 1943), 71-72.

27   Charles H. Fairbanks, ''The Ethno-Archaeology of the Florida Seminole,'' in William C. Sturtevant, ed., *A Seminole Source Book* (New York, 1987), 169-77; William C. Sturtevant, ''Creek into Seminole,'' *ibid.*, 98-105.

recruited them, and between native and non-native inhabitants in the environmental context — the lower Mississippi is more promising yet. Here, where British West Florida met Louisiana, native inhabitants, displaced Acadians, and New England settlers came into close proximity. Again, the exactness of parallels with Nova Scotia should not be laboured or exaggerated, for the ethnic diversity of the lower Mississippi region was the greater of the two by a considerable margin. Native cultures alone were diverse, with the competing Choctaw and Chickasaw representing only two of the peoples present in or near the Mississippi valley at the time. Non-native populations were also varied, with slavery having brought a large number of Africans and Afro-North Americans to join British, French and Spanish inhabitants. Also, the presence of the British-Spanish border was a creation of the Peace of Paris in 1763 that was not replicated in Nova Scotia, where the effect was to eliminate boundaries between politically hostile European empires rather than to create them. Historiographically, however, Nova Scotia and the lower Mississippi valley in the 1760s and 1770s share the doubtful distinction of having long been slighted by historians who mistrusted their anomalous borderland status. In both cases, the attention that *was* given by members of the "imperial" school was often overlooked by later scholars. An early and important scholarly study of West Florida was Cecil Johnson's *British West Florida, 1763-1783* published in 1942 as the revised version of an earlier Yale doctoral thesis completed under the direction of Charles McLean Andrews. A later work, unconnected with the "imperial" school but emphasizing the significance of the 1763 treaty, was Robert L. Gold's *Borderland Empires in Transition*, published in 1969.[28] Louisiana, never a part of the British Empire, did not attract the attention of the "imperial" school, but had its equivalent for its earlier years in the exhaustive narrative treatments of Marcel Giraud.[29] More recently, new questions have been raised regarding the lower Mississippi experience, and they have come from two principal historiographical directions. Significantly, both have emphasized human relationships with the physical environment.

The first of these historiographical initiatives involved the study of relations between native and non-native inhabitants. Patricia Dillon Woods's 1980 study of *French-Indian Relations on the Southern Frontier, 1699-1762* was followed by a number of works by Patricia K. Galloway. In 1983, Richard White published an ambitious comparative study of the experiences of the Choctaw, Pawnee and Navajo, making use of dependency theory to explain the processes of social and environmental change that affected each of the three peoples.[30] To this increas-

---

28 Cecil Johnson, *British West Florida, 1763-1783* (New Haven, 1942); Robert L. Gold, *Borderland Empires in Transition: The Triple-Nation Transfer of Florida* (Carbondale and Edwardsville, 1969).

29 Marcel Giraud, *Histoire de la Louisiane Français*, 4 Vols. (Paris, 1953-74).

30 Patricia Dillon Woods, *French-Indian Relations on the Southern Frontier, 1699-1762* (Ann Arbor, Mich., 1980); Patricia K. Galloway, ed., *LaSalle and his Legacy: Frenchmen and Indians in the Lower Mississippi Valley* (Jackson, Miss., 1982); Galloway, "Choctaw Factionalism and

ing range of sophisticated studies should be added James H. Merrell's prize-winning *The Indians' New World*, which, although it deals with the experience of the Catawba of the Carolina piedmont rather than with the lower Mississippi, offers a range of subtle methodologies in its analysis of the strategies adopted by native people to respond to the environmental and other changes brought by non-native society and their success in safeguarding their cultural integrity while doing so.[31]

The other major direction from which recent studies have approached the lower Mississippi relates to the cautious revival of interest in the "frontier" experience that has animated a number of social historians in studies ranging geographically from northern New England to the southern backcountry. While rejecting the Euro-American ethnocentrism and the faith in the progress of civilization that were prominent in Frederick Jackson Turner's famous formulation of 1893, such scholars have emphasized the responses of settlers to the unfamiliar human and natural environments of frontier areas, the distinct social forms and mores that arose from these encounters, and the importance and the fluidity of frontier relations between native and non-native peoples.[32] Regarding the lower Mississippi valley, the most sophisticated example of such work can be found in Daniel H. Usner, Jr.'s studies of "the frontier exchange economy." It was in the eighteenth-century development of "a cross-cultural web of economic relations," Usner argues, that "many later subsistence activities and adaptive strategies were rooted."[33] To these works dealing with native/non-native relations and with the frontier experience can be added two others that have recently dealt with the lower Mississippi valley from different but not unrelated perspectives: Carl Brasseaux's 1987 study of *The Founding of New Acadia: The Beginnings of Acadian Life in Louisiana, 1765-1803*, and Robin Fabel's *The Economy of British West Florida, 1763-1783*, published in the following year.[34]

Interesting as these works may be, what do they have to offer to Planter Studies? Some significant insights, I suggest, and at more than one level. Most visible are the opportunities for specifically comparative research. These would include the

Civil War, 1746-1750," *Journal of Mississippi History*, 44 (1982), 289-327; Richard White, *The Roots of Dependency: Subsistence, Environment, and Social Change Among the Choctaws, Pawnees, and Navajos* (Lincoln, Nev., and London, 1983).

31 James H. Merrell, *The Indians' New World: Catawbas and their Neighbors from European Contact Through the Era of Removal* (Chapel Hill, N.C., 1989).

32 See Gregory H. Nobles, "Breaking into the Backcountry: New Approaches to the Early American Frontier, 1750-1800," *William and Mary Quarterly*, 3rd ser., 46 (1989), 641-70.

33 Daniel H. Usner, Jr., "The Frontier Exchange Economy of the Lower Mississippi Valley in the Eighteenth Century," *William and Mary Quarterly*, 3rd ser., 44 (1987), 191. See also Usner, "Frontier Exchange in the Lower Mississippi Valley: Race Relations and Economic Life in Colonial Louisiana, 1699-1783," PhD thesis, Duke University, 1981.

34 Carl A. Brasseaux, *The Founding of New Acadia: The Beginnings of Acadian Life in Louisiana, 1765-1803* (Baton Rouge and London, 1987); Robin F.A. Fabel, *The Economy of British West Florida, 1763-1783* (Tuscaloosa, 1988).

negotiations conducted with the government of British West Florida by the Connecticut-based Company of Military Adventurers. Originally composed of Connecticut veterans of the British conquest of Cuba of 1762, who intended to take advantage of the British government's promised largesse in the form of land grants to disbanded soldiers in the newly-acquired colonies of North America, the Company began serious efforts in the early 1770s to achieve this goal in West Florida. By the end of 1773, nineteen townships had been mapped out, with four selected for immediate settlement, and the first group of what would eventually number some 400 New England families had set out for the Mississippi by way of Pensacola. Although the settlements of these southern Planters never produced the populous and prosperous communities that their leaders envisaged, their experience formed part of the economically-motivated outmigration from New England in which the Nova Scotia Planters were earlier participants.[35] Among the Acadian settlers in Spanish Louisiana, such phenomena as chronically troubled relationships with native inhabitants, participation of some hundreds of Acadians in an insurrection of 1768 which succeeded in expelling a Spanish governor who had insisted on Acadian settlement at the dangerously isolated upriver post of San Luis de Natchez, and the steady development of Acadian slaveholding in the 1760s and 1770s, invite comparison with the strikingly different roles of Acadians in Planter Nova Scotia.[36]

For the Choctaw, the departure of the French from Louisiana had certain stabilizing results. Internal divisions as to whether to ally militarily with France or great Britain, which had led to civil war in the 1740s, were now laid to rest, as were disputes with the Chickasaw. Both peoples now allied with the British of West Florida. The costs, however, were measured in terms of British encouragement for new and destructive wars with the Creek, the end of French gift-giving with the consequent undermining of the authority of diplomatic, or civil, chiefs, and an intensification of a market-driven trade in which newly-arrived British traders exchanged liquor for deerskins. Depletion of the white-tailed deer in turn intensified conflicts with the Creek over disputed hunting grounds. Together with the encroachments of non-native settlers in increasing numbers, this environmental change greatly narrowed the maneuvering room of the Choctaw vis-à-vis any and all of the European colonial powers. Thus, although the British regime departed from West Florida in 1783, these results could not be undone. As for the Micmac, though not of course for precisely the same reasons, the changes formalized in 1763 had brought new pressures to the Choctaw and much straitening of choice in matters of resistance and accommodation.[37]

Even more fundamentally, however, both the study of Planter Nova Scotia and that of the lower Mississippi valley in the same era confirm the validity and

---

35 Johnson, *British West Florida*, 139, 143; Bailyn, *Voyagers to the West*, 484-88; D. Clayton James, *Antebellum Natchez* (Baton Rouge, 1968), 17.

36 Brasseaux, *The Founding of New Acadia*, 86-89, 180-84, 188-92.

37 Usner, ''The Frontier Exchange Economy,'' 172-80; White, *Roots of Dependency*, 69-88.

importance of calibrating the societal and environmental history of eighteenth-century North America with the imperial reorganizations of the 1760s, in the interests of defining the great societal realignment that took place between the Seven Years' War and the American Revolution. The environmental and societal changes set in train during that period in the lower Mississippi region — as in East Florida — had lasting implications, even though the British regimes in the Floridas were conspicuously impermanent. The changes set in motion in Nova Scotia similarly could not be undone even though their significance might be obscured by the later influx of Loyalists. For the Planters themselves, a desire for continuity frequently emerged as characteristic of their removal to Nova Scotia: continuity not in the sense of stasis, but in the opportunity to pursue economic goals in a social and political environment comparable to New England. The government of Nova Scotia, in turn, was eager in 1758 and 1759 to proclaim that this was a realistic aspiration. The reality was that this kind of continuity was impossible to achieve fully, and difficult to achieve at all. It was as difficult for New Englanders in Nova Scotia or West Florida, as it was for displaced Acadians on the shores of the Gulf of St. Lawrence or in the bayou country of Louisiana, or for the Micmac or Choctaw whose strategies of alliance had been undermined. All of these peoples, and the others whose lives were affected by the forces unleashed by geopolitical events, now had to adapt to human and physical environments that were unfamiliar at best, unwelcoming and ultimately destructive at worst.

To conclude, then, I suggest that one of the lessons of the period from 1758 to 1775 is that geopolitical changes do make a difference and therefore that the preoccupations of the ''imperial'' school should not be dismissed. It is not so surprising that L.H. Gipson perceived the significance of the Planter migration when others did not. Gipson and other likeminded historians were not indifferent to such issues as migration, community formation and cultural interaction although their treatment of these matters was muted by their transcendent belief in the importance of the British Empire and its political institutions. Modern scholars would be unlikely to share that belief, just as they would be unreceptive to the Turnerian portrayal of the frontier as the cutting edge of civilization in its struggle with savagery. Nevertheless, just as new uses have recently been found for the notion of the frontier, and Turner widely reread if not rehabilitated, so there may be scope for a cautious dusting off of the works of Andrews, Gipson and the others. The prerequisite in both cases is a sophisticated understanding of the motivations of peoples of different ethnicity, the relationships between them — especially between native and non-native — and of the interactions of human beings with their environments. From the perspective of the scholarly concerns of the 1990s, the importance of the great imperial events such as the fall of Louisbourg and the treaty of Paris can only be fully realized in the context of the way in which they altered dramatically the framework within which the human agency of colonists and native people would be expressed, and in doing so set in motion processes of irreversible change in the human relationship with the environment. Viewed in this way, the importance of Planter Studies should be self-evident, and need fear no adverse comparison with the also important but quite different era of the Loyalist migrations. The Planter experience in Nova Scotia was crucial to the profound societal changes that took place in this part of North America in the 1760s and 1770s. The Planter experience, and that of the other peoples living in Nova Scotia at the time, also formed a noteworthy part of the great societal realignment that was taking place throughout those areas of North America that were affected by the imperial transfers formalized in 1763. In Planter Nova Scotia, continuity might be sought and, in a certain sense, found. The continuous history of Planter communities since the eighteenth century, and the persistent awareness of Planter heritage, are testimony to that. Nevertheless, the reality remains that Nova Scotia between 1758 and 1775 was in the grip of changes that were profound, lasting and of North American-wide significance.

Economic Fluctuations in Wartime Nova Scotia, 1755-1815

Julian Gwyn[1]
Professor of History
University of Ottawa

''War, along with harvest failures
and natural resource discoveries,
is to earlier periods in history
what oil shocks are to the 1970s
and 1980s.''[2]

I

From the 1740s until 1815 the economy of Nova Scotia was dominated by war and its immediate aftermath. It is clear that the mere attractiveness of good Acadian farmland, already cleared, was not enough to ensure the economic success of the new communities established in Nova Scotia, when some 2,400 New England immigrant families settled in the colony in the 1760s. Those settlements developed against a backdrop of international war. It must be remembered that the young colony, with the rest of the British Empire, was locked in what was, until 1758-59, a losing war with France.[3] Only with the transfer in 1763 to British hegemony of all of the Gulf of St. Lawrence region, including the entire Bay of Fundy, were recently-arrived Planters liberated from the threat of French power in North America. Yet the peace negotiated in Paris did not hold for long. In 1775 Britain was again preparing for war, this time with thirteen of her most populous North American colonies; and the effect of this long war and its aftermath had important economic consequences for Nova Scotia. This war proved as dangerous to Nova Scotia as the earlier war had been. If the power of France was not actually brought to bear against Nova Scotia, French naval forces were capable of landing a large army in New England in support of the American patriot cause, and of later successfully challenging the British navy in the Chesapeake.[4] Wholly incapable of defending themselves against incursions from New England, the population relied almost entirely upon forces sent from Great Britain. The end of war in 1783, again negotiated in Paris, brought a significant influx of Ameri-

---

1   The research for this paper was partly funded both by a federal government COSEP grant in 1983 and by research grants from SSHRCC between 1982 and 1984, for which I am very grateful.

2   Barry Eichengreen, ''Macroeconomics and History,'' in Alexander J. Field, ed., *The Future of Economic History* (Boston, 1987), 51.

3   See my ''Naval Power and the Two Sieges of Louisbourg, 1745 and 1758,'' *Nova Scotia Historical Review* (December 1990), 63-93.

4   The best of the recent accounts is David Syrett, *The Royal Navy in American Waters, 1775-1783* (Aldershot, 1989).

can refugees, creating all sorts of unwanted social tensions and economic competition — as well as opportunities — for the Yankees who had settled in Nova Scotia in the 1760s. It also significantly reduced the prestige and territory of Nova Scotia, when New Brunswick and Cape Breton were established as separate colonial administrations. The peace of 1783 proved less enduring than the one negotiated twenty years earlier. The renewal of warfare with France in 1792, which continued almost without stop until 1815, and with the United States between 1812 and 1814, again played havoc with the orderly economic development of Nova Scotia. A generation of war-induced disruptions after 1792 governed the markets, for which the New England Planters, the Lunenburg Germans, the returned Acadians, more recent Loyalist refugees and British immigrants actively competed.

In another way war brought particularly unsettling features to the Atlantic world. Owing to British military and naval weakness and the formidable alliances confronting her, it was never clear, until the peace treaties were negotiated, the extent to which British imperial interests could be defended or expanded. In none of these wars did British arms seize and hold the initiative, thus ensuring a victorious result from the outset. On the contrary, Britain seemed peculiarly inept, both from a military and naval standpoint, for several years after she engaged in war. In every instance she needed a long war to attain success or to avoid absolute disaster for her empire. This meant, among other things, by a declaration of war she was invariably inaugurating a particularly stressful time for the economy of the entire empire. The 1783 peace treaty of Paris as well as the 1802 peace treaty of Amiens had shown that Britain could suffer serious setbacks in the colonial sphere, and that even when colonial successes were achieved they could be overturned, if the war in Europe went badly for Britain and her allies. It was also clear that important British naval victories, such as occurred at the Saints in the Caribbean in 1782 or at Trafalgar in 1805, had little weight in peace making. They merely preserved the British from the threat of invasion, which the loss of naval superiority would have entailed. It is thus no exaggeration to claim that of the factors which fashioned Nova Scotia's economic destiny in these sixty years none was more important than war.[5]

This study should be viewed as part of an international historical concern, which is both large and continuing, for the social and economic impact of war. Focus has centered on the Atlantic economy before 1815,[6] with the economic impact of the wars of Revolutionary and Napoleonic France constituting a major preoccu-

---

5   This echoes comments made for Britain's economic destiny in the eighteenth century by Charles Wilson, *England's Apprenticeship, 1603-1763* (London, 1965), 313.

6   For an introductory to the subject see "Select Bibliography of Works on War and Economic Development," in J.M. Winter, ed., *War and Economic Development: Essays in Memory of David Joslin* (Cambridge, 1975), 257-92. The topic had been stimulated by the Great War of 1914-1918, which was analyzed intently in a remarkably rich series of monographs prepared internationally in the 1920s under the auspices of the Carnegie Endowment for Peace.

pation for historians of Britain.[7] Others, principally American scholars, have focused on the economic impact of the American War of Independence.[8] Historians of Quebec's society and economy have long been interested in *la guerre de la conquête,* though war as a factor in its economic development after 1792 is given little notice.[9]

There is regrettably still only slight interest in the economic development of Nova Scotia under these difficult wartime conditions;[10] nevertheless, the

7   The financial impact of the wars especially has long interested scholars. For recent work see J.L. Anderson, ''Aspects of the Effects on the British Economy of the Wars against France, 1793-1815,'' *Australian Economic History Review,* XII (March 1972), 1-20; A. Birch, ''The British Iron Industry during the Napoleonic Wars,'' in *The Economic History of the British Iron and Steel Industry 1784-1879* (London, 1967); François Crouzet, *L'Economic britannique et le blocus continental, 1806-13,* 2 Vols. (Paris, 1958); A. Hope-Jones, *Income Tax in the Napoleonic Wars* (Cambridge, 1939); Glenn Hueckel, ''War and the British Economy, 1793-1815; A General Equilibrium Analysis,'' *Explorations in Economic History,* X (1973), 365-96; and his ''English Farming Profits During the Napoleonic Wars,'' *Explorations in Economic History,* XIII (July 1976), 331-47; A.H. John, ''Farming in Wartime, 1793-1815,'' in E.L. Jones and C.E. Mingay, ed., *Land, Labour and Population in the Industrial Revolution* (London, 1967).

8   An important recent contribution is James F. Shepherd, ''British America and the Atlantic Economy,'' in Ronald Hoffman *et al., The Economy of Early America: The Revolutionary Period 1763-1790* (Charlottesville, 1988), 3-44. There is an excellent bibliography of pre-1984 imprints in John J. McCusker and Russell R. Menard, *The Economy of British America 1607-1789* (Chapel Hill, 1985), 383-459. Items not found there include Oscar T. Barck, *New York City During the War of Independence* (New York, 1931); Selwyn H.H. Carrington, *The British West Indies During the American Revolution: A Study in Colonial Economy and Politics* (Leiden, 1987) and his ''The American Revolution and the British West Indies' Economy,'' *Journal of Interdisciplinary History,* XVII (Spring 1987), 823-50; Robert W. Coakley, ''Virginia Commerce During the American Revolution,'' PhD thesis, University of Virginia, 1949; Thomas M. Doerflinger, *A Vigorous Spirit of Enterprise: Merchants and Economic Development in Revolutionary Philadelphia* (Chapel Hill, 1986), especially chapter 5, ''The Shock of War,'' 197-250; James A. Henretta, ''The War of Independence and American Economic Development,'' in Ronald Hoffman *et al., The Economy of Early America: The Revolutionary Period 1763-1790,* 45-87; Tommy R. Thompson, ''Marylanders, Personal Indebtedness, and the American Revolution,'' PhD thesis, University of Maryland, 1972.

9   Historical knowledge of Quebec's economy and society is as sophisticated as for any region in British North America. For a summary of recent scholarship, see Brian Young and John A. Dickinson, *A Short History of Quebec: A Socio-Economic Perspective* (Toronto, 1988), pp. 35 ff; and more specifically Alan Greer, *Peasant, Lord and Merchant: Rural Society in Three Quebec Parishes, 1740-1840* (Toronto, 1985); Jose Igartua, ''The Merchants and Negotiants of Montreal, 1750-1775: A study in Socio-Economic History,'' PhD thesis, Michigan State University, 1974; Paul McCann, ''Quebec's Balance of Payments, 1768-1772: A Quantitative Model,'' MA thesis, University of Ottawa, 1983; Dale Miquelon, *Dugard of Rouen: French Trade to Canada and the West Indies, 1729-1770* (Kingston, 1978); Françoise Noel, ''Gabriel Christie's Seigneuries: Settlement and Seigneurial Administrations in the Upper Richelieu Valley, 1764-1854,'' PhD thesis, McGill University, 1985, and her ''Chambly Mills, 1774-1815,'' *Historical Papers* (1985), 102-16.

10   The colony's economy to 1815 has been written largely from the perspective of Louisbourg, Halifax or New England merchant activity. Bertram A. Balcom, *The Cod Fishery of Isle Royale* (Ottawa, 1984); Donald F. Chard, ''The Impact of Ile Royale on New England 1713-1763,''

renewed interest in eighteenth-century Nova Scotia, heralded in part by the establishment of the Centre for Planter Studies at Acadia University, and the conferences held there in 1987 and 1990, ensures that this relative neglect has ended. It promises firstly to bridge the historiographical canyon now separating eighteenth-century Acadian and 'Anglo-German' Nova Scotia from the later Loyalist period. The prospect, secondly, is that the early economic history of this colony, whether in the fascinating community microhistories of the sort undertaken by Wynn,[11] McNabb,[12] Campbell,[13] Moody,[14] and MacNeil,[15] or in the

PhD thesis, University of Ottawa, 1976 and his ''The Price and Profits of Accommodation: Massachusetts-Louisbourg Trade, 1713-1744,'' in Philip C.F. Smith, ed., *Seafaring in Colonial Massachusetts* (Boston, 1980), 131-51; Walter Copp, ''Nova Scotia Trade During the War of 1812,'' *Canadian Historical Review*, XVIII (June 1937), 141-55, derived from his 1935 Dalhousie University MA thesis; Margaret Ells, ''The Development of Nova Scotia, 1782-1812,'' PhD thesis, University of London, 1937; Lewis R. Fischer, ''The Fruits of Stability: Merchant Shipping and Societal Growth in Pre-Revolutionary Halifax,'' in W.A.B. Douglas, ed., *Canada's Atlantic Canada* (Ottawa, 1984), 1-29 and his ''Revolution without Independence: The Canadian Colonies, 1749-1775,'' in Ronald Hoffman et al., eds., *The Economy of Early America*, 88-125, which is about Halifax; Julian Gwyn, ''War and Economic Change: Louisbourg and the New England Economy in the 1740s,'' in Pierre Savard, ed., *Mélanges d'histoire . . .* (Ottawa, 1978), 114-31; Christopher Moore, ''The Other Louisbourg: Trade and Merchant Enterprise in Ile Royale, 1713-1758,'' *Histoire sociale-Social History* (May 1979), 79-96 based on his 1977 University of Ottawa MA thesis; W.B. Kerr, ''The Merchants of Nova Scotia and the American Revolution,'' *Canadian Historical Review*, XIII (1932), 20-36; George Frederick Butler, ''Commercial Relations of Nova Scotia with the United States, 1783-1830,'' MA thesis, Dalhousie University, 1934. David Sutherland's University of Toronto Ph.D. thesis, the core ideas of which are found in ''Halifax Merchants and the Pursuit of Development, 1783-1850,'' *Canadian Historical Review*, LIX (1978), 1-17, and his many *Dictionary of Canadian Biography* contributions are excellent, although his interests are more on the socio-political world of merchants than on the economy. The wartime West Indies connection was treated by S. Basdeo and H. Robertson, ''The Nova Scotia-British West Indies Commercial Experiment in the Aftermath of the American Revolution,'' *Dalhousie Review* (Spring 1981), 53-69 derived from Robertson's 1974 Dalhousie University MA thesis; and Julian Gwyn, ''Rum, Sugar and Molasses in the Economy of Nova Scotia 1770-1854,'' in James H. Morrison and James Moreira, eds., *Tempered by Rum: Rum in the History of the Maritime Provinces* (Halifax, 1988), 111-34. The importance of war to economic change is obvious in Neil MacKinnon, *This Unfriendly Soil: The Loyalist Experience in Nova Scotia, 1783-1791* (Kingston, 1986), though economic matters constitute only a part of his subject.

11 Graeme Wynn, ''Late Eighteenth Century Agriculture on the Bay of Fundy Marshlands,'' *Acadiensis*, VIII (Spring 1979), 80-89; and his ''A Region of Scattered Settlements and Bounded Possibilities: Northeastern America 1775-1800,'' *Canadian Geographer*, 31 (1987), 319-38.

12 Debra McNabb, ''The Role of the Land in Settling Horton Township, Nova Scotia, 1766-1830,'' in Margaret Conrad, ed., *They Planted Well: New England Planters in Maritime Canada* (Fredericton, 1988), 151-60; ''Land and Families in Horton Township, N.S., 1760-1830,'' MA thesis, University of British Columbia, 1986.

13 Carol Campbell, ''A Prosperous Location, Truro: 1770-1838,'' MA thesis, Dalhousie University, 1988.

14 Barry Moody, ''Land, Kinship and Inheritance in Granville Township, 1760-1810,'' Paper presented to the Planter Nova Scotia Conference, Wolfville, Nova Scotia, October 1990.

15 Alan R. MacNeil, ''Early American Communities on the Fundy: A Case Study of Annapolis

larger focus of this essay, will be studied, not in isolation, but as part of a vast regional development in the northeast of North America.

II

This essay will analyze Nova Scotia's and Cape Breton's part in the economy of the Atlantic world during the first two generations of New England Planter settlement. It will also describe the changing nature of the colonial economy, employing price data to determine the long swings in the cycles of expansion and contraction; wage data to begin to form some idea of the relative changes in the standard of living; commodity trade and British public spending in Nova Scotia to determine changes in the balance of payments and hence the exchange rate. Finally, it will look at the expansion of shipping and shipbuilding, two important sectors of the colonial economy for which robust statistics can be generated. About agricultural production, the occupation in which most Nova Scotian families found themselves, little will be said. Nor are the fisheries subject to close scrutiny, even though they were depended upon by many families, who drew at least part of their livelihood from the sea.

A study of commodity prices in Nova Scotia reveals the major swings in the trade cycle, a subject much studied by British and American scholars, sometimes "with dazzling expertise."[16] Retail prices, of which a particularly rich collection survives for Nova Scotia, especially from the early 1770s, form the basis of what follows in this section, as wholesale prices are generally not available until 1813. A sample of 50 commodities from the counties of the Annapolis Valley and the Minas Basin between the years 1764 and 1820 form the basis of this study.[17] Of these, 37 commodities for the period 1773-1815 were selected on account of the relative completeness of the information. Prices in 1773-1775 were grouped to calculate an immediate pre-war average to serve as a base for a general price index. These then were compared with prices for the same commodities at different later periods, firstly for 1778-1782, the years of heightened inflation during

---

and Amherst Townships, 1767-1827," *Agricultural History,* 62 (Spring 1989), 101-19; and "Rural Society in Nova Scotia, 1761-1861: A Study of Five Townships in Transition," PhD thesis, Queen's University, 1991.

16 Ralph Davis, *The Industrial Revolution and British Overseas Trade* (Leicester, 1979), 11. For suggested intervals of expansion and contraction, see McCusker and Menard, *The Economy of British America,* 63 and W.W. Rostow, *British Economy in the Nineteenth Century* (Oxford, 1948), 33.

17 My collection of commodity price information up to 1815 includes as well those for Shelburne, Liverpool and Halifax. Halifax newspapers carried no price information until 1813, when the *Acadian Recorder* first appeared and immediately began publishing wholesale prices of goods regularly sold at auction in Halifax. This stopped in 1819, and no other newspaper resumed the practice until 1830. Thereafter Halifax wholesale prices are generally available on a weekly basis. Unfortunately, wood products are consistently absent from these lists. I turned to the newspapers of Saint John, New Brunswick hoping to find wholesale prices for wood products, but to my great surprise, in their lists of prices current, they too ignored such commodities.

the American War of Independence. Prices for 1784-92, the inter-war years, were then averaged, as were those of 1793-1801 and 1803-15, both periods of continuous war.

There are two ways to look at prices. The actual average prices can be compared, or they can be adjusted by assigning them a weight. For this paper actual unweighted commodity prices will be used. Between 1773-75 and 1778-82 there was a 70 per cent average price rise, ranging from a high of 346 per cent for tobacco, 162 per cent for rum and 155 per cent for salt to a low of 4 and 9 per cent for pepper and tea respectively. The average price for indigo and Souchong tea actually fell by almost 8 and 3 per cent respectively, unique experiences for the commodities studied here. The inter-war years, 1784 through 1792, were next calculated to establish the depth of the post-war depression. Commodity prices certainly declined dramatically, on average by 34.7 per cent. Yet such prices still remained on average 11.1 per cent higher than in the three immediate pre-war years. In this way war had the effect of permanently building significant price inflation into the colonial economy.[18] Renewed war, this time with Revolutionary and Napoleonic France, again forced up commodity prices, although on average they never again quite reached the wartime inflation of 1778-82. Prices rose an average of 15.1 per cent between 1793 and 1801, and by another 22.4 per cent in 1803-15 when compared with inter-war years 1784-92. By then prices were more than 56 per cent higher than those which had obtained in 1773-75. The data are found in Table 1 below.

Table 1
Annual Average Commodity Prices: Annapolis Valley & Minas Basin
(in Halifax pounds)
(unweighted)

Commodity	1773-75	1778-82	1784-92	1793-1801	1803-15
Apples (bush)	0.056	0.136	0.106	0.083	0.097
Barley (bush)	0.23	0.325	0.25	0.40	0.38
Beef (lb)	0.015	0.024	0.014	0.017	0.021
Brandy (gal)	0.40	0.50	0.415	0.613	0.563
Butter (lb)	0.028	0.06	0.042	0.047	0.06
Candles (lb)	0.045	0.075	0.051	0.054	0.063
Cheese (lb)	0.017	0.047	0.03	0.029	0.038
Cider (gal)	0.035	0.083	0.058	0.053	0.034
Codfish (qtl)	0.65	1.25	0.677	0.72	1.156
Coffee (lb)	0.07	0.10	0.067	0.075	0.095
Corn (bush)	0.225	0.435	0.235	0.294	0.394

18   This phenomenon had been observed by earlier historians, who studied several colonial American towns. See Arthur Harrison Cole, ed., *Wholesale Commodity Prices in the United States 1700-1861* (Cambridge, 1938).

Cotton wool (lb)	0.11	0.15	0.126	0.138	0.118
Eggs (doz)	0.035	0.051	0.042	0.03	0.05
Firewood (cord)	0.40	0.433	0.468	0.378	0.429
Flour/wheat (cwt)	1.20	1.89	1.08	1.19	1.95
Flour/rye (bush)	0.29	0.40	0.305	0.324	0.391
Hay (ton)	1.15	2.60	1.92	1.87	2.40
Indigo (lb)	0.051	0.047	0.038	0.047	0.084
Lamb/fresh (lb)	0.015	0.025	0.02	0.017	0.017
Molasses (gal)	0.15	0.338	0.154	0.267	0.24
Mutton/fresh (lb)	0.015	0.03	0.019	0.016	0.018
Oats (bush)	0.077	0.168	0.111	0.116	0.148
Peas (bush)	0.21	0.40	0.24	0.28	0.46
Pepper (lb)	0.18	0.187	0.153	0.17	0.168
Pork/fresh (lb)	0.025	0.029	0.022	0.026	0.025
Potatoes (bush)	0.068	0.081	0.077	0.072	0.089
Raisins (lb)	0.044	0.06	0.05	0.06	0.077
Rice (lb)	0.013	0.024	0.014	0.014	0.022
Rum (gal)	0.223	0.61	0.262	0.427	0.411
Salt (bush)	0.21	0.535	0.23	0.298	0.293
Shingles (1000)	0.65	0.90	0.54	0.70	0.86
Soap (lb)	0.04	0.09	0.048	0.055	0.048
Sugar (lb)	0.035	0.08	0.03	0.05	0.05
Sugar/brown (lb)	0.029	0.045	0.039	0.06	0.045
Sugar/loaf (lb)	0.04	0.096	0.05	0.106	0.084
Tallow (lb)	0.042	0.073	0.04	0.034	0.055
Tea (lb)	0.22	0.24	0.208	0.22	0.183
Tea/Souchong (lb)	0.525	0.51	0.40	0.49	0.42
Tobacco (lb)	0.039	0.174	0.065	0.086	0.112
Veal/fresh (lb)	0.017	0.024	0.021	0.015	0.017
Wheat (bush)	0.21	0.48	0.30	0.43	0.52
Wool/sheep's (lb)	0.075	0.10	0.059	0.078	0.097
Index	100.0	170.2	111.1	127.9	156.5

There thus was a sharp price inflation during the American war, of 70 per cent; and the peace brought prices rapidly downward, by about 35 per cent. The new war with France, which between 1812 and 1814 also encompassed the United States of America, witnessed renewed inflation, by 40.8 per cent, as an annual average between 1793 and 1815 inclusive. The details follow.

III

To what extent did wages keep up with such substantial and extensive price changes? Wages moved in the same general direction as prices but with differing amplitudes both in the wartime booms and the post-war depression. Table 3

Table 2
Commodity Price Indexes, 1773-1815

Years	Unweighted	% Change
1773-75	100.0	—
1778-82	170.2	70.2
1784-92	111.1	(34.7)*
1793-1801	127.9	15.1
1803-15	156.5	22.4

*Bracketed figures indicate a price decline.

illustrates the movement of average daily wages for 16 occupations. If we compare these results with the unweighted commodity price index, it appears that these workers experienced a modest rise in real wages during the high inflation of the war years, 1778-82. Thus when commodity prices rose by 70.2 per cent, money wages rose by 83.2 per cent. Thereafter in the years of peace, though their

Table 3
Average Daily Wages: Annapolis Valley & Minas Basin
(in Dollars: $1.00 = H£O.25)

Occupation	1773-75	1778-82	1784-92	1793-1801	1803-15
Boy's work	0.20	0.30	0.25	0.30	0.50
Chopping wood	0.30	0.60	0.40	0.45	0.60
Common labourer	0.65	1.20	0.75	0.85	1.05
Digging	0.60	1.00	0.60	0.70	0.70
Dyking	0.70	1.25	0.80	0.90	1.20
Fencing	0.50	0.90	0.60	0.70	0.50
Framing	0.60	1.20	0.90	0.80	1.30
Haying	0.50	1.00	0.60	0.75	0.90
Hoeing	0.40	0.70	0.45	0.60	0.80
Mason	0.80	1.40	1.00	1.40	1.50
Mowing	0.60	1.00	0.75	0.75	1.00
Planting	0.40	0.70	0.45	0.60	0.80
Ploughing	1.00	2.00	1.40	1.60	2.00
Reaping	0.40	0.80	0.65	0.70	0.80
Sawing	0.60	1.00	0.65	0.80	0.90
Ship's Carpenter	1.00	1.80	1.50	1.20	2.00
Average Wage	0.58	1.06	0.74	0.83	1.03
Unweighted Index	100.0	183.2	127.4	143.1	178.2

money wages fell, commodity prices fell more steeply. Thus between 1784 and 1792, when prices, though declining, remained 11.1 per cent above those of 1773-75, money wages were 27.4 per cent above those of the pre-war years, thereby allowing for a very modest rise in real wages. When prices rose in the 1790s, wages also rose and again outstripped the commodity price rise. Thus as money wages declined, prices fell more steeply, again leaving wages workers relatively better off than before the war. In the first decade of the wars with revolutionary France the gap between prices and wages narrowed. Commodity prices rose by 15.1 per cent and wages only by 12.3 per cent. Yet in comparison with the pre-1776 economy in Nova Scotia, real wages still had considerably advanced. Real wages resumed their upward thrust between 1803 and 1815, when commodity prices rose an average of 22.3 per cent, while money wages rose by 24.5 per cent.

What did this mean for Planters and their descendants? This depended on their occupation and where they lived. If they were farmers dependent on labour, their position deteriorated during the hostilities of the first American war. Thereafter it marginally deteriorated further as the real incomes of their workers rose, despite the very high prices their agriculture surpluses obtained. Twenty of the commodities, generated by the farmers of the Annapolis Valley and the Minas Basin, have been studied separately to determine the magnitude of their price changes.[19] Table 4 contains the details. The same pattern of high wartime prices, established in the general commodity price index, in comparison with relatively lower prices in peacetime was reflected also in this index of agricultural prices.

Table 4

Price Movements in Agricultural Commodities:
Annapolis Valley & Minas Basin

Interval	Unweighted Index	% Change
1773-75	100.0	—
1778-82	190.3	90.3
1784-92	130.2	(31.6)*
1792-1801	145.5	10.5
1803-15	181.6	24.8

*Bracketed figures indicate a decline in prices.

If the wages of only agricultural labourers, employing the wage index constructed for agricultural occupations — chopping wood, digging potatoes, fencing, haying, hoeing, mowing, planting, ploughing with a yoke of oxen and reaping — are considered, the story is somewhat different from that of wage earn-

---

19 The commodities included apples, barley, fresh beef, butter, cider, eggs, firewood, hay, fresh lamb and mutton, oats, peas, pork, potatoes, tallow, fresh veal, wheat and raw wool.

ers generally in the 43 year period. As Table 5 indicates, agricultural wages peaked below the average level of agricultural commodity prices during the American Revolutionary War. After the war, when prices declined from their average

Table 5
Index of Agricultural Wages, 1773-1815

Interval	Wage Index	% Change
1773-5	100.0	—
1778-82	183.7	83.7
1784-92	116.3	(36.7)*
1793-1801	145.9	25.5
1803-15	159.2	9.1

*Bracketed figures indicate a decline in wages.

wartime heights, agricultural wages fell more steeply. The long war with France at first saw real wages recover, as was evident in the period 1793-1801. Money wages also advanced in the years 1803-15. Yet such wages failed to keep pace with the prices of agricultural commodities, which also moved rapidly upwards to reach a level just below that of the late 1770s and early 1780's. When money wages were out-stripped by the rise in agricultural prices, real wages for agricultural labourers generally declined. The advantage thus went to farmers who employed agricultural labourers and their families. The analysis of price and wage movements allows us to plot the periods of inflation and deflation in the economy generally, even though the focus is specifically on the Annapolis Valley and the Minas Basin counties. Evidence for Halifax and the rest of the colony, in so far as it exists, supports the general movements of Nova Scotia's business cycle, outlined here.

IV

The colony's economy was driven by two principal factors, the extensive growth of population and the strategic importance placed upon it by the British government, partly as a result of its rivalry with the power of France, and partly from the emergence of the United States, as a less than friendly neighbour. In 1755, the year active hostilities reopened with France, Cape Breton and peninsular Nova Scotia held a population of not less than 25,000 souls. There were at least 14,000 Acadians.[20] There were fewer than 3,800 English, including the soldiers, principally in the Halifax area, and another 1,600 Germans around Lunenburg, with an estimated 2,000 Micmac throughout the colony and on

---

20 N.E.S. Griffiths, *Context of Acadian History: Society, Politics and Culture, 1603-1789* (Kingston, forthcoming).

French Cape Breton. The population of Cape Breton with the garrison numbered about 5,000.[21] There was a catastrophic decline in population with the expulsion of the bulk of the Acadians in 1755. By 1767, even after several years of new settlement from New England, the population of peninsular Nova Scotia and Cape Breton was estimated at only 11,800. Fifty years later it had reached 89,700, more than a sixfold increase. Table 6 has the details. There were in 1767 only some 13,540

Table 6
Nova Scotia Population Distribution: 1767 and 1817 Compared

Regions	1767		1817	
Halifax	3,695	31.4%	16,497	18.4%
Eastern & Cape Breton	866	7.4	23,728	26.5
Southwest	3,290	27.9	18,166	20.3
Fundy	3,928	33.3	31,305	34.9
Total:	11,799	100.0%	89,696	100.0%

Note: There was no census in Cape Breton in 1817. Its estimated population was 8,000, or 8.9 percent of the total population. In 1838 and 1851, it formed 17.4 percent and 19.8 per cent respectively of the reunified colony's population.
Source: *Census of Canada 1870-71,* Vol. IV, 60-62, 82.

acres under cultivation or 1.1 acres per head of population. The extent of the livestock of the province can only be guessed at, but the year before in Cape Breton, there were but 269 head of all kinds from goats, sheep and swine to horses, oxen, cows and calves, or less than 0.4 per then head of population, estimated at 707.[22] The only significant new immigration before the war of independence, was the arrival of some 1,000 Yorkshire folk mainly to the Chignecto peninsula.[23]

---

21 Some 1,687 souls were enumerated in 1752. Christian Pouyez, ''La population de l'Isle Royale en 1752,'' *Histoire sociale-Social History,* VI (November 1973), 147-80. When the garrison fell to the British in 1758, there were 3,031 military and 2,606 naval prisoners. See Gwyn, ''Naval Power and the Two Sieges of Louisbourg, 1745 and 1758.''

22 In General Thomas Gage's despatch, 23 December 1766, Shelburne MSS, V. 51, 53-54, William L. Clements Library (hereafter WLCL), Ann Arbor, Michigan. See as well ''Population of Nova Scotia 1766,'' Public Record Office (hereafter PRO), CO 217/44, fol.20. For an even earlier estimate see the report of Charles Morris, the Chief Surveyor, to Jonathan Belcher, the lieutenant governor of Nova Scotia, Shelburne MSS, WLCL, V. 48, 299-333. We have no agricultural census statistics for 1817, but in 1827 for peninsular Nova Scotia there were 292,009 acres of ''cultivated land,'' or 2.4 acres per capita. See *Census of Canada 1870-71,* Vol. IV, 94, also the *Acadian Recorder,* 5 April 1828.

23 Charles Bruce Fergusson, ''Pre-Revolutionary Settlements in Nova Scotia,'' *Collections of the Nova Scotia Historical Society,* 37 (1970), 5-22.

Steady, if unspectacular natural increase, the arrival of Loyalist refugees between 1775 and 1784,[24] together with disbanded soldiers and their families, dramatically raised the population of peninsular Nova Scotia so that by 1791 there were some 55,500 people, with 1,500 more in Cape Breton. Both Nova Scotia and Cape Breton during these momentous years endured significant emigration as well. Many of the Loyalist refugees, having spent a short time in the region, went elsewhere. A significant body of black Loyalists departed for Sierra Leone. The most celebrated collapse was the town of Shelburne, which from a boom-town of 12,000, shrank to less than 1,000 within a decade, and to 374 by 1816 with many leaving the colony altogether.[25] Still, natural growth continued and was aided by immigration from the British Isles, so that by 1801 the population perhaps numbered 66,000 with the British military and naval forces, including less than 3,000 in all of Cape Breton. Ten years later, in 1811, peninsular Nova Scotia may have numbered 71,000 souls, again including the British military garrison and naval forces, and Cape Breton, owing to recent arrivals of Highlanders, had grown to 5,000, for a total of some 76,000. By 1815 there were probably not less than 80,000 people in Nova Scotia and Cape Breton together.[26] These estimates are summarized in Table 7.

Table 7
Estimated Population of Nova Scotia & Cape Breton, 1755-1817

Year	Nova Scotia	Cape Breton	Total
1755	20,000	5,000	25,000
1767	11,100	700	11,800
1791	55,500	1,500	57,000
1801	63,000	3,000	66,000
1811	71,000	5,000	76,000
1815	74,500	5,500	80,000
1817	81,700	8,000	89,700

Except at the time of the influx of Loyalist refugees, population growth in Nova

24 MacKinnon, *This Unfriendly Soil,* 31-32.

25 Evidence for refugees returning to the USA is cited in MacKinnon, *ibid.,* 176. See Marion Robert-son, *King's Bounty: A History of Early Shelburne, Nova Scotia* (Halifax, 1983), which deals only with this early boom period and not the rapid decline to insignificance, which is the more important history of the place. For the blacks, see James W. St. G. Walker, *The Black Loyalists: The Search for a Promised Land in Nova Scotia and Sierra Leone, 1783-1870* (New York, 1976).

26 There is no population estimate in MacKinnon, *This Unfriendly Soil.* Emigration to the United States was an endemic problem for Nova Scotia and Cape Breton. It was a subject regularly com-mented upon from the very foundation of Halifax in 1749 and after the incorporation of Cape Breton into the British empire in 1763. There is a typical example, for instance, in 1805-06, es-pecially among fishermen, cited in Ronald H. McDonald, ''Nova Scotia Views the United States, 1784-1854,'' PhD thesis, Queen's University, 1974, 44-45.

Scotia was not impressive, when compared with other North American colonies. Elsewhere populations had been doubling in the eighteenth century every 25 years, and continued to do so for a time in the nineteenth century.[27] Yet in the almost 35 years between 1784 and 1817, Nova Scotia's population had grown only an estimated 70 per cent. The proximate cause of such relatively slow population expansion, as with an earlier example of population retardation in the pre-1760 New York colony,[28] can largely be assigned to the uncertainties created by war.

From the 1755 Acadian expulsion to the arrival of the Loyalist refugees in large numbers, population expansion had been painfully slow and by no means steady. The economic and social costs to Nova Scotia for the deportation of Acadians in their thousands were staggering. The political decision to remove the bulk of the Acadian population almost wholly undermined the colonial economy, an act of econocide — to employ Seymour Drescher's term for the British decision to end the slave trade and slavery in the empire — unparalleled in British colonial history either of the seventeenth or eighteenth century.[29] It is arguable that it set the seal of backwardness on the Nova Scotia economy, from which, at least in its agriculture, it had not recovered by 1815. In economic terms, it was doubtless one of the most destructive political decisions ever made in British America. It perhaps retarded Nova Scotia's development by two generations, a set back as considerable as Massachusetts had endured from the bloody King Philip's war in 1675-76.[30] In a colonial setting this was virtually an unendurable economic burden. Neither the arrival of the New England Planters from 1759 onwards, nor later of settlers from the British Isles and after 1776 of American Loyalist refugees, brought agriculture in the colony to the state it had achieved by 1755: that of producing substantial annual surpluses.[31] Certainly it is not until well after 1815

27   Robert V. Wells, *The Population of the British Colonies in America before 1776: A Survey of Census Data* (Princeton, 1975).

28   New York historians formerly believed that the colony's development had been retarded by the system of landholding, where much of the usable land in the Hudson river valley had been assigned in large blocks, called manors. It is nevertheless clear enough that the upper Hudson and much of the Mohawk river valley, despite their known agricultural advantages, were only very thinly populated until the French power in Canada was broken in 1759-60. Thereafter these were the fastest growing regions in the colony of New York, and competed with Nova Scotia for large numbers of settlers from relatively overpopulated places in New England. See Julian Gwyn, ''The Impact of War on the New York Economy, 1755-1763,'' unpublished paper, presented to the Department of Economic History, University of Exeter, March 1976.

29   Seymour Drescher, *Econocide: British Slavery in the Era of Abolition* (Pittsburg, 1977).

30   Not one new town was established in Massachusetts for fifty years after 1675. See Jack Greene, ''Recent Developments in the Historiography of Colonial New England,'' *They Planted Well: New England Planters in Maritime Canada,* 70.

31   This view differs from that of MacNeil, who believes that the average farmer in two ''Planter'' townships had reached the comfortable status as defined by Jackson Turner Main, *Society and Economy in Colonial Connecticut* (Princeton, 1985), 111. Yet in so doing they were only attaining the standard achieved more than sixty years earlier by Acadian farmers in 1704!

that the agriculture of the province began to acquire a reputation of the sort it had possessed during the era of the Acadian custody of the soil.

Although the economic effect of the deportation has yet to be studied in detail, several comments can be made. Acadian livestock had largely been slaughtered for the benefit of the British and colonial forces then in Nova Scotia. A second large deportation of the French and Acadians occurred in 1758, this time in Cape Breton, following the capture of Louisbourg. Once the British garrison there was greatly reduced in 1760, that island lost much of its remaining population, as its former economy had utterly collapsed. Until at least 1784 it was, like Newfoundland, little more than a collection of fishing stations. When the New England Planters arrived in peninsular Nova Scotia in the 1760s, the Acadian fields and meadows were found to have largely reverted to nature. In many places dykes, which had been neglected for a minimum of five years, had either been washed away or breached. The homesteads had everywhere been burned, along with the barns. This massive loss of agricultural capital found no parallel either in the Seven Years' War or in the American Revolution, except perhaps in South Carolina after 1779.[32] It was not soon replaced for the evidence points to the ineffectiveness as agriculturalists of many of the New England settlers, and hence the continued poverty. Nevertheless as population grew, so too did overall production, overseas commerce and domestic consumer demand. It was this sheer population growth which principally fuelled economic growth, as it did in any pre-industrial society.

Yet owing to Nova Scotia's strategic importance, the actual shape its economy acquired from the founding of Halifax in 1749 through to the end of war in 1815 was significantly influenced by public spending especially on the part of the British government. Only 22 of the 60 years which encompass this study were those of peace. High wartime spending characterized British public finance, and Nova Scotia, among British colonies, was the recipient of an inordinate share of this largesse. On average throughout the 60 years between 1756 and 1815 some £152,300 sterling was spent *in* Nova Scotia and Cape Breton by successive British governments. It did not make Nova Scotia popular with some members of the British Parliament. Edmund Burke considered Georgia and Nova Scotia to be economically the most backward of Britain's colonies in America. He called them creatures of the Board of Trade and Plantations. Georgia "had cost the nation very great sums of money," while Nova Scotia "was the youngest and the favourite child of the Board."

> Good God! What sums the nursing of that ill-thriven, hard-visaged and ill-favoured brat has cost to this wittol nation! Sir, this colony has stood us in

---

32 Jerome Nadelhaft, "The 'Havoc of War' and its Aftermath in Revolutionary South Carolina," *Histoire sociale-Social History,* XII (May 1979), 97-121; *The Disorders of War: The Revolution in South Carolina* (Orono, 1981); E.J. Cashin, "But Brothers, It is Our Land we are Talking About," in Ronald Hoffman *et al., Uncivil War: The Southern Backcountry during the American Revolution* (Charlottesville, 1985), 240-76.

a sum of not less than £700,000. To this day it has made no repayment. It does not even support those offices of expence, which are miscalled its government; the whole of that job still lies upon the patient, callous shoulders of the people of England.[33]

British public expenditure *on* Nova Scotia was far greater, but such benefits accrued to merchants in the British Isles, and are beyond the scope of this paper. The details of this British spending are summarized in periods of war and peace.

Table 8
British Public Expenditure in Nova Scotia and Cape Breton
1756-1815
(Sterling values)

	Military	Naval	Civil	Totals	Annual Average
1756-63	550,300	102,900	330,800	984,000	123,000
1764-75	401,700	154,400	73,300	629,400	52,500
1776-83	880,000	139,100	34,600	1,053,700	131,700
1784-92	591,300	244,500	247,100*	1,082,900	120,300
1793-1815	4,269,500	825,400	291,500	5,388,400	244,900
1756-1815	6,692,800	1,468,300	977,800	9,138,900	152,300

* Includes an estimated £159,000 received by peninsular Nova Scotia's and Cape Breton Loyalists by way of parliamentary compensation for their losses, a sum equal to 47 per cent of the £336,753 granted to claimants in British North America.

Much of these funds did not stick for long to the fingers of Nova Scotians, whether they were the Halifax merchants or the suppliers of hay and straw to the British military garrison outposts in the colony. The failure of Nova Scotia's agriculture to meet the needs of this internal market is an important element in estimating the relative importance of such spending to the colony. Much of what the British army and navy needed, when stationed in Nova Scotia, could not be supplied from within the colony. Instead it depended on imports principally from Great Britain but also from other continental colonies, the Caribbean and from the United States. In this way, British spending within the colony directly stimulated imports into Nova Scotia, and thereby helped to balance overseas payments. It also placed business in the hands of merchants, especially those of Halifax, and were, particularly in wartime, on a scale that would have been out of the ques-

---

33 11 February 1780. *The Parliamentary History of England from the Earliest Period to the Year 1803* (London, 1814), XXI, 59.

tion had enduring peace instead descended on the Atlantic world after 1763 or 1783.

William Forsyth, one of several Scottish businessmen who emigrated to Nova Scotia after 1783, is a case in point. A large importer of Scottish goods, he also exported to the British Isles, the United States and the Caribbean. When the French wars greatly disrupted his business he shifted his principal activity to supplying the much enlarged wartime Halifax garrison and to dealing in prize goods. In 1788 he had secured a seven-year contract to supply masts and spars to the British navy.[34] In this way the real economic benefits accrued not to the colonial merchants, who acted more as consignees or commission agents than as importers in their own right, but to suppliers overseas, who were based principally in London. One example was the partnership of James Foreman and George Grassie, two Scotsmen who had been sent to Halifax in 1789 by Brook Watson, who then dominated the British export market to Nova Scotia. Though both made colonial fortunes they were modest by the standards of their London-based principal.[35] Another example was Andrew Belcher, who acted as the chief agent in Halifax for Alexander Brymer's London-based commercial interests, and imported some £140,000 between 1792 and 1810, an average of £7,400 annually.[36] Brymer had himself arrived in Halifax in the 1770s with about £1,000 capital and departed for London in 1801 apparently worth £250,000! His example was later followed by others, who, having made a fortune in the colony, returned finally to England, there to invest and enjoy their wealth.

For most years between the founding of Halifax and 1815, the details of Nova Scotia's commerce are known only for trade with the British Isles. Trade with the United States, with other British North American colonies, the Caribbean, the Channel Islands and Europe south of Cape Finisterre, is undocumented. We have most details for 1768-72, when it amounted to very little, and for 1789-1808, when it was more considerable. Trade with the United States, owing to smuggling, was probably seriously under-recorded, while commerce across the Bay of Fundy with New Brunswick went almost wholly unrecorded. The details of Nova Scotia's trade with the British Isles are given in Table 10. Every year the colony ran a large deficit in its commodity trade with the British Isles, principally owing to the large volume of imports carried there from London, Liverpool and Glasgow. In the war years 1756-63 the trade deficit with the British Isles averaged £57,600 annually. In the twelve years that elapsed between 1764 and 1775, when trade declined for Nova Scotia, the average deficit on their account with the British Isles also fell

34 David A. Sutherland, "William Forsyth, 1749-1814," *Dictionary of Canadian Biography*, V, 327-29, Michael Wallace, another Scotsman, acted as wholesale dealer in British imports from 1779. He first undertook government business when he became agent for the repatriation to Sierra Leone of black Loyalists, and from 1793 was principally a military contractor. See David A. Sutherland, "Michael Wallace, 1744-1831," *ibid.*, VI, 798-801.

35 David A. Sutherland, "James Foreman, 1763-1854," *ibid.*, VIII, 299-301.

36 David A. Sutherland, "Andrew Belcher, 1763-1841," *ibid.*, VII, 62-64.

to £31,400. With the disruptions to normal trading patterns to British North America occasioned by the non-importation movements in North America, the American declaration of independence and the subsequent long war, Halifax temporarily became the most important port in British America for British exports. Normally Nova Scotia took about 1 per cent of all British exports to North

Table 9
Nova Scotia's Balance of Overseas Payments with the British Isles
1756-1815
(Official London Custom House Values expressed in sterling)
(Annual Average)

Years	Net Trade with UK† 1	UK Spending in NS 2	Balance 1-2
1756-63	(£57,600)*	£123,000	£65,400
1764-75	(31,400)	52,500	21,100
1776-83	(313,100)	131,700	(181,400)
1784-92	(177,300)	120,300	(57,000)
1793-1815	(249,200)	244,900	(4,300)
1756-1815	(173,700)	152,300	(21,400)

† British exports & re-exports to, less imports from, Nova Scotia.
* Sums in brackets indicate an unfavourable balance against Nova Scotia.

Sources: PRO, CUST 3/49-71, CUST 4/5-10, CUST 8/1-3, CUST 14/1-25, CUST 15/86-119, CUST 17/1-30.

America, while in 1776, 1777, 1778, 1779 and 1780 the colony took respectively 25.4, 50.2, 28.3, 15.4 and 12.9 per cent. By 1781-82 the situation had reverted more or less to what it had been in the early 1770s, and Nova Scotia absorbed only 2.4 per cent of all British exports to North America. In 1783 it rose somewhat to 6.7 per cent. Nova Scotia's deficit in trade with Great Britain and Ireland averaged £313,100 for each of the eight years of the American war. This was far above the annual average of £131,700 spent by Britain in the colony for civil, military and naval costs over the same period. The difference would have had to be made up by the sale of at least £181,400 annually of such imports, and the provision of shipping services. Most would have been re-exported to Quebec and some to the West Indies or wherever British arms allowed some sort of colonial trade to occur. As we lack details of the wartime trade from Nova Scotia to the West Indies or any other part of the world, we cannot precisely know its magnitude. The only port to profit from this increased war-induced trade was Halifax, which always dominated the British import trade generally and the commerce with the Caribbean specifically.

The clearest evidence that the colony was able to balance its payments is found in the movement of the exchange rate between sterling and Nova Scotia's currency of account, known as Halifax currency. The rate of exchange was the market value of the drafts of Nova Scotia's merchants in Great Britain and elsewhere, or of their drafts in the colony. Whenever the balance of payments tended to favour Nova Scotia and specie was readily available in the colony's places of business, the rate of exchange favoured the colonists. By contrast, when the balance of payments moved against the colony and specie became scarce, then the rate of exchange favoured British merchants and army or naval paymasters. The precise movement of the exchange rate was also determined by the cost of transporting bullion. The commercial par of exchange was the market value in Nova Scotia of the foreign coins which circulated within the colony. Throughout this period par value between Halifax currency and sterling was H£1.11 to £1.00.[37] Incidentally, to pay the troops stationed in Nova Scotia the British regularly supplied their deputy paymasters with silver coin. For instance, in the twenty years between 1757 and 1776, records indicate that some £387,690, or £19,385 annually, most of it in wartime, was shipped to Halifax.[38] This represented about 24 per cent of all estimated official British spending in the colony. It enabled Nova Scotia, unusual in any British colony, to remain free of public debt.

What then was the history of the exchange rate in Nova Scotia between the 1750s and 1815? Data exist for all years except 1773-74. Between 1757 and 1783 the exchange rate favoured Nova Scotia's merchants on average every year except 1762, 1777, 1778 and 1781. The war years 1776, 1779-80, 1782-83 found Halifax exchange largely at par with sterling. In 1784-87 it rose somewhat above par indicating difficulties with the balance of payments.[39] From then until 1798 the exchange rate was at par or hovering not far above it. The situation changed dramatically in the seventeen years between 1799 and 1815. At that time only on four occasions did the annual average exchange rate reach par or slightly above par. In 1799-1802 it fell to an average of £106.71, in 1806-08 to an average of £108.04, and in 1810-15 to an historic low annual average of only £96.60. These were years when there was a large surplus on the colony's balance of payments. Merchants, who supplied the British with goods and services within the colony, all of it in aid of the war effort, were extremely well placed to expand capital by trading profitably. Since they lived in Halifax, much of the prosperity of these late war years centred there.[40] As late as 1838 an Assembly committee remembering these hal-

---

37 A.B. McCullough, *Money and Exchange in Canada to 1900* (Toronto, 1984), 149. See his Table 41 "Halifax Prices of Sterling Exchange on London, 1957-1879," 265-81. He borrowed the data for 1757-83 from my Table 6 "Rate of Exchange: Halifax on London," "The Impact of British Military Spending on the Colonial American Money Markets, 1760-1783," *Historical Papers* (1980), 96-97. There is an extended discussion in John J. McCusker, *Money and Exchange in Europe and America 1600-1775: A Handbook* (Chapel Hill, 1978).

38 PRO, A 01/75/99-190/593.

39 McCullough, *Money and Exchange,* Table 40, 266-69.

40 It was this perhaps which induced Archibald MacMechan to describe the period 1812-15 as the "Golden Age of Halifax Trade." See "Halifax in Trade," *Canadian Geographical Journal,* III (September 1931), 156.

cyon days wrote with a sense of longing for their return, "Halifax may yet become in peace, what it was in the years 1812 to 1815, during the American war."[41]

Yet export markets, the usual route to such prosperity, remained small and difficult in wartime. Nova Scotia's export trade to the British Isles was very limited, rarely exceeding £5,000 in any year before 1784. This had been the case from the very founding of the port of Halifax. For instance, between 1749 and 1763 no less than two-thirds of the vessels clearing the port of Halifax could not find a return cargo and sailed in ballast. Even between 1764 and 1775, almost 30 per cent of the vessels still cleared the port in ballast.[42] It is clear both from the trade figures and those relating to British public spending in the colony, that Nova Scotia and Cape Breton had great difficulty generating exports for overseas markets. If the years 1791-94 are typical, average annual imports from all places, except other British North American colonies, were valued at £219,550, while annual average exports came to only £81,725, leaving an annual average commodity trade deficit of £137,825. Exports amounted only £1.4 per capita, compared with £12-£15 for Newfoundland, £9 for South Carolina, and £5-£6 for the British West Indies, £3 for Virginia and Maryland more than twenty years earlier between 1768 and 1772.[43] If re-exports are added to this sum, the figures change little. The colonies of Nova Scotia and Cape Breton were clearly only partly oriented to overseas trade in this early period of their development, with an economy largely subsistent in nature.

An examination of its exports reveals the core of its difficulties. The most important export was cod, dry and wet. Here Nova Scotia competed directly with Newfoundland for a market in the West Indies, and in every year Nova Scotia held but a small portion of this trade in low grade fish. For better grades of fish, which annually formed only a small proportion of fish exports, Nova Scotia also competed poorly in the markets of the Channel Islands and Europe south of Cape Finisterre. The market next in importance was that of the British Isles, principally in England, through the ports of London and Liverpool. The chief exports to Great Britain were wood products, furs and skins, while the main re-exports were raw sugar, rum and molasses as well as mahogany and the products of the southern whaling fishery. As a supplier of wood products Nova Scotia was only of marginal importance before 1815, facing the heavy competition of both the Canadas and of New Brunswick. As a supplier of furs and skins Nova Scotia was a far less important source than either the Hudson Bay or the Canadas, which dominated the market. Since the colony had no obvious advantage in the Atlantic staple trade it fell back on British public spending, the proximate cause of what prosperity existed in Nova Scotia before 1815.

---

41   *Journals and Proceedings,* 1838, Appendix.

42   Fischer, "The Fruits of Stability," 13.

43   See James Shepherd, "British America and the Atlantic Economy," *The Economy of Early America,* 7.

V

Perhaps it was through shipping services on behalf of merchants elsewhere or by the sale of newly-built vessels abroad, that Nova Scotia and Cape Breton were able to balance their payments. Surviving sources lend themselves in various ways to the study of the colony's shipping before 1815. The earliest shipping register — the Naval Officer's list — began with the opening of the port of Halifax in 1749, and noted details of individual ships, their crews and cargoes as they entered and cleared the port.[44] At first a Naval Officer was assigned only to Halifax. This meant that any vessel wishing to carry on trade, other than tramping from one coastal port of Nova Scotia to another, had to sail first to Halifax to register with the British appointed Naval Officer, and when making for Nova Scotia from a port outside the colony had first to enter via Halifax, however inconvenient, before sailing to its port of destination. Clearly vessels trading from Nova Scotia's Fundy ports to the nearby ports of New Brunswick (from 1784) and Maine rarely bothered to register their movements with the Halifax official. In this way, for instance, references to gypsum, an important export item from this region,[45] do not appear in the Naval Office lists. Nor did vessels from the ports along the southwest coast, later known as Digby, Yarmouth and Shelburne counties, make a great effort to register with the Naval Officer in Halifax. This means that the evidence from the Naval Office shipping lists is especially useful only for Halifax, Sydney and Arichat, where such officials also later resided, and their adjacent coasts. This source is further limited by the fact that complete accounts of trade for Halifax exist only between 1749 and 1766, and for the years 1812-19.[46] For 1768-72 this source can be supplemented by evidence collected by the American Board of Customs. Between 1772 and 1812 there are two other sources of value. The earlier is a shipping list of vessels paying fees to maintain lighthouses as they became established along the coast. The earliest was for the Sambro lighthouse at the entrance to Halifax harbour. Though there is partial data from 1778, the earliest complete annual statistics date only from 1786-87.[47]

The gap in our information is partially filled finally by statistics collected by

44   For the port of Halifax between 1749 and 1775, see the analysis by Fischer, ''Revolution without Independence: The Canadian Colonies, 1749-1775,'' in *The Economy of Early America*, 88-125, and Gwyn, ed., *Nova Scotia Naval Office Shipping Lists, 1730-1820* (Yorkshire, 1981).

45   Gerald S. Graham, ''The Gypsum Trade of the Maritime Provinces: Its relation to American Diplomacy and Agriculture in the Early Nineteenth Century,'' *Agricultural History*, 12 (July 1938), 209-23.

46   Full annual data also exist for the port of Sydney in 1795-97, 1803, 1805-11 and 1814, and for the port of Arichat for 1795-07, 1803-05, 1808-11 and 1814. Thus only for 1814 are there comparable data for the three ports of Halifax, Sydney and Arichat, too narrow a focus for useful comparison.

47   Similar information exists for the ports of Shelburne for 1793-97, 1807-08, 1810-15, for Yarmouth in 1797, 1808-15, and for Liverpool in 1805, 1808-15, where shipping activity was far less than at Halifax and the average vessel size much smaller.

the customs officer in Halifax. In general, the colonial authorities governing Nova Scotia were negligent in the extreme when it came to collecting useful information about trade and navigation, which clearly was of fundamental importance to the economic well-being of the province. The only statistical summary on shipping and trade ever prepared in this era by the Nova Scotia authorities was ordered in 1829 to provide details for the port of Halifax between 1801 and 1828. Finally, the Customs House in London received annual information from 1788 onwards about vessels entering and clearing the port of Halifax. Shipping information for the port of Halifax, drawn from these several sources, is summarized in Table 10. What emerges is a distinct trend from smaller to larger vessels, from schooners and brigs to topsail vessels well in excess of 100 tons burthen. As well as defining a clear trend to larger vessels, the statistics add to our knowledge of the cyclical history of the port as measured both by the changing annual average number of vessels entering Halifax and by the average annual tonnage. When the average annual tonnage data are measured by population growth, Halifax stagnated between the 1750s and the turn of the century; and only during the American war of 1812-14, when the port became the focus of unusual activity was there any significant expansion, when measured by the overall population growth of the colony.

Table 10
Incoming Shipping: Halifax, 1750-1815
(Excludes coasting trade)

Years	Mean # of Vessels	Mean Tonnage	(per capita)	Mean Size (tons)
1750-55	189	8,740	0.44	46.2
1756-63	194	8,700		44.2
1764-66	107	5,175		48.4
1768-72	131	6,694	0.56	51.1
1786-87	290	17,837		61.5
1790-91	170	13,872	0.24	81.6
1795-96	246	21,379		86.9
1799-1801	278	29,458	0.43	106.0
1802-07	240	23,218		96.7
1808-10	364	38,341		105.3
1812-15	530	73,480	0.92	138.6

Source: PRO, CO 217/44 for 1750-66; CO 221/28-32 for 1812-15; CUST 6/1 for 1768-72; Public Archives of Nova Scotia (hereafter PANS) for 1786-87, 1790-91, 1795-96, 1799-1801, 1808-10; PANS, RG 13/40 for 1802-07.

Were such vessels owned by Nova Scotians, or were Nova Scotian merchants purchasing the services of others to import and export their commodities? The sources are not well placed to provide a ready answer. The Naval Officer's Shipping List indicates that before 1749-66 the vast bulk of the vessels entering the port of Halifax were owned by non-Nova Scotians. By 1812-15 there has been a decided swing toward colonial ownership. Details on the size of the merchant fleet owned by Nova Scotians before 1790 are incomplete. Our knowledge thereafter relies on an annual report sent to London by the colonial officials, which information derives from the official ships' registry begun in Halifax, Shelburne and Sydney in 1787. The Nova Scotia fleet expanded unevenly, with the element registered in Sydney, Cape Breton, growing more rapidly than that owned and registered in Shelburne and Halifax.[48] The details can be found in Table 11.

Table 11

Merchant Fleet of Nova Scotia & Cape Breton, 1790-1808

(Enumerated on September 30th of each year)

Average	No.	Tons	Average Tonnage	Seamen	Average Men/Vessel
1790-92	444	22,404	50.5	1,881	4.2
1793-95	469	20,693	44.1	1,878	4.0
1796-98	534	23,614	44.2	2,070	3.9
1799-1801	610	28,695	47.0	2,382	3.9
1802-04	693	37,492	54.1	3,177	4.6
1805-08	684	33,205	48.5	2,623	3.8

Source: PRO, CUST 17/12-30.

Between 1790-92 and 1805-08 the tonnage capacity of the fleet rose by about 48 per cent, from about 22,400 to 33,200 tons annually, though the number of vessels rose by 54 per cent from 444 to 684. Many of the vessels were very small indeed, with one-third in 1790-92 being under 20 tons, and by 1805-08 such small craft formed about 12 per cent of the fleet. By 1790 almost 20 per cent of vessels were prizes taken during the American war. In general the merchant fleet of Nova Scotia and Cape Breton was composed of very small vessels, whose average size rarely exceeded 50 tons. Such vessels were useful principally in the fisheries, and as coasters, or the inter-colonial trade of the Gulf and St. Lawrence river, and in the Caribbean trade routes. Few traded directly with Europe and the Mediterranean, where trade was better carried on in larger vessels. At least until the end of 1808 there is no evidence of an upsurge in Nova Scotia's capacity to offer freighting services to the world.

Associated with this evident long-term rise in shipping activity in the port of

---

48   Details of the merchant fleet registered at Arichat from 1787 to 1815 are found in A.P. Tousenard, "Growth and Decline of Arichat, Nova Scotia, 1765-1880," MA thesis, Dalhousie University, 1984, 30, 41.

Halifax and the expansion of Nova Scotia's and Cape Breton's merchant marine was the development of shipbuilding as an important colonial industry. Before 1784 shipbuilding scarcely existed in the colony. As one report to the British Board of Trade remarked, "They have not yet built any ships beyond the small craft employed in the fishery, & other services upon their own coast."[49] The legislature voted subsidies for shipbuilding, and in 1786 some sixteen vessels, averaging about 75 tons each, were launched with benefit of such largesse.[50] There are no reliable statistics on annual launchings of newly-constructed vessels in Nova Scotia before 1787, while only from 1801 do we know the regions along the coast where the vessels were launched. As Table 12 shows, there was a sharp decline in shipbuilding, when measured by head of population, between 1787-90 and 1809-11, having peaked in 1800-1802.

Table 12
Nova Scotia & Cape Breton Shipbuilding, 1787-1815
(Annual Average)

Years	#	Tons	Mean Tonnage	(per capita)
1787-90	44	2,646	60.1	0.047
1791-93	30	1,670	55.7	0.029
1794-96	28	1,614	57.6	—
1797-99	33	2,069	62.7	—
1800-02	46	4,200	91.3	0.063
1803-05	54	3,332	61.7	—
1806-08	39	2,253	57.8	—
1809-11	34	2,801	82.4	0.037
1812-15	38	2,653	69.8	0.035

Source: PRO, CUST 17/12-30 for 1787-1808; PANS, RG 13/40 for 1809-15.

Of the 561 vessels, totalling 43,257 measured tons, launched between 1811 and 1815, 174 (31 per cent) amounting to 16,583 (38.3 per cent) in tonnage, were built in ports of the Annapolis Valley and Minas Basin. Shipbuilding was a severely cyclical industry, which war, owing to losses in actions with privateers and to the captures of enemy vessels, made even more volatile. It prospered best in peacetime conditions, or, if there was a war on, without Nova Scotia being a belligerent. Unfortunately, Nova Scotia found itself at war each time British interests determined on it, dragging the rest of the empire with it. Such peaks as there were

---

49 "State of Nova Scotia" (1784), PRO, BT6/84. 52-53.

50 Gerald S. Graham, *Sea Power and British North America, 1783-1820. A Study of British Colonial Policy* (London, 1941), 47. The pre-1820 shipping industry in British North America is briefly surveyed in Eric W. Sager and Gerald E. Panting, *Maritime Capital: The Shipping Industry in Atlantic Canada, 1820-1914* (Kingston, 1990), 23-46.

in shipbuilding were achieved in 1802 and 1811-12. Steep declines in newly launched tonnage occurred in part when many enemy vessels were captured and sold cheaply at auction after being condemned as prizes of war by the Halifax Vice Admiralty Court. This was especially the case in 1808-09 and 1812-13. The year 1812 was the worst of all those surveyed here for shipbuilding with only twelve new vessels amounting to merely 575 tons. This sharp decline stemmed directly from the successes against American shipping upon the outbreak of war, and the consequent purchase at auction of American prize vessels by Nova Scotian speculators.

How large an investment was this? Shipbuilding between 1788 and 1815 amounted to some 72,367 tons, which at an estimated £5 per ton implied a gross amount of perhaps £362,000 ($1,447,000) or less than £13,000 ($52,000) annually. This was by far the largest capital investment in any sector of the economy, except perhaps in agriculture. Some of these vessels were sold in the British Isles and the West Indies, although the annual trade reports ignored them. Whatever was earned from such sales, when the costs associated with purchases by Nova Scotian shipowners abroad are subtracted, helped balance Nova Scotia's payments with Great Britain and later the United Kingdom.

Shipbuilding had of course been stimulated not just by expanding trade and population, but by losses suffered both from the hazard of the weather, and from the caprice of war. Perhaps as many as one vessel in five either foundered or was captured while owned in Nova Scotia. The most complete study of the losses from war at sea, suffered by vessels in Nova Scotian waters, deals with the American war of 1776-83. Some 223 vessels, averaging 85 tons each, were seized either on their passage or cut out of Nova Scotia's numerous harbours.[51] These bald figures represent a loss of $15 a ton of about $285,000 in capital for the vessels alone, and perhaps half as much again in the value of cargoes, a total sum of perhaps $425,000 or £85,000. As the bulk of these vessels were far larger than was normally owned by Nova Scotians, we can conclude that most were British owned or owned by Loyalist Americans elsewhere in what still remained of British America. Of these losses, 53 alone had occurred in 1776, and were, it has been argued, an important element in influencing New England Planter families to alter their initial willingness to support the patriot cause during the war of indepen-

---

51 See John Dewar Faibisy, "Privateering and Piracy: The Effects of American Privateering upon Nova Scotia during the American Revolution," PhD thesis, University of Massachusetts, 1972, Appendix entitled: "A Compilation of Nova Scotia Vessels Seized During the American Revolution and Libelled in the New England Prize Courts." See as well his "Yankee Raiders and the Republican Incursion into Nova Scotia, 1776-1777," *The Log of Mystic Seaport*, 29 (1977), 82-91. Not all Nova Scotians suffered. Alexander Brymer dominated the prize proceedings of the Halifax Vice-Admiralty court during the war of independence, while representing prize crews, and was owner of one very successful privateer. See J.B. Cahill, "Alexander Brymer, 1745-1822," *Dictionary of Canadian Biography*, VI, 89-90. John Butler joined other Halifax merchants in outfitting the privateer *Revenge* in 1776. See Alan Dunlop, "John Butler (d. 1791)," *ibid.*, IV, 116-17.

dence. In the midst of war some Planters petitioned the Massachusetts General Court itself, and stressed their sympathy with the American patriots' revolutionary principles, while begging to have their seized property returned to them.[52] Their disappointments helped turn them against their former compatriots. Others lost their vessels and cargoes while exporting supplies from Nova Scotia to New England, contrary to British wartime regulations.

Direct attacks on the Nova Scotian and Cape Breton mainland also helped to turn erstwhile supporters of the patriot cause against the Americans. Every coast of the colony was visited by Yankee landing parties who penetrated deeply into the Bay of Fundy and along the entire South shore: Liverpool, LaHave, Cape Sambro but a few miles from the Halifax lighthouse, and even into the Northwest Arm itself. They ranged along the Eastern shore and along the Strait of Canso and attacked shipping there before descending on the few isolated fishing communities along the Northumberland Strait. Of those who lost heavily at the hands of American privateers, Simeon Perkins of Liverpool is the best known. Yet he himself continued investing in privateers as late as 1805.[53] In the later wars with France no such embarrassments were endured along the Nova Scotia coast. Instead numerous losses were suffered by Nova Scotia's shipowners, especially in the Caribbean at the hands of enemy privateers. There was a recurrence of activity by American warships and privateers between 1812 and 1814, and again Nova Scotians suffered losses.[54] These have yet to be studied in detail.

There is some evidence that American losses in the war of 1812-14 were far more serious than those suffered by Nova Scotians. Kert identified not less than 191 prizes taken by 21 of the 27 privateers outfitted by speculators from Nova Scotia.[55] Of these, 16 were restored to their owners by the vice admiralty court and the 175 remaining were condemned as prizes and the vessels and their cargoes sold at auction. As many as 47 of these were taken alone by one vessel, and another 95 were accounted for by seven other privateers. Neither the net value of such prizes is known, nor whether profits were achieved by the majority of investors. Yet obviously the resulting successes added to Nova Scotia's merchant fleet, while depressing the shipbuilding industry both there and in Cape Breton.

---

52 Abraham Knowlton, 13 November 1776; Azariah Uzuld, 24 December 1776; Joel Webber and Josiah Harris, 27 October 1777. Massachusetts Archives, Vol. 166, 27; 267, 372; 181, 400. Cited in Faibisy, "Privateering and Piracy," 69-70.

53 C. Bruce Fergusson, "Simeon Perkins, 1735-1812," *Dictionary of Canadian Biography*, V, 663-65. Malachy Salter, who owned the only sugar refinery in Nova Scotia, lost his only vessel to a Salem privateer in 1777. See Susan Buggey, "Malachy Salter, 1716-1781," *ibid.*, IV, 695-96.

54 The Rhode Island privateer, *Yankee*, alone took 40 vessels in six cruises. How many, if any, belonged to Nova Scotian shipowners, is not clear. See Donald MacIntyre, *The Privateers* (London, 1975), 178.

55 Faye Margaret Kert, "The Fortunes of War: Privateering in Atlantic Canada in the War of 1812," MA thesis, Carleton University, 1986, see appendices, 140-51. She used the records of the Halifax Vice-Admiralty Court, National Archives, Ottawa, RG 8, Series IV. Enos Collins served as a

VI

This brings our analysis to an end. What general conclusions can be drawn from this range of evidence? The first point to be raised is that not everything that happens in wartime is caused by war. There would have been swings in prices and wages, pressures on population growth, cycles in trade, balance of payment difficulties and important movements in the exchange rate, fluctuations in shipping and shipbuilding, without war. It is arguable, for instance, that the 1807 parliamentary decision, uninfluenced by the then prevailing wartime conditions, to abandon the slave trade was of more significance to the future economy of the Caribbean or at the Cape of Good Hope, than anything British arms had accomplished since the outbreak of war in 1792. Owing to Nova Scotia's interest in the Caribbean this was later to prove of enormous importance to trading patterns, when, as a result, sugar production in the British Caribbean began to falter.[56] Another example of an important decision taken in wartime, but not because of the war, was the unexpected and unilateral resolution by the Americans to withdraw in 1807 from the British West Indies carrying trade. This decision, caused not by war but by deteriorating relations with the United Kingdom, allowed the British North American colonies, led by Nova Scotia, to play a larger role in the West Indies market.[57] Such examples can be readily multiplied.

Yet in the case of Nova Scotia war was an important cause of change. It had a dramatic impact on population growth and retardation. In the first instance, the expulsion, as an act of war, of the bulk of resident population between 1755 and 1758, and their urgent replacement with loyal settlers from New England was highly disruptive to steady economic growth. Secondly, war and the peace treaty which ended it directly caused American Loyalists to become refugees. The sudden nature of their arrival and the extent of their numbers created further disorder, which was not confined to the economic sphere. They, together with perhaps 2,000 disbanded soldiers, were just numerous enough to begin to knit the colony together for the first time, transforming it from the scattered and rather isolated coastal settlements which had characterized the colony since 1755. In this way also the racial mix of the province's population was profoundly altered before 1790 by the influence of war. The later accretions of Scottish highlanders and Irish had little directly to do with war, but rather with the diminished economic prospects at home, the first wave begun in the midst of war, the second owing to the severe

---

lieutenant in the successful privateer, *Charles Mary Wentworth,* in 1799 and later did well from three privateers he owned. See Diane Barker and David A. Sutherland, ''Enos Collins, 1774-1871,'' *Dictionary of Canadian Biography,* X, 188-90; ''Joseph Barss, 1776-1824,'' *ibid.,* VI, 37-38.

56   Perhaps the best account for the economics of the Atlantic slave trade from the 1780s is David Eltis, *Economic Growth and the Ending of the Transatlantic Slave Trade* (Oxford, 1987).

57   See my ''Rum, Sugar and Molasses in the Economy of Nova Scotia 1770-1854,'' *Tempered by Rum: Rum in the History of the Maritime Provinces,* 117-18.

post-war depression, which bankrupted so many small holders in Ireland as elsewhere.

For Nova Scotia, war had a direct impact on the economy. It caused high levels of inflation by creating shortages, redirecting workers out of productive employment into the army and navy, disrupting overseas commerce, forcing up insurance and shipping rates. This occurred in Nova Scotia as elsewhere. Inflation was further advanced by greatly increased public spending, which resulted in an over rapid expansion of the money supply to meet wartime needs. It added to the funded long-term national debt in Great Britain and occasioned considerable and unexpected public spending in Nova Scotia.[58] It raised taxes far above peacetime levels. It gave a powerful resonance to shipping as exports suffered, and imports rose. This had dramatic effects for Nova Scotia, when in 1777-78 Halifax became an important entrepôt for all American imports from the British Isles. The successful establishment of American independence by force of arms forced Nova Scotia's natural trading partners in New England, New York and Pennsylvania outside the imperial trading community, demarked by the Navigation Acts. This was an appalling loss, and perhaps more than any other element defined the limits of Nova Scotia's future economic growth. Now Nova Scotia faced tariff walls, where before trade had been conducted without such impediments. Compensation was found only partially in the continued open access to the British Caribbean markets.

To begin to estimate the extent of Nova Scotia's losses one has only to produce for comparison's sake the essential facts relating to the economic development of Nova Scotia in this era with perhaps the weakest economic unit within the Union, namely the colony and state of Georgia. Like Nova Scotia, Georgia, it will be remembered, had also been a British military colony established for strategic defensive reasons. Just as Nova Scotia was designed to protect Massachusetts against the power of France, so too Georgia's initial role was to defend South Carolina against the power of Spain. It, like Nova Scotia, had received regular infusions of British public spending to sustain itself from its very foundation as a new colony. Its capital, Savannah, like Halifax, had been built at the cost of British taxpayers. Its civil administration, like that of Nova Scotia, was also financed by the British. In the crisis with Parliament in the 1770s, many Nova Scotians might have been tempted to switch their loyalty from the crown, but with a British army in Boston, Massachusetts had been unable to bring suitable pressure to bear on Nova Scotia. By contrast, Georgia had been badgered into support of the revolutionary Continental Congress by patriots from neighbouring South Carolina.[59] With a large loyalist body of opinion, Georgia's support for

---

58 Between 1812 and 1815, Nova Scotia had outstanding treasury notes amounting to only £17,475 or less than five shillings per capita, which represents the total provincial public debt. See J.S. Martell, "A Documentary Study of Provincial Finance and Currency 1812-36," *Bulletin of the Public Archives in Nova Scotia*, II (1941), 50.

59 Frances Harrold, "Colonial Siblings, Georgia's Relationship with South Carolina During the Pre-Revolutionary Period," *Georgia Historical Quarterly*, LXXIII (Winter 1989), 707-44.

the patriot cause was restrained, though ultimately the majority of its political leadership cast its lot with the American republic. Georgia, as the scene of much bitter combat, suffered far more losses from the war in the form of fleeing slaves and actual physical destruction from military action, than anything Nova Scotia had endured. Yet it soon recovered. Its pre-1776 exports were certainly worth more than those of Nova Scotia, and its free population was larger, so making the per capita value of those exports roughly on a par with Nova Scotia. With South Carolina, Georgia found a ready market for its exports of indigo, rice and cotton, both before 1776 and after 1783. Nova Scotia's struggling economic existence contrasts poorly with the vigour of that experienced by Georgia after 1783, with its reestablished plantation economic system.[60]

For Nova Scotia, little recompense for the loss of the New England commercial connection could be found in trading with Newfoundland, New Brunswick and Prince Edward Island, which possessed advantages over Nova Scotia in fish, wood products and agriculture respectively. As each of these colonies remained in such a primitive and struggling economic condition in the post-1783 world, even together they proved to be very inadequate markets on which to build a rich commerce for Nova Scotia. The inability of each of these separately or together to dominate the one good market open to them, that of the British Caribbean, is the clearest indication of their economic backwardness, the primitive nature of their infrastructures, their lamentable shortage of capital, diminished by the unfortunate fiasco at Shelburne.[61] Had overseas commerce flourished, the mercantile fleet of the colony would have expanded instead of stagnating in the 1780s and 1790s. As well shipbuilding would have earlier become more important. In wartime shipbuilding depended in great part on the losses suffered balanced by the number of prizes taken. For Nova Scotia the balance sheet has been imperfectly established both for the wars of 1776-83 and 1792-1815. It appears that losses were greater than successes throughout the American war of 1776-83 and in the wars with France until well into the first decade of the nineteenth century. In the later stages of that war, when it merged with the second American war, the balance seems to have shifted in favour of Nova Scotian shipowners. This resulted, not from the establishment of an effective colonial naval force at sea or from the prominence of Nova Scotians as privateersmen, but by the work of the British navy, financed as ever by the heavily burdened British taxpayer. Evidence indicates a rapid

---

60 See especially Kenneth Coleman, *The American Revolution in Georgia, 1763-1789* (Athens, 1958) and his *Colonial Georgia: A History* (New York, 1976); and for the economy James C. Bonner, *A History of Georgia Agriculture 1732-1860* (Athens, 1964); Julia F. Smith, *Slavery and Rice Culture in Low Country Georgia, 1750-1860* (Knoxville, 1985); George B. Crawford, "Preface to Revolution: Agriculture, Society and Crisis in Georgia, 1840-1860," PhD thesis, Claremont Graduate School, 1987.

61 According to Charles Morris, some £500,000 in capital had been wasted there. By October 1816 there were but 374 souls in the town and its suburbs. Anthony Lockwood, *A Brief Description of Nova Scotia . . .* (London, 1818), 74. For a contemporary description of Shelburne at its height, see [S. Hollingsworth], *The Present State of Nova Scotia* (London, 1787), 130.

expansion of the mercantile fleet from 1812 through 1814, when the Halifax Vice Admiralty court did so much prize business.

Finally, British public spending in the colony, especially high in wartime, remained throughout the period down to 1815 the most important form of economic activity, and played an unusually large role in defining colonial economic priorities. The closer in the economy one could place oneself to such government spending the greater the prospects of wealth. It was an internal market of unusual value, especially for those close to government, while for those on the periphery, which meant the vast bulk of the population, it was of little or no importance. As the basis of sustained economic growth it was exceedingly ephemeral and inadequate. This, to the vast disappointment of many colonials, the economic development of the colony after 1812-15 subsequently demonstrated so eloquently.[62]

---

62 See my " 'A Little Province Like This': The Economy of Nova Scotia under Stress, 1812-1853," *Canadian Papers in Rural History,* VI (1988), 192-225, and "Golden Age or Bronze Moment? Wealth and Poverty in Nova Scotia: the 1850s and 1860s," *Canadian Papers in Rural History,* VIII (forthcoming).

Nova Scotia and the American Revolution:
A Study of Neutrality and Moderation in the Eighteenth Century

Donald Desserud[1]
University of New Brunswick, Saint John

Influenced by the Principles of humanity and the just rights of Mankind in civil Society, we tremble, at the Gloomy prospect before us, We feel for our Gracious King, We feel for our Mother Country of which many of us are Natives, We feel for the British American Race, once the most Loyall, Virtuous, and happy of mankind . . . .[2]

This is a paper by a political scientist who wishes to learn more about the relationship between neutrality and moderation, specifically in the context of eighteenth-century Enlightenment thought. It is my argument that I can learn more about the politics of neutrality and its relationship with moderation by examining the political culture of Nova Scotia during the American Revolution, for during this time questions of neutrality and moderation were more than academic curiosities; they determined the lives and livelihood of a considerable number of citizens. Furthermore, in Nova Scotia neutrality and moderation were profoundly linked with the eighteenth-century ideas of political virtue and corruption. It would seem appropriate, then, to examine these concepts in the context of our understanding of virtue and corruption in the eighteenth century.

Civic Humanism and the American Revolution
Bernard Bailyn and J.G.A. Pocock have sought to explain the ideological origins of the American Revolution in terms of an Anglo-American civic humanist tradition.[3] By their analyses, the American Revolution was a struggle against the

---

1 I would like to express my gratitude to Drs. Elizabeth Mancke, Ann Condon, Julian Gwyn, Graeme Wynn and George Rawlyk, participants in the Planter Studies Conference, and to Drs. Theresa Chudy, Chris Doran, Harry Taukulis and Rod Hill, of the University of New Brunswick at Saint John Eighteenth-Century Society, for helpful comments on earlier drafts of this paper. I would also like to express my appreciation to my research assistant, Ms. Dawn Bourque, for her assistance and uncommon good sense in editing this paper.

2 From an address by the Nova Scotia Assembly to the British Parliament, 1775, in J.B. Brebner, ''Nova Scotia's Remedy for the American Revolution,'' *The Canadian Historical Review*, XV (June 1934), 171-81.

3 The standard interpretations of the American Revolution in terms of Enlightenment thought are by Carl Becker, *The Declaration of Independence* (New York, 1922), and by Gordon S. Wood, *The Creation of the American Republic* (Chapel Hill, 1969). Bernard Bailyn's interpretation can be found in his *The Ideological Origins of the American Revolution* (Harvard, 1967); *The Origins of American Politics* (New York, 1970); in his introduction to *Pamphlets of the American Revolution*, 2 vols. (Cambridge, Mass., 1965); and his *Voyagers to the West* (New York, 1986). His clearest statement of this thesis, however, is his ''Political Experience and Enlightenment

tyranny of a corrupted British parliament; the republic that the revolutionaries fought to erect in its place was supposed to recapture the civic virtues of the classical republic:

> Virtue, once endangered, was compelled to fall back on itself, and there was no remedy which Americans could seek short of *rinnovazione* and *ridurre ai principii*; a return to the fundamental principles of British government or — once that was seen as containing the seeds of its own corruption — of the constitution of the commonwealth itself; an attempt to reconstitute that form of polity in which virtue would be both free and secure.[4]

Bailyn explains that the ''American Provincials'' were ''remarkably well-informed students of contemporary social and political theory.'' Through the non-conformist connection, commonwealth radicalism ''continued to flow to the colonists, blending, ultimately, with other strains of thought to form a common body of advanced theory.'' The consequence was a revolution spurred on by intellectuals who used ideas in a deliberate and conscientious manner.[5] The ideas they used, while not uniform or without dissent, were nevertheless remarkably consistent. Corruption had overtaken modern political institutions and destroyed the legitimacy of imperial rule. A new republic must be resurrected in its place, one which would return to the ancient and lost values of citizenship and virtue, of liberty and participation in rule.[6]

Ideas in Eighteenth-Century America,'' *American Historical Review*, 67 (1961-62), 339-51. For J.G.A. Pocock's interpretation, see the various essays in *Politics, Language and Time* (New York, 1973); in *Virtue, Commerce, and History* (Cambridge, 1985) and ''The Americanization of Virtue,'' ch. xv of *The Machiavellian Moment* (Princeton, 1975), 506-52. See also ''The Classical Theory of Deference,'' *American Historical Review*, 81 (1979), 516-23. For a stimulating account of the ideological origins of the Loyalists, see Janice Potter, *The Liberty We Seek; Loyalist Ideology in Colonial New York and Massachusetts* (Cambridge, Mass., 1983). Dr. Potter's study presents, with considerably greater clarity (and depth), a mirror image to my own, and I am indebted to her thesis supervisor, Dr. George Rawlyk, for bringing this study to my attention.

4   The reason why ''virtue was compelled to fall back on itself'' was, Pocock explains, because the very language of their rhetoric forced them to now see England as alien, and virtue as recoverable only through revolutionary activity. Nova Scotia seems to have avoided this rhetorical trap. See *The Machiavellian Moment*, 507-508.

5   See Bailyn, ''Political Experience and Enlightenment Ideas in Eighteenth-Century America,'' 343-45: ''Thus, throughout the eighteenth century there were prominent, politically active Americans who were well aware of the development of European thinking, took ideas seriously, and during the Revolution deliberately used them in an effort to reform the institutional basis of society,'' (345). The most comprehensive studies of the politics and culture of this period are to be found in Caroline Robbins, *The Eighteenth-Century Commonwealthman: Studies on the Transmission, Development, and Circumstance of English Liberal Thought from the Restoration of Charles II until the War with the Thirteen Colonies* (Cambridge, Mass., 1959) and Isaac Kramnick, *Bolingbroke and His Circle: Politics of Nostalgia in the Age of Walpole* (Cambridge, Mass., 1968).

6   See Bailyn, *Pamphlets of the American Revolution*, Vol. 1, xi-xiii; and Pocock, ''Civic Human-

But while these ideas were consistent in their condemnation of corruption, the nostalgia for the past did not in itself present a simple and clear alternative. The values and ideas expressed in this civic humanist ideology, despite the simplicity of the pamphleteers, were never homogeneous, and, as Bailyn's definitive study on pamphlet literature of the American Revolution has so ably demonstrated, were fraught with inconsistencies and self-contradictions. To have liberty, to be free, may mean to be free from interference in my right to conduct my own affairs, or to be free to participate in the decisions of the state. It may mean the right to speak and think as I please, or it may mean the right and responsibility to bear arms so that I may participate in a citizen's militia to defend my country.[7]

It is Pocock's claim that during the eighteenth century there occurred a synthesis, as it were, of two dominant and hitherto exclusive paradigms: one deriving from the natural law tradition, which was structured around the notion of private rights of individuals under the protection of the law; the second, from the classical republican tradition, which was structured around the ideals of a republic based upon self-directed, virtuous citizenship.[8] The consequences of this merging of traditions can be seen in the liberal-capitalist ideology that emerged from the eighteenth century.[9] Activities such as commerce, condemned for their corrupting influence only a few generations before, were now praised for producing, in Montesquieu's words, "frugality, economy, moderation, work, discretion, tranquillity, order and rule."[10] Commerce was now a moderating influence, it calmed and softened mores.[11] Indeed, moderation became as important a value as liberty itself. But moderation, as a concept (like that of neutrality), tends to be ignored by Enlightenment scholars who see the civic humanist debate as a black and white conflict between the ancients and the moderns. As Reed Browning explains, there is a tendency to assume far too much simplicity in the divisions we ascribe to this time period.[12] And yet it was moderation, not revolutionary ideology, that the American Provincials would have found in Montesquieu.[13] According to Mon-

---

ism and its Role in Anglo-American Political Thought,'' in *Politics, Language and Time*, 53.

7   See Pocock, *Machiavellian Moment*, 466.

8   See Pocock, ''Civic Humanism and its Role in Anglo-American Political Thought,'' 53.

9   As Pocock explains, ''[t]he defence of commercial society, no less than the vindication of classical virtue, was carried out with the weapons of humanism. The 18th century presents us with legal humanism or humanistic jurisprudence, whose roots were ... being employed against the civic humanism of the classical republicans.'' Pocock, ''Virtue, Rights, And Manners — A Model for Historians of Political-Thought,'' *Political Theory*, 9 (1981), 366.

10   *Spirit of the Laws*, Book V, ch. 6. See Nannerl Keohane, ''Virtuous Republics and Glorious Monarchies: Two Models in Montesquieu's Political Thought,'' *Political Studies*, XX (1972), 387. For an excellent discussion of this transformation, see Albert O. Hirschman, *The Passions and the Interests: Political Arguments for Capitalism before Its Triumph* (Princeton, 1981).

11   Pocock, ''Varieties of Whiggism from Exclusion to Reform: A history of ideology and discourse,'' *Virtue, Commerce and History*, 219.

12   Reed Browning, *Political and Constitutional Ideas of the Court Whigs* (Baton Rouge, 1982), 11ff.

13   See Sergio Cotta, ''Montesquieu, la séparation des pouvoirs et la constitution fédérale des États-Unis,'' *Revue internationale d'histoire politique et constitutionnelle* (1951), 225-247; and

tesquieu, without moderation, there *could be* no liberty.[14] It was this moderation, this reasonableness which was as much a part of the revolutionary ideology of the thirteen colonies as was the desire for liberty and republicanism. Indeed, it was a moderate, balanced government that the Americans eventually erected to bring republican values to the new world, a system based upon a separation of powers,[15] and in no small part derived from Montesquieu.[16]

When we turn to Nova Scotia during this time, we see, on a much smaller scale, the same confluence of forces and ideologies as occurred in the other thirteen colonies. We find an extremist form of individualism which, in some circumstances at least, manifested itself as an evangelical revivalism.[17] We find, without question, examples of mercantilist conspiracy and, particularly in the case of the much-maligned Governor Legge, rather rabid and insensitive loyalty to Britain.[18] And we find examples of revolutionary fervour and ideological republicanism.[19] But

---

Lawrence J. Forno, "Montesquieu's Reputation in France, England, and America (1750-1800)," *Studies in Burke and His Time*, 15 (1973), 5-29.

14 "La liberté politique ne se trouve que dans les gouvernements modérés." *l'Esprit des Lois*, XI.4. On Montesquieu's 'moderate' concept of virtue, see D.J. Fletcher, "Montesquieu's Concept of Patriotism," *Studies on Voltaire and the Eighteenth Century*, LVI (1967), 541-555.

15 See Bailyn, *The Pamphlets of the American Revolution*: "The American writers were profoundly reasonable people. Their pamphlets convey scorn, anger, and indignation; but rarely blind hate, rarely panic fear. They sought to convince their opponents, not, like the English pamphleteers of the eighteenth century, to annihilate them" (17).

16 See note 13 above.

17 See M.W. Armstrong, "Neutrality and Religion in Revolutionary Nova Scotia," *The New England Quarterly*, IX (March, 1946), 50-62; also in G. A. Rawlyk, ed., *Historical Essays on the Atlantic Provinces* (Toronto, 1967). All page references will be to the Rawlyk collection: "To assume, therefore, that while their brothers in the Thirteen Colonies were engaged in a life and death struggle for the high ideals of 'Life, Liberty and the pursuit of Happiness,' Nova Scotians were unmoved by any higher consideration than safety and profits is unfair."

"The emotional extravagances of the enthusiasts ... [were] the marks of men and women who refused to conform to contemporary standards and wished to demonstrate their own alliance with a power which was superior to all human conventions. *The same individualism which found expressions in other molds in the Thirteen Colonies, activated the religious extraverts to the northern outpost.*" (39-40, 42; emphasis added).

18 V.F. Barnes, "Francis Legge, Governor of Loyalist Nova Scotia, 1773-1776," *New England Quarterly* (July 1931), 420-47; W.B. Kerr, "The Merchants of Nova Scotia and the American Revolution," *Canadian Historical Review*, (April 1932), 20-36; and *The Maritime Provinces of British North America and the American Revolution* (New York, 1941).

19 "The great contest between *Britain* and *America* has hitherto been only treated with speculation amongst us [residents of Chignecto]. A spirit of sympathy, I presume, for our brethren on the Continent, reigns in the breasts of the generality of the inhabitants. With gladness and cheerfulness would we be active in the glorious struggle, had our situation and circumstances been any way such that there was the least glimpse of success." Anonymous Letter to General George Washington, 8 February 1776. This appears in many different sources, and has achieved the reputation of being "oft-quoted." See, for example, Paul W. Bennett and Cornelius J. Jaenen, eds., *Emerging Identities: Selected Problems and Interpretations in Canadian History* (Scarborough, Ontario, 1986), 137; and G.A. Rawlyk, *Revolution Rejected; 1775-1776* (Toronto, 1968), 19. See also F. Kidder, *Military Operations in Eastern Maine and Nova Scotia During the Revolu-*

we also find examples of moderation, and it is significant that, after the shouting was over, it was the moderate factions that carried the day. Nova Scotia was, after all, only ostensibly loyal during the revolution; Nova Scotians, to use Brebner's felicitous phrase, were for the most part "Neutral Yankees."[20] Responding to Governor Legge's attempts to raise a militia to defend Nova Scotia against the Yankee rebels, the inhabitants of Cumberland explained: "Those of us who belong to New England, being invited into the Province by Governor Lawrence's Proclamation it must be the greatest piece of cruelty and imposition for them to be subjected to march into different parts in Arms against their friends and relations. Still should any person or persons presume to molest us in our present situation, we are always ready to defend ourselves and property."[21] Similarly, the people of Yarmouth petitioned: "We do all of us profess to be true Friends & Loyal Subjects to George our King. We were almost all of us born in New England, we have Fathers, Brothers and Sisters in that Country, divided betwixt natural affection to our nearest relations and good Faith and Friendship to our King and Country, we want to know, if it may be permitted at this time to live in a peaceable State, as we look on that to be the only situation in which we with our Wives and Children, can be in any tolerable degree safe."[22]

By so attempting to remain neutral, and thus avoiding participation in this political event, Nova Scotians seem to have rejected (or indeed been unaware of) politics. Thus, their ostensible loyalty to Britain during the revolution has been seen more as a product of their *apolitical* character rather than their patriotism. Indeed, scholarship on Nova Scotia's refusal to participate in the American Revolution has tended to concentrate upon three theories, all of which emphasise this supposed lack of political involvement of Nova Scotia decision-makers. Brebner's thesis stresses the isolation and frontiersmanship of early Nova Scotia. The rigours of the Nova Scotian frontier did not give the settlers the time to be concerned with such weighty political matters.[23] Professor Rawlyk's attractive

---

tion (Albany, 1867), particularly "Resolutions of the Maugerville Inhabitants, May 1776," (64-65); and W.B. Kerr, "Nova Scotia and the Critical Years, 1775-76," *Dalhousie Review (1932/33)*.

20 "They refused to fight their blood brothers. ... They felt incapable, even when willing, to take overt action to destroy British control. They were desperately concerned by the interruption in their economic intercourse with New England. The Nova Scotian settlers were weak and exposed, and knowing this, like the Acadians whom they had supplanted, asked that the belligerents treat them as neutrals." J.B. Brebner, *The Neutral Yankees of Nova Scotia* (1937; rpt. Toronto, 1969), 275.

21 Quoted in Rawlyk, ed., *Revolution Rejected; 1775-1776*, 28; and Bennett, ed., *Emerging Identities*, 140.

22 This too has been widely quoted; in Rawlyk and Bennett, cited above, and in Brebner, *Neutral Yankees of Nova Scotia*, 291; and Kerr, "Nova Scotia and the Critical Years, 1775-76," 102. The original reference is to Public Archives of Canada, Nova Scotia Series A, Vol. 94, 300.

23 See Brebner, *The Neutral Yankees of Nova Scotia*, 261. Of course, Nova Scotia did experience some of the revolutionary fighting as some groups found common cause with their Yankee brethren. See Kidder, *Military Operations in Eastern Maine and Nova Scotia During the Revolution*, and Kerr, "Nova Scotia and the Critical Years, 1775-76."

thesis is that it was not so much frontiersmanship nor isolation that convinced Nova Scotians to reject politics, but rather the appeal of evangelicism, promoted by such charismatic figures as Henry Alline.[24] Politics, a profane activity, was rejected in favour of the more sacred activities of revivalist religion. Others have concentrated upon the commercial activities of eighteenth-century Nova Scotia. Ruled by a merchant class concerned primarily with making a profit, Nova Scotia decided to take advantage of the new opportunities for trade with Great Britain.[25]

Yet, to be neutral is not (necessarily) to be apolitical, for neutrality can very well be an example of moderation. This becomes all the more probable when we recall that, at least according to Montesquieu, moderation was the *raison d'être* of English politics;[26] similarly, moderation may well have been a value of importance to Nova Scotians who had to choose between supporting either their Yankee relatives or their British colonial masters, both of whom presented ample evidence of corruption.[27] Further, the remoteness of the community does not in itself account for a lack of political involvement, and recent studies on culture of the Planter and other pre-Loyalist communities suggest that remoteness did not mean a lack of sophistication.[28] The involvement of eighteenth-century Nova Scotian

---

24 Gordon Stewart and George Rawlyk, *A People Highly Favoured of God* (Toronto, 1972). See also Armstrong, ''Neutrality and Religion in Revolutionary Nova Scotia''; *The Great Awakening in Nova Scotia 1776-1809* (Hartford, 1948); and W.P. Bell, *The ''Foreign Protestants'' and the Settlement of Nova Scotia* (Toronto, 1961). See also the various essays collected in Margaret Conrad, ed., *They Planted Well; New England Planters in Maritime Canada* (Fredericton, 1988).

25 Barnes, ''Francis Legge, Governor of Loyalist Nova Scotia, 1773-1776''; E.P. Weaver, ''Nova Scotia and New England during the Revolution,'' *American Historical Review*, 10 (1907), 52-71; Kerr, ''Nova Scotia and the Critical Years, 1775-76,'' *The Dalhousie Review*, 489-495; and ''The Merchants of Nova Scotia and the American Revolution,'' *American Historical Review*, X (1904), 52-71; and Brebner, ''Nova Scotia's Remedy for the American Revolution.''

26 See my ''Beyond Virtue and Honour: Montesquieu's Analysis of the English Constitution,'' PhD thesis, University of Western Ontario, 1989.

27 Consider, for example, the many references in Simeon Perkins' diaries to the American privateers and to the British press gangs. Harold A. Innis, ed., *The Diary of Simeon Perkins, 1766-1780* (Toronto, 1948). It is also worth noting that the attitude of the New Englanders towards Britain was somewhat different than the attitude of Nova Scotians, for the simple reason that New Englanders tended to see their prosperity as being the result of their own fortitude. In Nova Scotia, many settlers received their land (farms already cleared by the expelled Acadians) as gifts from the Crown. As well, Nova Scotian merchants, at least, would probably have seen New England as the source of their chief competition. Viola Barnes' thesis on the merchant control of Nova Scotia as an explanation for Nova Scotian neutrality refers to the ''economic bondage to New England under which the Province had suffered since the French and Indian War.'' See Barnes, ''Francis Legge, Governor of Loyalist Nova Scotia, 1773-1776.'' See also Kerr: ''It would seem, then, that the decisive fact in Nova Scotia was the almost total want of sympathy among artisans, fishermen, and farmers for the American cause. ... From every point of view it appears that Nova Scotia's New Englanders remained cold and impervious to the feeling of nationality which was impelling the thirteen colonies.'' ''The Merchants of Nova Scotia and the American Revolution,'' 34, 36.

communities with evangelical revivalism begs rather than answers the question of whether these same people were ideologically motivated in their behaviour. Finally, questions concerning the commercial aspects of Nova Scotia's decision to remain neutral throughout the revolution should not be seen as supplanting political concerns, for, as we are now accustomed to seeing, commercial interests and political interests went hand in hand in eighteenth-century Britain,[29] and did so surely in eighteenth-century British colonies.

In all of the theories to explain why Nova Scotia did not participate in the American Revolution, the central argument is that non-participation was evidence of a lack of will, or indeed lack of ability, to understand the political implications of the struggle that was going on around them. Like the Acadians they displaced, the Nova Scotians at the time of the American Revolution are accused of being *apolitical*.[30] Furthermore, this argument depends upon a premise which is seldom stated or proven, that neutrality is in itself an apolitical activity. But it is my argument that rather than being a rejection of politics, neutrality was (or could well be) a logical response, and indeed was a response quite in keeping with the civic humanist tradition Bailyn and Pocock identify as being of such importance to the ideological origins of the American Revolution. Since the rejection of corrupt forms of authority and a return to a simpler regime in which individuals relied upon their own sense of virtue is the basis for the civic humanist argument, it seems quite possible that this could, under certain circumstances, take the form of a suspicion of all forms of authority, be they Yankee or British. But first we must consider the concept of neutrality itself.

The Politics of Neutrality

Neutrality receives a surprising lack of attention in political science literature.[31] One looks in vain for a full-length examination of neutrality as a concept unto itself, the way we would look at liberty or individualism.[32] So let us consider what we mean when we describe someone or some people as being "neutral." We can think of someone as being neutral with regards to their attitude

---

28   We are fortunate now to have several studies on Planter culture, all of which demonstrate the sophistication and urbanity of eighteenth-century Nova Scotia. In particular, see Elizabeth Mancke, "Town and Empire: The Politics of Early Nova Scotia"; and Thomas Vincent, The Image and Function of Women in the Poetry of Affection" in this volume.

29   See Pocock, "The Eighteenth-Century Debate: Virtue, Passion and Commerce," ch. xiv of *The Machiavellian Moment*, 462.

30   Much more work also needs to be done on challenging the assumption that Acadian neutrality was an example of their apolitical character.

31   Will Kymlika, "Liberal Individualism and Liberal Neutrality," *Ethics*, 99 (1989), 883-905; Wojciech Sadurski, "Theory of Punishment, Social Justice, and Liberal Neutrality," *Law Phil*, 7 (1988), 351-73; Donald Wacome, "Liberty, Equality, and Neutrality," *Reason Papers*, 13 (1988), 67-83; Robert B. Thigpen and Lyle A. Downing, "Liberalism and the Neutrality Principle," *Political Theory*, 11 (1983), 585-600.

32   The closest I was able to find is a collection of studies on impartiality in university teaching; Allen Montefiore, ed., *Neutrality and Impartiality* (Cambridge, 1975).

towards a piece of art, for example. To describe oneself as being neutral is to say that one neither likes nor hates the work. Yet someone who described their attitude towards a piece of art or towards a performance of drama or music as being neutral nonetheless would be implying that there was disagreement about the merits of the work; they simply decided not to take sides. In fact, neutrality presupposes a conflict and a position with relation to that conflict. We do not consider someone neutral with respect to something of which there cannot be at least two contending sides.

What does it mean to declare oneself neutral? Notice when we use the word "neutral" we are already implying that this is an action. While it is true that someone may be able to be described, perhaps retrospectively, as "neutral," generally we think of someone as having "declared" themselves neutral; in other words, that they made a public statement to that effect. It is this declaration which distinguishes neutrality from impartiality. Impartiality is passive; it requires no such declaration (although one might mask neutrality with a claim to impartiality with the hopes that the combatants will ignore one's role), nor does it require any particular skill to maintain impartiality. Impartiality is akin to remoteness. Further, we consider that certain actions are necessary and appropriate before someone is able to continue to claim that they are neutral. The least of these is that they refrain from aiding one side at the expense of the other, unless they are prepared to provide similar service to the other side.[33]

Notice as well that it is not a condition of neutrality that someone be disinterested in the outcome; indeed, we would expect the opposite.[34] Surely Switzerland was interested in whether or not Nazi Germany was successful in the Second World War (even Switzerland could not be expected to rely upon her legendary mountain passes to protect her from Germany should Germany have succeeded in conquering Europe); yet Switzerland, in action and deed, was certainly neutral. Switzerland better fits the definition of neutrality then, perhaps, would a resident of, say, Tahiti.[35] Being completely without any interest in the conflict or not

---

33 Kolakowski explains that neutrality "presupposes a conflict and at the same time that the neutral person is not a party to it." Further, a person can be said to be neutral "only when [he] purposely behave[s] in a such a way so as not to influence its outcome." Leszek Kolakowski, "Neutrality and Academic Values," in *Neutrality and Impartiality*, 72-73.

34 Allen Montefiore distinguishes neutrality from 'indifference' and 'detachment': "To illustrate these distinctions by way of just one example: faced with appeals for help from two conflicting political parties I may decide to remain *neutral* between them, that is to say to do my best to provide them with help or hindrance in equal degree. This is quite compatible with my retaining a strong personal preference in favour of one side rather than the other; that is, I may in no way be *indifferent* to the outcome of the conflict. In making up my mind to remain neutral, however, I may have considered the matter in an entirely *detached* spirit, by reference, for instance, to my legal or other institutional responsibilities and abstracting wholly from my own personal preferences." (*Neutrality and Impartiality*, 5.)

35 Or, as Charles Taylor suggests, the residents of Alpha Centauri. See "Neutrality in the University," in *Neutrality and Impartiality*, 128-48.

being affected by the outcome or the events would not suggest neutrality; it would suggest, rather, remoteness.

Now let us consider different levels of neutrality. Following from the example above, consider the similar position of Tahiti in relation to the (continuing) Canadian debate over the constitution. Surely to use "neutral" to describe Tahiti's position is to misuse the word, for Tahiti has no interest in the outcome, is not affected by the events or the outcome and is not in a position to affect the events or the outcome. But consider how very different the example of the neutrality of a child caught between arguing parents. The child is certainly affected by the events and outcome of the conflict, but is powerless (in all likelihood) to affect its outcome. In this situation, the use of the word neutral seems more appropriate. Yet it is still a different kind of neutrality than we would use to describe the activities of, say, a hockey referee. The referee is interested in the outcome of the game (otherwise, we can assume, he would not have bothered to show up at the rink), he is affected by the outcome and the events (for he must respond and make decisions according to what is taking place on the rink), and he is quite able to affect the events and the outcome (by his rulings). Nevertheless, we would still think of him as being neutral. In the previous case, the child is simply unable or unwilling to participate in the event; in the second, an active and astute involvement in the event is absolutely necessary to remain neutral. The point of a referee is not simply to allow the two teams to avoid punishment, but to treat each equally.[36] But in this last case, neutrality implies an active and astute involvement in the conflict, indeed, an involvement which may well require a greater understanding of the issues at hand than required of either one of the combatants.

What this argument suggests is that we need two different, albeit related, definitions of neutrality. One should include in its definition the example of the child caught between two fighting parents; the other the example of the hockey referee. Let us, for lack of better words, call the first *a*political neutrality, the second, political neutrality. In the first (and although this flies in the face of my experience with my own children), we mean that neutrality, different from remoteness, in which the neutral party is unable to affect the outcome and as such must await its resolution, all the while being profoundly affected by the conflict. The second, political neutrality, refers to that neutrality when the neutral party can and must maintain communications with both sides, and must behave in such a manner as to avoid helping one side at the expense of the other, or helps and hinders each in an equitable fashion, but cannot *avoid* being actively involved in the dispute.[37]

---

36 "A neutral referee will, roughly speaking, be one who works with the clear and well trained intention of helping or hindering either side in completely equal measure *with respect to his application of the rules of the game*, whatever the nature of the performance that either side may produce in the course of it." Montefiore, *Neutrality and Impartiality*, 9.

37 An objection will be raised, then, to my use of the hockey referee as an example. But the referee cannot decide to avoid the game once he is on the ice participating; his choice is limited to not attending in the first place.

Political neutrality, further, would seem to require considerable political skill to be successful, a skill which would require a sound understanding of the issues at hand, and the character of the combatants. Finally, political neutrality cannot be extremist. In fact, it is hard to imagine how we can even conceive of extremism coupled with neutrality. Certainly political neutrality would require resoluteness and determination, but the ability to maintain contact with both sides, and to understand the issues of the conflict and the character of the combatants would imply an ability to maintain a sense of balance and equity. Simply put, political neutrality requires, indeed demands, moderation.

The question arises, then, as to which type of neutrality was found in Nova Scotia. The image of Nova Scotia being caught between America and Britain like a child caught between fighting parents is a common one at this time. The image of the American colonies behaving like errant children, unappreciative of their mother Britain, or alternatively, of the child who must now boldly and nobly strike out on her own, is also quite common.[38] But the question of political neutrality and Nova Scotia goes beyond the literary conceits of the pamphleteers. Let us return to Bernard Bailyn and his description of the political culture of eighteenth-century America as being indicative of classical republicanism:

> In every colony and in every legislature there were people who knew Locke and Beccaria, Montesquieu and Voltaire. But perhaps more important, there was in every village of every colony someone who knew such transmitters of English nonconformist thought as Watts, Neal, and Burgh; later Priestley and Price — lesser writers, no doubt, but staunch opponents of traditional authority, and they spoke in a familiar idiom. In the bitterly contentious pamphlet literature of mid-eighteenth-century American politics, the most frequently cited authority on matters of principle and theory was not Locke or Montesquieu but *Cato's Letters.* ... Through such writers, as well as through the major authors, leading colonists kept contact with a powerful tradition of enlightened thought.[39]

Even a cursory examination of the newspapers and pamphlets of Nova Scotia at this time reveals that Bailyn's description applies as much to Nova Scotia as it did to the thirteen colonies, and Bailyn's description of the American provinces as "remarkably well-informed students of contemporary social and political theory" surely applies to the contributors to the *Halifax Gazette.*[40] The *Halifax*

---

38 For example, *Nova Scotia Chronicle*, "in short, let us [Britain] do as an unhappy parent would do with a disobedient child, who had well nigh ruined him; turn him out to the wide world and disinherit him, until he shewed signs of reformation." ["Philo-Britaniæ," Vol. I, No. 1, 3 January 1769, 4.]

39 Bailyn, "Political Experience and Enlightenment Ideas in Eighteenth-Century America," *American Historical Review*, 67 (1961-62), 344.

40 Bailyn, "Political Experience and Enlightenment Ideas in Eighteenth-Century America," 343. One is struck with the subtlety of the arguments presented in the paper at this time. See, for

Gazette and the *Nova Scotia Chronicle* which followed it bear a marked similarity to, for example, the *Craftsman* of a few years before. Even during the so-called "missing decade,"[41] these papers are replete with references to 'Machiavel,' Voltaire and Cato. Articles are copied from Yankee and British newspapers and are signed with pseudonyms such as *Libertas*, *Marcus Aurelius* and Cicero's correspondent, *Atticus*.[42] One writer, claiming to be a descendant of Atticus, compares the deliberations of the American colonialists to those of the Roman senate:

> When I read over their Remonstrances, Resolves, Addresses, and Instructions, I cannot but consider myself as reviewing the transactions of the Roman Senate, and the masterly drawing of a Tacitus, or a Macauly, and of the pleadings of an Atticus, Cicero, Cato, Brutus, and a Cassius, together with the rest of the Illustrious Assertors of Roman Liberty in their time of public Danger; alike nervous simplicity and masterly argument, the product of a refined and exquisitely sensible mind, animating both; in short, I cannot figure to myself a more just picture than that of the souls of those Romans having with time transmigrated into the bodies of these Americans, to leave a second immortal memorial on this planet, of the inestimable worth of that Liberty, which is the source of true religion, virtue, science, commerce, and every social and amiable enjoyment, that tends to the perfection of our natures. …
>
> Almost every Person, so far as my acquaintance extends, that has taken the pains of reviewing that has been offered on both sides, agree that the Writers against the Colonies, ought, in point of dullness and weakness of arguments, to be recorded and celebrated in another Dunciad.[43]

The point here is that the political culture of Nova Scotia at this time was so rich

---

example, *Nova Scotia Chronicle*, Vol. I, No. 10, 28 February-7 March 1769, 173, where the question of whether the House of Commons, by virtue of it being the people's assembly, or Parliament, including King, Lords, and Commons, possesses sovereignty. The article is reprinted from the *Public Advertiser*, and the author, Thomas Pownall, would go on to become governor of Massachusetts. See J.A.W. Gunn, *Beyond Liberty and Property* (Kingston, 1983), 187.

41   See Stewart and Rawlyk, *A People Highly Favoured of God*, particularly 43-44: "For the Nova Scotia Yankees this period [1763 -76] was the missing decade. It was during these years that the other American colonies left Nova Scotia behind while they created for themselves a new sense of identity and constructed a new version of their position and purpose in the world." Stewart and Rawlyk correctly point out that the same revolutionary rhetoric often appeared in Nova Scotia during this time; however, they argue that it was "hedged with limitations and weakened with self-doubt." I agree with the first of these assertions and challenge the second. It was certainly hedged with limitations, as would be in keeping with their moderate attitudes. "Self-doubt," however, implies more than the evidence is capable of supporting.

42   Cicero was upheld as a model for moderation, against the extremes of the despotic Caesar, on the one hand, and the overly virtuous Cato, on the other.

43   "From the *Public Ledger*," *Nova Scotia Chronicle*, Vol. I, No. 10, 28 February-7 March 1769, 74.

in its relationship with eighteenth-century political philosophy that neutrality in Nova Scotia could not have been apolitical; that is, it could not have been of the kind that would preclude a knowledge and involvement with the issues at hand. More to the point, this culture was one in which the values of moderation were constantly being articulated. Further examination of Nova Scotia political culture bears this out. The best way to describe how the *Halifax Gazette* and its successor, the *Nova Scotia Chronicle*, presented the conflict leading up to the American Revolution is as a debate; that is, they printed articles, letters, speeches, from both sides.[44] A diatribe by Philo-Britaniæ was followed by a reply by Philo-Americanæ; a speech by a defender of the Boston Assembly by a letter from one wishing Americans would understand the British position. Some articles are clearly metaphorical; some present with charming simplicity an Oriental perspective reminiscent of Montesquieu's *Persian Letters*.[45]

In the first part of the decade preceding the Revolution, the Halifax paper is dominated by the question of taxation without representation. The majority of the articles present the pro-American viewpoint, with most articles reprinted from Boston and Philadelphia papers, and from the British *Public Advertiser* and the *Public Ledger*.[46] The following quotation is fairly typical:

> It has always been a principle in the laws of Great Britain, that the property of the subject was never to be taxed without his own consent; and it has always been considered that the people of the colonies were as much subjects to the crown of Great-Britain as the immediate residents in England. — At any rate, our colonies must be free-men, or they must be slaves; that is, they must have the same equitable title to protection, with ourselves, or they must not. — If we allow them the same right to protection, why do we attempt to load them with taxes diametrically opposite to their inclinations; and if we will not allow them a claim which nature and reason so evidently demand, are they to be condemned for espousing the

---

44 However, the number of articles in favour of the American side, *before* actual revolution was called for, outnumber those supporting the British side.

45 From 14 March through to 25 April 1769, [Vol. I, No. 12-18] the *Chronicle* carried a seven part series on "Chinese Morals"; "Translated from an Ancient Manuscript found among the Archives of a Temple Built on the Top of the Mountain called Pautala, in the Province of Lassa, in the Country of Barantola, adjoining to China; supposed to be wrote by Confucious, or some of his Contemporary's [*sic*]." It is a long and tedious piece, in which, rather heavy handedly, the virtues of temperance are contrasted favourably with passions. The issue which carried the last instalment also carried "The Visions of Mirza" in which prudence is exalted. Mirza was one of Usbek's correspondents in Montesquieu's *Persian Letters*. "The Vision of Mirza, the Son of Mirza translated from the original Arabick," *Nova Scotia Chronicle*, Vol. I, No. 18, 25 April-2 May 1769, 139.

46 On the press of the eighteenth century, and these two publications in particular, see Gunn, "The Fourth Estate: The Language of Political Innovation," ch. II of *Beyond Liberty and Property*, particularly 88-91. For the Halifax press, see Brebner, "The Profits and Pains of Neutrality," ch. 10 of *Neutral Yankees of Nova Scotia*, 255-310.

general cause of humanity, and resisting a despotism which we ourselves should resist, were we unhappily plunged in the same miserable situation.[47]

Reprinting a letter from Philadelphia, the *Chronicle* gave its readers some insight into how the American problem was being received in London:

> American affairs wear a very gloomy aspect. We cannot pretend to say what measures the Parliament will adopt, but we are very sure the ministry are against you. The merchants here (whose influence in the House of Commons with respect to America is very great) are much alarmed at the resolves of the people of Boston and New York, to import no more British manufactures. If this should become general, it would do more than all your petitions and remonstrances. The popular voice at present is against you. They insist upon their right to tax America, and offer no other argument to support this than that "You are the Colonies, and they the Mother Country," Some of the wisest Politicians imagine vigorous measures will be pursued with you. Doctor Francklin [sic] is indefatigable in his endeavours to serve his country. I heard him say a few days ago, in a large company, "Britain has no right to tax the Colonies, and never had such right, and I trust will never have it."[48]

The *Public Advertiser* was not so friendly towards the colonies, however, and the *Chronicle* reprinted a letter signed "For the Good of the Whole" which suggested the Americans had to consider the welfare of the entire empire, not just of their provinces:

> May the Americans be brought to believe, may they be convinced, that any distinction now introduced or continued among his majesty's subjects, must in the end, prove prejudicial to the whole; and may they clearly understand, that an obedience to the authority of one sovereign legislature, composed of king, lords and commons, is the surest, nay the only, preservation of British freedom.
>
> If liberty is what they seek, they will find it no where if it is not in the British constitution as happily re-established and recovered by the glorious revolution; in the British constitution as now flourishing under the auspices of his present majesty; and to whom allegiance is an insult if offered as subjects independent of the established and only legislature, which have, and

---

47 "From the *Public Ledger*," *Nova Scotia Chronicle*, Vol. I, No. 6, 31 January-7 February 1769, 41.
48 "Letter from a Gentleman in London, to his Friend in this City [Philadelphia]," *Nova Scotia Chronicle*, Vol. I, No. 7, 28 February-7 March 1769, 77.

ever ought to give their assistance for the defence and protection of his extensive dominions.[49]

Similarly, an extract from "The Constitutional Right of the Legislature of Great Britain to tax the Colonies" explains that the demands of the colonies were tantamount to a usurpation of parliamentary sovereignty:

> As a body corporate, under a charter, [the colonies] may, like other corporate bodies, make laws for their own utility and government. But no royal charter can be pleaded in bar of the supreme sovereignty of the state, in its legislative capacity. That would raise a charter above an act of parliament: the power of the king above that of the legislature; which would dissolve the constitution, and annihilate liberty.[50]

By the end of the decade, there is a subtle change in focus. The balance which typified the earlier editions is still present; however, now the articles tend to be more concerned with disassociating the newspaper from the extremists, be they British or American. In other words, in the mid 1760s, moderation meant printing both sides of the controversy. By 1774, moderation meant printing primarily articles from moderates, be they American or British. Nevertheless, the sympathies that the editors had with the cause is apparent, and few readers would have been fooled by the ruse of pretending to print seditious information only to demonstrate just how bad American rebel newspapers could be:

> As a specimen of the language with which the minds of the deluded Americans are poisoned against the government, by some of our weekly news-papers, the following passage is selected from Holt's paper [of New York] of August 18:
> "We are assured that Captain William Bull, in a sloop from this place, but last from the West-Indies, is arrived at Wilmington, North-Carolina, and that the inhabitants of that place have bought his vessel, and are loading her with provisions for the support of the town of Boston; which ought to be supported at the expense of the last mite, and even the last drop of Blood in North-America, for their noble stand against the oppression and tyranny of a miserable and corrupt, debauched, an almost bankrupt administration, devoid of sense, humanity, and every principle superior to that of mere brutes; an administration, compared with whom a common highway robber is almost a saint."[51]

---

49 "From the *Public Advertiser*," *The Nova Scotia Chronicle*, Vol. I, No. 17, 18 April-25 April 1769, 130.

50 "Extract from *The Constitutional Right of the Legislature of Great Britain to tax the Colonies*," *Nova Scotia Chronicle*, Vol. I, No. 18, 25 April-2 May 1769, 144.

51 *Nova Scotia Gazette and Weekly Chronicle*, Vol. V, Tuesday, 1 November 1774, n.p.

If we examine the political culture of Nova Scotia during the eighteenth century, we see a diversity of ideas and philosophies. But what dominates is a respect for moderation. This takes the form of articles praising political moderation, so, for example, speeches by Edmund Burke in support of the colonial cause are printed in full. It also takes the form of moral essays and allegorical tales on the values of moderation in general.[52] And finally, it takes the form of rather detailed and subtly argued essays about the values of liberty and moderation.

The *Halifax Gazette* on 13 December 1764 described a pamphlet ''handed about in some of the Coffee-Houses in Town, under the Title of 'Nouvelles Lettres du Chevalier D'Lon.'' The personal misfortunes of the Chevalier[53] were surely of less interest to the *Gazette*'s readers than the clear message that Nova Scotians, no less than this foreigner, enjoyed the 'rights of Englishmen.' [54] ''Liberty,'' writes the pamphlet's author, ''forms the basis of the English government'' and English law, wherein this liberty is to be found, ''are but a development of the primitive and natural laws.''[55] The Chevalier explains that even foreign nationals enjoy the full protection of the law; the rights of Englishmen are extended even to a French nobleman. The Chevalier appealed to William Pitt, and the *Gazette*'s editors thought it wise to explain why: ''The name of *Pitt* is, in England, the glory and the ornament of the Country, in the same manner as Cato's name was in Rome, when the Roman Republic was in its highest degree of splendor; Cato could not outlive Liberty, nor Liberty outlive Cato: The former, as well as the other, deserves and ought to be looked upon as the intrepid asserter of English Liberty.''[56]

---

52 See *Nova Scotia Chronicle*, Vol. I, No. 19, 2-9 May, 1769, for a debate about the merits of the ancients versus the moderns, and for an allegorical tale, in which Modesty, the daughter of Knowledge, meets Assurance, the offspring of Ignorance. See also Vol. I, No. 21, 16 May-23 May; ''Case of Great-Britain and America, addressed to the King, and both Houses of Parliament'': ''The affairs of Great-Britain and her colonies are at a crises. If our justice or our moderation dictate to us the making of concessions, they should be made whilst they can yet be *imputed* to our moderation, or our justice.'' [original emphasis]

53 He was, we are told, in hiding in London while his Parisian enemies, agents of the French crown, were preparing the kidnap him and return him to France.

54 This was a common theme. See, for example, ''From the *Gazetteer*, 13 August 1768'': ''I Think as well of, and wish as well to our fellow subjects in America, as I do to any of those in England; and would wish the same privileges and immunities which are enjoyed by Yorkshiremen, to be equally enjoyed also by Boston and New England men.'' However, the writer goes on to add a qualification ''so far, I mean, as the distance they are removed to will admit of, and allow as practicable.'' The writer concludes that the best way to receive these rights and privileges is within the empire, not by allowing its enemies to benefit from its division. *Nova Scotia Chronicle*, Vol. I, No. 1, Tuesday, 3 January 1769, 1.

55 The pamphlet is divided into letters to various English nobleman, seeking their protection. This quotation is taken from the letter to the Rt. Hon. Lord Mansfield.

56 *Halifax Gazette*, 13 December 1764 (No. 189). Americans (and Nova Scotians) were quite familiar with Cato because of the popularity of *Cato's Letters* by John Trenchard and Thomas Gordon. For an excellent discussion of 'Catonic' attitudes in the eighteenth century, see Browning, *Political and Constitutional Ideas of the Court Whigs*, ch. 1, ''The Catonic Perspective.''

In 1769 the *Nova Scotia Chronicle* published a letter from Philo-Britaniæ, reprinted from the Public Ledger.[57] Philo-Britaniæ wished to simplify the American problem and "cut the debate short" by asking several pointed questions. First, are Americans subjects of Great Britain? Second, do they wish to continue as subjects or "erect themselves into free states, independent on the mother country?" The third questions asks them to define what they mean by the word 'subject' and to explain what "degree of subjection, they would yield to Great Britain." Finally, the Americans are asked whether they see themselves as subjects of Parliament or vassals of the King directly, "in the same manner as Hanover." If the Americans are not willing to be subjects as all Englishmen are, Philo-Britaniæ continues, then, "let an act be passed to disenfranchise all natives of America, to cut them off from the rights and privileges of Britons, that they may henceforth be considered as aliens and foreigners. ... In short let us do as an unhappy parent would do with a disobedient child, who had well nigh ruined him; turn him out to the wide world and disinherit him, until he shewed signs of reformation."

The editors thought it best to print Philo-Americæ's reply from the *Public Advertiser* side-by-side with that of Philo-Britaniæ. "No," the writer answered in reply to the first query, Americans are not subjects to Great-Britain, "unless being subjects to the King of Great-Britain makes us British Subjects; if so, we are also Subjects of France and Ireland, for the King of Great-Britain is also King of France and Ireland as well as Great-Britain." As to the second query, America expects to continue as a subject to the King, "and as Proof of our Subjection to his illustrious Person, and our Attachment and Regard to the Constitutions, Privileges and Immunities we have received," expects to continue receiving these privileges and immunities. Indeed, "we ever have and ever will contribute to support the same with our Lives and Fortunes," but not without a price, rather "expecting and depending that all other Parts of his Majesty's Dominions will contribute in Proportion to their Advantage and Abilities for the same Purpose; and such a Dependence for mutual Advantage have we on Great-Britain."

The third query is answered by explaining that by the word "subject" Americans understood that they owed allegiance to their King, but "we are subject to him only in such Particulars wherein our Subjection is required." The "Degree of Subjection" is therefore voluntary, "and is in Proportion as Great-Britain Acts conformable to the general Good of the whole Empire, particularly in our commercial Interests." Finally, to be a subject is not to be a vassal, Philo-Americæ explains; in no sense are they arguing that by freeing themselves from the domination of the British Parliament do they mean to become, like the people of Hanover, vassals of the King. Now, if this answer would suggest to Philo-Britaniæ

For an equally sound discussion of Cato's Letters, see Pocock, *Machiavellian Moment*, 467-77, and Gunn, *Beyond Liberty and Property*, 19ff.

57 "From the *Public Ledger*," and "Philo-Americæ to Philo-Britaniæ," *Nova Scotia Chronicle*, Vol. I, No. 1, 3 January 1769, 3-4.

that America was no longer willing to ''continue [as] loyal, dutiful Subjects, under the protection of King, Lords and Commons, trusting to the Wisdom, Equity and Moderation of that august Legislature,'' then by all means, the writer continues, pass your act, disenfranchise us as Englishmen, but you will never disenfranchise us as Americans; ''in short, [we shall be] disinherited by Great-Britain, and deprived of receiving any Assistance from her, but owned and beloved by the King, as dutiful and loyal Subjects, who under the benign Influence of his Majesty's Favour, are well able to support ourselves, whose Lives and Fortunes ever have and ever shall be devoted to the Support of his Majesty's Royal Person, Crown and Dignity.''

In the next issue, a letter was printed explaining the separation and balance of powers in the British constitution.[58] The monarchy, the writer explains, is the essence of the British constitution. ''Our northern[59] system of government originally, however the branches of power might be divided, all proceeded from, and ultimately depend on, the kingly office.'' To lose the King is to lose the font of authority, and to degenerate into chaos. Remember, the writer continues, what happened the last time Britain got rid of its King. Nevertheless, the powers of the King must be limited.

> On the other hand, the increasing of Royal Power, beyond it[s] just bounds, is equally full of evil, and what can it serve? Has not Majesty enough to give; or, is wanted to screen the slave who promotes it, from the justice of the laws: — when once the balance is destroyed, and the laws lose their force, the King is equally unsafe. A Monarch of Great Britain has a most peculiar advantage, even in having his power bounded by laws, — A weak Prince can never benefit himself, any more than his vassals, by despotism; the more unlimited his power, the greater the danger to himself and people.

A prince is ''bounded by the abilities of his people.'' Hence, a wise prince will ''cultivate the arts; he strives with industry to lessen his own power, and makes subjects of slaves.''[60] Liberty is a precious gift, but it must be given in small dosages; just as by degrees citizens can be ''brought to submit to slavery,'' so too by degrees must they be brought to relish liberty. The role of the prince is as a gardener, his subjects ''like flowers taken from the field.'' What is to be avoided is haste and sudden change, for it is through such haste that societies decline into ''ignorance, barbarity, and slavery.'' Far better to be the ''head of a mighty and free people'' whose very liberty and vigour promotes the glory of the king:

58 ''Monarchy,'' *Nova Scotia Chronicle*, Vol. I, No. 2, 10 January 1769.

59 A possible reference to Montesquieu's popular description of the English constitution as having been founded in the Germanic woods. Indeed, Montesquieu's influence is apparent throughout this debate. See *Spirit of the Laws*, XI.6.

60 It is the responsibility of the prince to understand his people; unlike a despot who needs know only his own strength.

> As the constitution of Great Britain is founded upon the justest observations of nature, it is therefore more likely to retain its vigour, and have a longer duration than any yet formed
>
> Lacedemon was a strain upon nature; Rome was an assembly of violent humours, that were with difficulty kept together by common danger; Carthage, and many others, were lost by a jealousy of, and contention about, the supreme power, which in Britain is happily fixed. The admirable virtue of country, which so often shone forth in those Republicks, with the most noble Enthusiasm, has with us constant opportunities of signalising itself; nor has it shone in Britain with diminished glory.[61]

Just as humans are motivated by their passions, so too are systems of governments, and just as we have opposing passions to check one another, so too does the "ballance of power, and check upon the passions" prevent the British system of government from developing too rapidly. It is true that this balance "may sometimes impede our activity," but activity without such a check would be destructive. The English system has developed slowly, over time, and "the Enthusiasm of one branch is checked by the prudent coolness of the other; extremes are avoided, and though the growth may be held back, it gives time to gain strength and consistancy as it advances."

The writer had obviously read his Montesquieu. What is important, however, is the balance that he supplies to the first two writers. Here the *Chronicle* has set up a debate, whereupon one side is asking why the American colonies see themselves as not being subject to Parliament. Do they wish to owe allegiance directly to the king, and then cease to enjoy parliamentary protection becoming vassals, rather than subjects, like those of Hanover? To this it is replied that to be subjects, and true and proper subjects, is all the Americans wish, but to do so is to enjoy the rights and privileges of citizenship that accompany such subjection. The American colonies are not subjects of Great Britain; to be so is to imply that each citizen of America is somehow inferior to those of Great Britain. Further, to be subject to Parliament without the same representation in that Parliament enjoyed by British citizens is to violate the ancient British system. All the Americans want is to be treated as equal subjects, and to be allowed to follow their own interests. The liberal-capitalist ideology is clearly expressed here, for to so allow the Americans this liberty is to increase the prosperity of the realm. By pursuing their own commercial interests, the general good is served as well. But it is a Nova Scotian who provides the balance. The essence of the British constitution is the monarchy, and this is the source of the authority of the constitution. It is a balanced constitution, because from that source, powers are divided and distributed. To destroy the monarch is to destroy the very source of liberty,

---

61 This was a popular metaphor at this time and is found, for example, in Bolingbroke's *Patriot King*, where English virtue, protected by the parliamentary system, remains forever burning brightly. See Browning, *Political and Constitutional Ideas of the Court Whigs*, 41.

and to invite chaos and disorder. Yet, the monarchy's powers must be limited, through laws. Indeed, the monarch's powers are better served through these laws. It is in the monarch's interest to limit his powers, and to allow his subjects to grow and develop with a minimum of interference. Unlike a despot, a king gains when his subjects become prosperous and independent. More to the point, to rule in such a manner is to rule naturally; that is, it is to avoid ruling against the natural interests of the people. Only by ruling in this way can a regime hope to survive. What allows the British constitution to prosper is its balanced constitution which prevents excesses, and pits passion against passion, impetuousness against coolness. The result is a slow, even development, one in keeping with the spirit of the nation.

It was a slow and even development that prompted the elected members of the Nova Scotia Assembly to petition the British Parliament and recommend reforms of their constitution. In the summer of 1775, the summer of Bunker Hill, the Nova Scotian Assembly humbly begged leave to address their gracious sovereign and both houses of Parliament, "at this dreadfull, and alarming Crisis, when civil discord, and its Melancholy Consequences are impending over all British America." The purpose of the address was to offer advice on solving the American problem.[62] The Assemblymen were for the most part moderate men. They recognized the importance of trade to Nova Scotia, and they recognized its importance to the British Empire. They understood that stable government was necessary for prosperous growth and they sympathized with the Crown's frustration with the American colonies. Yet they also knew that trade and exploitation were not necessarily the same thing, and they could see how financial interests could easily become the motive for political corruption. Like their more rebellious Yankee cousins, they were primarily concerned with the distribution of power in the constitution of their government.[63] But while they too saw the merits of a shift of the locus of power into the hands of the elected assembly, they argued in favour of a balanced constitution in which the commercial and political interests were sufficiently separated to prevent the concentration of both commercial and political power in the same hands.

In the spirit of a Montesquieuan moderate government, the Assemblymen advocated a separation leading to a balance of powers. The address provides a four part plan; reform of the taxation system, coupled with reform of the executive, the legislative and the judicial branches of government. First, tax reform is called for. Taxes, the Assemblymen suggest, should be in proportion to the wealth of the colony, and hence should appreciate as the wealth of the colony increases. But rather than base these taxes on a gold or sterling standard, which would then mean that revenue would go up or down depending upon the international exchange on gold or silver, the Assemblymen suggest that taxes be based on

---

62 Brebner, "Nova Scotia's Remedy for the American Revolution."
63 See Bailyn, *Pamphlets*, Vol. 1, "The theory of politics that emerges from the pamphlets of the pre-Revolutionary years rests on the belief that what lay behind every political scene, the ultimate explanation of every political controversy, was the disposition of power" (38).

imported luxury goods, except for those produced by the British dominion. Further, the rate would be fixed every ten years. Taxes, the Assemblymen argued should be based upon a formula which encouraged the province to increase its wealth, not to punish it for prosperity. Remember, the Assemblymen explained, that "this province having no Manufactories or Lucrative Commerce, must ever have a scarcity of Specie."

Second, reform of the appointment of the governor is recommended. Neither the Governor nor the Lieutenant-Governor, should be appointed from the residents of Nova Scotia; rather he should always be from away, and his term should be fixed: "the Ambition of affluent Individuals in the provinces to Acquire Governments have led to faction and partys, subversive to the peace and happiness of the people, the good of the Province and the Honor of Government, probably the present disputes in America, may have been promoted by this Cause." The advantages of such an arrangement may not be noticeable immediately; however, what this would do is prevent any Nova Scotian from building an empire with which to seize power as governor, and then, presumedly, rule in his own interests. By always being appointed from outside of Nova Scotia, no governor would be expected to have developed a network of allies. This measure is further enhanced by limiting the term to three years;[64] by being appointed for only three years, no governor would have the opportunity to develop an empire while in office or become the captive of a particular interest group.

The result would be a shift of the locus of power away from the governor to the legislative bodies. The question remains, however, whether it would come to rest in the elected Assembly or the appointed Legislative Council. The Assemblymen asked for reform of the Council as well. First, every member appointed to the council should have at least 1,000 pounds in debt-free property in Nova Scotia; a provision familiar to Canadians, as such a restriction still exists for members appointed to the Canadian Senate.[65] Each would be appointed for life. Further, no Councilman would be allowed to serve as a tax or other revenue collector, nor would any Assemblymen be so permitted. Again, the assumption is that this stipulation would prevent the Councilmen and Assemblymen from using their office to enrich their personal fortunes, and ensure that Councilmen would have common interest with Nova Scotians. As the conclusion of the Address explains: "Most Gracious Sovereign, we have unhappily experienced, that the redress of our Grievances and those requested Regulations, could not come from us in the Constitutional Mode of Laws, which must have passed a Council,[66] some of them without property in the Province or Interest in our Welfare."

By itself, the reform of the Legislative Council seems to be quite mild, but coupled with the reform of the appointment of the Governor (whose responsibility it was to appoint the Councilmen), the provision would have two effects. First,

---

64 Although apparently this measure was taken out of the address that was received by Parliament.
65 *Constitution Act, 1867*, Section 23.3-4.
66 The draft inserted "Composed chiefly of Custom House Officers and Seekers of Employment."

by insisting on a land qualification, a new governor could not arrive and immediately appoint his friends from wherever he came; therefore the protection against a governor using his office for his own purposes by not allowing him to build empires is protected. Without such a provision, the point would be lost, as a governor could indeed arrive with his carpet-baggers in tow, and promptly appoint them to the Council. With Councilmen appointed for life, the chance of a governor being able to stack the council with his own men would be virtually eliminated. Secondly, the removal of revenue collecting responsibilities from the Legislative Council meant that that body would not be able to use its security of office to its own benefit. The role of collecting custom duties would be in the hands of a separate branch of government, removed from the legislative branch at least in terms of personnel. They should be provided with salaries sufficient to allow them to avoid the temptation of bribery, and should report directly to the Governor, Council and Judges of the Supreme Court of the province. By having representation from each of the legislative, executive and judicial branches of government oversee operations, surely each would check the other and prevent abuses. The lower house, the elected Assembly, is to have elections every three years.[67] Further, it is to be called into session annually. Without a regularly assembled legislature, either no laws would be passed, or the executive would take over the legislative functions. On the other hand, the Assembly should not be kept in continual session (as would happen, for example, if members were merely replaced with by-elections). Furthermore, it should have neither the power to assemble itself nor to dissolve itself. The Assemblymen obviously recognized this power as an executive prerogative, and asked only that "no Governor [should] be allowed to dissolve, or Prorogue [the Assembly] when he shall be informed, that they are preparing a petition to our Gracious King, and Parliament of Great Britain."

The principle of the separation of powers is applied to the Judiciary as well. Judges, first of all, are to "have their Commissions during good behaviour in the same manner as in England." This implied that both houses of the legislature would have the power to remove a judge, if (and only if) they acted in concert; however, neither the Governor nor the Council acting alone would have such power. If they did, then the integrity of the judicial branch of government would be jeopardised. This would allow corrupt judges to be removed from office, without making them subservient to any single branch or assembly of government. By the further provision of having judges, like Governors, appointed from away, then they would presumedly remain disinterested: "We can trace the present unhappy disorders in America to the Want of a Regulation of this kind."

The result is a subtle reform of an existing system which produces a moderate government much more in keeping with the spirit of moderation found in Montesquieu than the American framers produced with their constitution. Indeed, Montesquieu's summary of his theory is in keeping with the Assemblymen's

---

67   The original draft suggested every year.

proposals: "The legislative body being composed of two parts, they check one another by the mutual privilege of rejecting. They are both restrained by the executive power, as the executive is by the legislative."[68]

The address of the Nova Scotia Assembly is not a revolutionary proposal, and despite the opposition it received from the Governor and the Legislative Council (who no doubt recognized the limitations on their powers), it was well received in London. In fact, Brebner tells us that many of the measures were passed, and that the king was pleased with the reforms. Inexplicably, it was never signed into law, having, as Brebner put it, "unaccountably ... dropped out of sight."[69] We next see it in the 1805 compilation of Nova Scotia statutes by Attorney General Richard Uniacke, with the marginal note: "This Act passed with a suspending clause, and His Majesty's pleasure has never been signified."[70] But, while not a revolutionary proposal, it is a moderate one, and it demonstrates, I believe, the astuteness of politicians who are trying desperately not to take sides. They are well aware of the problems and they have spent time considering the source of these problems. If this is an example of Nova Scotian neutrality, then surely it cannot be characterized as being apolitical.

Uniacke's reaction to the address passed with a suspending clause by the Assembly thirty years earlier is instructive. During the revolution Uniacke took arms against Britain on the side of the Yankee rebels in Jonathan Eddy's ill-fated army and was captured at Fort Cumberland (Beausejour), eventually standing trial in Halifax.[71] Uniacke's fighting days were over, and he worked from then on to keep Nova Scotia neutral in the struggle. Uniacke's preface to his compilation of Nova Scotian statutes is unusually reflective.

Written with the threat of the Napoleon army ever present in the minds of Englishmen, Uniacke declares that Nova Scotians live in very troubled times. All the principles upon which a virtuous society are based were in danger of being subverted.

> The chief end of all human institutions is the preservation of men's lives, liberties, and properties. Our ancestors have manifested their wisdom in framing Laws peculiarly adapted to those great purposes, and their courage in defending those Laws, upon every occasion, has been equally conspicuous. English Subjects exhibit, in the history of mankind, a people possessing a form of Government, under which their lives, liberties and properties, are secured in a way that no other nation or people have yet experienced.[72]

---

68   *S.L.*, XI.6.
69   Brebner, "Nova Scotia's Remedy," 173-74.
70   *Statutes at large, etc., 1758-1804*, compiled and edited by Richard John Uniacke (Halifax, 1805), 204. Hereafter cited as Uniacke. [Cited in Brebner, "Nova Scotia's Response," 174.]
71   See Brebner, *The Neutral Yankees of Nova Scotia*, 283-85. See also Brian Cuthbertson, *The Old Attorney General: A Biography of Richard John Uniacke* (Halifax, 1980).
72   Uniacke, v.

"We have," continues Uniacke, "the most powerful motives to cultivate the virtues, manners and habits, of our ancestors." And it is the duty of Nova Scotians to "diligently cultivate those laws, manners, habits and customs, of the Mother Country. ..." For it is the British who continue, in this age of corruption, to "exhibit to the world a national character that will be venerated while virtue and honour exist in the human breast." When you add to this the fact that Nova Scotians enjoy a "mild and moderate government," it would seem that Nova Scotians are very fortunate indeed. Citizenship in Nova Scotia is protected in two ways. The first comes from the obligation that every citizen has to participate in the making of the law, through elections and the votes, and in the administration of that law, through jury duty and justices of the peace. The second comes from the equal protection that law affords: "Every person in this Province should consider it his duty to imitate, with the greatest care, this excellent example, and thereby effectually provide for the equal and impartial administration of the Law; which is the only equality that man can enjoy in civil society."[73] What is to be avoided is apathy; what is to be encouraged is participation.

"Man's advancement," Uniacke explains further, "either in vice or in virtue is gradual." So, as a consequence, citizens must guard against the slow relaxation of mores. This slow relaxation comes from want of knowledge, specifically, knowledge of the law. The purpose of his compilation is to permit every citizen to read for themselves what the law is and govern themselves accordingly.[74] To suggest that men can find their own way, without guidance, is in Uniacke's view, pernicious:

> None but the ministers of fallen angels would wish to deprive man of the grateful sensations he feels through life ... both by precept and by example, [of] the principles of religion, morality, virtue, and honour. ... Were man left to seek for first principles after his mind was filled with the cares and pleasures of the world, it requires little judgment to conclude, that at that period those important rules would find but little room for a permanent foundation in the human breast, and the man who laboured under the influence of such an education, would be the slave of his passions, and the ready perpetrator of every species of wickedness.[75]

Uniacke is not typical of Nova Scotians during the American Revolution. But

---

73 Uniacke, vii.

74 "the development of the individual towards self-fulfillment is possible only when the individual acts as a citizen, that is a conscious and autonomous participant in an autonomous decision-making community, the polis or republic. ... The individual's prospect of fulfilling his moral and rational nature consequently depended upon his ability to partake in political decisions within a particularized and secular framework." Pocock, "Civic Humanism and its Role in Anglo-American Political Thought," *Politics, Language and Time*, 53.

75 Uniacke, ix. See also Uniacke's address to the Colonial Secretary, 1806, cited in D.C. Harvey, "Intellectual Awakening of Nova Scotia," in Rawlyk, ed., *Historical Essays*, 102.

he is an example of someone who was making decisions during this time, and making them, as Bailyn indicates, with a sound knowledge of Enlightenment thought. What I am arguing is that there were many more like him, and that their decisions also demonstrated a sound knowledge of Enlightenment thought. Let us return to our two concepts of definitions of neutrality, political and apolitical. There is no doubt that there were factions in Nova Scotia who wished only to avoid being dragged into the conflict, feeling powerless to control their own destinies. And I am quite sure that other concerns, like economic self-interest, often dominated the strategies of other groups, many of which were in positions of power. But what I am arguing is that there is a profound difference between choosing neutrality and employing strategies accordingly, on the one hand, and avoiding conflict by hiding until the fighting is over, on the other. Furthermore, I maintain that the first of these, political neutrality, brings with it moderation in deed and thought, and that this seems to be quite in keeping with the traditions of Enlightenment thought traced by scholars of civic humanism. Therefore, Nova Scotia neutrality, and so Nova Scotia's response to the American Revolution, can yet be seen in terms of the ideas and beliefs of the Enlightenment, specifically that tradition of thought in which moderation became the guide for wise political activity. I am proposing that the civic humanist thesis propounded by Bailyn and Pocock has greater application in Nova Scotia at this time than has previously been thought; that far from being a rejection of politics and political things, neutrality in Nova Scotia was its logical extension.

Mi'kmaq Land in Southwestern Nova Scotia, 1771-1823

Bill Wicken[1]
McGill University

Until 1760 the Mi'kmaq maintained territorial control over most parts of Nova Scotia. During the late eighteenth and early nineteenth centuries this situation was irrevocably shattered and, as the non-native population increased, the settlers' fear of the Mi'kmaq people receded. Immigrants and colonial officials, who had long considered the Mi'kmaq an impediment to economic expansion, could now afford to ignore them. Although government officials in Halifax would have preferred to see the Mi'kmaq disappear by intermarrying with the Europeans, the Mi'kmaq as a culturally distinct people survived and officials were confronted with determining how to deal with them. Some Mi'kmaq attempted to make that decision for the government by petitioning the Lieutenant-Governor for title to land that they and their kinspeople had inhabited before the arrival of the Europeans. Many non-Mi'kmaq peoples frowned upon these endeavours arguing that the Mi'kmaq were a lazy, shiftless lot who had neither the skills nor the capability to exploit the land profitably. In effect, Mi'kmaq land petitions to government between 1784 and 1830 reveal a conflict between an expanding European population eager to occupy the principal harbours and agricultural lands of Nova Scotia and an indigenous people who, despite their numeric inferiority, attempted to retain possession of their lands.

Land petitions were the initial stage of a costly and lengthy process through which individuals sought exclusive proprietary rights over specific plots of land. As the petition was often written by a Justice of the Peace, this necessitated not only paying for his services but also travelling to one of the principal villages in the colony where the Justices lived. Once the petition had been received in Halifax, a warrant was issued to the Surveyor-General's Office to survey the land for which a petition had been made. The survey could be carried out by the Surveyor-General himself but was usually done by one of his deputies who were located in each of the colony's principal regions. After the survey had been completed, a copy of it was sent to the Surveyor-General of the King's Woods who ensured that the land requested did not include forests reserved for the King's Navy. A certificate to this affect was then issued, a draft grant was prepared by the Provincial Secretary's Office, the Attorney-General affixed his signature as did the Lieutenant-Governor, and a grant was issued to the petitioner.[2] Though it sounds

---

1   I would like to thank Louise Dechêne, Toby Morantz and Carman Miller for their helpful comments made in the preparation of this paper as well as the staff of the Public Archives of Nova Scotia whose enthusiasm for history has created the ideal intellectual atmosphere for researchers. Any errors in fact or interpretation are my sole responsibility.

2   Margart Ells, ''Settling the Loyalists in Nova Scotia,'' *Canadian Historical Association Report,* 1934, 105.

deceptively simple, the land granting process rarely operated smoothly. Problems arose in part because of periodic alterations in colonial policy but also because the government was inadequately staffed to deal competently with the flood of paper which swept through its doors, particularly after the arrival of the Loyalists during the early 1780s.

Between 1784 and 1830, seventeen Mi'kmaq families petitioned the Lieutenant Governor for a grant of land.[3] On a per capita basis, fewer petitions were submitted by the Mi'kmaq than by the non-Native population. This reticence probably resulted from the costly nature of the process,[4] but also because Mi'kmaq saw few merits in petitioning for land that they already occupied. Requesting a land grant would be tantamount to asking for something which they already possessed. Those who did submit petitions likely did so because they felt threatened by encroachments upon their lands by non-Natives.

Among those who sought government protection from the expanding white settlements were Jean Baptist and Joseph Elexey, Mi'kmaq residents of Shelburne County who on 6 May 1823 requested a grant of land on behalf of themselves and ''Twenty other Indian Families.'' The memorial read:

> Your petitioners were formerly settled at Eel Brook in this [Argyle] Township and was drove off by the Lands being granted and since that have settled on three different tracts of Land and have also been removed in the same manner at Last your petitioners settled on a Tract of Land up the Tusket River Twenty Miles from Salt Water the Last season we built one House and a number of Hutts and raised one hundred Bushel of potatoes, Some Indian Corn and considerable garden Stuff Last (fall) three men came on the Land with the intention of taking possession your petitioners having been so often removd, beg you Excellency will take the (case) into your consideration and grant them the Land they now occupy or such other Lands as you Your Excellency may think proper.[5]

The Elexey family's petition is unique for two reasons. First, unlike the other petitions submitted by Mi'kmaq families, it clearly indicates an ongoing struggle with non-Natives over occupation of the land, an aspect of post-1760 Nova

---

3 These petitions are contained in RG 20, Series A, Public Archives of Nova Scotia (PANS), and do not include Cape Breton Island. Some Mi'kmaq did request that land be given to them but these do not appear as formal land petitions but rather as personal appeals to the Lieutenant-Governor. Most of these appeals can be found in RG 1, Vol. 430, PANS. I have not included these petitions in my statistics.

4 Great Britain, Public Record Office (PRO), Colonial Office Series 217 (CO 217), Vol. 63, 77f, National Archives of Canada, (NAC), MG 11, Microfilm Reel # B-1043, List of Fees upon Grants of Land now taken in Nova Scotia as Transmitted by Governor Parr in December 1784.

5 PANS, RG 20, Series A, Vol. 88, Microfilm # 61, Petition of John Baptist Elexey to Sir James Kempt, 6 May 1823.

Scotian history hinted at in the historical record but rarely recorded.[6] Secondly, there is sufficient extant documentation from the late eighteenth century to partially reconstruct the events which led to their appeal to government in 1823.

The Elexey family's ancestors lived along the coastline between the present-day sites of Yarmouth and Shelburne in southwestern Nova Scotia and are referred to in pre-1760 documentation as the ''Cape Sable Micmac.'' Census information for this area is sporadic with the earliest data in 1708 indicating 97 Mi'kmaq men, women and children. This figure is likely a low one since at the time the census was taken some people may have been away fishing, hunting or visiting relatives in other villages.[7] A similar population, however, is given for 1722.[8] Thirteen years later, 50 men capable of bearing arms are recorded as living in the region.[9] In 1708 men able to bear arms constituted 30 per cent of the total Mi'kmaq population in Nova Scotia while in 1722 this figure was slightly higher at 31.6 per cent. By using these percentages, it is possible to postulate the number of Cape Sable Mi'kmaq in 1735 at between 158 and 166 people. Similar demographic data for the rest of the eighteenth century is not available although there are various sources which can be used to partially reconstruct the population.[10] While this information is still in the process of being analyzed,[11] the data does suggest the continuous occupation of the Cape Sable region by several key families throughout the latter part of the eighteenth century.

An abundance of fish and game in the area likely provided sufficient food resources to maintain Mi'kmaq residence along the coastline during the spring, summer and fall.[12] Large congregations of kin-related individuals during this

---

6 For example, in about 1823, Thomas Hammond, who because of his marriage to a woman from Gold River, decided to move there from his native Shubenacadie, requested ''some vacant lot where he would not be subject to the encroachment of the white people.'' PANS, RG 20, Series A, Vol. 89, Thomas Hammond to Sir James Kempt, (1823).

7 Recensement générale(sic) fait au mois de Novembre mile Sept cent huit de tous les Sauvages de l'Acadie qui resident dans la Coste de l'Est Et de ceux de Pintagouet et de Canibek, Famille par Famille . . . from a manuscript in the Edward E. Ayer Collection, Vol. IV, No. 751, Newberry Library, Chicago. The NAC has a typescript, MG 18, F 18.

8 France, Archives des Colonies (AC), CIIB, Correspondance Générale, l'île Royale, Vol. 6, 77f, NAC, MG 1, Microfilm Reel F-135, Recensement des Sauvages dans l'isle Royalle et de la peninsule de l'acadie qui sont deservis par les Missionaires du Séminaire des missions étrangeres Etablis a Québec fait par M. Gaulin prêtre Missionaire desd. Sauvages en 1722.

9 AC: G1 466, Archives D'Outre Mer, #71, NAC, MG 1, Microfilm Reel F-768, Recensement fait ce Cette present année du Nombre des Sauvages Miquemaq portant les armes conformement aux memoires des missionaires et aux declarations quem'en ont fait les anains et chef de chaque village,'' 1735.

10 *Cape Sable Vital Records*, 1799-1841 ed., Leonard H. Smith (Clearwater, Florida, 1979) and Registre de l'Abbé Charles-Francois Bailly, 1768 à 1773 (Caraquet), ed. Stephen A. White (Moncton, 1978) among others.

11 Bill Wicken, ''Social Change and Continuity in Mi'kmaq History, 1689-1749,'' PhD thesis, McGill University, forthcoming.

12 AC: CIID, Correspondance Générale, Acadie, Vol. 4, 85-85v, NAC, MG 1, Microfilm Reel F-171, ''Memoire des coste de L'acadie,'' 12 October 1701.

time period, however, may have been an informal arrangement, peaking during certain times of the year — for example, during the spring and fall anadromous fish runs — and declining during other periods when food resources were less plentiful. During the late fall, groups of three or four families likely migrated into the interior to engage in the winter hunt for moose and deer as well as for fur bearing animals such as the beaver. The skins of these animals provided material for clothing, shelters and coverings as well as serving a number of other material and religious functions in Mi'kmaq society. The length of the winter hunt probably varied according to the availability of fur bearing animals as well as according to the needs of individual Mi'kmaq. Though some Mi'kmaq may have spent more time in the interior in search of furs for exchange with traders than they had before the arrival of the Europeans,[13] the rich marine and fowl life inhabiting the southwestern coast may have tended to minimize the length of these hunting trips.[14] Dispersal likely occurred but may have been more of a movement along the coastline than it was into the interior.[15]

Among those exchanging European goods for the furs that the Mi'kmaq brought to the coast in the period before 1750, were the Acadians whose ancestors had first settled in the region during the early seventeenth century. In 1708 there were 66 Acadians living in the general area of Cape Sable, engaged principally in the fish and fur trade.[16] Their expulsion from the area by the English in 1756 facilitated the migration of New England fishermen who in the early 1760s, began establishing permanent roots on the southern shores of Nova Scotia.[17] Principally located at Yarmouth, Argyle and Barrington the Planter population totalled 502 people in 1762.[18] Thirteen years later, there were 240 families of English and Acadian descent living in the region. As most officials during this time calculated six people per family, this would suggest a total population of 1,440.[19]

Increasing migration into southwestern Nova Scotia was likely a factor in a

13 Patricia Nietfield, "Determinants of Aboriginal Micmac Political Structure," PhD thesis, University of New Mexico, 1981, 375.

14 "Il y a une grande quantité d'oiseaux de Mer, qu'on ne peut l'Imaginer, et tout l'hiver à la côte du Cape de Sable, les oyes, Canards...." ("During the winter time," notes a memoire written in March 1712, "there is a great quantity of seabirds, more than one can imagine, all winter along the coast of Cape Sable, geese, ducks.") AC:CIID, Vol. 10, (no pagination), NAC, MG 1, Microfilm # F-176, Memoire au sujet de l'accadie," Mars 1712.

15 See Dean Snow, *The Archaeology of New England* (New York, 1980), 303 for a discussion of this point.

16 NAC, "Recensement générale fait au mois de Novembre mile Sept cent huit."

17 NAC, MG 40: Q17, Monckton Papers, Microfilm #A-1715, Jeffrey Amherst to Lieutenant-Colonel Monckton, 24 August 1756.

18 PRO, CO 217, Vol. 19, 149f, NAC, MG 11, Microfilm #B-1028, "General Return of the Inhabitants in the several Townships Settled at Cape Sables," June 1762.

19 NAC, MG 23: A1, Dartmouth Papers, Vol. 1, p. 349, Abstract of the Number of Families Settled in Nova Scotia, August 1775. See also Boston, Massachusetts Historical Society, F.L. Gay Collection, Mascarene Papers, Vol. 5, 136, A List of the Acadian families September 1790.

"license" being issued to Francis Alexis "Chief of the Tribe of Cape Sable Indians" on 22 June 1771 by William Campbell, the Governor of Nova Scotia.[20] The "license" gave Alexis and his people the 'right' to improve lands near Eel Brook in Shelburne County, likely the same land referred to in the Elexey family petition of 1823. Under the terms of the agreement, Alexis was given "leave to Fish, Hunt and Improve lands under the Usual Instructions particularly in the Creek — called Ell (sic) Creek without hindering or Molesting any other Subjects who may have to fish there also."[21]

The meaning of this "license" is ambiguous. Did it provide the Alexis family with inalienable rights to the land around Eel Creek? Alternatively, as was sometimes the case with land set aside for the Mi'kmaq to hunt and fish, were these lands given at the pleasure of government? In this latter scenario, the government could re-establish its control over the land whenever it wished, as well as any improvements made on it since the license had been granted.[22] The commission specifically mentions that the Alexis family was not to hinder others who may wish to fish near Eel Creek and thus would suggest that exclusive proprietary rights were not extended to the Cape Sable Mi'kmaq, although further research might provide a clearer understanding of the government's intent.

If dissembling the government's interpretation of the 1771 "agreement" is fraught with dangers, even more so is the case in attempting to reconstruct what the document might have meant to Francis Alexis and his people. As other research has demonstrated, native understanding of agreements reached with unilingual white government officials often differed with what the written English version of the agreement implied.[23] The difference depended upon how each group perceived the land and their relationship to it. The Mi'kmaq, like many Algonkian speaking peoples, did not consider themselves to have exclusive proprietary rights over the land they occupied. Rather, they shared the land with its other inhabitants, the animals, birds, fish and plants. By doing so, Mi'kmaq ensured their own survival as well as that of other living organisms. To the Mi'kmaq, a license of occupation, as described in the 1771 commission issued to Francis Alexis, extended their relationship with the land to the English-speaking peoples who had come into their territory. Henceforward these peoples were to be governed by the same laws as were other inhabitants. Viewed from this perspective, the 1771 commission and subsequent licenses of occupation issued to various Mi'kmaq groups in 1783-84, appear less as agreements delineating the

20   The actual wording used by Campbell is "commission." I have interpreted this as being similar to licenses of occupation.

21   PANS, RG 1, Vol. 168, p. 155, Commission of William Campbell to Francis Alexis, Chief of the Tribe of Cape Sable Indians, 22 June 1771.

22   My thanks to Mike Powers of the Provincial Crown Lands Record Centre in Dartmouth, Nova Scotia, for pointing out differences in how lands were set aside for the Mi'kmaq.

23   For example, see Richard Price, ed., *The Spirit of the Alberta Indian Treaties* (Montreal, 1979).

'rights' of the Mi'kmaq than as establishing the laws by which the English were to share the land with its other inhabitants.[24]

That the English broke the terms of that 1771 agreement with the Cape Sable Mi'Kmaq is suggested by subsequent events. In 1773 the Reverend John Breynton of Halifax and Mr. Ronald McKinnon of Shelburne County requested that the Executive Council make a decision regarding a River lot "called Eel Brook running through their Lands in the Township of Argyle an exclusive right to said Riverlet being Claimed by the Indians."[25] The memorial was deferred for "further consideration," probably as a result of a prohibition upon the granting of land in April 1773 by the Board of Trade, the governmental body in England responsible for administering Nova Scotia.[26] With the re-institution of land granting as a result of the Loyalist migration, the Council found in favour of Breynton and in January 1785, he received a grant of 700 acres to land adjoining Eel Lake.[27] Breynton's success in obtaining title to the land adjoining Eel Brook may suggest why Charles Alexis, a Mi'kmaq spokesperson journeyed to Halifax eighteen months later and received from the Lieutenant-Governor a license on behalf of the Cape Sable Mi'Kmaq "to occupy their lands and usual Hunting Ground unmolested."[28] Though the location of these grounds is unknown, the fact that Alexis obtained a license of occupation is significant as it accounts for his complaints in 1793 to George Henry Monk, then Superintendent for Indian Affairs in Nova Scotia that "the French people (formerly the French neutrals) and some English have taken away the land that he had cleared and made a Garden of — that he had on a former complaint to Governor Parr recd a promise that his Land should be restored to him but he was deceived."[29] In May of the following year Charles Alexis returned to Windsor and complained "that they cannot go to work on their lands without it being made their own."[30]

Alexis' complaints reflect the difficulties which the Mi'kmaq confronted when faced with an expanding European population. Even though horticulture was an integral part of Mi'kmaq economic activities, for most people fishing and hunting continued to be the most important source of food. Consequently, even though crops were planted, the area adjacent to them may not have been occupied year round. This facilitated encroachment by non-Mi'kmaq peoples who in requesting legal title from the Lieutenant-Governor could argue that, at the time of their arrival, the land they now resided upon had been "vacant" or, as was often the

---

24 See PANS, RG 1, Vol. 430, #23 1/2 for the 1783-84 licenses.

25 PANS, RG 1, Vol 189, 104, Executive Council Minutes, 5 November 1773.

26 Margaret Ells, "Clearing the Decks for the Loyalists," *Canadian Historical Association Report,* 1933, 52-53.

27 PANS, RG 20, Series A, Land Grant, Vol. 11, The Reverend John Breynton, 21 January 1785.

28 PANS, RG 20, Series A, Vol. 17, License of Occupation to Indians of Cape Sable, 22 June 1786.

29 NAC, MG 23: G11-19, Monk Papers, Vol. 3, p. 1047, Microfilm #C-1451, 10 December 1793.

30 NAC, Monk Papers, MG 23: GII-19, Vol. 3, p. 316, George Deschamps to George M. Monk, 26 May 1794.

case, the land they sought next to their own was ''vacant and unimproved.'' This did not mean, however, that the land was not occupied but only that it was not inhabited year-round by individuals practising European forms of cultivation. In addition, the outbreak of smallpox, measles or whooping cough in nearby white settlements resulted in the temporary migration of resident Mi'kmaq populations.[31] These two factors in addition to an apparent unwillingness on the part of some, if not most Mi'kmaq, to fence their land made white encroachment upon their lands easier.[32]

Analogous land conflicts emerged between the Cape Sable Mi'kmaq and non-Natives over fishing rights. Settlers attempted to regulate access to the inland fisheries, allotting river lots to individual owners who could then use their favourable position to fish. This system, however, tended to limit the catch of those lacking river frontage or to those located further downstream. Mi'kmaq resident in the area made at least two complaints regarding their lack of access to the fisheries. In April of 1800, the Court of Sessions in the Yarmouth and Argyle District of Shelburne Country proclaimed that ''Charles Alexander the Indian Chief with the other Indians have a priviledge in common with the white people of Fishing in all Streams in this district,'' likely as a result of a complaint by Alexander.[33]

This appeal to the local magistrates appears to have had little affect and, shortly thereafter, the Mi'kmaq took their complaints to Lieutenant-Governor John Wentworth in Halifax. On this occasion at least two separate petitions were made; one by Bartlett Alexis and six other Mi'kmaq who complained of their problems in gaining access to the fishery at Salmon River,[34] and a second by Samuel Alexis petitioning for a grant of land at Eel Brook. Wentworth was sufficiently concerned to write to the Commissioner for the Relief of the Indians, Michael Wallace, on 28 September 1802, informing him that the Cape Sable Mi'kmaq by ''their own account. . .are a sober and industrious people, who plant and fish for subsistance.'' They have, however, been troubled by white people who ''claim the land. . .these Indians and their ancestors have lived [upon] and occupied for many years.'' In addition, he stated, they have suffered in consequence of white people setting their nets ''across the Brooks and small rivers, which entirely prevent any Fish running up the Streams — and of course deprive the upper residents of any share.'' Wentworth urged Wallace to write to the magistrates in the district requesting that they not only lay land out to the Mi'kmaq so as to deter encroachment

31 See for example, PANS, RG 1, Vol. 430, #52, Rob. Barry, Henry Guest, Samuel Roxby, Ford Welson (Shelburne) to George Grace, 24 February 1807.

32 In 1815, James Walker complained of a Mi'kmaq called Philip ''who has abundance of as good land as any in St. Margaret's Bay if he will only Fence and improve it.'' PANS, RG 1, Vol. 430, #155, James Walker to Henry Cogswell, 7 October 1815.

33 PANS, RG 34-324, Records of Sessions, Yarmouth and Argyle District, County of Shelburne, 1789-1816, 1, April term 1800, p. 89.

34 PANS, RG 1, Vol. 430, #71, Joshua Frost to John Wentworth, 1801.

by non-Native peoples but also take measures to "prevent the destruction of the fisheries."[35]

The response of the magistrates of Shelburne County was curt. Meeting in April of 1803, the sessions pointed out that the land for which Francis Alexis petitioned was already granted. As for the complaint of Bartlett Alexis, further investigation by the Sessions revealed that he was only interrupted in gaining access to the fishery by one person, thus making the "complaint unworth of further notice." They were convinced that "so far from the complaints of the Indians being well found, that they ever enjoyed and exercise as great if not a greater share of privilege claimed Than any of His Majesty's natural born Subjects resident in the District."[36]

These disagreements between the Lieutenant-Governor's office and Shelburne County civil officials illustrates an important political division within the colony. As the representative of the Crown, the Lieutenant-Governor was responsible not only for encouraging economic activity but also for ensuring the military security of Nova Scotia. Balancing these two responsibilities was an often difficult task, particularly during periods of war between England and France when colonial officials expressed concern that the Mi'kmaq might be persuaded by the French government to attack English settlements.[37] Conflicts between settlers and Mi'kmaq therefore became a cause of concern for the Lieutenant-Governor and required his immediate intervention. In 1795 when a group of Mi'kmaq camping near Windsor, "in such numbers as to give apprehensions to the People," took several sheep belonging to local residents, Wentworth wrote to George Monk asking him to enquire into the matter. If necessary, Monk was to incarcerate the Mi'kmaq in Fort Edward and to keep them there as hostages. Ideally, however, they were to be wooed "to our cause in such a manner that the peace of our scattered inhabitants may not be disturbed by them and also that they will join us, in case of an invasion" by the French.[38] As late as April 1798, Wentworth assured the Duke of Portland in London that despite the severity of the winter and the few animals remaining in the woods, the Mi'kmaq "were highly sensible of the relief extended to them, and I am persuaded they will be vigorously faithful in fighting any Enemy that may attempt to invade this Country."[39]

Such a concern for the loyalty of the Mi'kmaq prompted an attentiveness to their well-being that had been lacking during periods of peace and economic expansion. Indeed, Wentworth's suggestion in July 1793 of victualling and clothing a

35 PANS, RG 1, Vol. 430, #117, John Wentworth to Michael Wallace, 28 September 1802.

36 PANS, RG 34-324, Records of Sessions, Yarmouth and Argyle District, April term 1803, 114-15.

37 PANS, RG 1, Vol. 48, #105, John Wentworth to Henry Dundas, 23 July 1793. There is no evidence that the French were inciting the Micmac to attack English settlements.

38 PANS, RG 1, Vol. 50, John Wentworth to Lieutenant-Colonel George Henry Monk, 18 October 1793.

39 PANS, RG 1, Vol. 52, #54, John Wentworth to the Duke of Portland, 24 April 1798.

number of Mi'kmaq so that they might be available to resist an invasion of Nova Scotia actually assumed a tangible form through Monk's distribution of food and clothing to scattered groups of Mi'kmaq between 1793 and 1798.[40] Monk, however, was more concerned with maintaining the English Crown's alliance with the Mi'kmaq than he was in ensuring their future prosperity. The disbursement of food not only helped to sustain peaceful relations but also became a means through which the "loyalty" of individual Mi'kmaq was ascertained. Failure to provide an adequate demonstration of fealty to the Crown could result in being refused supplies.[41]

Moreover, Monk's location at Windsor in the center of the colony provided him with an advantageous position to survey possible political and military intrigues among the Mi'kmaq, a situation that was of concern to colonial authorities. In late January 1794, Monk wrote to Wentworth that the Mi'kmaq appeared to be more dissatisfied and restless than he had ever known and that "some of the more intelligent among them make circuitous visits to the different tribes, and give false reasons for such long and unusual Excursions."[42] Conferences held between Charles Alexis and other Mi'kmaq, particularly those inhabiting St. Margaret's Bay prompted Monk's attention. He noted in his Letterbook in November 1797 that "Charles Alexe has passed from Cape Sable by St. Margaret's Bay and Halifax Windsor and the South Mountain to Annapolis — an uncommon tract of very great distance compared with the usual and direct way by St. Mary's and Digby."[43] Three years previously, Monk had been concerned by the similarity between statements expressed by Charles Alexis and James Paul, both stating their unhappiness with the English policy of providing clothing and provisions while settlement proceeded but curtailing these disbursements once the land had all been settled.[44] This had prompted Monk to believe that Alexis had conferred with other Mi'kmaq, suggesting some form of political structure outside the control and influence of colonial officials.[45]

If anything, Monk's apprehensions illustrate the tenuousness of English settlement throughout the colony. With a population which likely did not exceed 3,000, of whom only a fraction inhabited southwestern Nova Scotia, the Mi'kmaq

---

40 A detailed record of these disbursements can be found in Monk Papers, MG 23: G11-19, Vol. 4.

41 Illustrative of this point is the case of James Paul who when denied provisions by Monk in January 1794 expressed the view that "if King George was so poor that he could give no more to Indians, the Indians better take nothing." Monk papers, MG 23: G11-19, Vol. 3, p. 1050. This remark so outraged Monk that he denied Paul all future assistance until he came to him and made a formal apology. See L.F.S. Upton, *Micmacs and Colonists: Indian-White Relations in the Maritimes, 1713-1867* (Vancouver, 1979), 83-84.

42 PRO, CO 217, Vol. 65, 150f, NAC, MG 11, Microfilm #B-1044, Monk to Wentworth, 23 January 1794.

43 Monk Papers, MG 23: G11-19, Vol. 3, 1084, 12 November 1797.

44 *Ibid.*, 1049-50, 12 January 1794.

45 *Ibid.*, 1047, 10 December 1793.

continued to live as a politically sovereign people during the late eighteenth and early nineteenth centuries.[46] The alliance established between themselves and the English during the 1750s and 1760s had not ceded Mi'kmaq land to the English Crown even though England claimed title to it through the Treaty of Utrect (1713) and later the Treaty of Paris (1763). Licenses of Occupation issued to the Cape Sable Mi'kmaq in 1771 and in 1786 established rules of conduct through which they would share the land with the non-Mi'kmaq peoples. As the numbers of these settlers increased after 1760, they came into conflict with this agreement, impinging upon Mi'kmaq access to the land and fisheries. Mi'kmaq complaints elicited some response in Halifax where officials were wary of antagonizing a people who had the ability to establish alliances outside the scope of colonial control. Eventually, however, the Cape Sable Mi'kmaq had no choice but to cede de facto control over portions of their land as the Elexey family petition of 1823 so graphically illustrates in their complaint that they had been forced off their lands on three previous occasions. These lands had likely been located on or near the seashore and had been a continuation of pre-1760 residence patterns. Forced into the interior, and by now aware that previous agreements regarding joint occupation of the land were no longer respected by the English, they appealed to the Lieutenant-Governor for a grant of land twenty miles from the sea. However, that request appears never to have been answered.

---

46   For a discussion of Mi'kmaq population, see Virginia Miller, ''The Decline of Nova Scotia Mic-
      mac Population,'' *Culture* II(1982), 107-120.

Bound for Nova Scotia:
Slaves in the Planter Migration, 1759-1800

Gary C. Hartlen
Queens County Museum

In 1758 and 1759 Charles Lawrence, the servant of the Lords of Trade and Plantations, sent out a call to the New England colonies for settlers.[1] Within a year, migrants from Massachusetts, Connecticut and Rhode Island began to move to the Nova Scotia frontier. They came because the offer of land, utensils and other incidentals of relocation were too attractive to refuse. These New Englanders brought with them their slaves.[2] For many Planters, Nova Scotia became their "New Jerusalem." However, the black slaves, who had accompanied them, saw little change for the better in their lives.

Lawrence explicitly acknowledged the institution of slavery in his second proclamation of January 1759 which promised that: "One Hundred Acres of wild Wood-Lands will be allowed to every Person, being Master or Mistress of a Family, for himself or her self; and Fifty Acres for every White or Black Man, Woman or Child, of which such Person's Family shall consist, at the actual Time of making the Grant...."[3] According to the census taken in 1767, there were over 100 "negroes" in the colony, half of them in Halifax.[4] Planter communities clearly did not support a large slave population but slaves could be found in many of the outlying townships, and it is quite possible that this early census failed to account for all of the black "servants" resident in the colony.

Lawrence's offer of free land in Nova Scotia must have been very appealing to large families living in mid-eighteenth century New England. The vacated Acadian lands in the Annapolis Valley and Chignecto region attracted farming families. A few black slaves were, not surprisingly, found in most of the agricultural townships. The fishermen came from Massachusetts, particularly from the Cape Cod area, to gain early access to the Grand Banks cod fishery.[5] These families located in towns and villages from Yarmouth to Chester on Nova Scotia's southern coast. Large fishing families felt similar economic pressures as agrarian families, but in addition to subsistence farming, these New Englanders fished, felled timbers, built vessels and traded. The slaves they brought with them were investments in their future prosperity.

In this paper, slave ownership by a number of individuals will be discussed.

1   D.C. Harvey, "The Struggle For New England Form of Township Government In Nova Scotia," *Canadian Historical Association Annual Report*, 1933, 17.

2   Janet Mullins, *Some Liverpool Chronicles* (Liverpool, N.S., 1936), 28-29.

3   Public Archives of Nova Scotia (hereafter PANS), MG 100, Vol. 47, #50.

4   Nova Scotia Census, 1767, PANS, MG 100, Vol. 120, #1.

5   H.A. Innis, ed., *Select Documents In Canadian Economic History, 1497-1783* (Toronto, 1929), 178-86.

Case studies are based on probate records, diary entries and other assorted contemporary legal documents. An attempt was made to discover the extent to which slavery existed in Planter Nova Scotia, who owned slaves, who these slaves were and how they lived. It should be admitted at the outset that finding written evidence of slavery during the Planter period was very difficult. One reason may have been that slaves were accepted on much the same terms as hired labour. The hardships faced when establishing new communities on the Nova Scotian frontier blurred the part played by each individual person, either slave or freeholder. The work of house raising, crop planting, harvesting, shipbuilding, fish catching and surviving in an unfriendly natural environment was hectic and always urgent in eighteenth-century Nova Scotia. Although blacks, either slave or free, could never be allowed to forget their "place," they were lumped into the category of servants, women and minors for land granting purposes and were considered appropriate wards for "protection" of the male head of the household.

Simeon Perkins from Norwich, Connecticut, joined the movement to Nova Scotia in 1762.[6] His first wife, Abigail, had tragically succumbed during the birth of their only child, Roger. Simeon started a business in Liverpool, Nova Scotia, with the blessing of his dead wife's father, who agreed to join him in the firm of Backus and Perkins. Along with supplies and implements, Simeon brought with him several slaves. Black Boston, one of these newcomers, was actually a crew member on one of Perkins's vessels in the coasting trade.[7] Simeon Perkins will be cited often in this paper. The references are taken mostly from his diary, which is one of the most informative first person sources available for this period. The shape of governments, religious controversy, contemporary business and industry, social and family affairs are all covered by 54 years of almost daily entries by this plain but literate man.[8]

In 1764, the Nova Scotia government put into place legislation which established a land deed system for real property and a regular court of probates for the distribution of the estates of deceased individuals.[9] This development closely touched Simeon Perkins who became the Registrar of Deeds and also served as a clerk of the Court of Probates in Queens County in that year.[10] The interest in land, which Perkins exhibited before his arrival, was shown by most of his compatriots as well. The accumulation of wealth through the acquisition of property was one motivation which had drawn these people from their New England origins. The dealings in land and the proprietary bickering found in early settlement minutes indicate that property was important to the early settlers.[11]

---

6   Simeon Perkins, *The Diary of Simeon Perkins*, Vol. 2, ed., D.C. Harvey (Toronto, 1958), 11.

7   Mullins, *Some Liverpool Chronicles*, 28.

8   The Diary of Simeon Perkins has been published in five volumes by the Champlain Society between 1948 and 1978. It has extensive notes provided by its three editors, H.A. Innis, D.C. Harvey and C.B. Fergusson.

9   Court of Probates Records, Queens County, Will Book I.

10   *Ibid.*, 2.

11   Township of Liverpool, Proprietor's Book, Queens County Record Office.

It can be argued that the Planters came to Nova Scotia because they desired a better life. They also felt that this move brought an opportunity for greater wealth. Recent studies have shown that the use of probate records can determine increasing assets with the resulting growth of wealth. Alice Hanson Jones, in her pioneering study of New England wealth, uses probate records as an investigative tool in defining wealth in Colonial America.[12] The conclusions drawn by Professor Jones are suggestive for the estates recorded in Nova Scotia after 1764. So, too, are the conclusions reached by Siddiq Fazley in his study of probate administration in Nova Scotia.[13] Although both of these sources have a more ambitious structure than this modest paper, they point to important assumptions that must be considered in any examination of slavery in Planter Nova Scotia: firstly, that slave ownership was considered part of a Planter's family wealth; and secondly, that this was part of a movement to increase the overall wealth and status as part of the individual's worth.

Using the methods employed by Jones, do inventories of Planter wills in Nova Scotia show that slaves were counted as "goods" in Planter estates? Could we tell if wealth increased or if ruin was more common than success? The search through will books in several communities founded by Planters, was interesting but inconclusive, and it proved impossible to find sufficient evidence upon which to base general conclusions about the role of slavery in the Planter economy or the nature of culture and society among Planter slaves.[14]

The drive for wealth may have been the reason why Simeon Perkins increased the size of his household by one "negro boy" on 12 July 1777. Perkins tells us: "I settle with Captain John Williams of Bermuda. He falls in debt £33.8.5 for which I take his Bill upon Messers. Musson, Trot & Co. merchants in said place. I settle with Mr. Merces and pay him for a negro boy, and sundry other goods to the amount of £51.8.5. The boys name is Jacob which I have altered to Frank. He is about 10 or 11 years old. Price 35 pounds."[15]

The casual way in which Perkins refers to his "negro boy" indicates how "normal" owning black slaves was to merchants and traders in the business community of Liverpool. These same capitalists added the book value of the blacks they had purchased to the total worth of their estates when they passed away. However, the fact that no purchased slaves are evident when the lists of goods are examined in estate inventories points to one of the weaknesses of using the probate methodology for measuring wealth or locating black slaves. Many of the people who died in Nova Scotia before 1800 had either not gathered an estate large enough to put into a will or for some other reason had died intestate. Dying intestate

---

12 Alice Hanson Jones, *The Wealth of a Nation to Be: The American Colonies On The Eve of The Revolution* (New York, 1980), 23.

13 K. Fazley Siddiq, "Nineteenth Century Wealth Transfers in Nova Scotia: The Administration of Probate," *The Nova Scotia Historical Review*, 9, 2 (1989), 23.

14 More than five hundred wills were consulted in registry offices and evidence of slave holding was rare.

15 Simeon Perkins, *The Diary of Simeon Perkins*, Vol. I, ed., H.A. Innis (Toronto, 1948), 158.

appears to be very normal in Nova Scotia at this time. There was no probate inventory available when Simeon Perkins died in 1812 and therefore this method would not establish him as a slave owner. Only his diary gives to us evidence to the contrary.

A perusal of His Majesty's Court of Probate proceedings in Queens County from the creation of the court in 1764 until 1800 failed to find evidence of any slave ownership. Again the problem arises from the source itself. When the existing probate records were searched, few were found with inventories of goods. It is not surprising that slaves were not recorded if no inventory was made of the other goods and chattels; nevertheless, the absence of black slaves in these registers, given the Perkins example, does not mean that slaves were not present.

Searches were also made of the probate papers and other documents in Annapolis, Kings, Colchester, Yarmouth and Lunenburg counties. The result of those investigations were similar in experience to Liverpool. Slave ownership did not often find its way into written documents. The few cases that emerge from these elusive sources are suggestive. In Truro, Matthew Arnold, sold "one Negro Boy named Abraham now about twelve years of age, who was born of my negro slave in my house in Maryland, For and in consideration of fifty Pounds Currency." This sale took place on 29 July 1779 in Truro, in the County of Halifax.[16] There was also the well-known sale by Joseph Northrup of Falmouth, Kings County, of a black man named Mintur to John Palmer of Windsor on 24 August 1779.[17] Mintur is mentioned again in the Owen Scrap Book in a document titled "Slavery Days in Nova Scotia." According to Owen: "In the days of Mintur, the possesion of slaves in the province by the sea ... was by no means unusual. In fact 'to keep slavery' was looked upon as a distinct mark of respectability."[18]

Simeon Perkins was asked by the government of Nova Scotia to join Magistrate Samuel Hunt to produce a census, in 1787, for Queens County. This census gave details of the whole county showing 1434 souls residing therein.[19] Of this total, 50 black people are noted in the summary, which is recorded in Perkins's diary, on 30 April 1787. The arrival of the Loyalists may well have accounted for this apparently substantial increase in the number of blacks in the area.

The probate records of Kings County produced evidence of slave-owning in 1802. An England-born gentleman, Benjamin Belcher of Cornwallis Township, recorded a will which was settled on 17 May 1802. Belcher's extensive estate lists land, cash, provisions, goods, stock, farming utensils, household goods, wearing apparel, books and "Negroes." The value of his slaves was listed as 175 pounds sterling. Each of the named individuals was valued with their clothes and bedding. The worth ranged from 55 pounds for a mature boy named Prince to ten

16   PANS, Truro Property Book I, 2, #68.
17   PANS, MG 1, 14, #113.
18   PANS, MG 1, Vol. 733A, Owen Scrap Book, No. 2, 111.
19   Nova Scotia 1770 Census (some 1773 and 1778): *Report of the Board of Public Archives of Nova Scotia*, December 1934 (Reprint Chicago Genealogical Society, Chicago, 1975), 30-37.

pounds for a young girl named Cloe.[20] Belcher made a sizeable bequest, in this same will, of 200 pounds for the construction of an Anglican church in Cornwallis, with a "gilt lettered" copy of the Lord's Prayer and the Creed, to be placed in the chancel. He then lists the slaves and the members of the family who are to receive them into their custody upon his death. Belcher may have had some remorse when he stated:

> My children unto who I have Intrusted these Negro people with never to sell, Barter or exchange them under any pretension except it is for whose bad or heinous offenses as will render them not safe to be kept in the family and that to be adjudged by three Justices of the Peace in said Township [Cornwallis] and in such case on their order they may be disposed of and I further request as soon as those young Negroes shall become capable to be taught to read they shall be learnt the Word of God...[21]

The last matter of business to be dealt with by Belcher in his will had been the disposition of his living assets. The moral and ethical quandary he faced is evident in the way he expressed his wishes for the future of his slaves. This genuine concern was from a man who was a large property owner living in the heartland of the farming Planter entrepreneurs.

Slavery and slave-owning appeared to be both comfortable and unsettling to a simple philosopher like Benjamin Belcher. The practices and existence of slavery do not seem to have disrupted his developing social, political or religious ideas, and giving them freedom upon his death never seems to have been a practical alternative. Nevertheless the disposition of an individual's property upon their death had been and always is difficult. The disposition of slaves was no less complicated.

David Randall, a Planter from Stonington, Connecticut, died in 1784 in Wilmot township, Annapolis County.[22] Randall's will was processed through the Annapolis Court of Probate on 18 July 1785. The division of property in Randall's estate was quite normal. His wife Keziah and his eldest son shared equally the real property of the legacy. The matter-of-fact manner which David had used to settle his other assets is worth noting. The will stated:

> I give Keziah, my said wife, a red Milch Cow with cut horns and my black mare and also the use of my Negroe Wench Sukey during the life of my said wife and after the Death of my Wife I give my said Negro Wench to my said daughter Sarah Newcome & Grand Daughter Mary Shay to be by them sold and the money arising from the sale to be equally divided between them share and share alike.[23]

---

20 Court of Probate, Kings County, 1802, 54th Proceeding, Inventory of the Estate.

21 *Ibid.*, Will of Benjamin Belcher, 6-7.

22 Esther Clark Wright, *Planters And Pioneers* (Hantsport, 1978), 168.

23 Court of Probate, Annapolis County, Will Book I, 18 July 1785.

In passing Sukey, first to his wife, and then to his daughter and granddaughter, for sale shows that Randall ignored the rising anti-slavery sentiment in Britain as the eighteenth century reached its close. There was no obvious pressure from his Planter neighbours to change the existing practice in Nova Scotia. Slavery continued as it always had, legally sanctioned, religiously separated and studiously avoided as a topic of discussion or as something to write about. It appears that eighteenth-century New England traditions were followed with little modification. Planters gave no thought to abandoning slavery as a horrible practice when they arrived on new soil to begin new lives. Any attempt to establish a new moral, political and ethical framework in Nova Scotia occurred alongside the unhealthy practice of owning slaves.

To Declare and Affirm:
Quaker Contributions to Planter Nova Scotia

Allen B. Robertson
Queen's University

The New England Planter migration to Nova Scotia marked the beginning of a unique English-speaking society in the fourteenth colony. Religion figured prominently as one of the forces which moulded the emerging culture. To date, critical analyses of the spiritual development of the Planters have been dominated by the attention given to Congregationalists, Baptists and schismatic off-shoots of both groups, in addition to Methodist in-roads. Smaller faith groups have been relegated to the periphery of most studies.[1] The Quakers (also known as the Religious Society of Friends), therefore, have not received recognition as vital contributors to the colonial social matrix. A re-examination of extant records suggests that this pacifist sect may have influenced Planter Nova Scotia to a greater extent than has hitherto been recognized. Quakers may well have encouraged the receptiveness of the general populace to the evangelistic message of Nova Scotia's first Great Awakening and subsequent revivals. Inspired speakers, the freedom of women and antisacramentarianism as expressed during and after the Awakening had ready models in Quaker teachings.[2] Though Quakerism found an audience in Nova Scotia, Quakers themselves were gradually absorbed into the surrounding populace. The Bridgetown Meeting was the only Planter enclave of Friends to persist as a distinct society into the mid-nineteenth century. By examining the relationship between Quakers and other evangelical denominations, it is possible to trace the contribution of the Quakers in Nova Scotia's religious heritage and to explain the fate of Quakerism in the province.

Members of the Society of Friends were present in both the agricultural and fishing townships established in 1759-60. At Barrington Township there were several households of Nantucket Quakers who had arrived in 1762 to pursue the fisheries.[3] In the Annapolis Valley and around the Minas Basin farmer and artisan

---

1   Gordon Stewart and George Rawlyk, *A People Highly Favoured of God: The Nova Scotia Yankees and the American Revolution* (Toronto, 1972); David G. Bell, ed., *Newlight Baptist Journals of James Manning and James Innis* (Hantsport, N.S., 1984); Allen B. Robertson, ''Methodism Among Nova Scotia's Yankee Planters'' in Margaret Conrad, ed., *They Planted Well: New, England Planters in Maritime Canada* (Fredericton, 1988), 178-89. The Baptist Heritage in Atlantic Canada series has published several significant contributions to Maritime religious historiography with special attention to Congregationalists, Baptists, Allinites and Methodists.

2   Stewart and Rawlyk, *People Highly Favoured*, 121-39; George A. Rawlyk, *Ravished by the Spirit: Religious Revivals, Baptists, and Henry Alline* (Montreal, 1984), 80-89, 120-32.

3   Edwin Crowell, *A History of Barrington Township and Vicinity, Shelburne County, Nova Scotia 1604-1870* (Yarmouth, N.S., 1923), 94, 95, 111-12, 200-201. Crowell (and one of his sources, Dr. Geddes) appears to infer Quaker adherence based on common surnames in Nantucket of known Quakers with similar surnames in Barrington.

Friends could be found in Wilmot, Granville, Cornwallis, Falmouth and New-port.[4] Other members surfaced at the provincial capital of Halifax. The earliest province-wide census to record religious affiliation, that of 1827, was taken well after the influx of Loyalist and British immigrants to the colony. It is difficult, therefore, to arrive at any substantive figures for Planter Quakers for the pre-1783 period. Quaker meeting minutes are not known to be extant for those same years. The only surviving meeting records are for the post-1786 Dartmouth Nantucket Whalers' colony.[5] One is led to late census returns, genealogical records and other scattered sources to provide material for a Planter Quaker profile. Outside Barrington Township they were very much a minority compared to other denominations. Nonetheless their individual profiles at times more than made up for what they lacked in numbers.

Rhode Island and Massachusetts appear to have provided the main sources for Planter Quakers in Nova Scotia. The townships of Falmouth and Newport were planted by Rhode Islanders, and one of the two agents originally sent to negotiate with the governor and council for settlement terms, John Hicks, came from an influential Quaker household.[6] His maternal grandfather had held high government office in Rhode Island while a great-uncle had governed the colony.[7] John Hicks himself had served as a Justice of the Peace at Charlestown. During the initial years at Falmouth the township records show Hicks to have played a leading role in local government. After his removal to Granville Township in 1765

4 Allan C. Dunlop, comp., *Census of Nova Scotia — 1827; Census of District of Pictou — 1818* (Halifax, N.S., 1979); W.A. Calnek, *History of the County of Annapolis* (1897; rpt. Belleville, Ont., 1972), 526-27, 318-20; A.W.H. Eaton, *The History of Kings County, Nova Scotia* (1910; rpt. Belleville, Ont., 1972), 317, 460; Elizabeth R. Coward, *Bridgetown, Nova Scotia: Its History to 1900* (Kentville, N.S., 1955), 125-27; John V. Duncanson, *Falmouth — A New England Township in Nova Scotia* (Windsor, Ont., 1965), 83, 92, 160-61, 184-85, 267-68.

5 "Minutes of the Nova Scotia Meetings of the Society of Friends ... 1786-1798," Public Archives of Nova Scotia [PANS]: Micro: Churches: Dartmouth: Quakers. For a fuller history of the Dartmouth Quakers see: Gene Keyes, *The Quaker Whaler House in Dartmouth* (Dartmouth, N.S., 1990). Quakerism did make an official mark on the province in 1759 when the Assembly adopted current English legislation which permitted affirmation as a substitute for swearing in legal proceedings: "By the Act 1759. 33, G.2, C.2.1.P.L.48. Quakers are permitted to make solemn affirmation where an oath is required by law...: 'I (A.B.) do solemnly, sincerely, and truly declare and affirm' ": Beamish Murdoch, *Epitome of the Laws of Nova Scotia*, 2 Vols. (Halifax, 1832), Vol. 1, 183.

6 Duncanson, *Falmouth*, 11-12, 267-68; Franklyn Hicks, "John Hicks," *Dictionary of Canadian Biography*, IV, 350-51. The inventory of Hicks's estate 27 February 1790 was taken by Robert FitzRandolph and Samuel Moore, "two of the people Called Quakers & Did Declare and affirm" [the validity of the inventory]: John Hicks, 1790, #12, Registry of Probate for Annapolis County, Annapolis Royal. Surveys of Shelburne, Kings and Annapolis counties have not yielded other Estate Papers which provide references to a Quaker presence; set legal terms and forms appear to have eliminated religious distinctions in Wills, Courts of General Sessions records, Deeds, etc.

7 "Walter Clarke," *Dictionary of American Biography*, IV, 163.

he held the distinction of becoming the first known Quaker to serve in the provincial House of Assembly (1768-70).[8]

Hicks's profile was more public than that of other Friends whose standing resided more in local community repute. Among the latter were the farmers Stephen Akin at Falmouth and Perry Borden (who later moved to Cornwallis). Borden's Quaker father from Tiverton, R.I., had been hired to survey the Minas Townships.[9] The Rhode Islander Stephen Chase, also of Cornwallis, left one of the few surviving pre-1783 Quaker marriage records, those for his third and fourth wives in 1764 and 1776 respectively.[10] In Annapolis, Wilmot and Granville, the Parker, Young, Moore and Phinney households supplemented the Hicks family, in addition to the Spurrs and Sangsters. The Barrington Friends proved to be transient settlers. Following the end of the Revolutionary War the majority returned to Nantucket to avoid further impressment troubles, and to more readily pursue whaling. Only a handful of the enclave's residents remained behind. The Gardners, Chapmans, Swains, Pinkhams and Covels have been identified as Friends households; the latter four families still had Quaker adherents in 1827.[11]

These few names represent, of course, many Quakers when spouses and children are included. Conversion and out-marriage into other faith groups on the other hand depleted Friends' numbers. One late record (which mixes nineteenth-century Planter and Loyalist families' descendants) is found in the 1861, 1871 and 1881 federal census returns for Annapolis County; here the figures for Quakers drop successively from 65 to 41 to 12.[12] A century earlier, though, at Falmouth in 1770, SPG missionary Bennett stated that there were 4 Quaker families and one Quaker-Baptist family in his parish charge of 36 households, representing approximately 24 Quakers.[13] Research continues in an effort to identify individual Quakers in the province prior to Confederation.

The Quakers who came to Nova Scotia were far more identifiable than other Planters by their particular garb, language (use of thee and thou), pacifism, restrictive marriage practices and silent meetings. Marriage had come to be a means of creating a semi-closed Quaker society. All candidates for marriage were visited by delegates to judge mutual suitability and to determine if both individuals were indeed Quakers.[14] To marry out of meeting was to invite expulsion from the

8   Shirley Elliott, *The Legislative Assembly of Nova Scotia 1758-1983: a biographical directory* (Halifax, 1984), 94. Elliott and her predecessor C. Bruce Fergusson erroneously identified the Loyalist Lawrence Hartshorne (d. 1822) as the first Quaker in the Assembly in the 1790s; *ibid.*, 91.

9   Duncanson, *Falmouth*, 184.

10   Eaton, *Kings County*, 226-27.

11   Arthur G. Dorland, *The Quakers in Canada, a History* (Toronto, 1968), 32-33; Dunlop, *Census of Nova Scotia*.

12   Calnek, *Annapolis*, 318-19. There was a Quaker presence in Pictou though it appears to have been founded by Loyalists. See Dorland, *Quakers*, 36; In "List of Pupils — June 1849" 2 Quakers are listed, PANS: Micro: Places: Pictou Academy, Reel 2.

13   Duncanson, *Falmouth*, 83.

14   Dorland, *Quakers*, 13-15.

society. Difficulties arose in Nova Scotia over the absence of formal meetings to regulate Quaker courtship and marriage ceremonies. Stephen Chase's two marriages were duly attested to by witnesses in Quaker fashion. There is no evidence, though, to prove that any of these signatories were practising Friends.[15] In another example, Stephen Akin of Falmouth appears to have married out of meeting, while his children married into other denominations.[16] Correspondence of the 1790s between visiting Friends and Thomas Green (a Dartmouth settler who had moved to Annapolis) indicates that although meetings were held in the area none were recognized officially by Philadelphia or Rhode Island Meetings.[17] Out-marriage by Planter and Loyalist attendants as well as possible military service by the latter may explain the reluctance of the American Quakers to give their meetings official standing. It is significant, in spite of a lack of strict adherence to Quaker marriage regulations or official standing, that Friends in Nova Scotia endeavoured to maintain both social and religious practices as a means of preserving their identity. The journal kept by Friend Joseph Hoag on his 1801-1802 tour of Nova Scotia attested to the persistence of Quakerism forty years after the Planters had arrived. It is particularly noteworthy that Hoag regularly had large turnouts for his preaching sessions and meetings in Annapolis and Digby counties, and at Halifax and Dartmouth.[18]

Late eighteenth-century Quaker enthusiasm did not prevent the eventual decline in numbers. In this century Elizabeth Coward in the 1950s quoted an elderly resident of Clarence in Annapolis County who recited oral memories about Quaker women's bonnets and the long silences at the meetings as Friends waited for "the Spirit to move them."[19] This was Quakerism at the edge of memory. By 1901, indeed, there were only 28 Quakers listed in the federal census returns for Nova Scotia.[20] These later figures and wistful recollections might lead one to question the relevance of examining Quakerism other than as a historical curiosity that

15   Eaton, *Kings County*, 226-27.

16   Duncanson, *Falmouth*, 161-62.

17   Dorland, *Quakers*, 35.

18   Christopher Densmore and Doris Calder, "The Journal of Joseph Hoag: A Quaker in Atlantic Canada, 1801-1802," *Newsletter Canadian Friends Historical Association — Supplement*, 39 (Seventh Month 1986). Hoag had relatives in Cumberland County, N.S., the family of Nathan Hoag who had settled in the area as Loyalist refugees from Westchester, N.Y., *ibid.*, 4; Marion Gilroy, *Loyalists and Land Settlements in Nova Scotia* (Halifax, 1980), 39; "Cumberland County: Barronsfield, Elysian Fields, Francklin Manor, Maccan and Nappan...," PANS, Micro: Places: Beausejour Museum: Reel 1, re: Births of the children of Nathan and Abigail Hoeg [Hoag], 10, 22 of Register 1.

19   Coward, *Bridgetown*, 125.

20   *Fourth Census of Canada, Vol. 1: Population* (Ottawa, 1902), 144. There were sufficient numbers of Friends in the 1880s, however, to warrant frequent visits from New England Friends, as noted in the writings of Quaker historian Rufus M. Jones (1863-1948) of Maine: "It was a very common and ordinary matter for New England Friends to drive to the 'Provinces,' especially to Nova Scotia, on religious visits, and, as soon as the railroads made travel easy and rapid, there was an almost unbroken stream of circulating ministry." Douglas V. Steere, ed., *Quaker Spirituality: Selected Writings* (New York, 1984), 268-69.

passed almost imperceptively from the provincial scene. Their impact, however, came in the later 1700s and early 1800s when Quaker numbers were higher. The language and practices of Quakers, it is argued here, enlarged the receptiveness of Nova Scotians to New Light revivalism from the 1770s to the 1790s.

The pre-1776 Congregationalists and Baptists in the Planter townships expected to have Sunday services, conducted by an educated clergyman, if available, in a meeting house. That same individual also oversaw the vital rites of passage — baptism, marriage and funerals, as well as the all important communion services for those who "owned the covenant." Bereft of a minister, settlers were left only with family prayers and Bible reading (if literate).[21] This did not serve, however, to create that special social bond forged in shared religious beliefs as expressed in the regularly constituted society. Quakers by contrast had dispensed with the sacraments and formally educated clergy. Assembled together in silence they shared simultaneously individual and communal receptiveness to the Inner Light. It was the community of believers who assisted in marriage and burials, and inculcated the peculiar Quaker customs.

Quakerism is a form of group mysticism in which those assembled together seek union with God and their neighbours to achieve unity in the Light. Historian Howard Brinton has succinctly stated the varied names given to that Inner Light in this fashion:

> The energizing center of the whole movement was the Inward Light, the Inward Christ, that of God in every man, the Power of God, the Witness of God, the Seed of the Kingdom, the Pure Wisdom which is from Above ... the Society of Friends escaped anarchism because its members realized that this Light was a superindividual Light which created peace and unity among all persons who responded to it or "answered it in one another. ..."[22]

Meetings regulated the believers in that special unity and prevented schism. Within the meeting both men and women could speak out if so directed by the Light. Leaders in contemplation, so-called "Quaker preachers," likewise could be men or women since there was no differentiation in spiritual natures.[23] In common with other branches of Protestantism Quakers studied the Bible and were well schooled in its language, imagery and witness. To it they added works such as Jacob Boehm's mystical writings, and Robert Barclay's late seventeenth-century apology for Quakers.[24]

---

21 J.M. Bumsted, *Henry Alline, 1748-1784* (Toronto, 1971), 14-15.
22 Howard H. Brinton, *Friends for 300 Years: The History and Beliefs of the Society of Friends since George Fox Started the Quaker Movement* (Wallingford, PA, 1965), 14; P.W. Martin, *Experiment in Depth: A Study of the Work of Jung, Eliot and Toynbee* (Boston, 1955), 230-31, 239-40.
23 Brinton, *Friends*, 90, 150.
24 *Ibid.*, viii; Steere, *Quaker Spirituality*, 24. Robert Barclay of Pennsylvania was the author of

The question remains as to how these beliefs may have had a role in Nova Scotia's evangelical heritage, especially as espoused by Henry Alline and Wesleyan Methodists. Allinites, New Light Baptists and Methodists all held to a belief in the Fall of Man, the Atonement and a need for individual dramatic conversion experiences. All three groups also accepted direct divine spiritual inspiration in preachers. They differed in acceptance of self-proclaimed prophets who took both Allinite inspiration and Wesleyan arminianism to the furthest extreme in antinomianism. George A. Rawlyk in his several studies of Alline has stressed the importance that Alline attached to experiential religion.[25] The Spirit was all, far surpassing church doctrines, sacraments or the usual Biblical interpretations. Even Scripture was to be understood not in a literal but in a spiritual sense so that the Spirit itself might impress the reader with divine truth. Allinite extremists in the 1790s, known as New Dispensationists, went so far as to deny church regulations and the validity of the Bible as the sole source of authority. Mrs. Randall of Cornwallis, the prophet-foundress of this movement, included the denunciation of marriage in her revelations. This variant of antinomianism spread rapidly through the Planter townships.[26]

It took the unrelenting preaching of orthodox New Light Congregationalists and Baptist ministers such as Thomas Handley Chipman and John Payzant to counter the New Dispensation Scheme. They could not, however, reclaim all Allinites who maintained Henry Alline's stand on Free Will. Some of these latter were absorbed by Methodists and others persisted as Free Will Baptists and strict Allinites.[27] The rapidity with which the New Dispensation Scheme had been propagated, or the earlier spread of the Great Awakening of Alline, attested to a receptiveness on the part of many settlers to unorthodox beliefs. This acceptance has been variously attributed to the rejection of Calvinism as found in Congregationalism and Old Light Baptist teaching, a spiritual disequilibrium induced by the American Revolution, the rebellion of women against a patriarchal society, and the desire for any novel preaching in isolated communities. To this list of plausible reasons must be added exposure to or familiarity with Quakerism and allied sects by the Planters of Nova Scotia.

The New England Planters could not have been unaware of Quakers prior to arrival in Nova Scotia given Quakers' old dominance of Pennsylvania and Rhode Island politics and society. In the province of Nova Scotia the Quakers in the town-

An Apology for the True Christian Divinity (1680), a work considered indispensable next to the writings of Quaker founder George Fox; Barclay's great-grandnephew Thomas Barclay (son of the Anglican rector of Trinity Church, New York City) was a Loyalist settler in Nova Scotia and Member of the Assembly for Annapolis County and Township: Calnek, *Annapolis*, 311, 344-48; George L. Rives, *Selections from the Correspondence of Thomas Barclay* (New York, 1894), 1-2.

25 Rawlyk, *Ravished By the Spirit*, 8-9, 15; George A. Rawlyk, ed., *Henry Alline: Selected Writings* (New York, 1987), 9-10, 28.

26 Rawlyk, *Ravished By the Spirit*, 81-89; Bell, *Newlight Baptist Journals*, 11-12, 14-19.

27 Robertson, ''Methodism Among Nova Scotia's Yankee Planters.''

ships certainly were visible enough to attract attention. Alline himself recorded in his journal that in Falmouth Friends were on occasion held up to ridicule:

> I remembered, that at a certain time some years ago, when I was in company with some young women, who were making a derision at people's waiting for the moving of the Spirit, I joined with them in the laughter and mockery ... when I was convinced that I had made a mock of religion, and made light of speaking reproachfully of the *moving of the Spirit: he [the devil] said it was the Spirit of God I had made a mock of, and therefore was lost forever.* ...[28]

Alline believed that the Quakers and himself waited on the same Spirit. The antisacramentarianism of Quakers, however, also drew unflattering comments. Alline on demoting the importance of outward forms before the pre-eminence of conversion prompted a Cornwallis resident in a 1780 letter through the Horton-Cornwallis Newlight Church to state that Alline was "guilty of Quakerism."[29]

A more positive response to Friends is found in the diary of Simeon Perkins. That Connecticut merchant in Liverpool Township recorded the visit of travelling Quaker preachers in 1786. Joseph Moore of New Jersey and Abraham Gibbons of Pennsylvania spoke in the New Light meeting house to a large gathering of which Perkins was one. He observed, "They appear to be very steady, sensible men, and seem to be esteemed and loved by people in general that have conversed with them." The previous day's diary entry had likewise noted, "Their discourses were plain, and I do not know that they deviated much from the Gospel."[30] Perkins's comment on the Gospel and Alline's on the Spirit in relationship to Quakers points to the crucial matter of language and perception. Quakers used Scriptural vocabulary and imagery. Auditors, whether Baptists, Congregationalists, Methodists or Presbyterians, responded to Quaker usage of Biblical language by placing that vocabulary in familiar contexts. They heard Gospel preaching and they did not always perceive the unorthodox meaning of the Quaker preachers behind the discourse.

It has been repeatedly observed that Alline's hearers often missed his Free Will message because they re-heard his preaching in a calvinistic Congregationalist mind-set. This resulted in the bifurcation of the Allinite Great Awakening between those who grasped Free Will and those who heeded only revivalist Newlightism. Perkins's experience with Moore and Gibbons was another example of failure to comprehend that a speaker was not representing orthodox Christianity. Michael P. Winship, in his provoking article, "Encountering Providence in the Seventeenth Century: The Experience of a Yeoman and a Minister," saw the same

---

28   James Beverley and Barry Moody, eds., *The Life and Journal of the Rev. Mr. Henry Alline* (Hantsport, N.S., 1982), 51.

29   Bell, *Newlight Baptist Journals*, 44.

30   *The Diary of Simeon Perkins*, [Various editors], 5 Vol. (1948-78), Vol. 2 (1780-1789), 336.

problem in colonial Massachusetts: ''The surviving sources indicate that members of the laity seem to have been content to have their spiritual aspirations and experiences expressed within the bounds of a discourse whose terms were set by the ministers. But while the ministers set the discourse, close examination will show that not all the terms of the discourse were used or understood in the same way by both ministers and laity.''[31] Quaker preachers drawing on the Bible could be assured of an audience even when these were composed of non-Quakers.

The Great Awakening of 1776-84 in Nova Scotia and New Dispensationism took place among a populace already familiar in some fashion with ''waiting on the Spirit'' as exemplified by Friends who kept family meetings or met as neighbours. In addition to traditional Quakerism, Connecticut settlers brought with them a knowledge of another faith group which had arisen near New London among one of the colony's wealthiest families. The Rogerenes adhered to a mix of Seventh Day Baptist and Quaker teachings as combined by John Rogers (1648-1721) of New London in the late 1600s. The sect, also known as Quaker-Baptists, was militant in its denunciation of Church-State ties. It espoused silent prayer, total immersion of adult believers, communion, faith healing and Quaker style marriages.[32] Members of the leading Rogerene households — Rogers, Bolles, Waterous and Whipple — all had representatives who settled in Horton and Cornwallis Townships in Nova Scotia.[33] In the year of Connecticut Planter migration to Nova Scotia the Rogerenes were undergoing another period of persecution which culminated in the so-called Rogerene Countermove, a form of demonstrative non-violent protest.[34] Relatives in Nova Scotia would have kept apprised of events back in Connecticut as would their Horton-Cornwallis neighbours.

The Rogerene insistence on separation of Church and State, suspicion of educated clergy, and the call to a particular way of life to denote identity in a Christian community resonated with the New Light evangelical message of Henry Alline.[35] The observance of silent prayer and reliance on the Spirit to guide one in faith or during persecution had direct parallels with Quaker teachings. Both

---

31 Michael P. Winship, ''Encountering Providence in the Seventeenth Century: The Experiences of a Yeoman and a Minister,'' *Essex Institute Historical Collections*, 126, 1 (January, 1990), 26.

32 Ellen Starr Brinton, ''The Rogerenes,'' *The New England Quarterly*, 16 (March 1943), 3-19; John R. Bolles and Anna B. Williams, *The Rogerenes: Some Hitherto Unpublished Annals belonging to the Colonial History of Connecticut* (Boston, 1904); F.M. Caulkins, *History of New London* (New London, CT, 1852), ch. XIV: ''The Rogers Family, and The Sect of Rogerenes''; William G. McLoughlin, *New England Dissent 1630-1833: The Baptists and the Separation of Church and State*, 2 Vol. (Cambridge, MA., 1971), Vol. 1, 249-53, 255, 257, 260-61; Richard L. Bushman, *From Puritan to Yankee: Character and Social Order in Connecticut, 1690-1765* (New York, 1967), 57, 164.

33 Eaton, *Kings County*, 72-76; Alice Rogers Nieman, *Windham Hill is Home: A Rogers Genealogy* (Halifax, 1989), 9-18.

34 Brinton, ''The Rogerenes,'' 12; Bolles and Williams, *Rogerenes*, 284.

35 Isaac Backus, *A History of the Baptists in New England*, 2 Vols. (1777; rpt. Boston, 1871), Vol. 1, 382.

groups, then, previously familiarized Planters with a version of Alline's renewed call for New Light conversion raptures in the Spirit of God. New Light Baptists found in a similar way that the idea of immersion as public witness had a long tradition among Planters outside strict Baptist circles. This observance and the communion service marked the Rogerenes as unorthodox Quakers. They in effect were intermediaries and transmitted certain Baptist and Quaker ideas to the Minas Basin settlers.

The Rogerenes did not rely solely on public witness to pass on their beliefs. Their founder John Rogers and his successors were prolific propagandists who made ready use of the printed word to disseminate their particular ideas. John Rogers himself in 1705 had published *An Epistle to the Churches of Christ Call'd Quakers*; in it he was sympathetic to Friends but decried the denial of water-baptism and the Lord's Supper.[36] Unfortunately it remains a subject of conjecture whether such pamphlets circulated in Nova Scotia. At the least Rogerene relatives in Horton-Cornwallis were themselves familiar with some of the vocabulary borrowed from Quakerism. Furthermore historian Arthur J. Worrall in his examination of early eighteenth-century Connecticut Quakers has pointed out that Rogerenes knew themselves not to be in competition with, and so not hostile toward, Friends.[37]

The Great Awakening in Nova Scotia had elicited comparison by contemporaries to its namesake in New England during the 1730s-40s. Personal knowledge of that event did not ensure immediate receptiveness to the Allinite revival message. Nonetheless it meant that the Planters did not believe themselves to be encountering an alien process outside their world view. Aggressive sectarian preaching also was not unknown; the Rogerenes were a noticeable example. What has been overlooked is that the Quakers themselves had periods of revival. One of the most recent prior to the arrival of the Planters in Nova Scotia took place in 1750-52. The English Quaker preacher Mary Weston toured New York and New England as a reforming Friend using the familiar language of election, reprobation and original sin before her mixed audiences. During her swing through New England large numbers of sympathetic hearers attended her meetings.

---

36 John Rogers, *An Epistle to the Churches of Christ Call'd Quakers* (New York, 1705); Brinton, "The Rogerenes," 5-6, 9.

37 Arthur J. Worrall, *Quakers in the Colonial Northeast* (Hanover, NH, 1980), 115-16. The Rogers family of Horton Township on the Gaspereaux Mountain by the 1790s had Quaker neighbours. Armisted and Mary Fielden of Masham, Yorkshire, had emigrated with their six children in 1774 to Nova Scotia. Unlike the majority of the Yorkshire migrants who went to the Cumberland area the Fielden family moved into Horton. Former neighbours, William and Mary Parker, also Friends, settled in Hants County, as did two brothers of William Parker. The full impact of these Yorkshire Quakers on their neighbours remains to be assessed in its own right. W. C. Milner, "Records of Chignecto," *Collections of the Nova Scotia Historical Society*, 15 (1911), 44, 62; William F. Parker, *Daniel McNeil Parker, M.D. His Ancestry and a Memoir of His Life* (Toronto, 1910), 31-33; Lancashire and Yorkshire Quaker Registers, re: birth, marriage and children of Armisted Fielden — extracts provided courtesy of Keith Fielden, Southgate, London (June 1991).

Figures ranged from 1500 at Nantucket and 2,000 in Salem, to over 4,000 at Newport, Rhode Island, with the Governor in attendance.[38] The message to seek God in the Spirit of Truth was not confined to New Lights and Rogerenes.

It is one of the intriguing features of colonial Nova Scotian religious history that, in spite of fierce sectarian rivalry, most touring preachers could be assured of admittance to a community's church or meeting house. In part this generosity reflected an interest in evangelical preaching that was almost catholic in spirit. Resident ministers always ran the risk of losing adherents to the new doctrinal messages of the visitors. On the other hand these withdrawals may have been uncommitted worshippers not firmly convinced of familiar doctrines. Those members of a church who went to hear a strange preacher and did not abandon their particular denomination were the listeners who sieved and rejected unharmonious aspects of an itinerant's sermon.

Quakers were not immune to the dangers of travelling revivalists. Methodism's stress on personal salvation, group prayer meetings and reliance on the Spirit to instill Holiness, drew young Quakers into the fold, as did its rival the New Light Baptists. The 1827 Census reveals, for example, that the Barrington Swain family which had five Quaker households also included Swains who were Methodists (nine households) and Baptist (one household). Similarly in Wilmot Township the Phinneys had become divided among Quakers, Baptists, Methodists and Anglicans. The Hicks of Wilmot and Annapolis had almost all become Baptists while only the house of Weston Hicks retained allegiance to its Quaker heritage.[39] Marriage by Quakers to Quakers to establish Quaker households, and converts to the faith (by ''conviction'') only partly counterbalanced the outward loss. That same resonating set of beliefs and vocabulary used by Quakers and Rogerenes which had opened the receptivity of Planters and the later Loyalists to Nova Scotia's emerging revivalist tradition remained a two way gate into or out of Quakerism and Protestant evangelicalism.

In 1801-1802 the Quaker Joseph Hoag toured Eastern British America. Hoag noted in his journal that he was importuned repeatedly to linger as a Quaker leader to regularize meetings. He was received warmly in Dartmouth and Halifax, and in the lower Annapolis Valley townships. The attendants at meeting were both Friends and the curious, either Planters, Loyalists or later immigrants. Hoag's reception in Cornwallis was less warm when he spoke in the Baptist meeting house in November 1801: ''The gathering was not large. The inhabitants mostly fixed in the Baptist belief that it seems heavy getting along amongst them.''[40] A few days later he received a far larger turnout in the Horton Baptist assembly hall: ''Many of other societies coming in, there was an open door for labor. I was much enlarged. The doctrines of truth went for clear and appeared to be well received

---

38   Worrall, *Quakers in the Colonial Northeast*, 74. It should be noted for comparison that Rogerene women ''gifted by the Spirit'' were encouraged to take a vocal part in religious meetings; Bolles and Williams, *Rogerenes*, 208.

39   Dunlop, *Census of Nova Scotia*, 109, 88, 54.

40   Densmore and Calder, ''Joseph Hoag,'' 11.

by the people.''[41] At Horton, in what became Wolfville in the 1830s, Hoag's audience came from a more compact settlement where meeting houses of several denominations were nearer together, necessitating more tolerance in the trading centre at Mud Creek. Here, as well, the older resonance with forms of Quakerism seems to have persisted longer.

At the opposite end of the Valley, in the back country of Wilmot, Joseph Hoag met with another experience. Two months before his return to the United States in the spring of 1802 he visited three Quaker families who had emigrated directly from Britain. For 28 years they had not met with Friends in Meeting. Hoag sadly observed: ''The old people appeared to retain the trait of Friends in language, dress and deportment. The children were gone from it except those of the youngest brotheres [sic] who had settled a number of miles [nearby] were in the practice of sitting down with their children on first day which the others omitted.''[42] These families were like so many Hoag had seen who, ''seemed as sheep without a shepherd.'' Hoag witnessed the beginning of Quakerism's decline as a distinct society in Nova Scotia though he may not have been fully cognizant of it given the reception he had had of large audiences in Halifax, Dartmouth and Digby.[43]

Quakerism was not the cause of the Allinite Great Awakening. Congregationalists, Baptists and Methodists all followed their particular sectarian paths into the nineteenth century. Along the way they absorbed both Quakers and remnant Quaker-Baptists. The revivals which followed the Awakening perpetuated vocal, enthusiastic outpourings and hard-driving sermons quite unlike the silent assembly of Friends in pursuit of the Truth. The past was not entirely or immediately annihilated though, in spite of the success of these main stream faith groups. The seed bed of eighteenth-century revivalism in the Planter townships had been prepared by the New England Great Awakening led by Methodists and Congregationalists, the Quaker Awakening of 1750-52, acquaintance with both Quaker and Rogerene teachings, and the existence of religious plurality and official tolerance in Nova Scotia. The later declension of Quakerism by absorption into evangelical churches infused into the dominant evangelical denominations the Quakerite concept of the necessity for regular communal worship, the spiritual equality of all people and the idea that women could perform valuable services for the social and ecclesiastical community. Quakers showed the more enthusiastic revivalist denominations that conversion and conversation with the Spirit of God did not have to occur always in the whirlwind or the earthquake. Seekers after Truth could find the Light in the still small voice.

---

41 *Ibid.*, 12.
42 *Ibid.*, 18.
43 The Annapolis County enclave of Friends maintained communications with Vassalboro, ME, Friends until the 1840s. Daniel Smiley of the latter place wrote to Joseph FitzRandolph of Bridgetown, N.S. (20 February 1841) following a visit to Nova Scotia: ''I have often remembered the few Friends that compose the little meeting at Annapolis with feelings of affection and solicitude. O that you may be enabled to hold all your meetings in the power of God.'' PANS, MG 1, Vol. 238, #23.

HIER RUHET IN GOTT:
Germanic Gravestones in Nova Scotia[1]

Deborah Trask[1]
Assistant Curator
Nova Scotia Museum

In 1749, after the War of the Austrian Succession, the British set out to establish a firm footing in Nova Scotia, an area they had governed half-heartedly since 1713. Governor Shirley of Massachusetts was influential in the plans for colonization of Nova Scotia. In 1749 he wrote to the Lords of Trade about settlers:

> They should not in this case be all foreign Protestants; tho' as great a Number as can be had from the Protestant Swiss Cantons, Palatines and other Northern parts of Germany, which have increased Pennsylvania within the past twenty years with perhaps 100,000 inhabitants, and who are all good settlers, should have due Encouragement to transport themselves into the Province.[2]

Between 1749 and 1752 more than 2,000 such ''Foreign Protestants'' landed at Halifax, the new British garrison town in Nova Scotia. They were recruited by the British government from principalities suffering severe economic problems, religious persecution or war in south-western Germany and the Montbéliard district of France and Switzerland. The political intention seems to have been to counter the French and Catholic presence in Nova Scotia by populating the interior with people who, for the most part, spoke German and were Lutheran or Calvinist. In 1753 some 1,500 of these new immigrants were moved down the coast to Lunenburg.

In some fields there has been an assumption that assimilation into the predominant English culture began immediately.[3] After all, the settlement of Lunenburg itself was named, not for their origins, but for the royal house of Brunswick-Lüneburg, ancestral home of King George I of England. Yet many of the first documents of the settlement are in German. Early church records of the township are in German. Of the early estate inventories and wills which have survived, many were also written in German, although the settlement of account papers, presumably prepared by clerks in the court of probate, are all in English. In 1788, Anton Heinrich, known as Anthony Henry, a Halifax printer, noted in

---

1   An earlier version of this paper was presented to the 1988 conference of the International Association for Gravestone Studies, Franklin and Marshall College, Lancaster, PA.

2   Quoted in Winthrop Pickard Bell, *The ''Foreign Protestants'' and the Settlement of Nova Scotia* (1961; rpt. Fredericton, 1990), 11.

3   Michael Bird and Terry Kobayashi, *A Splendid Harvest: Germanic Folk and Decorative Arts in Canada* (Toronto, 1981), 22.

the introduction to his German almanac for that year that many of the younger generations of the foreign Protestant settlers in Nova Scotia were affecting an "aversion for" the German tongue.[4] Judging from the original documents for Lunenburg, this may not have been the case in that new settlement. In fact, some traces of the language still remain. In 1964 the Nova Scotian author Norman Creighton wrote the following comment on Lunenburg County:

> In the surrounding countryside, you still hear people — especially members of the older generation — speaking with a distinctive 'Dutch' (Deutsch) accent, which has a lilt as cheerful as a hooked rug. The wonder is that any trace of it is left. They came from Germany, these pioneers, at a time when George II ruled Britain and Hanover. They settled the rocky shore with little more to furnish a house than the family Bible, still cherished in many Lunenburg homes. But nobody can read it anymore because it's in German.[5]

One such family Bible, in Mahone Bay, contained this entry (1870 translation):

> 1737 — I, John Philip Heyson, was born October 20th in District Ushberg, in the Kur Palatine. The town was called Hering; and, in 1751 — moved to this country. 1759 — married Magdalene Zwicker, March 4th, 1760 — March 19th, are my two sons born into the world, and March 21st brought to holy baptism, and the names of Frederick Heison, my father, and of my father-in-law Peter Zwicker, given to them.[6]

The author of this brief history, John Philip Heyson, died in 1813. Although he counts as a first generation settler, by the time of his death English gravestones were acceptable in Lunenburg Township, and so a sandstone tablet, carved elsewhere, marks his grave. In the old burying ground in Mahone Bay, near his home at Oakland, a tiny local slate stone marks the grave of his grandson and namesake, who died 25 January 1797, age 6 days, as recorded in the Burial Records of the Dutch Reformed Church, Lunenburg.[7] This is a crudely carved local slate, barely comprehensible, but particularly poignant, with its Germanic heart motif.

For the purposes of this paper, I have used the term "Germanic gravestone" to refer to any gravestone found in the region of Lunenburg County between the LaHave and Martin's Rivers (the area of original "foreign Protestant" settle-

4   Bell, *Foreign Protestants*, 585.

5   Norman Creighton, "Land of the Jolly Ox," *Sun Life Review*, 21, 2 (April 1964), PANS V/F, Vol. 135, #33.

6   Mather Byles DesBrisay, *History of the County of Lunenburg* (1895; rpt. Bridgewater, 1967), 389.

7   Records of the Dutch Reformed, later Presbyterian Church, Lunenburg, PANS, Micro: Churches, Lunenburg, partial translation MG 4, Vol. 86.

1. J.P.H., 25 January 1797. Stone for John Philip Heyson, slate, Mahone Bay, N.S. (Nova Scotia Museum collection: P133.167.20 Photo: Deborah Trask)

ment)[8] which either marks the grave of a first generation ''foreign Protestant'' or is inscribed in the German language. For my data base, I found 12 stones inscribed in German which pre-date 1810, and an additional 5 stones for early German settlers. There are two more stones for the first generation settlers, Heinrich and Susanna Oxner, near Five Houses (LaHave),[9] which I have not yet seen. Thus, of the nearly 1500 original settlers of Lunenburg, I have found only about one per cent of graves in the County with contemporary inscribed gravestones which clearly commemorate the first generation.

The oldest surviving stone is dated 1780, and marks the grave of Anna Catharina Barbara Schmidt Zwicker, the wife of Peter Zwicker the 2nd, who died at age 40 and was buried at Mushamush (now Mahone Bay).[10] The stone is local slate, lined off for lettering and shallowly carved with crude upper case letters. Spacing between the words is marked with a vertical row of three dots, and whenever the line was filled, words were split and carried over to the next.

8   Bell, *Foreign Protestants*, figure 8.

9   Noted in ''Cemeteries of Lunenburg County,'' Lunenburg County Genealogical Society: ''This cemetery is situated near the edge of the land by the beach above the old wasserlot. One has to walk quite a distance.''

10 Records of the Lunenburg (Zion) Lutheran Church, 367, PANS, Micro: Churches.

2. Ana Cathariena Zwicker, 1780, slate, Mahone Bay, N.S. (Nova Scotia
Musuem collection: P133.167.5 Photo: Deborah Trask)

From about 1775 on there were skilled stonecarvers making gravestones in Halifax, and these markers would have been available to those who could afford both to commission a stone and to arrange for its transportation. Philip Augustus Knaut came from Saxony. He kept one of the earliest stores opened in Lunenburg, and represented the county in the first provincial assembly. He was also a furrier, sawmill owner and trader. He became wealthy dealing in furs, and had trade connections in Halifax, so it is not surprising that the stone for his wife, Ann, who died in 1780, came from there. Carved in sandstone by the Scottish stone carver James Hay in Halifax,[11] this stone at Lunenburg is in marked contrast to the crude local slate gravestone for Catharina Zwicker who died the same year in Mahone Bay.

The pair of stones for Peter Zwicker 1st (died 1789 at the age of 78) and his wife Maria Magdalena (died 1787, aged 79) stand in Bayview Cemetery in Mahone Bay, originally the "burying ground at Mushamush." These are slate, beautifully but shallowly carved in Gothic script, but otherwise undecorated. The Maria Magdelena Zwicker stone reads (in translation):

> Here rests in God
> Maria Magdelena Zwicker
> born in Palatinate (Electorate)
> in Zeistham(?) close to Landau
> died 11th October 1787
> She has been married for 52
> years, 6 months and has been blessed
> with 49 children and grand children and
> great grand children, of whom
> 9 have died in the Lord,
> and 40 afterwards [left to mourn her?][12]

The Zwickers were members of the Reformed Church at Lunenburg. Behind them stands a pair of stones for Christian and Anna Regina Ernst, who died in 1798 and 1801 respectively. Although these are also unadorned and inscribed in German, the carver has used a vertical, uppercase Roman script. The Ernsts were members of the Lutheran Church, and when Anna Regina was buried at Mushamush, 2 November 1801, the Lutheran Burial Register recorded her interment as the 49th of 55 in that church that year.[13] If those other graves were marked at the time, only the gravestone for Anna Regina Ernst has survived. The

---

11 For more on the work of Hay, see Deborah E. Trask, *Life How Short, Eternity How Long, Gravestone Carving and Carvers in Nova Scotia* (Halifax, 1978), 58-68.

12 I am grateful to Heidi Grundke, Halifax, for her patient assistance in translating from the German Gothic script some of the barely decipherable eighteenth-century gravestones.

13 Records of the Lunenburg Lutheran Church, 367, PANS, Micro: Churches.

3. Maria Magdalena Zwicker, 1787, slate, Mahone Bay, N.S. (Nova Scotia Musuem collection: P133.167.7 Photo: Deborah Trask)

will of Christian Ernst is also written in German.[14]

Another interesting stone, shallowly carved in Gothic script, undecorated local slate with German inscription, marks the grave of Katharina Zwicker, wife of John George Zwicker. She died the same year as her father-in-law, Peter Zwicker 1st, 1789, aged 35. It seems likely that the stones for Peter Zwicker 1st, Maria Magdalena Zwicker and Katharina Zwicker were all carved by the same hand. The stone for Johonnes Rehfus, died 1798, also shallowly carved, undecorated local slate with German inscription, is more crudely inscribed in a cursive script — difficult to do with a chisel, which may account for the brevity of the inscription.

The most glorious Germanic stone is for Johan Georg Eisenhauer, slate, 1805, ornamented with a wonderful dancing tulip. This, like the Ernst and Zwicker stones, includes detailed biographical information, such as where he came from, birthdate, when he came to Nova Scotia, wedding date, number of children and death date. A translation of the inscription reads:

> Here rests Johan George
> Eisenhauer. Born at
> Wilhelmsfeld in Germany
> Anno 1733. 22 January.
> Comes to NOVA SCOTIA 1751,
> Marries 1759. Lives in
> wedlock 46 years. Begets
> 13 children, dies 1805, 10th June

The will of Johan George Eisenhauer is also written in German.[15] Another document from the Eisenhauer family is the baptismal record for his son Johan George Eisenhauer, baptised in 1772.[16] The paper is watermarked 1804, and so was probably lettered about the time of the gravestone, perhaps by the same hand. George Eisenhauer's step-brother, Adam Hebb, pre-deceased him by two years. Hebb had a sawmill on the LaHave River, and his gravestone at the "burial ground near the Cove Marsh" at the present community of Dayspring is a sandstone tablet, perhaps carved in Halifax, with an image of a relief-carved classical funerary urn, typical of that period, and an English inscription but a German epitaph.[17] The epitaph is a poem or song, beginning (in translation): "Come, O death, thou sleep's dark brother."

---

14 Will of Christian Ernst, written 1796, registered at probate 10 May 1802, PANS, Lunenburg County Wills: RG 48, Reel 842.

15 Will of George Eisenhauer, registered at probate 18 June 1805, PANS, Lunenburg County Wills: RG 48, Reel 842.

16 Baptismal record for Johan George Eisenhauer, baptised in 1772, ink on paper, watermarked 1804, PANS: Canon Harris papers: Eisenhauer.

17 The gravestone for Adam Heb, sandstone, 1803, Dayspring, has been overcleaned by a zealous descendant, obliterating much of the epitaph. A transcription is printed in DesBrisay, *History of the County of Lunenburg*, 387-88.

4. Johan George Eisenhauer, 1805, slate, Mahone Bay, N.S. (Nova Scotia
Museum collection: P133.167.17 Photo: Deborah Trask)

There are two earlier Germanic gravestones inscribed in English, both in Lunenburg and commemorating members of the Jung family. The oldest, for Mary Elizabeth Jung who died in 1784 aged 21, is a crudely carved slate, with the inscription panel cut back quite far and with tailed swirls on the more elaborately carved shoulders. The stone for George Jung, died 1794 aged 23, has a heart in crossed floral stem tympanum design, with flat chisel-cut inscription on slate. George was the eighth child of Andreas Jung, who had come from Litzelinden in Weilburg (Rhineland, north of Frankfort), and who authored an account of the Lunenburg Zion (Lutheran) Church, 1770-1785, referred to by Bell as the "Jung manuscript."[18]

Other stones inscribed in German are found in Lunenburg. The graves of Kathrina Maragreta (Zöller) Lässle, age 34, and her infant daughter Maria Sovia, both of whom died in 1808, are marked with simple slate stones beautifully carved in Gothic script. The young husband and father, Heinrich Lässle (or Henry Lesley, in its anglicized form) died the following year, but his grave is not marked.[19] The slate stone for Johan Michael Silber, who died in 1810 aged 23, is the latest inscribed in German.

Stones from Massachusetts Bay were also available on the South Shore. The nearby Planter settlement of Liverpool maintained close economic ties with Massachusetts and Connecticut, as did other Planter townships. The old (Congregationalist) burying ground at Liverpool contains a remarkable variety of late-eighteenth-century gravestones: carved slates from the area around Massachusetts Bay and sandstones from the Connecticut River. The Nathan Freeman stone at Lunenburg (slate, 1801) is for a young man from Liverpool whose family chose to have a New England stone rather than a local or Halifax one. The people of Lunenburg township could have had gravestones from New England as easily as from Halifax, yet very few graves are marked, and of those that are, most appear to be of local material and production.

When Peter Zwicker the 2nd died in 1813, the same year as his brother-in-law, Philip Heyson, he was very specific in his will:

> It is also my will that after my decease, my six sons . . . shall erect and place for me a *Tomb Stone* beginning with this Inscription, here Lieth Interred, Peter Zwicker the Second of Lunenburg Nova Scotia etc. and if in case I should happen to die away from home, I desire to be buried at the Mush a Mush burying ground, in failure of which my said sons shall forfeit and pay unto the Reformed Church of Lunenburg the sum of *twenty five* pounds currency.[20]

---

18 Bell, *Foreign Protestants,* ch. 77.

19 Will of Henry Lesley, yeoman, written 10 February 1809, registered at probate 20 February 1809, PANS, Lunenburg County Wills: RG 48, Reel 842. Presumably he was a son of Marcus Gottfried Lässle, probably born about 1772.

20 Excerpt from the will of Peter Zwicker, written 5 October 1811, registered at probate 13 November 1813, PANS, Lunenburg County Wills, RG 48, Reel 842.

5. Adam Heb, 1803, sandstone, Dayspring, N.S. (Nova Scotia Museum collection: P133.169.2 Photo: Deborah Trask)

6. Kathrina Maragreta Läsle, 1808, slate, Lunenburg, N.S. (Nova Scotia Museum collection: P133.169.4 Photo: Deborah Trask)

This is a very unusual request to be found in a will. Presumably he felt that it was important to ensure that his grave would be marked, when the custom even at this late date was not necessarily to do so. His sons followed his wishes, though not quite to the letter, and he is buried beside his wife, marked by a sandstone gravestone inscribed in English, with compass star motifs on the tympanum.

The stone for another brother-in-law of Philip Heyson, the first generation Henry Koch (or Cook) who also died in 1813 at Lunenburg, is a similar sandstone with incised compass star shoulder designs. A much cruder stone exists for one of his descendants, an unnamed infant boy who died in 1848 at First South. The Germanic heart motif appears on the locally carved descendant's stone, not the purchased stone used for the first generation. The stone for Reb. Eliz. Meissner who died in 1802 at age 19 is a slate inscribed in English with what may be a New England style winged cherub on the top and a Germanic heart motif at the base. She was the wife of Casper Meissner 3rd, and so was at least third generation herself. The meaning of the second date on this stone is unclear.

Casper (or Jasper) Heckman, grandson of Casper Heckman 1st, tavern keeper, and son-in-law of Peter Zwicker 2nd, died in 1802, age 40. His slate stone at Lunenburg is inscribed in English, and has a strange spindly tree design off centre in the tympanum. Although it is tempting to infer that this refers to his profession of vintner, it is most likely a crude version of the tree of life.

On forms of functional artifacts other than gravestones, Germanic folk art images flourished into this century. Michael Bird and Terry Kobayashi have pointed out that "Tulips, hearts, compass stars and geometric designs characterize many Lunenburg County artifacts, and these motifs resemble those of Pennsylvania German folk art. . . . The most striking Germanic decorative work appears in the motifs and inscriptions carved into grave markers. . . forms which proclaim their own dates."[21] In fact, there are very few Germanic grave markers in Lunenburg County, and those which survive are, for the most part, unadorned except for teutonic Gothic script. This is in sharp contrast with Pennsylvania German gravestones of the same period, which are usually carved in high relief more often with an image and no inscription. Germanic imagery on gravestones in Lunenburg County, although not present on stones for the first generation, continues to the present, but no longer with any conscious cultural association.

When considering the Planter period in terms of individual immigrants, we find in early gravestones a combination of primary document and artifact. Gravestones are, in material culture terms, extremely vulnerable to vandalism and destruction by the elements, if nothing else. Their very survival from the Planter period is therefore remarkable. As I have told this conference previously,[22] it is generally accepted that about ten per cent of eighteenth-century graves are still marked. In some Planter communities, depending on whether or not there was a line of communication with New England (as in Yarmouth), or a local supply of good stone (as in Horton or Cornwallis) this figure might be as high as 20 per cent. Lunenburg, though not a Planter settlement, was a planned settlement which predated the New England Planter communities by less than a decade. Far fewer than ten per cent of the Lunenburg eighteenth-century graves are marked. Was this because it was that much older a community? There was a lot of resentment by the French and the native populations of Nova Scotia against the new British garrison town of Halifax in the first years of that settlement. One story has it that the Indians quickly realized that the new settlers got quite upset when their dead were dug up, and to avoid this harassment the settlers stopped marking graves and moved the burial ground to within the stockade, for a time. This past spring, during the early stages of the resetting project at the Old Burial Ground, Halifax, we found a stone for a child who died in 1752.[23] The stone, carved in Massachusetts Bay area at that time, was itself buried, perhaps so as not obviously to mark the grave. All the gravestones which have survived in Halifax and Annapolis, and which were carved before 1768, came from New England, a market not really

---

21 Terry Kobayashi and Michael Bird, "The Traditional Folk Arts of Lunenburg County," in Richard Henning Field, ed., *Spirit of Nova Scotia, Traditional Decorative Folk Art 1780-1930* (Halifax, 1985), 126-27.

22 Deborah Trask, " 'Remember Me As You Pass By': Material Evidence of the Planters in the Graveyards of the Maritime Provinces," in Margaret Conrad, ed., *They Planted Well; New England Planters in Maritime Canada* (Fredericton, 1988), 304-306.

23 Malachi Salter stone, 1752, slate, Old Burying Ground (formerly St. Paul's Cemetery), Halifax, uncovered May 1990.

7. Peter Zwicker 2nd, 1813, sandstone, Mahone Bay, N.S. (Nova Scotia Museum collection: P133.167.2 Photo: Deborah Trask)

accessible, or even perhaps desirable, to the first generation of German settlers. Was the permanent marking of graves not a Germanic tradition, as evidenced by the odd request in the will of Peter Zwicker 2nd? Certainly this does not appear to be the case in areas of Germanic settlement in Pennsylvania. More likely, the permanent marking of graves was not a priority to a community struggling to get established.

What becomes very clear is that the government ensured that excellent records were maintained for the individual settlers who came to Lunenburg Township: ship registers, victualling lists, land grants, wills and estate inventories, to name a few. The church records are also very detailed, including annual lists of communicants, marriages, baptisms with names of sponsors, burials with the place of burial and even the funeral text noted. A number of decorated paper records of vital events also survive.[24] But of all the documents of early settlement, those carved in stone are very rare indeed for Lunenburg, and so deserving of special attention.

24   See Deborah A. Young, *A Record for Time* (Halifax, 1985). This is a catalogue of an exhibition of decorated family and individual records, published by the Art Gallery of Nova Scotia.

A Scots-Irish Plantation in Nova Scotia:
Truro, 1760-1775

Carol Campbell
Truro, Nova Scotia

Patrick M'Robert, journeying up the coast of America from New York to Newfoundland, commented upon visiting Truro in 1774; "No people live happier among themselves than these seem to do," he concluded.[1] The next year the Lieutenant-Governor of Nova Scotia reported that the inhabitants of Truro were "a strong, robust, industrious people...settled on the best land, and the most flourishing because they are the most industrious."[2] What caused two such diverse observers to suggest that Truro was an exemplary settlement?

While there can be no single answer, a major contributor to Truro's contentment may have been the emphasis placed by its settlement association on kinship groupings and ethnic homogeneity within the township. Other Nova Scotian towns were also established by associations of future proprietors, but it would appear that these communities did not share Truro's blending of generational mix within family groupings, religious and ethnic homogeneity, and proprietorial residency requirements.[3] In Truro, agreement on societal goals, rooted in homogeneity, facilitated the balance between continuity and change. As we shall see, throughout the Planter period, consensus enabled social and economic institutions carried from New Hampshire to adapt with relative ease to the Nova Scotian environment.

The founding of Truro, Nova Scotia, was a small part of the third migration of Scots-Irish who had travelled from Scotland to northern Ireland and later to America, where large numbers settled in New Hampshire.[4] The Ulster heritage of the

---

1   Patrick M'Robert, *A Tour Through Part of the North Provinces of America* (Edinburgh, 1776, rpt. 1935), 20.

2   Lieutenant-Governor Mariot Arbuthnot to Lord Germain, 15 August 1776, Public Archives of Nova Scotia (hereafter PANS), RG 1, Vol. 45, Doc. 24.

3   For comparisons see Debra A. McNabb, "Land and Family in Horton, N.S., 1760-1830," MA thesis, University of British Columbia, 1986; Elizabeth Mancke, "Corporate Structure and Private Interest: The Mid-Eighteenth Century Expansion of New England," in Margaret Conrad, ed., *They Planted Well: New England Planters in Maritime Canada* (Fredericton, 1988); and A.R. MacNeil, "Early American Communities on the Fundy: A Case Study of Annapolis and Amherst Townships, 1767-1827," *Agricultural History*, 62, 3 (Spring 1989), 101-19.

4   Much of the genealogical data on Truro's grantees has been collected from various sources and entered into the Family Files at Colchester Historical Museum, 29 Young St., Truro, N.S (hereafter CHM). Other genealogical sources used in the preparation of this paper include Thomas Miller, *Historical and Genealogical Record of the First Settlers of Colchester County* (Halifax, 1873, rpt. 1983); Gwyneth Logan, Logan Grantees of Truro, N.S. (Vancouver, 1966); Ezra S. Sterns, "The Moore Families of Londonderry, N.H.," *The New England Historical and Genealogical Register* (Boston, 1897), 491-92; and "Crowell's Scrapbook," PANS, Micro: Places: New England.

majority of New Hampshire's pioneers encouraged the continuance of communal and familial networks, and expedited the establishment of territorial churches.[5] In addition, population pressures in New Hampshire encouraged the practice of older towns establishing frontier townships using the proprietary model of self-managed homogeneous communities.[6]

A New Hampshire township which was particularly prolific was Londonderry which founded, among others, the towns of Belfast, Maine; Bedford, New Hampshire; Coleraine, Massachusetts; Cherry Valley, New York; and Truro, Nova Scotia.[7] Londonderry, New Hampshire, had prospered during the 1750s by provisioning British forces and by encouraging household manufacture of an excellent grade of linen.[8] Immigration of Scots-Irish, both directly from northern Ireland and from other New England communities, coupled with a very high rate of natural increase, contributed to the growing population. By the second half of the decade fertile land had become so expensive that newcomers and young men could not afford the land-based lifestyle to which they aspired. As an alternative, during the French and Indian Wars, many of these men joined the volunteer militia.

When the French-English conflict resulted in the expulsion of the French from Acadia, one group from the hamlet of Derry in the Township of Londonderry, some of whom had served with Captain Alexander McNutt at Fort Cumberland, chose land on the shores of the Bay of Fundy in a region referred to as the Cobequid.[9] Disregarding the possibility of differences between Nova Scotian and

5   For the social and economic background of the Scots-Irish see Kerby A. Miller, *Ireland and the Irish Exodus to North America* (New York, 1985), particularly "Irish Emigration before the American Revolution," 149-67. The general topic of Scots-Irish emigration is covered in Maldwyn A. Jones, "Ulster Emigration, 1783-1815," in E.R.R. Green, ed., *Essays in Scotch-Irish History* (London, 1969), 46-68.

6   Jere R. Daniell, *Colonial New Hampshire: A History* (Millwood, N.Y., 1981), especially ch. 7, "Patterns of Growth, 1715-1765," 134-64, explains the use of the proprietary in New Hampshire.

7   Edward L. Parker, *History of Londonderry, Comprising the Towns of Derry and Londonderry* (Boston, 1851) gives a detailed account of the founding of Londonderry and its satellite townships. Other secondary sources which have been consulted include: Ralph Stuart Wallace, "The Scotch-Irish of Provincial New Hampshire," PhD thesis, University of New Hampshire, 1984; Charles Clark, *The Eastern Frontier: The Settlement of Northern New England, 1610-1763* (New York, 1970); and David E. Van Deventer, *The Emergence of Provincial New Hampshire, 1623-1741* (Baltimore, 1976). The most widely available primary source is George W. Browne, ed., *Early Records of Londonderry, Windham and Derry, New Hampshire, 1719-62* (Manchester, N.H., 1908).

8   Parker, *History of Londonderry,* 50.

9   A.W. Eaton, "The Settling of Colchester County, by New England Planters and Ulster Scotsmen," Royal Society of Canada, *Transactions.* 3rd. Ser., VI (1912), 212-60, remains the most comprehensive account of the settling of the Cobequid area. For McNutt's role in the Township Grant see Phyllis Blakeley, "Notes for article in *Dictionary of Canadian Biography,*" PANS, MG 1, Vol. 3005, Nos. 14-18.

New Hampshire settlement practices, this group determined to organize themselves into the New Hampshire ideal of an economically viable, self-managed community, independent from centralist control. To that end they formed a settlement association and began planning their migration in March of 1760.[10] Although no further details of pre-settlement planning are available, the results achieved imply that New Hampshire proprietary customs were closely followed.[11] In eighteenth-century New Hampshire the proprietary was deemed to be primarily economic and the main duties of the proprietors consisted of settling the township with suitable persons; distributing the land; and providing infrastructure, such as roads, sawmills and grist mills.[12] Development of the community suggests that Truro's settlers transferred these obligations to Nova Scotia.

In fulfilling their first responsibility, that of finding settlers, the proprietors of Truro retained the New Hampshire ideal of ethnic and religious homogeneity, reinforced by a territorial church centred around kinship connections; the Londonderry migrants were all Presbyterian, all Scots-Irish, and many were related. Emigration in family groups was strongly encouraged by settlement associations in order to ensure the presence of older, experienced leaders, strong-bodied youths, young families, and marriageable girls, as well as to provide emotional security for individuals. Perhaps to provide suitable future marriage partners for the closely-knit Londonderry kinship groups, Truro's proprietors obtained additional settlers from Governor Lawrence's Boston agent, Thomas Handcock. These were also all Presbyterians and, with the exception of two families, Scots-Irish. The resulting community was ethnically and religiously homogeneous, yet contained a relatively large group of unrelated young people.

Table 1: Age at Migration to Truro

	Male	Female
−10	38	32
−20	20	15
−30	7	9
−40	9	8
−50	8	7
50+	1	4

A second provision for the peopling of the future community was that proprietors requested land in the names of their minor sons. Grants in Nova Scotia ranged between one-half and two shares (250-1000 acres), with no individual

10 *Diary of Matthew Patten of Bedford, New Hampshire* (Concord, N.H., 1903), 76.

11 "Truro Township Record Book, 1770-1837" (hereafter TTB), PANS, Typescript Copy (MG 1, Vol. 150) and Original (MG 1, Vol. 150a).

12 Daniell, *Colonial New Hampshire,* 156.

obtaining more than two. By applying for land in the name of adolescent sons, Truro's proprietors were able to circumvent this ruling, thus ensuring both the availability of land for the second generation and the homogeneity of the population for many years to come.[13]

Table 2: Grantees Listed on the 1765 Grant[14]

Men with children over 5	16
Men with children under 5	13
Childless married men	6
Single young men	8
Minor sons of grantees	25
Widows	2

As we have seen, the proprietors fell into two groups: those from Londonderry, New Hampshire, and those who had emigrated from Boston. In acknowledgement of the benefits of communal cohesion, this division was perpetuated in Truro, probably by common consent.[15] The Township of Truro contained two small hamlets: Derry, peopled by those who had migrated from Londonderry Township, many of whom belonged to two extensive kinship groups, centred around the Archibald and Moor families, and Down, whose inhabitants had travelled from Boston in nuclear and extended family groups. (See Map 1) An indication that the proprietors correctly estimated the importance of family solidarity can be gleaned from the fact that those who sold their shares outright during the first ten years of settlement were without strong kinship ties in the community.[16]

The second proprietorial responsibility was land distribution. This appears to have been accomplished in the summer of 1760 when a proprietor-appointed surveyor divided the township into two hamlets with household, marsh and wood

13 Compare with Horton where, according to Debra McNabb ("The Role of the Land in the Development of Horton Township, 1760-1775," *They Planted Well,* 151), "there was a closing off of opportunity within the first generation."

14 Genealogical sources provided identification of 70 of a total of 84 Truro grantees. A list of the grantees, together with the number of shares they received, can be found in J.M. Murphy, *The Londonderry Heirs* (Truro, N.S., 1976), 99-100.

15 McNabb, "Land and Families," 25 states that Horton grantees could choose their neighbours by "drawing-in-company."

16 Examples are William Nesbit (a Halifax merchant, the one non-resident proprietor, presumably imposed by Halifax), Hezekiah Egerton, William Kennedy, John Jeffrys, Moses Blaisdell, John Crawford, John and Matthew Fowler, and Elizabeth Bell. William Kennedy and John Jeffrys eventually returned to Truro. PANS, RG 47, Reel 438, Book 1, Nos. 72; 106; 418; 19; 70; 69; 97; 148. It should be noted that Truro's extant registered deeds are not a complete record of all land transactions.

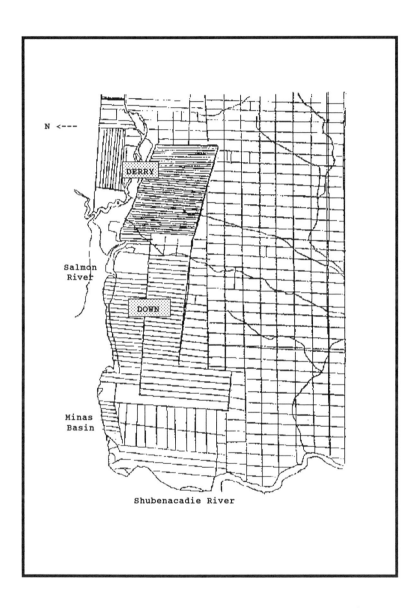

Map 1: A Plan of the Township of Truro surveyed by Thomas Harris, Truro, 12 August 1788 (based on the plan of 1765)

lots, and communally-held undivided backlands.[17] The pattern used was the Londonderry, New Hampshire, one of contiguous homesteads stretching back from the river, an alternative to the typical New England form of a central town-plot followed by Charles Morris in other Nova Scotian townships.

During the first decade further land distribution was restricted by the strength of the communal ideal, centred around the principle of common ownership of undivided land by resident proprietors. Communality is implied in all early land transactions recorded in the Truro Township Book. Land dealings were subjected to a majority vote of the town meeting; common land was sold to approved purchasers for upkeep of the meeting-house; and local records of land transactions were kept by town officers.[18] Non-resident land owners remained unwelcome; approval to purchase was only granted to those who were resident, or who intended to become so.[19] This provision may have originated in the Londonderry, New Hampshire, ruling of 1720 stating that all proprietors of the township must reside within its boundaries.[20] The original motive in Truro, as it had been in Londonderry, was probably to enhance communal solidarity and the result was that final division of the backlands was delayed until 1787 and no evidence of an overt challenge to communal authority over land disposal can be found before then.[21]

The third and most important responsibility of the proprietors was economic development. In order to build an undifferentiated agrarian economy of the New Hampshire model in Nova Scotia the proprietors had to induce certain tradesmen to migrate. These included a blacksmith and miller, both of whom were customarily offered extra land to offset their capital investment. In Truro, brothers-in-law Alexander Miller and John Morrison were each given one hundred acres of "mill

---

17   Patten recorded that he was chosen to be "one of their Commitees *[sic]* to go to Halifax to Got [sic] the grant and Survey the Land." A formal survey of Truro Township was carried out by Samuel Archibald in 1763 and a plan was drawn, presumably in conjunction with the effective grant of 1765. The 1788 map, which was the source of Map 1, was based on Archibald's plan and, with few exceptions, records the households of 1763. Patten, *Diary,* 76; PANS, MG 100, Vol. 240, nos. 19-30 and 19-31; TTB, 37; CHM Map File, "A Plan of the Township of Truro," surveyed by Thos Harris, Dept. Surveyor, Truro, 12 August 1788. Copied and Scaled down by Bruce McNutt, May 1983.

18   TTB, 1-37, *passim.*

19   An example of a purchaser who intended to reside in Truro was Henry Glen, the Scottish merchant, who was working out of Debert Village in Londonderry Township. In 1770 he purchased the grants of John and Matthew Fowler. While a house was being built for him in Truro, he rented the farm to Hugh Mitchell of Windsor. Apparently Glen was deemed to be a member of the community as he was one of the "freeholders and inhabitants" of Truro who signed the call to the Reverend Daniel Cock in July of 1770. TTB, 42; "Indenture between Hugh Mitchell and Henry Glen," PANS, RG 47, Reel 438, Book 1, 137; "Estate Papers of Henry Glen," PANS, RG 48, Reel 405.

20   Browne, ed., *Early Records of Londonderry,* 20.

21   Documentation for this challenge is found in various papers concerning the "Writ of Partition for the Township of Truro in the County of Halifax, 1788," PANS, MG 100, Vol. 240.

land'' and one-half of the ''mill stream,'' in addition to their regular grant.[22] Other tradesmen in the fledging community included a tanner, two shoemakers, a gunsmith, a cabinet-maker, a wheelwright, and at least seven weavers.[23]

Truro's initial progress owed much to these tradesmen. The mill, which tradition states used Acadian mill stones, began working and wood products were early exported to the West Indies.[24] Furs and hides were a second exportable forest resource and, although there is no concrete evidence of such a trade, the importation of ''250 pounds of bullet and shot'' from one supplier within a five-year period is suggestive, as is the fact that the community's young tanner, Matthew Archibald, was able to amass sufficient wealth to return to New Hampshire in 1767 to acquire a bride and many household furnishings.[25] While few traces of other tradesmen remain, census figures reveal an interdependent community where no single crop was universally grown.[26] Estate papers confirm the existence of trade between households of the type found in New Hampshire, with a local network of exchange of labour and goods.[27]

A pivotal economic feature of the first decade was the early success of the textile trade. The presence of at least seven weavers lends credence to the theory that the original long-term plan for Truro's economy was to replicate Londonderry's mix of agriculture with the household manufacture of linen. Flax was grown by many community members, spun by women and girls, and woven into cloth by the weavers.[28] The export of over two hundred pounds of linen from the Cobequid in 1767 indicates the early success of the trade, but, unfortunately for the plans of the proprietors, the times were inauspicious for development of a textile industry and in 1769 the Board of Trade ordered that the local manufacture of linen be halted.[29]

---

22 Morrison to Archibald, PANS, RG 47, Reel 438, No. 55.

23 Occupations of Truro's settlers are taken from early wills, deeds and Court records.

24 Miller, *Historical and Genealogical Record,* 19; *Gerrish v McNutt*, PANS, RG 39, Series C, Box 5, 1767. Three saw mills were established in Truro by 1767, suggesting that the lumber industry was deemed to be fairly profitable. ''General Return of Several Townships in Nova Scotia,'' 1 January 1767, PANS, RG 1, Vol. 443, No. 1.

25 *Jessome v Archibald,* PANS, RG 39, Series C, Box 10, 1772; Margaret Fisher, *Janet Archibald,* 8; Miller, *Historical and Genealogical Record,* 19.

26 ''Early census rolls of Nova Scotia,'' PANS, RG 1, Vol. 443, No. 32, 1771 census, Truro Township (hereafter 1771 census); No. 33, 1770 census Truro Township (hereafter 1770 census).

27 For example, ''Estate Papers of Andrew Gamble,'' PANS, RG 48, Reel 438. Patten's *Diary* provides an intriguing glimpse into the daily life of those who emigrated from New Hampshire to Truro.

28 There is no correlation between flax production, as recorded on the 1771 census, and the occupation of weaver. Wallace, ''The Scotch-Irish of Provincial New Hampshire,'' 256, states that the year-round nature of linen production made it particularly attractive to the Scots-Irish. He asserts that spinning was normally done by women. Patten and later Truro practice corroborate this opinion.

29 CO 217/45, docs. 109 and 161; I.F. McKinnon, *Settlements and Churches in Nova Scotia, 1749-1776* (Montreal, 1930), 92.

While many households were involved in several economic activities, to most these were merely supplementary to the main occupation: farming.[30] Following the Londonderry practice of supplying military establishments using nearby rivers as a means of transportation, Truro's settlers used the Shubenacadie River to supply the garrison at Halifax. The presence of a trader in each hamlet, David Archibald in Derry and John Savage in Down, facilitated the exchange of excess farm products for imported goods, such as metal wares, paints and indigo, barrels of rum, and large quantities of clay pipes and tobacco, through the Halifax market.[31] While each trader was the leading proprietor in his hamlet, neither had sufficient business acumen to survive, even in Nova Scotia's rudimentary economy.[32]

Although real economic progress evaded the grasp of Truro's pioneers, social concerns were well looked after. Throughout the Planter period, life in the township revolved, as it had done in New Hampshire, around three interlocking social institutions: family, church, and community.[33] Each of these components was rooted in the Ulster and New England past and each was adapted to suit the changed conditions in Nova Scotia. However, as the community matured in the early 1770s, changing conditions within and increasing influences from outside began to impinge upon the continuity of social institutions transported from New Hampshire. Within the township the large number of adolescents who had emigrated began to move into their twenties and establish new households, potentially upsetting the patriarchal balance of power; the arrival of a minister and several new settlers from Scotland began the slow diminution of Scots-Irish influence; and the sense of communal identity began to weaken. Outside influences included the imposition of central power through the Court of General Sessions of the Peace and the rise in land prices throughout Nova Scotia as a result of a significant increase of settlers from Britain.[34]

Continuation of family grouping of households within the township into the second decade suggests that the mutual support required in a wilderness setting strengthened the extended family.[35] Yet the patriarchal tradition of control over

---

30 1770 and 1771 census figures. Some indication of the progress of farming in the Cobequid is Governor Franklin's confidence in 1768 that those families "will be capable of furnishing many supplies and refreshments to the new settlers of Charlottetown." Franklin to Major-General Gage, CO 217/45, 121.

31 *Jessome v Archibald.*

32 Both Archibald and Savage had great difficulty paying their Halifax debts. See *Jessome v Archibald* and PANS, RG 39, Series C, Box 13, 1774, *John Butler v John Savage.*

33 For the New Hampshire experience see Daniell, *Colonial New Hampshire,* ch. 8, "Social Institutions: Family, Church, and Community in a Changing World," 165-89.

34 Bernard Bailyn, *Voyages to the West: A Passage in the People of America on the Eve of the Revolution* (New York, 1986), 372-73.

35 TTB, 14-18 gives a complete listing of the boundaries of the households of the hamlet of Derry in January 1774.

adult sons had suffered a setback as a result of the terms of the Truro land grant. Fathers could not even depend upon the labour of their single sons. The 1771 census records twenty young, single men living in their own households, eleven of whom were raising stock, and clearing land. An average figure of 9.9 cleared acres for these youngsters compares favourably with the town average of 13.4 acres per household. The signatures of fourteen young, single men on the 1770 contract of the Reverend Daniel Cock suggests that fathers accepted the inevitable, conceding to their sons the freedom they desired.[36]

There is some suggestion that the availability of land also led to a lowering of the age-at-marriage as possession of a working farm contributed to economic independence.[37] Typical of the holdings of young people who had emigrated as adolescents is the farm of William McKean (age 26) who on 3 October 1771 married Ann Archibald (age 20). William, an original grantee, had remained in the family home until 1770, but worked his own land, clearing thirteen of his 500 acres, and producing twenty bushels of wheat, thirty bushels of oats, and two bushels of peas that year. As well he had obtained a horse, a yoke of oxen, three head of cattle, six sheep, and two pigs.[38] Such a start conferred immediate autonomy upon a young couple and provided support for the family which, almost inevitably, started arriving within a year of marriage.

The pattern of natural increase begun in Londonderry continued in Truro, testifying to growing confidence in the community. During the first nine full years of settlement, 1762 to 1770, inclusive, 85 children were born. Included in this figure are the births of 15 children in 50 households during 1763, the second year of settlement. The community continued to be prolific into the 1770s with 105 births recorded from 1771 to 1779, inclusive.[39] As few, if any, births to transients are recorded in the Township Book, this figure reflects the continuing high birth rate of those who had emigrated as teenagers and married during the 1770s.

The deep-seated desire for religious sanction for all family occasions created a demand for a resident minister and a formal church structure; a demand which was finally filled with the appointment of the Reverend Daniel Cock, a Presbyterian minister from Greenock, Scotland. In July of 1770 an ad hoc committee of the town requested that "heads of families," meet to decide if Cock was acceptable as a minister, to agree upon the terms to be offered him, and "To see if they will desire Mr. Cock to appoint a Fast Day for the election of elders in this

---

36   TTB, 42.

37   For those who married between 1760 and 1770 the age-at-marriage is available for only three women and six men. The average is 23.4 for males, well below Greven's 26.8 for first generation Andover. However, given the relatively large number of young males capable of supporting a family in Truro during the 1770s this seems a realistic figure. For the relationship of possession of land to age-at-marriage see Philip J. Greven, *Four Generations: Population, Land and Family in Colonial Andover, Massachuestts* (Ithaca, N.Y., 1970).

38   Miller, *Historical and Genealogical Record*, 314-16; 1771 census; 1770 census.

39   TTB, 128-34.

town so that there may be a session constituted in the Congregation.'' Just how badly the congregation had fared without minister or elders is shown by the next request, ''To consider putting the place of public worship in some repair as barns will soon be inconvenient for the purpose.''[40]

The undifferentiated nature of social institutions enabled the minister to be paid by general assessment, enforced by town officers. The minister's contract, which was recorded as a town document, was signed by 50 men, each of whom accepted full responsibility for his share of the assessment, not knowing what it would be, demonstrating a trust in the system and an identification with the community as a whole.[41] Further evidence of the cohesion of the community's social institutions is seen in the role of the meetinghouse, which was used for both secular and religious meetings and was financed by the town. Money from the sale of small parcels of common land was used to finish the building and to buy ''glass, nails and painters colours.''[42] Town and church were regarded as one, and the assumption was made that residence in one meant membership in the other.

Although this assumption was retained into the next century, the restraints of communal ownership of land began to be felt in the early 1770s when emigration from the British Isles exerted pressure on land prices throughout Nova Scotia. The arrival of farmers and young tradesmen from Lowland Scotland provided both immediate and potential purchasers of land in Truro, generating the desire to divide the remaining common land.[43] Final division of the backlands was very thoroughly discussed in town meetings before it was decided to allow John Savage to make the division and to pay him 12,000 acres immediately adjoining the two hamlets for the service.[44]

A second indication of the changing attitude to land possession in the 1770s is found in the case of the schoolmaster. The original Truro grant had provided a school lot, for the public support of education. There is no record of its use before 1772 when the town appointed Robert McGowan to the position of schoolmaster. Judging by his personal library, McGowan was a well-read, professional teacher, far more learned than any pioneer community had the right to expect.[45] Although he was also a Scots-Irish Presbyterian, he displeased his employers so seriously that they voted in 1773 that ''Mr. McGowan shall have no land in this town.'' But apparently such a decree no longer hindered purchase, for McGowan bought ten acres of land and settled down in Truro where he died in 1779.[46]

---

40 TTB, 41-42.

41 *Ibid.*

42 TTB, 1-7, *passim.*

43 For examples, John Christie, a joiner, who arrived with the Reverend Mr. Cock and later purchased a farm. Miller, *Historical and Genealogical Record,* 243; ''Estate Papers of Henry Glen,'' PANS, RG 48, Reel 405.

44 TTB, 8-9.

45 ''Estate Papers of Robert McGowan,'' PANS, RG 48, Reel 415, Mc 53.

46 He may even have continued his school on a private basis. He is described as ''late School-Master in Truro'' in his estate papers.

Additional evidence of weakening communal bonds is found in the issue of the "common fence," which enclosed the whole interval and marsh from one end of the hamlet of Derry to the other. Formerly each proprietor had been responsible for the upkeep of the fence along his own house lot, but by January 1774 there had been widespread neglect of this commitment and a committee was formed to record the exact location and number of rods that each proprietor was required to maintain. While the community was still sufficiently unified to undertake such a major effort, formal edicts were necessary for what had once been undertaken as a natural part of communal obligations. The incident demonstrated the transitional nature of Truro's social and political institutions during the 1770s when traditional bonds were beginning to weaken and centralized authority had not yet developed.[47]

Halifax first challenged the authority of Truro's institutions through the Court of General Sessions of the Peace in 1770. Judging by the wording of the Township Book, the Court's appointment of town officers by an external body took town leaders by surprise. Although the imposed list was accepted, the theory that central authority could run local government was not, and a compromise was reached in 1772. The notation was made, "Officers chosen by the town and approved at the special sessions of the Court held at Onslow."[48]

Comparison of the 1770 list, "intruded . . . by the sessions" with the 1772 list, chosen by the town, reveals differing perceptions of the role of local government in the life of the community. The administration in Halifax, appropriating policy-making power, distributed town offices between thirteen older men. In contrast, the town preferred to retain its senior people for the influential positions of clerk, moderator, and members of the powerful ad hoc committees which called the meetings and set the agendas. The town's 1772 list, allocating 28 positions among 22 individuals, only one of whom was an older man, implies that town office was viewed as a vehicle for men of lower status to take part in public affairs. It was, doubtless, this democratic attitude which led Lieutenant-Governor Arbuthnot to refer disparagingly to the people of the region as "great levellers."[49] Halifax authorities, following orders from London, preferred the hierarchical Virginian-type of local government.[50]

Even within the town the careful balance of individual, familial and communal concerns, which had been the hallmark of the 1760s, was gradually superseded

47 TTB, 14-18.

48 *Ibid.*, 4.

49 Lieutenant-Governor Mariot Arbuthnot to Lord Germain, 15 August 1776, PANS, RG 1, Vol. 45, doc. 24.

50 D.C. Harvey, "The Struggle for the New England Form of Township Government in Nova Scotia," *Canadian Historical Association Report*, 1933, argues that township government was ended by V Geo III Cap. I, "An Act for the Choice of Town Officers and Regulation of Townships" of 1765. In contrast, the Truro Township Book chronicles a more gradual shift from the New England to the Virginian model of local government.

by centralizing influences. The appointment of church elders chosen from the small pool of available senior men contributed to the concentration of authority. At that time, families which did not have ranking males, for example the Moors, lost influence in the community, while those families with several older men, especially the Archibalds, gained prestige.[51]

While hindsight suggests that the concentration of familial power and the intrusion of centralized authority into local government marked the beginning of the change from New Hampshire proprietary township to Nova Scotian community, which was accelerated by the outcome of the American Revolution, the leisurely pace of such changes probably made them almost imperceptible. Until the beginning of the nineteenth century the homogeneity and shared life-experiences of Truro's people continued to bind them in a consensual society and the availability of land within Truro and nearby townships lessened the disadvantages inherent in such an inward-looking, localistic community.[52]

Truro's unwavering support of the Revolution, its complete rejection of the teachings of the charismatic Reverend Henry Alline, the exclusion of non-Presbyterian Loyalists, the continuation of town meetings under the guise of "Overseers of the Poor," and long term enforcement of universal church assessment indicate the continuing strength of the communal ideal among its people.[53] Following the lesson learned in New Hampshire, that a distant central government could be safely ignored, Truro's resident proprietors adapted the form of township government, which had been developed in the older Londonderry, to the Nova Scotian reality. While centralist institutions remained undeveloped, the extended family, the congregation, and the town formed integral parts of a whole, a community whose strength lay in its cohesiveness. By paying careful attention to the rights of individuals, families and districts within the township, and by using compromise rather than confrontation both internally and in dealings with Halifax, it had been possible to create in early Truro a consensual, harmonious society, a society where "a strong, robust, industrious people," could indeed "live happi[ly] among themselves."

---

51   Members of the Moor connection do not figure as prominently on membership lists of town office, while there is increasing Archibald participation in town affairs. See TTB, 13-52, *passim.*

52   Later development of the town is chronicled in Carol Campbell, "A Prosperous Location: Truro, Nova Scotia, 1770-1838," MA thesis, Dalhousie University, 1988.

53   *Ibid.,* 38-116.

Land, Kinship and Inheritance in Granville Township, 1760-1800

Barry Moody
Department of History
Acadia University

For many of the New England Planters who came to Nova Scotia in the 1760s, the land itself was one of the major attractions. But how did they perceive the land? What uses was it intended to serve? How did it influence family relationships? And what do the answers to these questions reveal about the nature of the Planters? These and a number of related questions led to an examination of the wills and deeds of Granville Township from 1760 to 1800, roughly covering the period of the first generation of Planter immigrants.[1]

Granville Township was laid out on the north bank of the Annapolis River and Basin, and stretched from the Digby (more properly Annapolis) Gut to present-day Paradise. The usable farmland is to be found in a fairly narrow strip between the North Mountain and the river, with the dyked marshes of the former occupants, the Acadians, providing the most fertile land. In 1759, the Township was granted to 138 applicants, most of them from Massachusetts and a few from New Hampshire.[2] The supplementary grant, made nearly two months later, added fifteen names, most of them from old Annapolis Royal families.[3] Confusion and uncertainty followed, with some of the original grantees taking up their lands and others not. The first grant, made to the recipients as tenants in common, was voided and a new grant was made in 1765 to confirm the ownership of those already in possession.[4] This new grant, however, was to individual landholders, rather than to all the proprietors jointly, as the first one had been.

In 1765 the township was laid out in long "house lots" 42 rods (approximately 700 feet) in width, running from the Annapolis River to the Bay of Fundy — roughly 500 acres. To each lot was added fourteen acres of marshland and a long narrow strip, again from shore to shore, called a fish or basin lot, eight rods wide, containing anywhere from 50 to 80 acres, located at the extreme western end of the township. Unlike the situation in nearby Annapolis Township, or in Horton and Cornwallis, the grantee possessed almost all of his land in one lot, rather than having it spread around the township. The development of the township and the

---

1   Granville Township was chosen for this case study because of the availability of the records and the paucity of previous work on this region. Only further research on other townships will enable us to determine whether Granville was typical or atypical of Planter townships in Nova Scotia.

2   W.A. Calnek and A.W. Savary, *History of the County of Annapolis* (Toronto, 1897), 194-97.

3   Calnek and Savary, *History of Annapolis*, 196-97. The members of the Winniett clan figured prominently in this grant.

4   The original grant, dated 30 October 1765, is now in Fort Anne National Historic Park, Annapolis Royal.

distribution of land among successive generations would be greatly influenced by this granting process.

Most of the deeds for the first several years are not to be found in the Office of the Registrar of Deeds. However, much trading of lots must have taken place during the early stages of settlement. Those who received more than one share were able to consolidate their holdings, with Colonel Henry Munro, for example, finally having his three lots in a row, #147, 148, 149, while John Hall and three of his sons grouped themselves on lots #26, 27, 28.[5] Since the grantees had drawn these lots, the settling of members of the same family in one area must have been by design, and the result of trade and purchase.

Even after the initial shifting around, the first settlers were clearly not content to merely clear their lands and farm them. In slightly more than 35 years, there were are over 800 separate transactions dealing with these 150 lots of land.[6] Few adult male residents of the township were able to resist the lure of buying and selling land, and some seem to have been almost obsessed with it. What they sold, and how they sold it, and for what they sold it, reveal a great deal about life in Granville Township in the eighteenth century, and provide one of the best opportunities we have to peer into the lives and minds of these ordinary Planters.

Throughout the first decade and a half after settlement, the proprietors continued to sell and trade entire lots, but new trends can also be observed. It is clear that one of the important functions of this new land, which had cost only an initial fee, was that it provided the means both to set oneself up in farming and to acquire additional land. Lots of land were increasingly mortgaged during this time period, and the money used to buy yet more land, or to purchase stock or perhaps to pay for the building of a house. Merchants in Halifax or Boston, the occasional relative back home in New England, or old families in Annapolis, in addition to more wealthy neighbours, were looked to as sources of funds. Amounts ranged from £25 to several hundred pounds, and most mortgages were expected to be repaid within a year or two, usually at 6 per cent interest. Even when mortgages were long overdue, however, there is little evidence of foreclosure. They were obviously considered good long-term investments, and indeed they were. Most were eventually released, although some more than thirty years after they were due. The mortgages clearly provided an important source of credit and cash in a new community, stimulating the local economy and allowing the proprietors to get on their feet. If there was any fear of the impact of the Stamp Act in Granville Township, it is not reflected in the number of transactions because, as is noted on the deeds, ''no Stampt Paper is to be had.'' The outbreak of hostilities in the colonies in 1775 signalled the abrupt ending of the extensive use of mortgages in Granville, reflecting the growing economic uncertainty in North America.

The land was also used to back a performance bond, as when in 1768 Jonathan

---

5   Public Archives of Nova Scotia, Record Group 20, Series C, Vol. 225, List of Granville Proprietors, n.d. [c1774-5]5.

6   Office of the Registrar of Deeds, Annapolis County, Lawrencetown, Books 1 to 11.

Leonard of Granville, housewright, used house lot 21 as a guarantee that he would deliver "twenty tons of Good English hay at one pound five Shillings pr Ton loose" to Benjamin Shaw at lot 12.[7] In a similar manner, Jacob Troop, "cordwinder," used his lot in the mid-1770s as a surety in the delivery of 400 pairs of men's and women's shoes to merchant Christopher Prince.[8] The £100 promised for the shoes had allowed Troop to buy his lot of land in the first place.

At times, the mortgages and bonds of performance took on a life of their own, circulating like money in a cash-starved community. Holders of mortgages conveyed them to others to cover debts of their own, or to buy property or goods. Occasionally, such transactions became rather complicated. In 1763 Thomas Day of Halifax mortgaged lots #71, 72, 73 and 74 to William Butler and John Bird of Halifax, merchants and partners. All three men died, and the mortgage was sold to Arthur Edie, James Laird and Alexander Anderson, in 1766, who sold it, in turn, to George Henry Monk in 1770. He "for and in Consideration of a Bond from Jonathan Leonard of Granville ... for the Sum of One Hundred and twenty Pounds with a Condition for the delivery of forty eight Tons of Hay" conveyed it to Jonathan Leonard in 1771.[9]

By the early 1770s, the focus of land transactions had shifted. Entire lots still sold on a regular basis, but now more attention was given to the 14-acre marsh lots. Clearly these lots were perceived to be the secret to successful farming in the township — rich land, without the stumps and rocks of the uplands, and within easy access of the river to facilitate the transportation of crops such as hay. Marsh lots were bought, sold and traded on a regular basis and divided and subdivided, until some were so small as to make their value or usefulness questionable. Prices crept up gradually, and before the end of the 1770s a 14-acre lot on the Belleisle Marsh — the largest and apparently most fertile marsh — might well sell for as much as a 500-acre lot of undeveloped upland.[10] The number of lots transferred, and the speed with which they were acquired and then disposed of, often at very little or no profit, makes one wonder if at times this were not as much a spring ritual, an abiding and fascinating activity for the men of the community.

The way in which certain individuals acquired and held on to land during this initial period of settlement indicates that they had other plans for the future. One lot of 500-acres alone was certainly more land than one person could ever expect to utilize during a lifetime. If he were able to bring more than 20 or 30 acres of this land into production, he would be doing very well indeed. Why would anyone need to possess more than the initial grant? Clearly some men were speculating, buying land at the very cheap prices of the 1760s and 1770s and hoping for a rise in price. During this time period, undeveloped 500-acre lots with no build-

7   Registry of Deeds, Book I, 48, Jonathan Leonard to Benjamin Shaw, 20 October 1768.

8   Registry, Vol. I, 181-84, Christopher Prince to Jacob Troop, 17 January 1772; and Jacob Troop to Christopher Prince, 17 January 1772.

9   Registry, Book I, 196-97, George Henry Monk to Jonathan Leonard, 4 March 1772.

10 See Registry of Deeds, Books II-IV, many references.

ings were selling for £20 to £40, often less than a shilling an acre.[11] In the Andover, Massachusetts, described by Philip Greven, by the 1730s land had risen to £14 per acre.[12] Shrewd foretellers of the future could see that while prices might not climb that high in Nova Scotia, they were bound to escalate in the years to come. Land was the safest kind of investment.

No one would have been able to guess just how suddenly the situation would change for townships like Granville after 1776. The American Revolution led to the sudden influx of Loyalists into Nova Scotia, and the rapid escalation of prices for cleared land and housing. In 1771, Isaac Forster Jr. sold lot 58 for £15; twelve years later, in the fall of 1783, Benjamin James "late of New York city" paid £466.13.4.[13] At the same time, Ferdinand Shafner sold Andreas Buhker [Bogart] "late of New York" lot 1 for 300 guineas, a property that he had paid £115 for only three years before.[14] The Rev. Asarelah Morse had made himself a nice little nestegg in November 1783, when he had sold his farm — lot 103 — for which he had paid £30 eleven years before, to Anthony Rhoades "late of New York" for £664.6.8.[15] Even allowing for substantial improvements that might have been made in the properties, and for the general inflation that was part of the period of war, these are still remarkable profits. Other transactions, while not quite as dramatic as these, show a very substantial change in property values in Granville Township as the land-hungry Loyalists arrived.

No man in Granville Township was as avid or shrewd a player in the land-speculation game as was Jonathan Woodberry, described variously in the deeds as doctor, surgeon, physician and gentleman. Born in Haverhill, Massachusetts, in 1737, he came first to Yarmouth before 1763 and then to Granville in 1767. Throughout the 1760s and 1770s he purchased all types of land in Granville and in neighbouring Wilmot Township, where prices were even lower. The good doctor purchased no less than fourteen and one-half full 500 acre lots (7250 acres), assorted separate marsh lots and fifteen basin or fish lots.[16] When the Loyalists arrived he sold most of his land in Granville and moved to Wilmot, where at the age of 74 he settled down with his new wife to sire a second family.[17]

It was Woodberry alone who saw the future value of the fish lots, those neglected strips of land apparently designed to provide the proprietors with convenient

11 Registry of Deeds, Book I, 19, John Easson to Alexander Robertson, 17 September 1764; 23, John Sinclair to Henry Munro, 21 June 1763; 24, Moses Banks to Henry Munro, 9 October 1765; 81, John Harris and John Davis to Samuel Harris, 7 November 1769.

12 Philip Greven, *Four Generations: Population, Land, and Family in Colonial Andover, Massachusetts* (Ithaca, NY, 1970), 129.

13 Registry of Deeds, Book I, 147-148, Isaac Forster Jr. to Thomas Treche, 12 April 1771; Book IV, 460-462, Peleg Little to Benjamin James, 24 September 1783.

14 Registry of Deeds, Book 4, 318-319, Christopher Prince to Ferdinand Shafner, 16 August 1780; Book 4, 506-508, Ferdinand Shafner to Andreas Buhker, 17 September 1783.

15 Registry of Deeds, Book I, 238-39, John Morrison Jr. to Asarelah Morse, 4 January 1772; Book V, 9-11, Azarelah Morse to Anthony Rhoades, 21 November 1783.

16 Most of Dr. Woodberry's transactions are to be found in Registry of Deeds, Books I, II & III.

17 Calnek and Savary, *History of Annapolis*, 637-38.

bases for the fisheries, using either the Annapolis Basin or the Bay of Fundy shores. Being fairly narrow — only 8 rods, or 132 feet wide — but ranging below 51 and 80 acres and possessed of no fertile marsh land, they were largely ignored during the first two decades of settlement. Woodberry was able to buy many of them for about two dollars apiece.[18] With the influx of the Loyalists, land of almost any type was saleable, and the long-despised fish lots took on added value. Throughout the 1780s, they sold for between £6 and £10 each, as Loyalists such as Cornelius and Tunis Bogart, and Ludwig Croscup bought three or four of them in a row and called it a farm. Woodberry and others who had held onto their original fish lots profited handsomely.

The land played another important, though perhaps less direct, role in the lives of the settlers. It was the land itself, and the nature of its distribution, that brought the New Englanders into intimate contact with people of different backgrounds and values. The government of Nova Scotia had indeed granted to the proprietors certain rights over the land and its distribution. But it was also that government, mostly Haligonians, which decided whose name should appear on that list of proprietors. Certainly most of them were New Englanders, but not all. There was a healthy sprinkling of government officials and friends, the military, and older residents of the colony. From the beginning, then, Granville Township would depart from the New England model. Outsiders and strangers, those people rural New Englanders had so long sought to exclude from their communities, would immediately be in the midst of those same transplanted New Englanders. In addition, as Jonathan Belcher whittled away at the power of the townships, they lost any control they may have had over the composition of the population of their community. There was no means by which they could prevent "strangers" from purchasing land and settling in their midst.

Shaws, Wades, Fosters and Troops, from Barnstable, Ipswich and Lunenburg, Massachusetts, found themselves settled next to Shafners, Balsors and Worsters from the Germanic states, McBrides, Rays and Milberrys from Ireland, and McKenzies and McGregors from Scotland. Twenty years later, Ruggles, Bogarts, Boehakers and de St Croixs from the eastern seaboard of the new United States flooded into the township, as the Loyalist tide surged into Nova Scotia. The intermingling of all of these people, and more, with the New England majority is clearly evidenced first in the land papers, and then in the marriage records of the township. From the very beginning, then, the Planters would inhabit a very different community from the ones they left behind them in New England. There the closed, corporate community was already in the process of breaking down; in Nova Scotia it shattered completely. Even if they had wanted to, they could not have duplicated in this colony the form of society which had characterized New England for its first one hundred years. Those who wished to see such a

---

18   See for example Registry of Deeds, Book II, 38, Israel Longley to Jonathan Woodberry, 29 October 1773; 39, Ezekiel Foster to Jonathan Woodberry, 29 October 1773; 40, Jeremiah Foster to Jonathan Woodberry, 29 October 1773.

societal form perpetuated would have to look elsewhere than Nova Scotia.

The land, and more specifically the amount of land available, also made a profound impact on family relationships and inheritance. Each proprietor of the township was granted 500 acres and, as has been seen, the cost of purchasing additional land remained very low for the first twenty years. Such amounts stand in sharp contrast to the property that the average inhabitant of many of the old, established New England towns could hope to own by the mid-eighteenth century.[19] These comparatively large tracts of land could be used for speculation, or security for loans, or in business transactions, but they also held out the important possibilities of being used to root families, through many generations, firmly in the soil of the township. The way in which fathers provided for sons, daughters and wives also reveals a great deal about the nature of the community that was being built on the banks of the Annapolis River.

Given the amount of land at his command, the costs of acquiring more, and the acreage needed to support a single nuclear family, the average first generation head of family in Granville Township held in his possession the wherewithal to determine the future of his sons, grandsons and possibly great-grandsons. Phillip Greven, in his study of Andover, Massachusetts, in the seventeenth and eighteenth centuries argues that when land was fairly plentiful, the first and second generation fathers used their ability to divide their estates among all of their heirs as a means of extending their control over their sons and strengthening the patriarchal form of family.[20] Most fathers held onto their lands until death, passing them on only in the form of inheritances. As the amount of land in any one branch of a family dwindled over the generations, the ability to promise land to all faded, and with it the power to control the next generation.

With the move to Nova Scotia, New England fathers once again possessed the means to reestablish that patriarchal power of which lack of land had deprived them. Five hundred acres was more than sufficient to provide a livelihood for a number of sons, and possibly even some sons-in-law. The generational cycle of patriarchal control could begin once again. If, however, New Englanders brought such an ideal with them to Nova Scotia, there is little evidence of it to be found in the deeds and wills of Granville Township. Many fathers of the first generation did what they could to establish their sons in their independence long before the time of their own deaths, but frequently this was done with few if any strings attached. Underlying all transactions seems to have been the desire for the orderly passing of the means of survival from parent to child, the desire to assist the child's start in life as much as possible, and the overriding fear of an old age devoid of both family support and sufficient material provision. There was little evidence of a general desire to extend control over the lives of the next generation, to build the patriarchal society that the amount of land made possible.

A number of vehicles were used for conveying property from one generation

---

19 Greven, *Four Generations*, 224.
20 Greven, *Four Generations*, 70-83.

to another; some individuals used all of these at various stages of their lives, while others used none at all. Some fathers chose simply to give to sons at a fairly young age the land necessary for their own advancement in life. For instance, in 1769 Amos Farnsworth deeded an entire 500 acre lot to his eldest surviving son Jonas.[21] The father was then 64, the son only 20. Jonas was unmarried, and the possession of a farm lot did not seem to hasten his marriage. He would wait for another five years before establishing his own family.[22] Likewise Moses Shaw gave his son Isaiah 100 acres of land on his 22nd birthday, in 1785.[23] Farnsworth was a Planter from Groton, Massachusetts, while Shaw was a Loyalist from New York, both now of Granville.

Other fathers preferred to sell to their sons at a minimal sum rather than to give it to them outright. Samuel Bent in 1793 conveyed 120 acres of lot 73 to his son Samuel Jr. for £20,[24] while in 1789 John Chute Sr. sold his son Benjamin a valuable marsh lot for the same low price.[25] Joseph Potter of Clements summed up well the reasons for such action in his deed of conveyance whereby he sold his son Israel an entire 500 acre lot in Granville in 1792. Aside from the £15 which changed hands, Joseph was doing this "for the Nattrual love and Affection" he bore his son and "for the Better Maintenance of him the said Israel Potter."[26]

Yet others transferred property between the generations for what would appear to be market value prices, if the records are to be believed. George Worster sold lot 28 to his two sons George Jr. and Jacob for £200 in 1783,[27] while William Longley handed his grant, lot 59, to his son for £30 in 1773.[28] As there is no record of any of the second generation mortgaging their properties in order to acquire them, it is probable that fathers frequently financed these purchases, if indeed the sons ever paid the full price listed.

Some parents chose to attach conditions to the conveyance, not so much, it would appear, to attempt to control the receiver as the gift. Fathers, it seemed, waited to be very certain that they had enough worldly possessions to last for the years during which they could not be productive farmers. Giving one's property away too hastily, even to one's children, might easily be bitterly regretted in old age or sickness. In 1778 Nathaniel Barns conveyed his farm lot 118, all stock and farming utensils, to his son Nathaniel, to take effect only after his own death and that of his wife.[29] John and Sarah White, in selling 100 acres to their son

21 Registry of Deeds, Book I, 126-27, Amos Farnsworth to Jones Farnsworth, 1 March 1769.

22 Calnek and Savary, *History of Annapolis*, 507-508.

23 Registry of Deeds, Book, V, 422, Moses Shaw to Isaiah Shaw, 11 October 1785; Calnek and Savary, *History of Annapolis*, 600.

24 Registry of Deeds, Book IX, 32-33, Samuel Bent to Samuel Bent Jr., 1 January 1793.

25 Registry of Deeds, Book IX, 34-35, John Chute Sr. to Benjamin Chute, 26 December 1789.

26 Registry of Deeds, Book X, n.p., at end of book, Joseph Potter to Israel Potter, 23 May 1792.

27 Registry of Deeds, Book IV, 365-67, George Worster to George Worster Jr. and Jacob Worster, 22 May 1783.

28 Registry of Deeds, Book IV, 397-91, William Longley to Israel Longley, 20 October 1773.

29 Registry of Deeds, Book IV, 364-65, Nathaniel Barns to Nathaniel Barns, 23 November 1778.

Timothy, specified that he was "not to sell the land to any stranger but may sell it [to] any of his family."[30] 27 Given that the Whites Sr. were transferring a portion of their own lot, and that whoever possessed it would live in intimate connection with them, passing and repassing over each other's lands, perhaps sharing common springs or brooks, such a condition made perfect sense. It was, however, an attempt to be generous and fair to a son while at the same time not placing the rest of the family in jeopardy — to control the land, but not necessarily the son.

As common as these varied means of conveyance were, it is clear from the records that less formal, extra-legal, means were also an important part of the picture. It was not a legal requirement for land transactions to be registered, although it is clear that it was common practice to do so. Legally binding arrangements were undoubtedly entered into between parents and children, but the record of these is now lost, or remains in the hands of descendants. For others it was probably merely an unwritten, and perhaps even unspoken, arrangement, acknowledged by all. In 1784, James Delap Sr. and Jr. sold the fish lot belonging to their home property. James Sr. had inherited the lot on the death of his son Thomas, in 1771.[31] However, there is no conveyance to joint ownership with James Jr. Neither is there a will or any other estate papers for James Sr. on his death in 1787. His only surviving son James merely "inherited" in a less formal, but equally effective, way. The property remained in the Delap family until the 1960s. A glimpse into this largely unrecorded world is given in a 1793 deed, whereby Jabez Snow conveyed two acres of marsh to Andrew Boaker. The history of this little piece of land is recorded there, for Jabez had given it to his son Josiah, who had in turn given it to his brother William. No legal documents were signed. Now, on Andrew Boaker paying to William £5.10, Jabez provided a deed recognizing the transaction. As long as property remained in a family, however, and there were no quarrels over possession, such documents would be unnecessary. How much of this informal trading went on is impossible to determine now, but it is clear that, in this way or some other, much property in the township never went through the formal process of registered deeds or recorded probate. On these grounds, then, and several others, the use of probate records as the basis for determining wealth in Granville Township is a rather questionable practice.

The options for eighteenth-century Granville parents were many, and some families availed themselves of several of them, as a means of securing the future, both for themselves and for the next generation. An examination of two Granville Planter families highlights some of the problems and attempted solutions. The ends sought were security and stability for the parents and material assistance for the children. The means varied from child to child, rather than from family

---

30 Registry of Deeds, Book VII, 71-72, John and Sarah White to Timothy White, 3 May 1787.
31 Registry of Deeds, Book V, 45-46, James Delap Sr. and James Delap Jr. to George Cornwell, 16 March 1784. Registry of Probate Office, Annapolis Royal, inventory of estate of Thomas Delap, 1771. Calnek and Savary, *History of Annapolis*, 499-500.

to family, and changed over time as well, as circumstances altered.

Josiah Dodge was born in Massachusetts in 1718, had fought at Louisbourg in 1758 and had helped lay out the township in 1759. He married three times, but his seven children were by his first wife.[32] He acquired by grant and purchase considerable property, but began to disperse it to his children fairly early in his life. His first son, Josiah Jr., was old enough to get a grant in his own right, probably with his father's assistance. In 1762 the father gave to his son an additional piece of land on which to build a house.[33] In 1773 he conveyed at no charge two full lots to his second son Asahel, born in 1751 and married in 1773. According to the deed, this was done "in order that my said Son may Inherit a part of my Estate."[34] The pitfalls of such generosity were made obvious the next year when Asahel sold one of the lots for $100.00, and thus the land — the means of survival and advancement — passed out of the control of the family.[35] That he was concerned about not only his sons was also made clear the same year when he signed over 120 acres to Israel Fellows, for the affection he bears his daughter Susanne Fellows, and £7. Susanna Dodge had married Israel Fellows, and they had obviously been living on this particular piece of land for some time, perhaps since their marriage.[36] The next year, Josiah provided for another daughter, Sarah, when he sold land, house and barn to his son-in-law Jonathan Leonard.[37] What Josiah thought when his son-in-law immediately mortgaged the property and lost it the following year is not recorded.[38] Then it was son Benjamin's turn, and here Josiah was somewhat more cautious. Although allowing him to build a house on the property, probably at his marriage in 1776, Josiah waited until 1789 to make Benjamin a "deed of gift" for 600 acres, the homestead, and even this carefully circumscribed bequest was not to take effect until after the father's death.[39] In his will, Josiah made minor provisions for two other daughters, who were to receive £15 each.

Like many of his contemporaries, John Hall, from Medford, Massachusetts, attempted to do what he could for his children during his lifetime, keeping in mind his own future requirements as well. Hall's children were somewhat younger than Dodge's but somehow he was able to acquire a separate grant for John Jr., only 18 in 1765, and half grants for Henry and Moses, 16 and 15 respectively[40] As

32 Calnek and Savary, *History of Annapolis*, 501-502; A.W. Savary, *History of the County of Annapolis, Supplement* (Belleville, Ont., 1973), 68.

33 Registry of Deeds, Book I, 34, Josiah Dodge Jr. to Josiah Dodge Sr., 10 June 1762.

34 Registry of Deeds, Book II, 80-81, Josiah Dodge to Asahel Dodge, 25 September 1773.

35 Registry of Deeds, Book II, 81-82, Asahel Dodge to Peleg Smith, 23 July 1774.

36 Registry of Deeds, Book II, 82-83, Josiah Dodge to Israel Fellows, 10 December 1773.

37 Registry of Deeds, Book III, 18, Josiah Dodge to Jonathan Leonard, 2 April 1774.

38 Registry of Deeds, Book III, 27-28, Jonathan Leonard to Robert Fletcher, 13 January 1775.

39 Registry of Deeds, Book VIII, 240, Josiah Dodge to Benjamin Dodge, 16 October 1789; Registry of Probate, will, Josiah Dodge, 1805; Savary, *Supplement*, 68.

40 Fort Ann National Historic Park, Annapolis Royal, Original grant, Granville Township, 30 October 1765; Calnek and Savary, *History of Annapolis*, 518.

Hall made clear in his will many years later, he had paid all charges for these grants and arranged for them to appear in his sons' names. This Hall considered to be "thare full Share," and no other provision was made for them in his will.[41] However, he apparently helped them in other ways. In 1774 John Jr. sold his father part of his lot for £25, probably to raise some much needed cash, having married only the year before.[42] Twelve years later, after the tremendous rise in land prices due to the influx of the Loyalists, the father sold it back to John Jr. for the same price.[43] Sons Aaron and Samuel received land in their father's will,[44] while the two daughters received a cow and a calf each. In addition, Hall probably assisted his daughter Elizabeth in several ways. About 1783, Hall married as his second wife Mary Harris, widow of John Harris of Annapolis. In that same year Hall's daughter Elizabeth married Mary's son Henry.[45] The new Mrs. Hall possessed considerable property in her own right — how is not exactly clear. As was now his right, John Hall and Mary sold some of this land to her son in 1787, possibly for money borrowed from Hall himself.[46] On the death of his second wife, John Hall, now 67, sold half of his home lot and half of the house, barn and "Syder house" to his son James, aged 23. But John married a third time, about 1790, and drawing up his will in 1791 left all of his furniture, farm implements and cattle to his son James, as well as care of the widow. Shortly before his death, and after drawing up his will, evidently needing money to deal with some of his debts, Hall sold the remaining half of his home lot, house and barn to his son Moses, of Boston.[47] These sales and gifts had depleted the estate that was to have been left to James. Most of the household effects and livestock had to be sold to pay the debts of the estate, and James, as administrator, had to pay £25 to the creditors merely to keep the property he had bought a few years before.[48] His brother Moses eventually sold James the other half of the house and lot.[49] But it was a hard way to come into one's inheritance.

In neither of these cases did events turn out exactly as the proprietor had intended. Estates dwindle, children and spouses die, children do not always use their inheritance as one would wish. However, these two examples indicate just how complex was the issue of orderly succession to property for the Granville Planters. Fathers strove to assist, to provide equally and fairly for their children,

41 Registry of Probate, will of John Hall, 1792.
42 Registry of Deeds, Book IV, 263-64, John Hall Jr. and Elizabeth Hall to John Hall, 3 December 1774.
43 Registry of Deeds, Book V, 464-65, John Hall to John Hall Jr., 12 June 1786.
44 Registry of Probate, will of John Hall, 1792.
45 Calnek/Savary, 518, 521-22; Registry of Probate, will of John Harris, 1772.
46 Registry of Deeds, Book VI, 171-72, John and Mary Hall to Henry Harris, 21 March 1787; Registry of Probate, will of John Hall, 1792, mention of money still owing from Henry Harris.
47 Registry of Deeds, Book VIII, 564-65, John Hall to Moses Hall, 13 July 1792.
48 Registry of Probate, will, inventory and list of items sold, estate of John Hall, 1792; Registry of Deeds, Book X, 109-10, James Hall to creditors, 15 October 1795.
49 Registry of Deeds, Book X, 53-54, Moses Hall to James Hall, 11 May 1796.

while at the same time protecting their own futures. There is little evidence here of attempts to control or manipulate the children, to play the patriarch.

Many fathers were cautious in dispersing their lands, but with good reason. Life was uncertain, and once the land was out of one's control, anything could happen. Unlike his contemporaries Hall and Dodge, John Chute waited until his death in 1791 to pass on his property to his sons, and this was probably just as well.[50] In 1786, his eldest son Samuel was drowned while crossing the Annapolis River, leaving a wife and nine children, the youngest 10 months old.[51] Samuel having died intestate, his widow was appointed administrator of the estate, a decision that immediately led to problems. Little more than a year after the death, the widow petitioned the Judge of Probate:

> That your Petitioner with a View of bettering her Situation lately married Dr. James Lynam, & as the Affairs of the Estate were in a very confused Train found herself necessiated to Empower her present Husband, to Act, & Settle the Accts of Said Est. in her Stead, But by the late Visible & Glaring Acts of Mismanagement & Squandering, Committed by the said Dr. Lynam, She has the Strongest Reason to fear her large Family's being soon reduced to poverty & want, Unless proper methods, are speedily taken to prevent the Consequences of his Irregularities.

She therefore petitioned that new trustees and guardians be appointed, to remove control from her hands and those of her husband. Those who wrote supporting the intent of the petition added the very practical consideration that "the large family within Mentioned, will Shortly become a parish Charge, unless timely & Effectual Methods are taken to prevent the Ruin of said Estate." The messy affair dragged on for sixteen years before the estate was finally settled.[52] If John Chute had given his son Samuel a share of the family estate prior to his death, it would have been swallowed up in the tragedy of that family's disintegration and passed out of the control of the family.

One area where parental control might have created tensions and caused problems was the role of the widow. Scholars have tended to look with either amusement or disgust at the apparently unfair and demeaning provisions made by husbands for their wives: "And to my wife I leave my best feather bed, her wearing apperal and the use of the west front room." We have, I think, not looked carefully enough at how such provisions actually worked themselves out in practical terms, and the role that the widow played in the evolving structure of the family. It is certainly a far more complex, and important, role than a superficial analysis might indicate.

Some husbands attempted to provide for both their own old age and that of their

---

50   Registry of Probate, will, John Chute, 1791.

51   Calnek and Savary, *History of Annapolis*, 491-9.

52   Registry of Probate, estate papers, Samuel Chute, 1786.

wives by attaching conditions to deeds of gift or sale to their children, or by other binding legal arrangements. In a formal bond, signed in 1784, James McGregor agreed to "obligate & bind myself heirs or Executors to take Care or Charge of my Father Thomas McGregor & Rosannah his wife, & do further oblige muyself heirs or Executors, that they shall be Decently provided with every Necessary that shall be Wanting for the Support of them."[53] George Worster Jr. bound himself for £130 to keep his parents "in a Genteel manner" during their lifetimes.[54] In such ways were sons constrained and restricted, often long after the death of the father, in exchange for property or other material assistance from their parents.

Almost without exception, the wills of Granville Township also provided a fair degree of power and security for the widows. Some husbands preferred to leave all of the property to the wife for life, as did Valentine Troop in August 1776, for his "well-beloved wife Cattee."[55] John Wade made a similar provision for his wife Hannah, leaving her all the household furniture absolutely, and the use of the entire real estate for as long as she remained his widow. Even after her remarriage she would be entitled to the use of one third of the real estate for life.[56]

Others provided that the widow should have a "living" from the property rather than control of it. This provision nonetheless provided her some control, as the property was now bound for her lifetime. Some husbands attempted to be even more specific. Sons were to receive their inheritance only if certain goods and services were provided for the widow. David Bent left his "beloved wife Mary Bent" two cows, his household furniture and one room in the house, and ordered that two of his sons were to "Provide for her meat, drink, clothing and all things needful for her both in sickness and in health."[57] Josiah Dodge provided that his wife Susannah should have the use and "improvement" of the dwelling house and part of the land, two good cows, use of the furniture, and be supplied with firewood, and four bushels of good wheat meal and two of rye meal yearly. When he added a codicil to his will fourteen years later, Susannah had already died, and he had remarried, so he ordered his son to provide in the same manner for his stepmother.[58] Although John Hall died insolvent, and his son James actually had to pay creditors himself, James was nonetheless required by the terms of his father's will to care for his father's wife, whom he had married only two years before, for her lifetime.[59]

Aside from the provisions of wills, which might bind sons for decades, the law clearly recognized the dower rights of wives, and these certainly extended to the lands of deceased husbands. When Abijah Parker died intestate in 1780, the Court

53 Registry of Deeds, Book V, 106, bond of James McGregor, 8 April 1784.
54 Registry of Deeds, 43-44, Bond of George Worster Jr., 12 February 1793.
55 Registry of Probate, will of Valentine Troop, 1776.
56 Registry of Probate, will of John Wade, 1813.
57 Registry of Probate, will of David Bent, 1796.
58 Registry of Probate, will of Josiah Dodge, 1805.
59 Registry of Probate, will of John Hall, 1792.

of Probate recognized Miriam Parker's dower rights in the estate. More than twenty years later the estate still had not been divided, and the children were thus prevented from coming into their shares of the inheritance.[60] A widow could voluntarily relinquish her dower rights, as did Sarah Munro, wife of one of the wealthiest men in Granville Township who died in 1780. This, however, was done only to protect her children's interest in the estate. In 1783 she had remarried and, as she later testified, her second husband had turned out to be "a Very profligate & Abandoned Character," preventing her from carrying out her obligations as administrator of her first husband's estate. Even then, it took 23 years from the time of their father's death before Henry Munro's children actually came into legal possession of his property.[61] That the widow held real potential power over the estate is made clear by examining some of the land transactions. When Richard Clark died in 1783 he left, by will, his wife Elizabeth one third of the home lot in Granville, and the obligation of the two sons Robert and Richard to provide a comfortable room in which to live and sufficient food and material possessions for her well-being. Her sons were to receive the rest of the estate. Eight years later her signature was still necessary for one of the sons to sell a small marsh lot.[62] Fifteen years after her widowhood and remarriage, Jane Sproul affixed her signature to a deed allowing a son by her first marriage to sell a piece of his father's property.[63] A widow, on occasion even after her remarriage, possessed the legal right to continue to control her former husband's property, in her own best interests, although not necessarily those of her sons. And since the widow's options were fewer — that is, she could not buy, sell or trade the property — she had less room to manoeuvre, and could make fewer concessions. The property could be frozen in a way that the husband, with more options, would not have tolerated.[64]

The resulting stress and strain on a family could be very real indeed. To be so close to full ownership, and yet so far away! When John Parsons died in 1778, he divided his property equally between his three sons, providing for a life income for his widow "Elliner." But to even post the bond necessary for the carrying out of the terms of the will, son James had to mortgage his inheritance. In the mortgage, the terms of the will concerning Eleanor were specifically mentioned as occasioning this act. Five years later the executor of the estate resigned in disgust, citing the actions of Eleanor and her son as the cause. He had found it necessary to replace one entire window in Eleanor's room "which said Ellenor and her Son broke to pieces by Sending Brick Batts or Stone at Each other." The docu-

---

60 Registry of Probate, estate papers of Abijah Parker, 1801.

61 Registry of Probate, estate papers of Henry Munro, 1780.

62 Registry of Probate, will of Richard Clark, 1783; Registry of Deeds, Book VIII, 424-25, Richard Clark to Joseph Cossins, 24 May 1791.

63 Registry of Deeds, Book X, 35-37, Matthew Roach to James Thorne, 22 March 1796.

64 For a discussion of widows' rights in South Carolina at a comparable time, see John E. Crowley, "Family Relations and Inheritance in Early South Carolina," *Histoire Sociale*, XVII, 33 (May 1984), 35-57.

ments are unfortunately silent about how long Eleanor and her sons thus lived happily together, but they virtually had no choice in the matter.[65]

Some widows were more clever in their approach to the entire matter of inheritance, especially if their positions were more tenuous by being stepmothers of the children who sought to inherit. When Thomas Walker died in 1773, he left his wife Ann with at least four children by his previous marriage, the youngest being only ten. The widow was appointed administrator of the estate, and maintained it and apparently raised the children. In 1784, when the youngest had reached the age of majority, the widow Walker purchased the claims to the estate of the three daughters for £60 each and then turned the estate over to the only surviving son Andrew, now 27 years old. However, in exchange for surrendering her dower rights, Ann Walker wrote into the deed that all household furniture was reserved to her alone and that she was to have "the use of the west room in the Mansion with Sufficient fuel & the use of two cows." Further, Andrew was not to sell any of the home property without his stepmother's consent.[66] The widow Walker effectively secured her future, or at least brought some security to it; it would be Andrew Walker who would have to live with the restrictions.

The information concerning land and inheritance indicate that the Planters in Granville Township showed little inclination to turn the clock back to a time when the father could use his control of the land to dominate the lives of his children. Nor is there any evidence to indicate that the traditional New England dislike of "strangers" was able to survive the short sea voyage to Nova Scotia. There would appear as well to be very little to differentiate these settlers of New England origin from their British, German or Loyalist neighbours when it came to matters of land use and inheritance. Whatever else the move to Nova Scotia might entail, there is little to indicate that it was seen by the Planters of Granville as a means to retreating to the old ways, or preserving traditional New England values and forms. If any sought such a haven, they were perhaps among those who quickly left the colony in the years immediately following the migration.[67]

What is revealed in Granville is that families were bound together in a complex and varied set of relationships — economic, familial and emotional. And these relationships, interwoven into the fabric of the community, had a profound impact on the daily lives of those concerned, more important perhaps than the "larger

---

65   Registry of Deeds, Book VIII, 57-58, James Parsons mortgages to William Clark as security for bond posted by Clark, 15 April 1788; Registry of Probate, will and estate papers of John Parsons, 1778.

66   Registry of Probate, estate papers of Robert Walker, 1773; Registry of Deeds, Book V, 208-15, James Delap and Sarah to Ann Walker, 24 February 1783; Peleg Little and Margaret to Ann Walker, 4 September 1784; Jane James to Ann Walker, 4 September 1784; Ann Walker to Andrew Walker, 4 September 1784; Calnek and Savary, *History of Annapolis*, 622.

67   Much more work will be needed in this area before we can confidently fit the Planters into the evolving picture of the American frontier of the eighteenth century. See Gregory H. Nobles, "Breaking into the Backcountry: New Approaches to the Early American Frontier, 1750-1800," *William and Mary Quarterly*, 3rd ser., XLVI, 4 (October 1989), 641-70.

issues'' of revolution and politics, and perhaps even religious revival. And at the centre of these relationships was often to be found the land. Until we have a more thorough knowledge of property, how it was controlled, by whom, in what ways, how it was transmitted from generation to generation, how it shaped, and sometimes destroyed community, we will still be a long distance away from a real understanding of the Planters.

The Material Lives of the Yeoman Planters of Kings County, Nova Scotia: A Preliminary Survey Based on Probate Inventories, 1761-1797

Richard Henning Field
Director, Dartmouth Heritage Museum

In March of 1775, George Mumford and Woodward Sanford went to the home of their neighbour, Widow Card, to inventory the worldly possessions of the late Richard Card of Newport, Kings County (now Hants County), Nova Scotia. To satisfy demands of creditors, and to protect the inheritance of Richard Card's ten children, an accurate account of the deceased's personal estate including livestock, household furnishings and tools was required. Mumford and Sanford probably went about their task with heavy hearts as they reflected on the life of their friend and neighbour. Both Card and Mumford hailed from Kingston, Rhode Island, and Sanford came from Newport in the same colony. In his will, Richard Card refers to himself as yeoman.[1] Born on 11 January 1717, he was the son of Joseph and Hope Card of Kingston, Rhode Island. Married twice, he died on 12 March 1775, and was outlived by his second wife Hannah who died some twenty years later.[2] The inventory of Card's estate compiled by Mumford and Sanford was submitted to the court and duly recorded on 12 April 1775.

As court-appointed inventory-takers, Mumford and Sanford were organized and meticulous in their duty. Beginning in the farmyard, they moved to the house and recorded Card's possessions in some detail, listing them room by room. Card's livestock included two oxen valued at twelve pound and ten shilling, and two cows valued at eight pounds. Other livestock listed were a horse, several sheep and geese. The high evaluation of the oxen is in keeping with estate values placed on teams of oxen in the late eighteenth century for other counties in Nova Scotia, including Lunenburg[3] and Kings County.

Completing their task in the farmyard, Mumford and Sanford moved into the house and began listing domestic furnishings. The Card inventory is one of the earliest Planter documents found to date which gives a room-by-room record of furniture and accessories. The Card house consisted of three rooms identified as the "Westerly Room," the "Easterly Room" and the "Chamber." This nomenclature describes a simple structure with hall/parlour configuration flanking a central chimney on the first floor, and a sleeping chamber on the upper half storey probably reached by a ladder or narrow set of stairs. Such a simple hall/parlour

---

1   Public Archives of Nova Scotia (PANS), Hants County, Loose Petitions, Estate Papers, Wills, 1761-1797, RG 48, Reel 561. Kings County papers are filed under Hants County.

2   Esther Clark Wright, *Planters and Pioneers* (Hantsport, 1982), 74.

3   For information on Lunenburg County see Richard Henning Field, "The Material Lives of Lunenburg German Merchants and Yeomen: The Evidence Based on Probate Inventories, 1760-1830," PhD thesis, Dalhousie University, 1990, 164-66.

room plan raises some interesting questions about Planter houses. The fact that Mumford and Sanford were so specific in identifying the sleeping "Chamber," but only named the other rooms according to their compass bearing, suggests that the functions of the "Westerly" and "Easterly" rooms were less specific and actually used for multi-functional family activities, assumptions supported by the objects listed in these rooms by Mumford and Sanford.

The house occupied by Richard Card and his family was typical of his Planter yeoman neighbours at the time of the inventory in 1775 based on an examination of 91 yeoman inventories for Kings County between the years 1761 and 1797 for individuals who migrated from Rhode Island or Connecticut. Examination of these 91 inventories suggests that most eighteenth-century Planter yeomen who left New England to settle in Kings County and other Planter townships lived in simple domestic settings with multi-functional room plans, and in actuality were reproducing earlier settlement patterns, house types and proxemic relationships found in the New England colonies of Rhode Island and Connecticut from which many of the Planters originated. Indeed, the hall/parlour house configuration was being replaced by more elaborate structures with increased space and specialized room function in both Rhode Island and Connecticut as early as 1725-30. In the early decades of the eighteenth century in New England "the old forms of construction were abandoned, or rather were transformed, and the pre-revolutionary style began; a style more easily recognized as 'Colonial,' and closely akin to that of the great houses which from 1750 to the end of the century gave its peculiar architectural character to the Atlantic seaboard."[4] Yet, the Planter settlers built simpler hall/parlour plan houses, suggesting that the same cycle of house development found in Rhode Island and Connecticut was repeating itself in late eighteenth-century Nova Scotia. Although further research must be conducted, preliminary investigations suggests that Planter Nova Scotia witnessed a compressed replay of much of the history of New England building. However, it must be kept in mind that the simple hall/parlour house remained a common rural form in New England into the 1840s. Daniel Norris at the 1987 Planter Conference hinted at this process when he speculated that the Stephen Loomer house in Canning, Kings County, developed into its present one-and-one-half storey gambrel-roofed New England/Dutch Colonial style from an original hall/parlour plan.[5]

By acknowledging this cycle of house development it becomes possible to clarify unexamined assumptions of earlier work on Planter architecture, and to establish a chronological study of the evolution of Planter house styles. For

---

4   Norman Morrison Isham and Albert F. Brown, "Early Rhode Island Houses," in Dell Upton and John M. Vlach, eds., *Common Places: Readings in American Vernacular Architecture* (Athens, 1986), 150.

5   Daniel Norris, "An Examination of the Stephen Loomer House, Habitant, Kings County, Nova Scotia," in Margaret Conrad, ed., *They Planted Well: New England Planters in Maritime Canada,* (Fredericton, 1988), 245-46.

example, the construction of the Calkin house near Grand Pré, Kings County, a structure which was personally examined before being relocated, contains what has previously been described as an ''Acadian cellar,'' a romantic notion based more on speculation and wishful thinking than fact. It is obvious that this earlier portion was part of the original structure of this house based on a simple two-room configuration which, like the Loomer house, was transformed at a later date into its present Dutch Colonial style.[6]

The Planter architectural landscape and the Planter domestic setting require closer examination, an exercise which might lead to a better understanding of the Planter ''mentality'' — their ideas, attitudes, assumptions and solutions — in the face of their new life after migration to Nova Scotia. Certainly, attitudes about the Planter cultural landscape must be reexamined and revised, particularly in light of the fact that recently there has been a tendency to draw conclusions about Planter life based on such elite architecture as the Loomer and Calkin houses as they exist in their present style. This is highly misleading and inaccurate as it disregards the ''hidden'' and simpler room plans from which such houses developed.

Recent studies by Michael Steinitz on housing in eighteenth-century Massachusetts is leading to a total reevaluation of architecture in that state, which according to Steinitz was a landscape ''characterized by much smaller and meaner dwellings than has been assumed up to this point.''[7] In other words, the Massachusetts landscape did not consist entirely of ''elite'' colonial house styles, but was composed of many smaller structures which simply did not survive the last two centuries, or were not sturdy or adaptable enough to be incorporated into later more elaborate houses. It is perhaps time to consider the Planter landscape in this context, and interpret structures such as Loomer and Calkin as endpoints in the chronological development of Planter houses.

The suggestion that Planter yeoman houses were much simpler and meaner in both internal and external appearance than previously thought, and that the Planter architectural landscape underwent a developmental sequence which repeated the house cycle found in Rhode Island and Connecticut is supported by two factors of information found in the 91 Kings County probate inventories studied. First, inventories such as that of Richard Card allows us to describe the house type based on the room by room listing of domestic effects recorded by the inventory takers; second, the total evaluation of furnishings and accessories found in individual inventories, the actual furnishings themselves (their type and style), and their placement in the domestic setting strongly supports the suggestion that most Planter yeomen lived in very simple, even harsh surroundings. The household of Richard Card evaluated at £78 and 18 shillings is one of the wealthiest of those

6   Heather Davidson, ''Private Lives from Public Artifacts: The Architectural Heritage of Kings County Planters,'' *ibid.*, 250-51.

7   Michael Steinitz, ''Rethinking Geographical Approaches to the Common House: The Evidence from Eighteenth Century Massachusetts,'' in Camille Wells, ed., *Perspectives in Vernacular Architecture* (Columbia, 1989), 20-21.

individuals who list themselves as yeoman. Only artisans and craftsman such as shoemakers and carpenters have estates worth more. For example, James Willson, carpenter, of Falmouth, Kings County, had an estate which was evaluated at £155/17/6 in February 1772.[8] Most yeomen, however, had estates worth much less than Card reflecting their inability to purchase space enhancing domestic objects. Of the 91 inventories examined the average estate worth was £31 and 10 shillings.

By turning our attention to the Card inventory, we can begin to better understand the Planter domestic household and how it worked. When Mumford and Sanford left the farmyard and entered the house in what they called the "Westerly Room," they found:

> wearing apparel
> one case of drawers
> one chest
> pewter dishes, basins, plates and spoons
> one looking glass
> one featherbed, bedstead and accessories

It is obvious from this listing that the "Westerly Room" held the best furniture and would be described as a multi-functional parlour used for sleeping, as a dressing room, and for dining and entertaining.[9] Once again we see a reversion to earlier domestic living patterns, activities and multi-functional room use as found in early eighteenth-century parlours in New England,[10] a pattern supported by evidence found in other Kings County inventories.

The estate worth of Richard Card at the time of his death indicates that he was better off than some of his neighbours. Not only did he have a number of valuable farm animals, but he was able to embellish his parlour with space enhancing objects, including the looking glass, chest and case of drawers. If he used his parlour for entertaining, as seems likely, then the outward display of these objects in the best room in the house would not be missed by his neighbours and friends. Chests in parlours would often contain important possessions such as fine linens and clothing, and the display of so much pewter also suggests that it was highly prized. The presence of the "case of drawers" helps to establish Card's social position and wealth. In New England "by the early years of the eighteenth century, chests of drawers could be found in the homes of wealthy merchants and in

---

8   PANS, Hants County, Loose Petitions, Estate Papers, Wills, 1761-97, RG 48, Reel 561.

9   These room functions are also supported by the objects listed in the "Easterly Room" which served as the kitchen/hearth room, and the "Chamber" which was only used for sleeping.

10   Abbott Lowell Cummings, "Inside the Massachusetts House," *Common Places: Readings in American Vernacular Architecture* (Athens, 1986), 222; Kevin Sweeney, "Furniture and the Domestic Environment in Weathersfield, Connecticut, 1639-1800," in Dell Upton and John M. Vlach, ed., *Material Life in America, 1600-1800* (Boston, 1988), 264.

the homes of artisans and yeoman farmers of middling status.''[11] The same is true of looking glasses. During the mid-eighteenth century a relationship between the possession of a looking glass and wealth still existed.[12]

Understanding the importance of the proxemic relationships found within the domestic setting between objects, space and people is one of the most important aspects in determining social class, and how the material context influenced and established social interaction and status. According to Robert Blair St. George:

> the less space and space structuring artifacts a person could afford. . .the more his use of space as a means of expression and as a tool in social interaction was limited. Certainly no social scientist or historian would doubt that all men, regardless of their accumulated wealth, arrange interiors according to deeply embedded cognitive patterns. . . . Depending on one's ability to produce it, space is a means of oppression and control as well as cognitive design. By structuring the many rooms of his house along the continuum from open to closed space, the wealthy yeoman could better suit a specific interaction or performance to an appropriate material setting. But the man who greeted Madam Knight at the door of his ''hut'' had no such advantage. With less rooms and less possessions, he was further along the road leading to social disenfranchisement. Inside his house, a scarcity of space forced him, as it did many others, to use furniture that combined more than one function.[13]

Richard Card at the time of his death was a Planter yeoman in social transition. He lived in a simple house but had control over his space. He was able to furnish his parlour with space enhancing objects and use it for social display and entertaining, and to some degree control the thoughts and actions of his guests. However, the other rooms in Card's house were not as socially ''open,'' and not as well furnished.

Moving into the ''Easterly Room,'' Mumford and Sanford entered the kitchen which was furnished with:

> iron pots and one iron kettle
> one pair of andirons
> one pair of candlesticks
> one pair of tongs and two iron trammels
> buckets and barrels

---

11   *Ibid.*, 270

12   *Ibid.*, 280

13   Robert Blair St. George, '' 'Set Thine House in Order': The Domestication of the Yeomanry in Seventeenth-Century New England,'' *New England Begins: The Seventeenth Century, Volume Two: Mentality and Environment* (Boston, 1982), 173.

one brass warming pan
carpenter's tools

This room contained the cooking hearth as indicated by the presence of the pots, kettles, andirons and trammels, and would have been the centre of most family-oriented activities as well as being used for the preparation and consumption of food. The hearth room was the all-purpose living area.

Finally, Mumford and Sanford moved into the sleeping "Chamber" which contained a bed, bedstead and accessories, and a cutless. This room had only one function and was furnished for that purpose alone, a fact which allowed Mumford and Sanford to specifically identify its purpose and call it by its proper name, "Chamber," while the multi-functional aspects of the other two rooms were more difficult to identify with specific names.

Although it is impossible to determine what furnishings were removed from the house by Card's wife and children prior to the taking of the inventory (family members usually removed a few personal belongings including furniture and accessories such as chests and mirrors), the absence of any listing for tables and chairs is curious but not uncommon. If they were removed by family members this would suggest that they had a higher social value than the looking glass, chest, case of drawers and pewter which were left behind — a highly unlikely possibility. The obvious explanation is that the Card household contained neither chairs or tables and that chests were used for these purposes, as well as built-in furniture which was normally not listed by inventory takers. However, built-in furniture is rare in Nova Scotia. It is found mostly in the Germanic tradition in Lunenburg county, where built-in benches were used as seating, but built-in tables never existed.

The fact that the Card household contained neither tables nor chairs should not be considered unusual. Of the 91 inventories examined for this paper, 11 do not list tables or chairs, which represents 12 per cent of the total, a figure that is in keeping with inventory studies for the same time period in New England. For example, Kevin Sweeney in his study of Weathersfield, Connecticut,[14] found that, in 1750, 12 per cent of the households did not have tables and 10 per cent did not list chairs. In 1760, the figures were 10 per cent and 9 per cent; in 1780 they were both 12 per cent; and, in 1790, they were 9 per cent and 11 per cent respectively.

These percentages by decades of selected furniture forms are in keeping with the figures found in Kings County between 1761 and 1797. Simply put, some Planter yeoman households were too poor to have tables and chairs. Chests and boxes filled these functions, a fact which supports the previous suggestion that many Planters lived in very simple houses with few possessions. Richard Card was not poor, but was more interested in objects which enhanced his social

---

14 Sweeney, "Furniture and the Domestic Environment in Weathersfield Connecticut, 1639-1800," 264.

position and allowed him some control over his domestic surroundings. Therefore, rather than tables and chairs, he owned a looking glass, chest and case of drawers.

If Card is considered a "middling" sort of yeoman, what about his poorer neighbours? As already suggested the types and quantities of furniture recorded indicate that most Planter yeoman households in Kings County between 1761 and 1797 were sparsely furnished and consisted of no more than two to four rooms based around a hall/parlour plan. The average domestic interior contained one or two beds with accessories, one or two chests with and without drawers, wearing apparel, some chairs and tables, tools, iron and/or brass pots and kettles, andirons, trammels, pewter, linen or woolen wheels, textiles and occasional books. Silver and china are notably rare or non-existent while earthenware is common.

Only occasionally does an unusual object stand out in an inventory which suggests the New England origins of the owner and household. For example, in the probate record of Thomas Akins of Falmouth, Kings County, yeoman, taken on 9 May 1775, there is listed "one great chair" valued at £0/2/6.[15] A "great chair" in the New England probate inventories of the mid- to late eighteenth century refers to a turned chair with rush seat and arms. It was normally used by the senior male head of the household. Great chairs began appearing in New England inventories as early as 1700 and reached a peak in the 1770s.[16] A "great chair" is a description and type of object specific to New England and identifies both the owner, and the inventory takers who used this name, as probably coming from one of the New England Colonies of Rhode Island, Connecticut or Massachusetts. By way of comparison, of the 900 inventories studied for Lunenburg county for the years 1760-1830 there was not one single listing for a "great chair."[17]

A brief examination of two other yeoman inventories will help us to visualize and better understand the Planter domestic environment. The inventory of Jeremiah Baker, also of Newport, Kings County, was taken on 28 November 1767 by James Mosher, Benjamin Willcocks and Samuel Albro and evaluated at 31 pounds and 12 shillings and contained:

one bed, one coverlet, 2 blankets, one pillow and one old bedstead	2/ 0/0
a low case of drawers and one chest	10/ 0/0
a small trunk, table and six old chairs	0/10/0
wearing apparel	1/15/0
two old guns	1/ 0/0
farming utensils	2/ 0/0
two brass kettles and one warming pan	1/17/0

---

15 PANS, Hants County, Loose Petitions, Estate Papers, Wills, 1761-97, RG 48, Reel 561.

16 Sweeney, "Furniture and the Domestic Environment in Weathersfield, Connecticut, 1639-1800," 269, 273.

17 See Field, *Lunenburg*.

two cows	8/ 0/0
one mare, saddle and bridal	4/10/06[18]

Almost all of Baker's estate worth is found in the case of drawers and chest at ten pounds, a higher evaluation than even his two cows, highlighting once again the social/functional value placed on such objects. This is particularly interesting if one notes that the lowest evaluation in the Baker inventory is for the trunk, table and six chairs, suggesting once again that tables and chairs were simply not that important in the Planter household.

The household of Stephen Chapman also of Newport, Kings County, is somewhat different. Taken on 7 November 1770 by Henry Knowles and Jonathan Card, Richard Card's oldest son, the estate was evaluated at 35 pounds and 14 shillings and included:

one mare and colt	9/ 0/0
three cows	9/ 0/0
one sow and three goats	9/ 0/0
three pewter basins, three platters, five plates,	
four porrigers and six pewter spoons	0/16/0
one pine table and two chests	0/10/0
two boxes and eight chairs	0/ 8/0
two linen flax wheels and one wollen wheel	0/15/0
one Bible and other books	0/15/0
one featherbed, bolster and pillow	2/10/0
two coverlets, two bed rugs, two blankets	
& two sheets	2/ 0/0
two beds, one trudle bed, one bolster and one pillow	1/ 0/0[19]

The Chapman household was well equipped, and although not worth as much as the Card inventory, is similar. It is interesting that the inventory takers listed two boxes with the eight chairs, and two chests with the pine table, again indicating that the chests could have functioned as tables and the boxes as chairs when required.

Yeoman households such as those of Card, Baker and Chapman are the norm between the years 1761 and 1797. They are sparsely furnished, simple two to four room houses, based on a hall/parlour plan reflecting earlier New England house styles and domestic living patterns. In most cases these structures no longer exist unless incorporated into later more elaborate buildings such as the Loomer or Calkin houses.

The study of the eighteenth-century Planter architectural and cultural landscape, domestic environment, furnishings, living patterns, and proxemic/social relation-

---

18   PANS, Hants County, Loose Petitions, Estate Papers, Wills, 1761-97, RG 48, Reel 561.

19   *Ibid.*

ships will require a complete examination of probate records for all Planter town-ships in Nova Scotia, and a realistic assessment of surviving Planter houses. There is little doubt that by employing material life methodology our understanding of the Planters will change, causing us to reevaluate some of our current thinking, and allowing us to deepen our understanding of Planter life in Nova Scotia. Hope-fully this preliminary survey of Planter inventories in Kings County will help to point the way.

Poet to Pulpit to Planter:
The Peregrinations of the Reverend John Seccombe

Gwendolyn Davies
Department of English
Acadia University

In December 1725, the Sophomore student, John Seccombe of Medford, Massachusetts, lost his job waiting on tables in the Harvard dining hall "for stealing & Lying" and "was publicly admonished in the Hall, degraded to the lowest in the class, and turn'd out of his waiter's place."[1] Sixty-seven years later in November 1792, the same John Seccombe, now a Planter in Nova Scotia and a dissenting clergyman, died in Chester universally lamented by all as "An affectionate husband, a tender parent ... a sincere friend. ... A great example of morality and religion," and "A perfect pattern of piety, patience, and resignation, through all the troublesome scenes and trials incident to this transitory life."[2] Between these two public moments in the "transitory life" of the Reverend John Seccombe stretch the pages of what might be a popular picaresque novel of the time, for like Henry Fielding's *Tom Jones* (1749), Seccombe was born of ordinary but genteel estate, enjoyed an exuberant youth amongst his adolescent peers, tasted the pleasures of high life on the road to success, was plunged into the abyss, flirted with the law and incarceration, and rose again to enjoy a denouement as a publicly useful citizen. That he also happened to be a poet, sermon-writer and diarist with a broadside poem so popular that it was still being republished 120 years after its initial circulation brings a level of embellishment to the subject of this paper that retrieves him from the pages of time and elevates him to a status beyond that of mere prankster, preacher or Planter.

John Seccombe was born in Medford, Massachusetts, 25 April 1708, into a family that had settled in New England in the 1670s. As *Sibley's Harvard Graduates* points out, Seccombe's waiting on tables at university "in that day of sharp social distinctions, suggests that his family was not then as wealthy as it later became."[3] His humble origins seem not to have inhibited the boisterous spirits of the young undergraduate. According to the Harvard College Records his public reprimand in university Hall "for stealing & Lying" in December of his sophomore year was followed three months later by another such incident: "Sacomb, was examin'd concerning two fowls suspected to be stoln, under Examination he was found guilty of horrid lying (though not of theft) for this he gave in a written confession which was read in the Hall, and he admonished."[4]

1   Clifford K. Shipton, *New England Life in the 18th Century: Representative Biographies from Sibley's Harvard Graduates* (Cambridge, Mass., 1963), 286.
2   *The Royal Gazette and the Nova Scotia Advertiser*, 27 November 1792, n.p.
3   Shipton, *New England Life in the 18th Century*, 286.
4   *Ibid.*, 287.

Public discipline does not seem to have had the desired cautionary effect on Seccombe, however. Only five months after his university commencement, the now resident graduate again appears on the Harvard record books, this time paying seven shillings with each of his friends "for contriving to take, & for taking the third Goose lately stolen on the Common."[5] In the boyish fashion of those literary picaros, Tom Sawyer and Huck Finn, Seccombe described in a letter to former classmate Nicholas Gilman on 30 March 1729 the turkeys, hats, books and monies all stolen by various pranksters around the college, adding that "All those that have ever played Cards at College have been found out" and that "I have bottled my Cyder so that I shall have I hope a good bottle for you when you come down or up to College."[6]

The tone of Seccombe's life changed dramatically in the summer of 1733 when he accepted the call of the new Congregational parish of Harvard, Massachusetts, for £300 settlement, £120 salary, the possibility of later adjustments, and an extra £20 in labour that Seccombe had bargained so he would not have to cut and sled his own wood. That his appreciation for fine food, good drink and jolly company had not changed is evidenced by the hundreds of pounds of food and many barrels of drink consumed in the raising of the meeting house in June 1733,[7] and, more particularly, by the innkeeper's expense account for Seccombe's ordination on 10 October 1733:

Joseph Willard's Bill for Expenses at the Ordination
Oct. 10th 1733.

The night before Ordination I supped Eleven of Mr. Seccomb's friends	£1..18..6
The next Morning I Breakfasted nine	1..11..6
The same Day Dined Eleven at 3/6	1..18..6
The same Day Breakfasted 24 Ministers and Messengers	4.. 4
The same Day Dined 38 Ministers and Messengers	6..13
The Keeping Mr. Seccomb's relations' 9 horses 2 nights	18
To Lodging nine Persons 2 nights at 4 p night	6
To six Gallons and 2 quarts of Wine at 10/6 p gallon	4...6..3
To Pipes and Tobacco 4/, Loaf Sugar and Nutmegs 5/	9
For my Journey and bringing up Liquor	10
For Keeping 38 horses Ordination Day at 6	19
For 27 Persons some Scholars and some Ministers' wives at Dinner	4..14..6
For 8 horses belonging to Scholars and others one day at 6	4
	28..12..3[8]

5   *Ibid.*

6   Nicholas Gilman Mss, Massachusetts Historical Society, John Seccombe to Nicholas Gilman, 30 March 1729.

7   Henry S. Nourse, *History of the Town of Harvard, Massachusetts, 1732-1893* (Harvard, 1894), 182.

8   *Ibid.*, 182-83.

"Some of the faded tell-tale vouchers," notes Henry S. Nourse in his *History of the Town of Harvard*, "lead us to wonder, supposing the ecclesiastical punch to have been of normal potency, whether anybody in town on ordination day went to bed quite sober."[9] The cost of entertaining Seccombe's family and friends no doubt was a heavy burden for the parish of 50 families to support, but "His parishioners must have been thrown into a very fever of wonderment," notes Nourse, "when, after a brief residence as a bachelor among them, he built, fronting upon the then lonesome common, a gambrel-roofed mansion, three storied in front, two storied at the rear, so imposing in size, rich in its appointments, and tasteful in the arrangement and adornment of its ample rooms and the grounds about it, that a century later it could reasonably be called "one of the most baronial-looking residences in the Commonwealth."[10] The occasion for Seccombe's extravagance was his marriage on 10 March 1737 into one of the most prestigious clerical families of Massachusetts. His bride, Mercy, was not only the daughter of the Reverend William Williams of Weston but also the granddaughter of the well-known Reverend Solomon Stoddard. Local legend had it that the bride's father had promised to furnish as large a house as the groom's father, now a wealthy Medford merchant, could build, and that, out of such a rash bargain, the young Reverend John Seccombe concocted the palatial furnished mansion that was the talk of the countryside.[11] With its imposing hall, broad staircase with twisted balusters, wainscotted rooms, deep window-seats, elaborate fireplaces, huge kitchen hearth, manicured gardens, and wide avenues of trees leading to the meeting-house and main road respectively, the house dominated the centre of the village. A 130 acre farm provided food and wood. After Seccombe received the gift of Grape Island from the Lancaster proprietors in February 1734, a large summer cottage also became the centre of rural entertainment for what Nourse has described as the "gay guests from the bay towns."[12]

Harmony did not rule long in the parson's seemingly perfect domain, however, for like Tom Jones and other protagonists in picaresque romances, Jonathan Seccombe's fortunes were threatened by his relations with the opposite sex. Nourse and Sibley both paint a picture of an ill-tempered, unreasonable Mrs. Seccombe who, says Nourse, "certainly welcomed, and perhaps invented, the malicious charge of unfaithfulness to his marriage vows, that finally separated her husband from his parish."[13] A twentieth-century perspective might well question the justification for such remarks, particularly given the fact that Seccombe appeared before his congregation on 1 January 1738/39 and "offered Christian satisfaction for his Offence."[14] The "offence" is never defined, although it is clear from the

9   *Ibid.*, 183.
10   *Ibid.*, 186.
11   *Ibid.*
12   *Ibid.*, 187.
13   *Ibid.*, 186. See also Shipton, *New England Life in the 18th Century*, 290.
14   Shipton, *New England Life in the 18th Century*, 290.

congregation's divided response to Seccombe's apology and from the continuing demands for his resignation "on criminal grounds" that the matter was serious.[15] It is also clear from the diary of the Reverend Ebenezer Parkman of Westborough, Massachusetts, that news of the Seccombe affair spread beyond the borders of Harvard and became inextricably bound up with what Parkman called the "Scandalous offences" of other ministers in the seven towns of that neighbourhood.[16] His diary entry for 7 February 1739 reveals a visit from Captain Jonathan Sawyer of Harvard "with the bitter and grievous Case of Mr. Seccombe their Pastor," a consultation that led Parkman to urge caution until both sides of the case were heard. Parkman concluded "that none of the Crimes charg'd against Mr. Seccomb (however those false Rumors were that flew about the world) were such but that upon his deep Humiliation and Reformation and endeavouring to Conduct Himself with Peculiar Care respecting the Youth of the Flock he might be, nay and ought to be, continued their Pastor."[17]

As is typical of the fate of protagonists in popular romance, challenges never occur in isolation. Exacerbating Seccombe's relationship with the church over his marital situation was the divisiveness that emerged in the late 1730s in the Marlborough Association of ministers over the Great Awakening then sweeping New England. When Seccombe invited the British revivalist, the Reverend George Whitefield, to preach to his Harvard congregation on 13 August 1745 as part of the New Light revival, a number of fellow clergy expressed their disapproval,[18] and the Association subsequently published a protest against Whitefield and his preaching style. Seccombe's signature is conspicuously absent from this document,[19] and the sympathetic response of Seccombe and his congregation to the Great Awakening is confirmed by two essays on religious revivalism published by Seccombe in Thomas Prince's *Christian History ... For the Year 1744*:

> Some while under the Spirit *of Bondage* were so sensibly affected with their Danger that they dare not close their Eyes to sleep lest they should awake in Hell: And would sometimes *arise* in *the Night* and go to the Windows under alarming Fears of Christ's sudden *Coming to Judgment*, expecting to hear the Sounding of the Trumpet to summon all nations to appear before him. ...
>
> I think I may say there has been *a great Shaking among the dry Bones*, and some that have been for a long Time *dead in Trepasses and Sins* appear to be made *alive* to God: sleepy Sinners have been awakened, stub-

---

15 Nourse, *History of the Town of Harvard*, 189. See also Shipton, *New England Life in the 18th Century*, 290.

16 Francis G. Walett, ed., *The Diary of Ebenezer Parkman: 1703-1782*, First Part (Worcester, 1974), 62.

17 *Ibid.*, 60.

18 *Ibid.*, 122.

19 Nourse, *History of the Town of Harvard*, 189.

born Sinners subdued, proud Sinners humbled, carnal Persons made
spiritual.[20]

Although in subsequent years Seccombe seems to have maintained good relations with his fellow clergy in the Seven Towns, there are reminders of the conservatism of his peers in 1747 when the Reverend Ebenezer Parkman notes in his
diary:

> Mr. Swift, Mr. Bliss, and Mr. Minot came to Ministerial Meeting. Mr. Sec-
> comb preach'd a Savoury and moving Sermon upon John 4, 41, 42. It seems
> indeed to have been Compos'd in A Strain which many would Term New-
> Light, but there was not much ground, if any at all for anyone to make
> Exception. But I saw plainly that it did not go down well with Some Gen-
> tlemen. I am heartily sorry that there are any Remains of the Bitter root
> among us.[21]

Whether it was "the Bitter root among us" that led to Seccombe's demission from
the Marlborough Association on 7 September 1757 or whether, as Nourse suggests, there were residual ripples from Seccombe's alleged misconduct with a servant in 1739 is unclear,[22] but Seccombe's last entry in the church book in Harvard
notes: "I was dismissed by my Pastoral Relation to the Church of Christ in Harvard on the Seventh day of September A.D. 1757, upon my request by the consent of an Ecclesiastical Council of Six Churches, and a Vote of a major part of
the Brethren of the Church in full communion."[23]

At this point in John Seccombe's career, the abyss threatened. Unemployed,
seemingly discredited, and certainly alienated from many in his congregation and
profession, Seccombe probably had few options other than to immigrate to
Chester, Nova Scotia, as part of the Planter exodus. His parting comment to his
congregation — that it would never have a minister whose relationship with it was
not prematurely concluded — was uncannily prescient, and may well indicate the
degree to which the town, not Seccombe, was at fault for the division.[24] Certainly Seccombe's career in Nova Scotia was marked by only the most harmonious
of relationships with his small Congregational parish in Chester, Nova Scotia,
and with Mather's meeting house in Halifax. In Nova Scotia he also enjoyed the

20 "Revival of Religion at Harvard in the County of Middlesex..." and "The Rev. Mr. Seccombe's
    Account of the Revival of Religion at Harvard finished" in Thomas Prince, ed., *The Christian
    History ... for the year 1744* (Boston, 1745), 13-14; 17-21.

21 Walett, ed., *The Diary of Ebenezer Parkman*, 156.

22 Nourse, *History of the Town of Harvard*, 186. See also Shipton, *New England Life in the 18th
    Century*, 291; S. Buggey, "John Seccombe," *Dictionary of Canadian Biography*, IV, 705; and
    Seth Chandler, *American Historical Discourse Delivered Before the First Congregational Society
    in Harvard, Massachusetts* (Boston, 1884), 1.

23 Nourse, *History of the Town of Harvard*, 194.

24 Shipton, *New England Life in the 18th Century*, 291.

respect of such old college classmates as Chief Justice Jonathan Belcher. Although he experienced a more modest life style than in the past (his three-quarter Cape Cod house still stands on Wake-Up Hill at Marriott's Cove),[25] he was able to acquire a lot in Chester township in 1760, another in 1765, more land and 12 acres of island in 1780, and a 30 acre lot known as the minister's lot.[26] Notwithstanding this acquisition of property, Seccombe found himself financially pressured in Nova Scotia. In 1761 he had assigned most of his American property to his brother Thomas in Medford for safekeeping,[27] and his magnificent estate of 120 acres of land with its fine mansion in Harvard had remained empty until April 1765 when it had finally been sold for a mere £600.[28] By 18 January 1770 such was Seccombe's economic distress that H.H. Gerrish and Malachy Salter of Halifax wrote to Andrew Elliot and Samuel Cooper in Boston seeking charitable relief for Seccombe:

> He has never had any Establish'd Salary, but receives about £20 per annum from his Parish, which contains a few Industrious, but poor People, He has expended all the Money he brought with him into this Country (and which we are inform'd was considerable) in Buildings & other improvements, on a new Farm, which has reduced him to very necessitous Circumstances: He has had some small relief from this Town. We cannot avoid Earnestly recommending this Gentleman, now advanc'd in years, — as an Object very worthy of a Charitable Assistance.[29]

A letter by Seccombe, written after returning to New England for a visit in 1769, emphasized the physical contrast between his old way of life and the new, particularly on the level of comfort and food:

> I have enjoy'd a good measure of health ever since I came into Nova Scotia, but have had it in a higher manner since I was last at New England. I took a great deal of pleasure and satisfaction in visiting my friends there, & very particularly at Harvard. I sensibly grew fatter and stronger than before, & continue so to this day. ... The grain, butter and other things,

---

25 "Nova Scotia homes honored," *Chronicle Herald*, 19 August 1989, 1-C.
26 See Public Archives of Nova Scotia (PANS), MG 100, Vol. 120, "Chester Documents," No. 39K, 15 April 1762; No. 39L, 4 May 1762; No. 39M, Chester 1784, Black Box, Lunenburg Co., folder 1, No. 37; and No. 39R, "Those To Whom Land Granted At Chester 31st October 1765." See also Index to Nova Scotia Grants, 1760 and 1765, 29750A, Chester Township, Book 6, 548; and "John Seccomb," 1780, 542A, Chester Township, 172. Also: PANS, MG 100, Vol. 120, "Chester Proprietors, 1802," file 36-36C.
27 Fred E. Crowell, "New Englanders In Nova Scotia," PANS Micro, "Biography: Crowell, Fred: Scrapbook; No. 89, "Seccombe," 97. See also New England Historic Genealogical Association, 6S70, Sub-group I, Series S, Mercy Seccombe to Willis Hall, Esqr., 11 October 1797.
28 Nourse, *History of the Town of Harvard*, 132.
29 *Ibid.*, 194.

which were given me by my friends at Harvard were very acceptable, & will be very beneficial to us ... you live in a country where there is a plenty of all the necessaries & comforts of life. It is far otherwise with us at Chester, for sometimes it may be said (of some at least) that they are in want of all things.[30]

Financially pressed as Seccombe was by the 1770s, he nonetheless seemed to enjoy a position of stability and respectability in Nova Scotia. As Susan Buggey points out, for 25 years he preached regularly at Mather's Meeting House in Halifax as well as in his own Chester congregation, finding in the Halifax church that it was "so natural to be with this people, that it seems almost as if I were their Pastor."[31] However, this was threatened when in December 1776, in the heat of the American Revolution, "Mr. Seccomb, a dissenting Teacher of Chester, being charged with preaching a sermon on Sunday the first of September last tending to promote Sedition and rebellion amongst the people at that place"[32] was arraigned before the Executive Council of Nova Scotia. Seccombe "asserted his innocence" before the Lieutenant Governor and Members of Council, but on the 6 January 1777 they "resolved that the said Seccomb shall give Five hundred pounds Security for his future good behaviour and that he shall be under injunction not to preach or pray or otherwise to officiate to any congregation until he shall have signed a recantation of the principles which he has been charged with to the satisfaction of Government."[33] The matter was obviously settled by recantation or neglect, for Seccombe seems to have still been preaching in Halifax until April 1784 when the Anglican Loyalist clergyman, the Reverend Mather Byles, Jr., noted in a letter to his sisters in Boston: "Mr. Russel, a Gentleman from Scotland, takes the charge of the Dissenting Meeting-house in this Town, known by the name of St. *Mather*, and called so in a late Map. Mr. Russel succeeds Mr. Secombe the famous Author of Father Abdy's Will who is superannuated and retires."[34] As late as 1788 Seccombe was still presiding at services in Chester, although one report described his body as being so enfeebled that he could not climb the pulpit stairs without help.[35]

Byles's mention of the poem, "Father Abdy's Will" confirms that Seccombe's reputation as a writer of verse had pursued him into Nova Scotia. Although he was not known to sustain his poetic activities in the province, his life may well be measured by the character and public nature of his literary endeavours. "Father Ab__y's Will" published in Boston in broadsheet form in 1731 while Seccombe

---

30 Shipton, *New England Life in the 18th Century*, 292.
31 Buggey, *Seccombe*, 705.
32 Executive Council Minutes, PANS, RG 1, Vols. 210-12, 23 December 1776, 332-33.
33 Executive Council Minutes, PANS, RG 1, Vols. 210-12, 6 January 1777, 333.
34 Byles Family Papers, Massachusetts Historical Society, Ms. N-38, 1784-1790, Box 2, file February-June 1784, 1 April 1784.
35 Crowell, *New Englanders in Nova Scotia*, 97.

was still resident at Harvard College was comic doggerel that celebrated the university's sweeper, Matthew Abdy, and, inadvertently, the young Seccombe's carefree collegiate years. Reprinted by the *Weekly Rehearsal*, 3 January 1732, the Harvard poem elicited a verse response from the Yale College sweeper in a poem originally attributed to Seccombe but later credited to John Hubbard of New Haven.[36] Governor Belcher sent the verses to London where *The Gentleman's Magazine* published the Harvard and Yale poems in the issues of May, June and October 1732,[37] and as late as 1782, the Loyalist Samuel Curwin was able to buy Seccombe's poem as a broadside in the streets of London.[38] "Father Ab__y's Will" was set to music in the eighteenth century and went into numerous broadside versions in North America, appearing as late as 13 February 1843 in the *Morning Herald* of Halifax and in 1854 in the United States.[39] Vernacular in language, jingo-ish in rhythm, and detailed in its lists of inheritances, "Father Ab__y's Will" has served as both a comic invention in its own day and as an eighteenth-century domestic record for our own time:

> A small tooth comb
> An ashen broom
> A candlestick and hatchet
> A coverlid
> Strip'd down with red
> A bag of rags to patch it.[40]

Once in Nova Scotia, Seccombe seems to have ceased writing the comic verses that had established his literary reputation and to have published instead a series of commemorative sermons marking either religious activity (the ordination of Reverend Bruin Romcas Comingoe on 3 July 1770 in Halifax) or death (the loss of the Honourable Abigail Belcher, wife of Seccombe's friend, Jonathan Belcher, on 20 October 1771 or of Mrs. Margaret Green, wife of Benjamin Green, on 1 February 1778).[41] These sermons, like his earlier New Light essays in New England, represent a more serious and intellectual side of Seccombe that also

---

36 Shipton, *New England Life in the 18th Century*, 287-88. See also "Father Abbey's Will; To Which Is Added A Letter of Courtship..." (Cambridge, Mass., 1854), 7-8; and "Certificate Respecting the Rev. John Seccombe, The Massachusetts Magazine, 7 (August 1795), 301-302.

37 "Father Abbey's Will," 8, 11.

38 Shipton, *New England Life in the 18th Century*, 288.

39 *Ibid.*, 288; "The Last Will of Mathew Abdy," Halifax *Morning Herald, or General Advertiser*, 13 February 1843, n.p.; and "Father Abbeys Will" (Cambridge, 1854).

40 "Father Abbey's Will," *The Massachusetts Magazine*, 6, 11 (November 1794), 696. A copy of the 1731 broadsheet is held in the American Antiquarian Society, Worcester, Mass., and various versions of "Father Abbey's Will" (sometimes published as "Father Ab__y's Will", or "Father Abdy's Will") are held by the Massachusetts Historical Society, Boston.

41 Buggey, *Seccombe*, 706.

found reflection in the books that he owned or in the respect in which he was held by scholarly clergymen like Ebenezer Parkman.

From a twentieth-century perspective, the most enduring example of Seccombe's writing lies in the diary that he kept as he travelled to Nova Scotia as a Planter immigrant and became settled in his new life. Originally dated 1759, the diary has in recent years been attributed to the year 1761.[42] It records everything from the division of lots in the new township of Chester to the texts of Seccombe's sermons in Halifax and Chester to the hanging of a young soldier in Halifax for desertion. This is not the diary of a Simeon Perkins or an Ebenezer Parkman, for it is not a journal written as a record of a community to be consulted as a resource years later. Instead, Seccombe's diary is first and foremost a mechanical record of day-to-day events "Designed," as he puts it on the first page, "only for the use & inspection of my Family." As such, it is a documentation of weather, his movements back and forth between Halifax and Chester, and the friends he meets. With an eighteenth-century man's bow to the science of his body, he even records his cathartics and purging. The most significant dimension of Seccombe's diary, however, lies its outstanding documentation of eighteenth-century Nova Scotian food and diet, for true to the fleshly enjoyments of his youth, the aging parson maintained a delight in food and drink. As an end to his peregrinations from Harvard poet to Harvard preacher to Nova Scotia Planter, it is comforting to have an enduring image of Seccombe dining at lunch at Mr. Blackden's on "Boil'd Beef & Pork etc — & Roast Duck, etc. etc." and in the evening at Mr. Fairbanks on roast pork, mutton, Apple pye, Baked Quinces and Pears, etc."[43] At various times, he experiments with eating beaver, revels in soused salmon and cucumber, and brews his own fresh lemon punch. What the diary lacks in literary elegance, it makes up for in candid detail. A comic versifier in his youth, Seccombe was no meagre observer in his later years. For both contributions, he deserves to take his place amongst literary historians and material culture specialists now turning their attention to eighteenth-century Nova Scotia.

---

42 [John Seccombe] "Journal" PANS, MG 1, Vol. 797C, #1, ts., 1. For the dating of the journal, see C.B. Fergusson, "The Diary of Rev. John Seccombe," PANS *Report* (Halifax, 1959), app. B, 18-45.

43 [John Seccombe], "Journal," 18.

A Planter Family:
The Bubars of New England and New Brunswick

John S. Bubar
Department of Plant Science
Nova Scotia Agricultural College

My family name, Bubar, came into use after my branch of the family settled on the St. John River. Others who did not settle there or who returned to the U.S.A. soon after the American Revolution use the spelling Bubier. This makes it possible to use the Bubar name to trace the migration of some pre-Loyalist settlers in the New Brunswick area and their descendants. Our name evolved from that of Joseph Boobyar, who arrived in Marblehead, Massachusetts, prior to 1668. His great-grandson Joseph Bubier (Bobor, Boober, Booby or Buber) joined Captain Francis Peabody's company and obtained property in the Maugerville settlement in the 1760s.

Born in Marblehead in 1728, Joseph moved with his widowed mother to Arowsick at the mouth of the Kennebec in the 1740s. He married Martha Grover of Georgetown in 1749 and they had eight or nine children born between 1750 and 1767.[1] Joseph and Martha purchased property on Parkers Island from the Plymouth Proprietors in 1760 and sold their property in 1764. The difficulties faced by the settlers in their dealings with the Proprietors, as described by Kershaw,[2] probably caused Joseph to seek new holdings for himself and his growing family by moving up the St. John River Valley.

Joseph Buber owned Maugerville lots 64 and 65 in 1761 which were sold to John Beardsley and Abner De Peyster respectively in 1786.[3] Joseph Sr. left New Brunswick about 1785.[4] Joseph Sr. and two sons, William and Christopher, were residents of Bowdoin, Maine in 1790.[5] The names of the "subscribers to bond for the preached gospel among us" in 1774, which brought the Reverend Seth Noble to Maugerville, include Joseph Jr. and Benjamin.[6] The absence of Joseph Sr. suggests he may have retained a residence in Maine and that Martha and younger children stayed there while older children developed properties on the St. John River. Joseph Sr. and the younger children who resided in Bowdoin did not adopt the Bubar spelling of the name.

Descendants of three of Joseph and Martha's sons use the Bubar spelling of the

---

1   Details on the origin of the names and genealogy of the ones residing in Massachusetts and Maine are found in M.M. Bubier, *Bubier Family Notes* (Providence, R.I., 1959).
2   G.E. Kershaw, *The Kennebeck Proprietors 1749-1775* (Portland, Me, 1975).
3   Letter from E.C. Wright, 16 March 1981.
4   Transcript of Evidence Given to a Commission by the Court of Chancery of the Province of New Brunswick, 1787-88, Provincial Archives of New Brunswick (PANB), RS-55.
5   Bubier Family Notes, 113.
6   Pickard papers — Maugerville Settlers, PANB, F-358.

name which makes it possible to trace their movements from the Maugerville settlement up to the present day. Since a detailed genealogy of these families is being
prepared,[7] I will limit myself to an overview of where the family went and some
of the reasons for their migrations.

The three sons were Benjamin, Joseph Jr. and John, born about 1750, 1752 and
1756 respectively. Two daughters, Mary (Polly) and Martha, also settled on the
St. John River and married brothers Icabod and Jeremiah Howland, sons of Joseph
Howland who also moved from the mouth of the Kennebec to the St. John.[8]

Benjamin was one of the residents of Maugerville who subscribed to the bond
in 1774 that brought the Reverend Seth Noble to Maugerville. He was considered
a rebel by the Loyalist settlers and was evicted in 1785 together with his wife,
Abigail, and daughter from a lot in Gagetown to which he did not have clear title.
His share of property at Lincoln was sold in 1779. He and a number of settlers who
were considered rebels in New Brunswick moved to the area of present-day
Bangor, where they were received as patriots and joined by their pastor Seth
Noble. Benjamin was still living near Milo, Maine, in 1834. His descendants
include the Reverend Benjamin C. Bubar, Jr., who campaigned for the Presidency
of the United States in 1976 and 1980 as the Prohibition Party candidate and two
Baptist ministers, John and David, featured in a 1975 *Time* magazine article.[9]
Another descendant, Dan Bubar of Schroon Lake, New York, went to Hungary
in 1990 as a missionary of the Faith Evangelical Free Church. It appears that Pastor
Noble had a strong influence on Benjamin who encouraged his descendants to
become ministers, evangelists and missionaries.

Little is known about Joseph Jr. He owned property in Maugerville, married
and raised a family believed to consist of three sons and three daughters. He died
sometime after 1795 and before 1819: at least the property in Maugerville was
owned by his son Stephen by 1819. Most of the Bubars currently living in New
Brunswick trace their ancestry to one or more of his sons.

Stephen Bubar, born about 1780, purchased property on the Nashwaak and
established a sawmill. His will indicates an estate valued at £2039/17/3 with
£1706/3/2 in claims against it. Each of the three sons and three daughters were
left £5 with the balance to his wife, Christianna. After she disposed of the
property, she moved upriver, presumably to be near her brother, the Reverend
Charles McMullen of Hartland. She remarried Benjamin Noble, grandson of Seth
Noble, and lived for the rest of her life in Lower Brighton, about five miles south
of Hartland.

Joseph Jr.'s son Samuel had a farm at Penniac on the Nashwaak, where he raised

7   Mr. George H. Hayward, 29 Leeds Drive, Fredericton, N.B. is preparing this genealogy and
     depositing copies in the PANB.

8   Roberta H. Johnson, Ruth B. Walsh and Elizabeth P. White, 1979; Joseph Howland of North
     Yarmouth, Maine, and Burton, New Brunswick (1717-96); *The Mayflower Quarterly* (May
     1979), 70-80.

9   *Time*, 5 May 1975.

five sons and ten daughters. The other son James of Durham Bridge on the Nashwaak had seven sons and two daughters. Many of their descendants remain in the area. Some moved to the Miramichi and others to Carleton County. Considerable intermarriage took place among these families, who maintained a strong affiliation through their churches.

Stephen's eldest son James appears to have moved to Maine. At least he disappeared from New Brunswick at about the same time as a James Bubier appeared in Bowdoinham, Maine.[10] Although the name was spelled Bubier, his descendants in northwestern Maine now spell the name Bubar. Some adopted the spelling Boober.

Stephen's son Charles purchased a farm on the south side of Hartland near his uncle Charles McMullen's farm. He married Sarah Noble and they had two sons and a daughter. Following Sarah's early death, he married her sister Hannah. The sons George and Charles disapproved of the marriage and apparently left home as a result of it. George arrived in Selkirk, Manitoba, in time to be taken prisoner by Louis Riel. His brother Charles joined him later and they both married and raised families there, where they were contractors and operated a boat on the Red River. George moved to Denver, Colorado, with his family in the 1880s. One of his sons carried the name to the State of Washington. Another joined the American Navy and his descendants tend to be found associated with locations of United States Naval bases. Charles moved to British Columbia and established a ranch at Midway, on the United States border south of the Okanagan Valley. They celebrate the centenary of their settlement there in 1991. It is the second ranch in the area to have been owned by one family for a century. Charles left a number of descendants that reside mainly in British Columbia and account for the occurrence of the Bubar name there.

Stephen's third son John married his cousin Charlotte Bubar from Penniac and established a farm still owned by a descendant with the same name just north of Hartland, New Brunswick. Three of their eleven children were deaf-mute suggesting that a recessive genetic deficiency is present that was expressed due to the inbreeding in the family. Three sons married and left descendants that carry on the Bubar name in Carleton County.

Two of Stephen's daughters, Elizabeth Ann Derrah and Mary Jane Tompkins, also married and settled in Carleton County where they each have numerous descendants. The other daughter, Charlotte Augusta Bubar, remained unmarried and was a pioneer school teacher in Bristol, Carleton County.

Stephen's descendants and a number of relatives from Maugerville and the Nashwaak cleared the land and continued to farm much of central Carleton County. They still work together in church and family groups carrying on the traditions of the original Maugerville Planter community.

Joseph Sr. and Martha's third son, John, was evicted from land to which he did not have clear title in Newtown in 1783. At that time he was married, and had a

---

10   Bubier Family notes — Section M.

log house and four acres cleared. John and his brother-in-law Ichabod Howland, petitioned for land on the Oromocto in 1790 but did not get it, nor did he and his brothers William and Christopher get land they petitioned for in 1785. He moved upriver and occupied land on the west bank of the St. John River two miles south of the present Beechwood dam site and finally gained ownership of land there in the 1820s. In the meantime he raised a family of three sons and four daughters. One son, David, is known as the Aroostook giant famous for his feats of strength.[11] He is probably the inspiration for the Paul Bunyan legend, which leads to the suggestion that it would be much more appropriate to have a monument to Paul Bunyan near the Beechwood Dam than it is to have one in Bangor, Maine. After John died in 1829 or 1830, his widow Elizabeth and son Charles moved to Aroostook County, Maine, near Caribou, where some of Charles's descendants carry on the name today.

Esther Clark Wright stated that the ''The Maugerville settlement was successful because it was formed by a closely knit group, with religious ties, and with experience in a not dissimilar environment.''[12] These same characteristics stood the displaced pre-Loyalist settlers in good stead as they moved on up the Nashwaak and St. John Rivers, returned to Maine or moved to the mid and far west. This study, using the Bubar name as a marker, helps to trace the movement of these settlers following the arrival of the Loyalists and shows how the ties established among the Maugerville settlers have been maintained for more than two centuries.

---

11   John Mason, ''David Bubier, The Giant from Aroostook,'' *Yankee Magazine* (June 1968).

12   Esther Clark Wright, *The St. John River and its Tributaries* (Wolfville, N.S., 1966), 121.

The Mapping of the Planter Settlements in Nova Scotia

Joan Dawson
Research Associate
Nova Scotia Museum, Halifax

Mapping has always been an essential tool of colonisation. Maps served to identify, for the benefit of the government of the colonising country, the areas over which their agents exercised control. In providing a visual image of those areas, maps might describe their physical appearance: their relief, vegetation and natural resources; as well as recording the developments brought about by the colonists as settlements, political boundaries and communication routes. They were also a useful way of describing future projects for which the colonial officials sought approval and funding. As sources of this type of information, maps are a valuable complement to the written historical documents of any period.

The coming of the Planters to Nova Scotia in the 1760s generated a number of maps which illustrate the changes brought about by their arrival. They range in size and scope from large maps of the peninsula of Nova Scotia and Bay of Fundy, through area maps including several townships, to plans of individual grants within a township, and the layout and allocation of town plots. They are located in Britain in the Public Record Office, and in Nova Scotia in the Public Archives, in the Department of Lands and Forests, in town offices, in museums and in private ownership. This survey will consider just a few examples of these documents.

Most of the ''Planter'' maps are the work of Charles Morris I, Chief Surveyor for Nova Scotia from 1749 until his death in 1781.[1] Morris was deeply involved in several ways with the establishment of the Planters in the province. Politically, even before his appointment to the Nova Scotia Council at the end of 1755, he had advocated the expulsion of the Acadians. After their departure, when the remaining inhabitants were deprived of the agricultural infrastructure which the Acadians had provided, Morris, in his capacity as Council member, recommended to the Board of Trade that New Englanders should be brought in to settle the province in their place. When this policy was adopted, it became his responsibility as Chief Surveyor to encourage and provide for the establishment of the would-be immigrants. His duties involved the selection of viable sites for settlement which would meet with the approval of the agents who visited Nova Scotia in 1759 in response to Governor Lawrence's offer of land. Once these sites were approved and the settlement process started, Morris supervised the laying-out of the town sites and the allocation of lots within the new townships. For several years thereafter he kept a close eye on their progress. His records took the form not only of written reports on the state of the townships but also of maps showing their location and resources.

---

1   For a summary of Morris's career, see Phyllis R. Blakeley, ''Morris, Charles,'' *Dictionary of Canadian Biography*, IV, 559-62.

Morris appears to have acquired his skill as a surveyor during his service as a military officer. An officer trained in surveying would be capable of representing on paper the important strategic features of terrain to be attacked or defended, the site of a fort or battery, or communication routes. In addition to describing the shape of the land, military surveyors were taught to observe its vegetation and other relevant features. In Morris's day, the most useful instrument for land surveying was a compass. (Instruments used in marine navigation and hydrography, which depended on a level horizon, were of little use in hilly, wooded country.) In the absence of a chain, distances could be determined by pacing, while a plane table and simple methods of triangulation might be used to construct area maps.

Charles Morris had, presumably, learnt such techniques while serving at Annapolis Royal in the 1740s. His early knowledge of the Fundy and Minas regions of Nova Scotia was acquired when, in 1748, he had been sent by Paul Mascarene, chief administrator of Nova Scotia, and Governor Shirley of Massachusetts to survey the upper part of the Bay of Fundy and to assess its potential for settlement. His superiors were impressed both by his mapping, and the accompanying report, "A breif [*sic*] survey of Nova Scotia."[2] When serious thought was given in 1749 to establishing Protestant settlements among the Acadian villages, Morris drew up plans showing how this might be done.

At that time, however, the establishment of Halifax took priority over other projects, and it became Morris's task to lay out Cornwallis's new settlement. The same year saw his appointment as Chief Surveyor for Nova Scotia. In the early 1750s he surveyed much of the South Shore and part of the Eastern Shore in search of a suitable place to establish the Foreign Protestants. When the site which was to become Lunenburg was selected, it was Morris again who laid out the town.

By 1755, Morris had travelled widely in Nova Scotia, making detailed maps of a number of areas. His map of the Peninsula of Nova Scotia,[3] (Figure 1) made in that year, shows clearly the state of development and settlement of the province at the time of the expulsion. This was the geographical background against which the new wave of immigration from New England was to take place, and this map will serve as a starting-point for our discussion. It represents a region where the majority of the population was clustered in the Acadian villages on the Annapolis Basin and River, the Minas and Cumberland Basins, and the western end of the peninsula. Halifax-Dartmouth, and the Lunenburg-LaHave area, were the only signs of British colonial development. With the departure of the Acadians, an already sparsely-populated province would become almost empty of European settlers.

Late in 1758, Governor Lawrence announced in the Boston *Gazette* that land in Nova Scotia was to be made available for settlement. The following January,

---

2   See Andrew Hill Clark, *Acadia: The Geography of Early Nova Scotia to 1760* (Madison, WI, 1968), 189n.

3   Charles Morris, "A Chart of the Peninsula of Nova Scotia ...," 1755. British Library, King's Maps CXIX, 57.

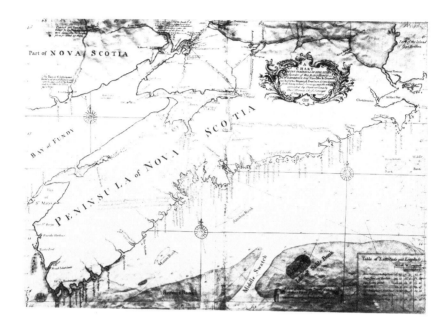

1. Charles Morris's 1755 map of Nova Scotia. (Courtesy of the British Library, London; Photograph: National Archives of Canada.)

the details of the offer were made known, and when the first group of agents representing prospective settlers visited the province in 1759, it was Charles Morris who accompanied them to view the potential settlements. They were soon followed by representatives for other would-be immigrants, and by the end of the year, the basis for the Planter settlements had been established.

In his capacity as Chief Surveyor, Morris was, of course, already familiar with the land which was being offered, having mapped much of it previously. The selection of sites was made under his guidance, and on the basis of information he had acquired during previous surveying expeditions. He personally supervised the settlement of the township lands, as well as mapping them. An extract from a letter from Lieutenant Governor Jonathan Belcher to the Lords of Trade, written on 3 November 1761, gives us some idea of Morris's role in the establishment of the settlements:

> The Chief Surveyor, My Lords, is so lately returned from Cobequid, where he has spent some time in disposing the Township in that District for a Settlement, and in opening a Communication by a Road from Chebernacadie River to Chignecto, that I cannot be furnished by this Opportunity with so exact an Account of the Settlements as I hope to lay before Your Lordships by the next Conveyance. In obedience to Your Lordships I now have the

honor to transmit three accurate Maps planned by the Chief Surveyor, of the Places already settled, and of those where Settlements are speedily expected, and also of the Lands on the River St. John. These maps will give Your Lordships a view of all the granted cleared lands in the Province.[4]

It is not clear which maps Belcher is referring to, but soon afterwards, on 11 January 1762, he again writes: "With these papers are ... humbly transmitted to Your Lordships a Chart of the Peninsula of Nova Scotia, containing delineation of the several Townships, and a Chart of the Basin of Mines and Cobequid Bay, with another of the District of Chignecto and a Plan of the Lands along the St. John River."[5] These maps are now in the Public Record Office in London.

The first map referred to is probably familiar to many people. A version of it, entitled "A Chart of the Peninsula of Nova Scotia by Chas. Morris Chief Surveyor 1761."[6] (Figure 2) appears in the Parks Canada publication *The New England Planters in Nova Scotia*,[7] It was probably made on Morris's return from

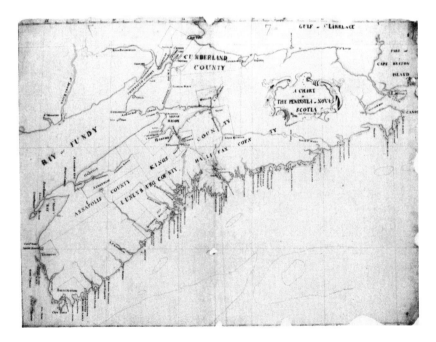

2.   Charles Morris's 1761 map of Nova Scotia, showing the Planter townships. (Courtesy of the Public Record Office, Kew. Crown copyright.)

4   Public Archives of Canada, *Report*, 1904 (Ottawa, 1905), [289].
5   *Ibid.*, [289]-290.
6   J.E. Candow, *The New England Planters in Nova Scotia* (Ottawa, 1986).
7   Public Record Office (hereafter PRO), CO 700, Nova Scotia No. 34 (1).

Cobequid at the end of the fall of 1761, as a record of his labours up to that time. It shows the division of the province into five counties (Annapolis, Kings, Lunenburg, Halifax and Cumberland) and indicates the boundaries of the townships of Sackville, Cumberland and Amhurst [Amherst] in the Chignecto area, Onslow and Truro further south, and Cornwallis, Horton and West and East Falmouth on the Minas Basin. Further west lie the townships of Granville and Annapolis, Yarmouth and Barrington, with Liverpool and New Dublin on the South Shore. The map also gives a general view of the province, and many other place names appear as well as the Planter settlements. Its chief contribution to the historical record, however, is to locate these new townships on the overall provincial scene, and to confirm that, by late 1761, their boundaries were established, to a great extent encompassing the lands earlier settled and farmed by the Acadians.

The other, more detailed, maps made by Morris at about the same time and also referred to in the Governor's letter, are specifically intended to give an account of the nature of the townships laid out for the Planters. One of them, entitled "Plan of the District of Chignecto,"[8] (Figure 3) shows the boundaries of the townships granted at Sackville, Cumberland and Amhurst [Amherst] on the isthmus between "Part of the Peninsula of Nova Scotia" and the "Lands beyond the Peninsula."

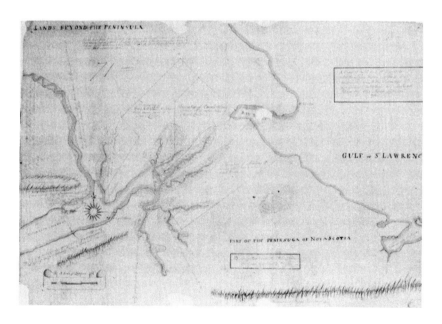

3 . Morris's plan of the Chignecto area, showing the townships of Amherst, Sackville and Cumberland, 1761. (Courtesy of the Public Record Office, Kew. Crown copyright.)

8 PRO, CO 700, Nova Scotia No. 36.

According to Lawrence's proclamation, an equitable distribution of resources was to be made among the grantees, with each share consisting of a proportion of upland, meadow and marsh. Morris indicates on the map the acreage of marshlands (much of which had previously been drained and farmed by the Acadians), not only within each of the new townships but also along the other rivers running into the basin. Along the coast in the Joggins area, a note is made of ''Coal Mines.'' The existing ''road'' to Bay Vert, which had been established by the Acadians, is also marked. Two areas of ''High barren unimprovable Mountains'' are shown, and there are notes about the adjacent coastlines. This is still a relatively small-scale map, giving no details about the grants to individuals within the townships, nor about the sites of the town plots proposed for the settlers. It is simply designed to convey to the authorities the location of the new townships, and something of their economic resources.

A companion to this map in the Public Record office is also mentioned in the Governor's letter and dated 1761. Entitled ''A Plan of the Minas Bason and Cobequid Bay with the Several Towns granted thereon,''[9] (Figure 4) it presumably represents the work that had kept the Chief Surveyor so busy in the fall of that year. Here Morris again shows the township boundaries and the acreage of marshland

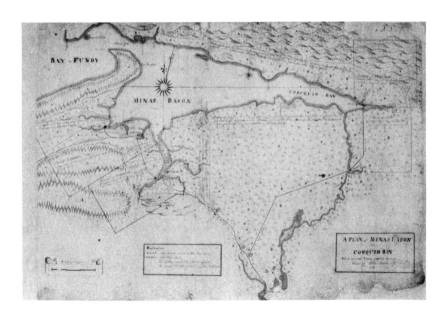

4. Morris's plan of the Minas-Cobequid area, with the townships of Onslow, Truro, Newport, Falmouth, Horton and Cornwallis, 1761. (Courtesy of the Public Record Office, Kew. Crown copyright.)

9   PRO, CO 700, Nova Scotia No. 35.

with which each township is endowed, as well as the unproductive mountainous hinterland. The townships shown are Onslow, Truro, Newport, Falmouth, Horton and Cornwallis; once again the area represents agricultural land developed by the Acadians.

Not all of the Planter townships are equally well documented, and there does not seem to have been a general map of the South Shore equivalent to those of the Minas-Cobequid and Chignecto maps. In 1762, however, Morris made a map of the Cape Sable area from Port LaTour to Pubnico[10] (Figure 5) showing the town of Barrington, at the focal point of the township, and a similar map of Lunenburg and LaHave Harbours.[11]

As well as maps which were essentially intended to show the location and resources of the settlements, plans were made — again, often by Morris, but sometimes by surveyors working under his direction — of the lay-out of the town plots which were supposed to form the centre-piece of each township, and the allocation of lots to individuals. Morris himself supervised much of the laying-out and planning of the new communities, whose inhabitants were each to have a lot in town in addition to their farm or water lots. A number of town plans (including copies, some of a later date than the original surveys) have survived, scattered among various public and private collections.[12] They reveal variations on a fairly standard layout, with blocks of houses in a grid, and open spaces or parades to allow for the Town Meetings required by the New Englanders, as well as glebe and school lots to provide for religious observance and education. Later, of course, the town sites developed in a variety of different ways as lots were exchanged or sold, and many settlers opted to live on their farmlands rather than in town houses.

One example of an early town plan is the unsigned ''Plan of the Town of Cornwallis containing 160 Half-Acre Lotts,'' (Figure 6) dated 1760, now in the Public Archives of Nova Scotia.[13] It is a simple layout, consisting of four numbered divisions, each with three blocks identified by the letters A, B and C. At the centre is the ''Perade,'' the public square typical of settlements of this period. Adjoining the parade are the customary lots set aside for the school, the glebe and the minister. The name of the holder of each lot is inscribed on the plan; there a few vacant lots. No attempt is made to provide orientation or topographical information or to locate the town in relation to hills, river or coastline. It is simply a record of the laying out of the lots and their ownership. The annotations C and H on many of the lots may have been added later as a record of the clearing of the land and

10   C. Morris, ''A Draught of the Coast of Cape Sable ...,'' 1762. PRO, CO 700, Nova Scotia No. 37.

11   C. Morris, ''A Draught of Lunenburg and LeHave Harbours ...,'' [1762], II, Ministry of Defence, Hydrographic Dept., Taunton, Admiralty B5814, Shelf Ff.

12   Town plans can be found in the Public Archives of Nova Scotia, the Provincial Crown Records Centre and various town offices.

13   Public Archives of Nova Scotia (hereafter PANS), F/239 — 1760 Cornwallis.

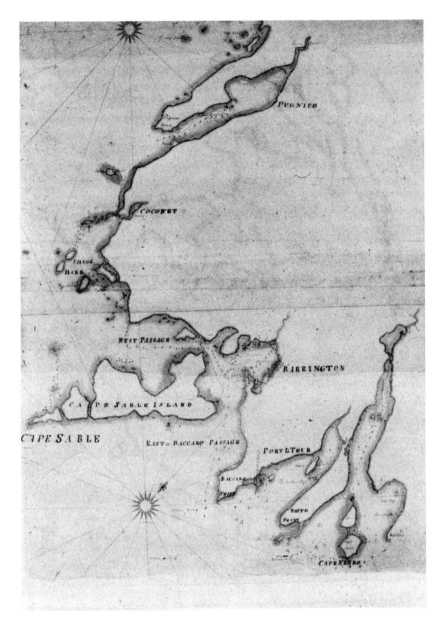

5. Morris's 1762 map of the Cape Sable area. (Courtesy of the Public Record Office, Kew. Crown copyright.)

6. The town of Cornwallis, 1760. (Courtesy of the Map Division, Public Archives of Nova Scotia.)

the construction of houses. The back of the plan contains a list of the persons to whom the lots were allocated.

Another example is a later copy, also in the Provincial Archives, of a 1760 plan for the rather larger town of Horton.[14] (Figure 7) The original plan was signed by Morris; the copy represents a town of six divisions, each consisting of four blocks, and including no fewer than three parades. A school lot and ministerial lot are provided, adjacent to the central and left-hand parades respectively. (Another copy of the plan, in the National Archives of Canada,[15] also shows a glebe lot in the first division, on a site left vacant in this example.) A burial ground lies just beyond the sixth division. A note beside the first division marks "Horton River" as a reference point for the location of the settlement. Presumably the more grandiose plan for this town was based on the larger number of expected immigrants — 200 proprietors as opposed to 150 at Cornwallis — though the provision of three parades seems perhaps excessive.

In Morris's "Report on Towns in Nova Scotia" dated 1762, he states of Horton: "This Township begun its settlement 1760; it was granted to Two Hundred Proprietors; the present Families now settled in this Township are in number One Hundred and fifty, containing Nine Hundred persons. ..."[16] Not only had the number of residents decreased from the original estimate, but given the propensity for people engaged in agriculture to live on their farms, the town plan had clearly been over-ambitious. In spite of Morris's provisions, by 1817 Lord Dalhousie would observe that "There is no town of Horton; it is a scattered settlement of neat common houses, small farmers, but rich in their way of life."[17]

The establishment of the Planters on the agricultural lands left by the Acadians was paralleled by the settlements in Western Nova Scotia and the South Shore, where fishing formed a large portion of the economy. These areas were also familiar to Morris from earlier surveys. He both supervised the establishment of settlers and made some maps of the districts concerned. Here, again, the towns did not always develop according to plan. Morris's early map of Liverpool, showing a projected town site further upstream than the settlement which actually developed, appears, with an accompanying commentary, in Allen Penney's study of the Simeon Perkins house.[18]

Morris had produced his "Draught of Lunenburg and LaHave Harbours ..." in 1762. The following year, a town plot for New Dublin[19] (Figure 8) was surveyed at the site of the present village of LaHave. It shows only the general area designated for the town, with no indication of the planned layout, and in fact the

14   C. Morris, "Plan of Horton Town Surveyed and laid out in June 1760 by Chas. Morris Chief Surveyor." PANS V7/ — 1760 Horton.

15   National Archives of Canada, National Map Collection, NMC 468.

16   PANS, RG 1, Vol. 37, doc. 13 3/4.

17   M. Whitelaw, ed., *The Dalhousie Journals* ([Ottawa], 1978-82), I, 45.

18   A. Penney, *The Simeon Perkins House: an Architectural Interpretation, 1767-1987* (Halifax, 1987), 21.

19   Anon., "The Plott of New Dublin," 1763, PANS, RG 20, Series "C," Vol. 90A, #3.

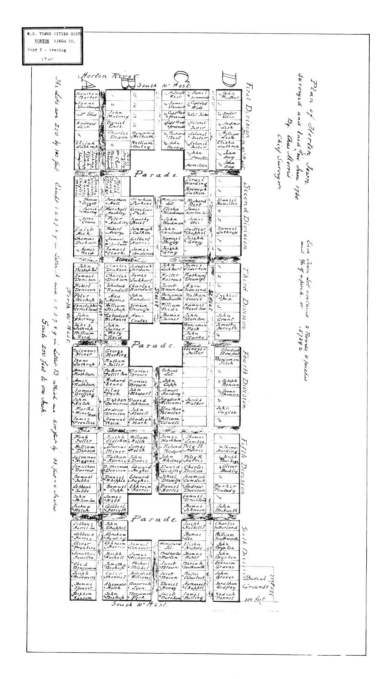

7. A copy of Morris's 1760 plan of Horton. (Courtesy of the Map Division, Public Archives of Nova Scotia.)

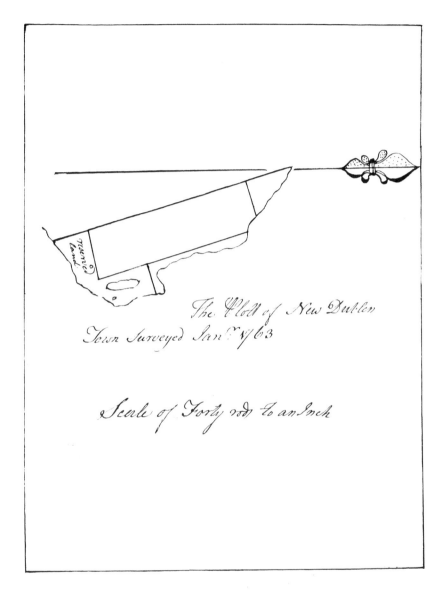

8. The town plot of New Dublin, 1763. (Courtesy of the Map Division, Public Archives of Nova Scotia.)

population of this area was established only slowly, with few of the original grantees actually settling their holdings. Another plan from New Dublin Township survives in the Fort Point Museum, accompanying a grant dated 1763, showing "Ferguson's Island,"[20] (now Moshers Island, one of the LaHave Islands in the New Dublin area) granted to one Henry Ferguson.

In contrast to the initially unsuccessful settlement of New Dublin, other South Shore communities established during this period flourished. In 1762 Morris drew up a plan for a grant in Chester Township to one Samuel Blackdon,[21] now in the Public Archives of Nova Scotia, which also holds a plan entitled "Chester, surveyed and laid out by Jonathan Prescott Esquire, Agreeable to the division of Allotments by the Governor-in-Council in the year 1764."[22] This plan, now in very poor condition, shows the street layout, with numbered lots and two open spaces (one later to be occupied by the Anglican church), the east and west harbours and the peninsula. A similar plan, made in 1858, shows many of the same features.[23] (Figure 9) Unlike some town sites discussed earlier, the Chester street plan has survived with little alteration until the present day. A 1766 map, unsigned but possibly by Morris,[24] shows Chester Township and the islands, with the layout of the town of Chester itself indicated.

The Chief Surveyor's work in establishing the Planters in Nova Scotia is best summed up by his large "Plan of the Peninsula of Nova Scotia with the County of Cumberland whereupon are delineated the Several Towns from the original Survey by Charles Morris, Chief Surveyor, 1764,"[25] of which the central section is reproduced here. (Figure 10) A much more detailed map than the 1761 "Chart of the Peninsula…," it shows a province in which the Planter settlements — which had increased in number since the earlier map — were developing alongside other land grants. The notes explain that "The Townships edged with Blue have been settled upon the Plan of Governor Lawrence's Proclamation." (The other colours identify grants made "in virtue of the King's Mandamus," grants to "sundry disbanded officers and others," and "Townships undertaken to be settled in Governor Wilmot's commands.") The map shows the boundaries of the Planter settlements, and indicates the sites of towns which were beginning to develop. In the western section, the word "Town" appears at the sites of Yarmouth, Barrington and Granville, while only the fort is marked at Annapolis. On the South Shore, Chester and Liverpool towns are named, though no town is marked at the proposed site of New Dublin, a testimonial to the honesty of Morris's reporting. "Town" indicates the locations of Cornwallis, Horton, Falmouth, Newport, Truro and Onslow, while Cumberland and Sackville townships each have a

20   Fort Point Museum, LaHave. Untitled MS map.
21   PANS, RG 20, Series "C," Vol. 90A, #2.
22   PANS, HG2, 239 — 1764 Chester.
23   Anon, "Chester," [1858], PANS, F/239 — 1858 Chester.
24   Anon, untitled, PANS, V7/230, c1766 Chester Township. The map is damaged and may originally have had both a title and an indication of authorship.
25   PRO, CO 700, Nova Scotia No. 38.

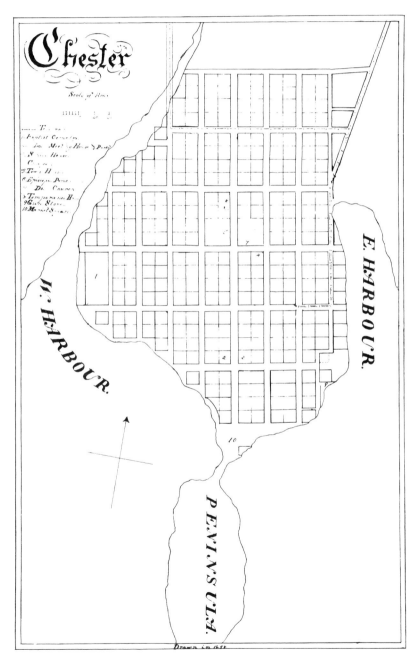

9. The street plan of Chester, 1858. (Courtesy of the Map Division, Public
    Archives of Nova Scotia.)

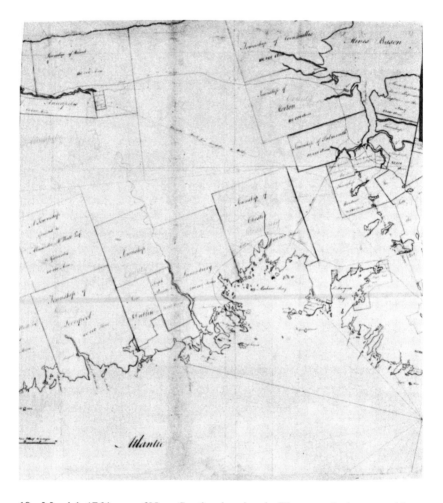

10. Morris's 1764 map of Nova Scotia, showing the Planter and other townships. (Courtesy of the Public Record Office, Kew. Crown copyright.)

"Town Plot." A comparison of this map with Morris's 1755 and 1761 maps of Nova Scotia reveals significant development, in terms of the establishment of administrative divisions, and actual and potential settlement, over the decade. Much of this development can be credited, either directly or indirectly, to Charles Morris.

The failure of many of the towns in primarily agricultural areas to develop along the lines planned by the Chief Surveyor and his associates seems with hindsight to have been inevitable. In the relatively peaceful 1760s, the need to live in densely populated palissaded communities such as early Halifax and Lunenburg gave way to the natural inclination of farmers to live on their lands, and the town plots passed into the hands of speculators and of the merchants and tradesmen who needed to be at the centre of the larger community. When, with time, towns began to grow, they were not necessarily centred on the sites originally selected by Morris, nor did they always follow his plans, but this should not detract from his achievements.

Morris's versatility as an administrator, surveyor and mapmaker would be hard for a public figure of today to emulate; yet he was not originally trained for a career in these fields, and indeed started his working life as a school teacher. Later, as an officer serving at Annapolis Royal, he apparently developed an aptitude for cartography. After his appointment as Chief Surveyor, he turned the skills he had learnt as a military officer to more general, civilian purposes, combining them with other administrative duties.

Charles Morris was, of course, not the first mapmaker to work in the region we now know as Nova Scotia, though he might be considered to have been its first town planner. As well as his depiction of the development of the province as a whole, his detailed representation of areas settled in the 1760s by the Planters under his supervision provides a lasting record of this episode in the province's history. His son, Charles Morris II, was to do the same thing twenty years later for the Loyalists — but that is another story.

Archaeological Evidence of Planter Material Culture in New Brunswick and Nova Scotia

Marc C. Lavoie[1]
Department of Tourism, Recreation and Heritage

This paper is an overview of the current archaeological work at Planter sites in New Brunswick and Nova Scotia. Discoveries and excavations are reviewed, comparisons are made and future directions are suggested. We are only beginning to understand the Planters from an archaeological point of view, but the information already gathered adds considerably to an overall understanding of this important chapter in the history of the Maritimes; and sites soon to be explored promise to yield information that will complement and supplement the potentially rich documentation from archival research, genealogies, museum collections, historical and geographical studies.

In 1983, the Nova Scotia Museum and a number of funding agencies sponsored partial excavations of Acadian domestic dwellings at Belleisle in the Annapolis Valley, Nova Scotia. These sites revealed the presence of rich cultural deposits, yielding a wealth of information on settlement patterns, architectural styles, construction materials, the contents of households, material culture, daily life and activities, trade networks and Acadian economy. Also, regional similarities and differences between contemporary Acadian sites were noted in the artifact collections and house styles.[2] Similar information can be obtained from the excavations of Planter sites.

Historical archaeology is the study of European-derived populations and indigenous groups, their daily activities, adaptive strategies, economic and socio-

---

1   I am grateful for the editorial comments received on earlier drafts of this paper by Dr. Christopher J. Turnbull, director, and Ms. Patricia Allen, assistant director, at New Brunswick's Archaeological Services in Fredericton, and by Dr. Brian Preston, archaeologist at the Nova Scotia Museum in Halifax.

2   The Belleisle archaeological project was directed by David J. Christianson for the Nova Scotia Museum. In 1984, Mr. Christianson completed a survey of the Annapolis Valley where he located a number of ruins; one cellar has been attributed to the Planter period. In 1986, Mr. Christianson and Dr. Brian Preston surveyed and test-excavated a number of locations in Nova Scotia for Acadian and more recent sites. In September 1990, Dr. Preston and Mr. Marc C. Lavoie tested a number of Acadian and Planter sites in Pré Rond, Granville Beach and Granville Ferry in Nova Scotia. See D.J. Christianson, *Belleisle 1983: excavations at a pre-expulsion Acadian site*, Curatorial Report No. 48, The Nova Scotia Museum, 1984; M.C. Lavoie, *Belleisle, Nova Scotia, 1680-1755: Acadian material life and economy*, Curatorial Report No. 65, The Nova Scotia Museum, 1987; B. Preston, *An Archaeological Survey of Reported Acadian Habitation Sites in the Annapolis Valley and Minas Basin Areas, 1971*, Curatorial Report No. 20, The Nova Scotia Museum, 1971; *Excavations at BeDi-2, Belleisle, Annapolis County, 1972*, Curatorial Report No. 21, The Nova Scotia Museum, 1972; and "Archaeological Field Work Summary Report," S.A. Davis *et al.*, *Archaeology in Nova Scotia, 1985 and 1986*, Curatorial Report No. 63, The Nova Scotia Museum, 1987, 229-57.

political interactions, within and between distinct, contemporary or concurrent populations, as reflected by their material culture. The term ''material culture'' is synonymous with ''material life,'' describing all artifacts: food, costume, lodging, technology, industry and the contents of households.[3] In the course of archaeological projects, researchers attempt to locate and identify the remains of specific historical groups, or produce an inventory of the range of historical occupations in a survey area or region. A variety of historical occupations can be identified in a single survey area, simply because many locales and regions have been visited, exploited and occupied by different groups over time. This variety offers much potential for the study of specific occupations and very interesting comparative studies, opening a window into the life of settlers in both New Brunswick and Nova Scotia. All of these different occupations are, or should be, of equal interest to historical archaeologists.

Historical archaeologists combine studies of artifacts, structural remains, faunal and floral analyses with archival, historical and geographical studies to produce an archaeological study of a site or a region. Material culture studies in themselves are extremely important. Every type of artifact has its own history, some artifacts being well documented in comparison to others. Generally speaking, the artifact is viewed as a three-dimensional document from two points of view: 1) Each artifact has recognizable and measurable attributes, information which enables archaeologists to gain insight into the age, origin and the intended use of a particular object;[4] 2) These artifacts are retrieved in a three-dimensional context, in a specific location at a site, and in combination with others. For example:

> Three joining [mended] fragments of a Rhenish stoneware chamber pot are found on a site, but they have been recovered from different locations and at different levels ... one was found beneath the original foundation of a house and must, therefore, have been deposited there before the house was built. The second comes from the upper fill of a well, which indicates that the shaft had ceased to function before the potsherd was thrown into it. The third piece was found in the silting of a shallow ditch ... one can deduce that

---

3   This definition attempts to reflect the general research concerns of historical archaeologists, combining them with Fernand Braudel's thoughts on material history. See F. Braudel, *The Mediterranean and the Mediterranean World in the Age of Philip II, Vol. 1* (New York, 1972), 13-22; and *The Structures of Everyday Life* (London, 1981), 23-29; J.F. Deetz, *In Small Things Forgotten: the archaeology of early American life* (New York, 1977), 4-24, 156-157; and S. South, *Method and Theory in Historical Archaeology* (New York, 1977), 1-29, 317-30.

4   Ivor Noël Hume has written extensively about this type of evidence. Writing about pottery, he outlined the type of information that is ideally available to archaeologists: ''A fragment of pottery the size of a finger nail can be readily identified as to its composition, its approximate date of manufacture, and sometimes even its factory. We know how it was shipped to the colonies, how much it was worth, and an inventory may give us the name of its owner.'' See I. Noël Hume, *Historical Archaeology* (New York, 1968), 13.

the well was out of use before the house was built ... [and] the ditch might be contemporaneous with the construction date of the house. ...[5]

Planter sites and artifacts have been known to archaeologists for a number of years. Until that time, archaeologists had recorded the location of a variety of pre-historic and historical sites as part of provincial and archaeological resources inventories, and in the course of independent, university projects. Over the past five years, however, systematic surveys and test-excavations at a small number of Planter sites have been completed in selected areas of New Brunswick and Nova Scotia. Also, Planter, Loyalist and later ruins were identified in the course of surveys and excavations for early trading posts, fortifications and domestic sites of the French/Acadian period (1605-1760) in both New Brunswick and Nova Scotia.[6]

Test-excavations have revealed the existence of a variety of contemporary and concurrent occupations, offering great potential for comparative studies. Generally speaking, Planter ruins are located at the margin of tidal marshes, meadows and river intervals, but on slightly higher elevations than Acadian occupations; they also differ in outline from a specific type of Acadian ruins.[7] Furthermore, the artifact samples from both types of ruins differ greatly from one another, indicating significant differences in occupational chronology, access to markets and sources of supply, probably a reflection of the trading networks, accessibility to markets or the availability of goods for sale in the northeast or in specific regions. Similar differences between Planter sites should be noticeable, and status differences as reflected by consumer preferences have been noted, as we will see below.

---

5   I. Noël Hume, ''Material Culture with the Dirt on it: a Virginia perspective,'' in I.M.G. Quimby, ed., *Material Culture and the Study of American Life* (New York, 1987), 25-26.

6   In the early 1970s, Dr. Brian Preston, recorded a Planter site in Pré Rond, Nova Scotia. Test-excavations at Castle Frederick (ca.1765-ca.1820) in Upper Falmouth, Nova Scotia, were completed by Dr. Stephen A. Davis and archaeology students at Saint Mary's University in 1988 and 1989, in the fall of each year. In New Brunswick, Mr. J. Russell Harper and Dr. Norman F. Barka excavated two structures associated with the Simonds, Hazen and White trading post in their search for Fort La Tour in the 1950s and 1960s. Mrs. Louise Hale and Mr. Scott Finley surveyed the Enclosure Provincial Park in 1988. Mr. Marc C. Lavoie surveyed the Beaubassin area in New Brunswick and Nova Scotia in 1986. See N.F. Barka, ''Historic Site Archaeology at Portland Point, New Brunswick, Canada, 1631-c1850,'' PhD thesis, Harvard University, 1965. J.R. Harper, Portland Point: crossroads of New Brunswick history, The New Brunswick Museum, 1956; ''Portland Point Excavations: preliminary report of the 1956 expedition.'' m.s., 1956, file, Archaeology New Brunswick, Fredericton. M.C. Lavoie, *The Archaeological Reconnaissance of the Beaubassin Region in Nova Scotia and New Brunswick — 1986*, The Council of Maritime Premiers Reports in Archaeology No. 7 (Fredericton, 1990).

7   At least two styles of Acadian houses are now recognized. Surface features for one style of house are easily recognized: the outline of the house walls, storage area and bake oven are evident on the surface. This house type has been identified in Nova Scotia at Upper Falmouth, Belleisle, New Minas and in the Granville area, and in New Brunswick at Fort Beauséjour. A second style of Acadian house is represented by rectangular or square depressions. See footnote 2, and A.

In 1990, New Brunswick's Department of Tourism, Recreation and Heritage sponsored a 17-week archaeological reconnaissance and test-excavations at the Enclosure Provincial Park. The park is located at the confluence of the Southwest and Northwest Miramichi Rivers, south of Newcastle (Figure 1). Historical information indicates that selected areas of the park were occupied from the 1750s into the present century by Acadian refugees (ca. 1756-1759), Planters (ca. 1765), Loyalists (ca. 1784) and by nineteenth-century and later occupants.

Historical information related to the Planter presence at the Enclosure Provincial Park is very interesting, but incomplete. Apparently, William Davidson and John Cort were established in that location sometime during the second half of the 1760s. These entrepreneurs established a commercial salmon fishery and were involved at various times in a lumber operation and the fur trade. John Cort erected a house at Miramichi Point which he bequeathed to his daughter Mary Ann O'Hara-Cort around 1783. William Davidson had a warehouse in the same

1. Miramichi Point photographed from the south shore of the Southwest Miramichi. The arrows indicate the known extent of the site to date and the tip of the point (from left to right). The site is located at the Enclosure Provincial Park, near Newcastle in New Brunswick.

Crépeau and B. Dunn, *The Melanson Settlement: an Acadian community (ca. 1664-1755)*. Research Bulletin No. 250, Parks Canada, 1986, 7-12; F. Korvemaker, "Report on the 1972 Excavation of two Acadian Houses at Grand Pré National Historic Park, Nova Scotia," Manuscript Report No. 143, Parks Canada, 1972, 13; Lavoie, *The Archaeological Reconnaissance of the Beaubassin Region*, 11-12.

location. The ruins of these structures have not yet been located. Furthermore, it is difficult to say who else might have been at the site with Davidson and Cort. However, they had a number of employees who could have been living at the point. The documentation also indicates that William More [sic] and George Sutherland resided at the point as early as 1769, but their relationship to Cort and Davidson is not understood.[8]

Only a small area of the park was surveyed, due to the wealth of archaeological finds discovered during the assessment: seven structures were identified and nearly 40,000 artifacts were recovered. The ruins identified to date are located towards the eastern limit of the point (Figure 2). Planter ruins are represented by

2. M. André Chiasson (left) and Mr. Christopher Blair (right) shovel-testing along pre-determined survey lines on a master grid, at the Enclosure Provincial Park. Since no maps from the 1750s and 1760s exist or have been located to date, this is a standard method of site location, the information being recorded on the master grid.

---

8   Davidson probably resided at The Elm Tree, a few kilometres from the point on the Southwest Miramichi. He removed himself from the area during the American Revolution, residing in Maugerville on the St. John River, from 1777 to 1783. A 1788 plan of the point shows the location of Cort's house and Davidson's warehouse. We are presently trying to match the period maps with modern plans in order to locate both structures at the point. See F. Thériault, "De La Point Boishébert à la Point Wilson," m.s., 1988, file, Archaeology New Brunswick, Fredericton. W.H. Davidson, *William Davidson, 1740-1790*, Historical Studies No. 6, The New Brunswick Museum, 1947.

structural remains associated with artifacts produced in the 1760s. Two Planter structures have been identified. The first is a small house or a storage shed erected on a brick and clay footing; it is about 4.5 by 7.0 meters (Figure 3). This house or shed appears to have been a flimsy structure, occupied for a brief period of time. Perhaps it was used as an initial shelter until more permanent structures were erected at the point. Artifacts recovered to date relate to food consumption, being represented by creamware bowls or plates, and an English Brown Stoneware mug.[9]

The second structure dates to the Acadian presence at Miramichi Point (ca. 1756 to 1759), but appears to have been reoccupied during the Planter period. Artifacts from the French Regime underlie or are mixed with early pearlwares, late English White Salt-Glazed Stonewares and Anglo-American coarse earthenwares —

3. The north profile of the excavation unit at the small Planter house or shed located at the Enclosure Provincial park. The arrow points to the pedestaled brick and clay footing truncated in the course of the excavations. (The photographic scale is 50 cm long.)

9   For a general discussion of most of the artifacts discussed in the present paper, see I. Noël Hume, *A Guide to Artifacts of Colonial America* (New York, 1969). Anglo-American coarse earthenwares are found at both Acadian and Planter sites.

artifacts which duplicate those found on other Planter sites.[10] They represent objects for food storage and consumption — plates, bowls and storage vessels. In 1991, our search for Planter occupations will continue at the Enclosure Provincial Park.

In 1982, a survey team from Archaeology New Brunswick identified the ruins of a small domestic dwelling in Gagetown. Unfortunately, the historical documentation on this particular house has not yet been compiled. Archaeological information, however, indicates that the house was occupied from around 1780 to 1820. It is a small rectangular structure, about 6 by 5 meters erected on a field stone footing and located on the top of a knoll overlooking the St. John River (Figure 4).

4. Dr. David Black stands in front of the small, late Planter or early Loyalist Period shanty identified in Gagetown, New Brunswick, in 1982. The cellar has been filled in with field stones, the result of field clearing after the house was burned, dismantled or abandoned. (The photographic scale is 50 cm long.)

---

10   It is plausible that structures related to the Acadian refugee camp at Miramichi Point were not set afire in the late 1750s, when the Acadian refugee camp was seemingly abandoned. These structures could have been reoccupied later by Davidson, Cort or their employees. It is also plausible that the foundations of Acadian structures were utilized again to erect new structures. The site appears to have been vacant for about five or eight years between the Acadian and Planter occupations, although it was visited by traders in the area. The practice of reusing old cellars to erect new structures was documented in southern New Brunswick in the fall of 1986. See "Journal of Charles Robin giving a day by day account of his work in Canada, 1767-1787," typed copy housed at the Village historique acadien, Caraquet, N.B. Personal Communication, M. Fidèle Thériault, Archaeology New Brunswick, Fredericton, November 1990.

Artifacts retrieved from the test-excavations include fragments of Anglo-American coarse earthenwares, English slipwares and early pearlwares; they represent objects for food preparation, service and consumption.

In the fall of 1986, another house occupied by Planters, Yorkshiremen or early Loyalist farmers was identified at Mount Whatley, near Sackville, New Brunswick (Figure 5). The Miner site is isolated from modern roads, farms and more recent, nineteenth-century ruins. This house is located conveniently near the Tantramar Marsh and a natural spring, and it must have been accessed from the marsh. Historical documentation has yet to be undertaken. However, the archaeological tests indicate that the house was occupied from about 1780 to 1830. It was a dwelling with a rectangular floor plan, about 10 by 15 meters.

Artifacts recovered from the Miner Site test-excavations include objects for food preparation, cooking and service: a tureen, bowls and plates in pearlware and white refined earthenware and an Anglo-American coarse earthenware pan or bowl. Glass objects include liquor bottles, a flask and a stemmed drinking glass. The pearlwares duplicate the type of pottery used by British officers at Fort Cumberland (Fort Beauséjour), indicating a similar source of supply, and possibly, delimiting the range of wares available in this region around 1780 and after. Furthermore, it is interesting to note that the ceramics display moderate use-ware, worn footrings and rims, and extensive scratches, plausibly indicating prolonged

5. Mr. Laird Niven records his finding in his fieldnotes at the Miner site in Mount Whatley, New Brunswick. The arrows show the approximate location of the corners of the house.

usage, the use of iron utensils, the possible absence of table cloths or the storage of plates in stack, or on their rims, on shelves or in a china cabinet.[11]

Both the Miner Site and the house at Gagetown represent either late Planter occupations or very early Loyalist occupations; extensive archaeological excavations would reveal their actual nature and age. Nevertheless, they represent very interesting sites for comparative purposes with earlier and later Planter occupations in both New Brunswick and Nova Scotia.

The preliminary work at the Simonds, Hazen and White trading post at Portland Point in Saint John yielded valuable information. These ruins are located between nineteenth-century refuse and the ruins of Fort La Tour.[12]

Trading activities at the post began in 1762 and continued until about the end of the eighteenth century. Excavations by Harper and Barka in the 1950s and 1960s revealed the presence of perhaps a house and a shed related to the Simonds, Hazen and White occupation. The house had a rectangular masonry footing, measuring 3.35 by 7.6 meters, while the shed, also erected on a masonry footing, was 3.2 meters long and 2.9 meters wide. Anglo-American coarse earthenwares, delftwares, English combed-slipwares, Chinese export porcelain, liquor bottles, a drinking glass and tobacco pipes were recovered during the excavations of the shed. These artifacts are typical of the Planter period. No artifacts were recovered from the house, however. The artifacts from the Simonds, Hazen and White trading post could represent either objects utilized by the occupants of the site, objects meant to be sold, or a combination of both. A comparative study of these objects with other Planter collections could provide answers to these questions.

In Nova Scotia, the excavations at Castle Frederick in Upper Falmouth have yielded a wealth of information about Planter everyday life. The site consists of a number of features and structures associated with pre-expulsion Acadians, Planters and later occupations. "Castle Frederick" refers to both the 8000-acre estate and mansion occupied by the cartographer and landowner Joseph Frederick Wallet DesBarres (1721-1824) his family, tenants, servants and co-workers, established at Upper Falmouth, around 1764 and after. From the time of his arrival at Upper Falmouth and until his departure in 1774, DesBarres busied himself in the coastal survey of the Gulf of St. Lawrence, the Maritimes and New England. He published a series of maps entitled The Atlantic Neptune between 1774 and 1784.[13] It appears that his estate was managed at various times by his

---

11 A number of interesting studies on the origins, range of forms and uses of pearlware vessels are available. See G. Miller, "Origins of Wedgwood's 'pearlware,'" *Northeast Historical Archaeology*, XVI (1987), 83-95; I. Noël Hume, "Pearlware: forgotten milestone of English Ceramic history," *Antiques*, XCV (1969), 390-97; L. Sussman, "Changes in Pearlware Dinnerware, 1780-1830," *Historical Archaeology*, XI (1977), 105-111; and "British Military Tableware," *Historical Archaeology*, XII (1978), 93-104. On use-ware, see D.M. Griffiths, "Use-Marks on Historic Ceramics," *Historical Archaeology*, XII (1978), 68-81. On the Miner Site, see Lavoie, *The Archaeological Reconnaissance of Beaubassin*, 9-10.

12 Barka, "Historic Sites Archaeology at Portland Point," 191-213.

13 For overviews of the life, professional, political and business achievements of DesBarres, see

mistress, Mary Cannon, especially from the time of his departure in 1774, into the nineteenth century. In 1770, a population of 93 was recorded on the estate, including tenants and employees of Acadian, English, Scottish, Irish, German and American origins.[14]

Archaeological surveys and test-excavations at Castle Frederick began in 1987; this work continued until the fall of 1990, and other excavations may be undertaken in years to come.[15] Partial excavations have been undertaken at three Planter houses: the castle and at two smaller structures believed to represent dwellings occupied by workers or tenants. The two smaller houses are rectangular structures, being represented by shallow, surface depressions or cellars, approximately 4 by 5.5 meters and 4 by 6.5. meters respectively. The smallest house yielded a limited number of artifacts: a pearlware plate sherd, brick fragments and unidentifiable nails. The larger structure has a small mound at its western end, representing a chimney collapse or a fireplace. Artifacts recovered from the excavations include fragments of English White Salt-Glazed stoneware, some with scratch-blue decorations, sherds of Jackfield ware, Whieldon black-glazed earthenwares, Anglo-American coarse earthenwares and fragments of early pearlwares. The production dates for these artifacts coincide well with the Planter presence in the area, from ca. 1764 to about 1820.

The castle consisted of a central, main section with eastern and western additions. This configuration is based on period sketches, surface features and the test-excavations (Figure 6). The entire structure must have been approximately 27.0 meters long and 9.0 meters wide at its widest point. Artifacts include fragments of Batavian porcelain, Chinese export and European porcelains, English White Salt-Glazed stoneware, varieties of early and late creamwares and pearlwares, English and Anglo-American coarse earthenwares, English slipwares, bottle, table and window glass, buttons, gunflints, architectural remains, and a precision nut and bolt — perhaps from a tripod for a survey instrument (Figures 7-9).[16]

R.L. Bishop, "An Eighteenth-Century Nova Scotia Observatory," *The Journal of the Royal Astronomical Society of Canada*, LXXI, 6 (1977), 425-42; G.N.D. Evans, *Uncommon Obdurate: the several public careers of J.W.F. DesBarres* (Salem, 1969); and R.J. Morgan, "Joseph Frederick Wallet DesBarres," *DCB*, V, 192-97.

14   J.V. Duncanson, *Falmouth: a New England township in Nova Scotia, 1760-1965* (Windsor, Ontario, 1965), 28.

15   Dr. Brian Preston assisted by a number of archaeologists completed surveys in this location beginning in 1987. Test excavations began in 1988. The author tested four structures during the summer of 1989. Finally, Dr. Michael Deal, Mr. Stephen T. Powell and students from Memorial University of Newfoundland in St. John's completed partial excavations of DesBarres's mansion in 1990. Technical reports are in preparation. See footnote no. 6.

16   This is only a summary of the finds from the 1989 and 1990 excavations. The architectural remains of the house were examined in detail during the 1990 field season; the report on this facet of the archaeology is in preparation by the author.

6. An aerial view of the ruins of DesBarres' mansion at Castle Frederick in Upper Falmouth, Nova Scotia. The workers are excavating a prepared limestone pad, representing the main entrance of the house, or more likely, the foundation of an observatory. The arrows point to the approximate limit of the eastern extension to the house.

By comparing the artifacts from the castle with those from the larger tenant's house it becomes clear that there are not only more artifacts from the former structure, but also a greater variety of wares, including wares not retrieved from the excavations at the tenant's house. Also, the range of artifacts at the castle is more varied than those from the other sites reviewed, both in New Brunswick and in Nova Scotia. This is not surprising, considering that DesBarres was more affluent than the occupants of the other sites, undoubtedly having access to a greater variety of objects because of his social status, his mobility and his probable connections with other affluent people in Nova Scotia and elsewhere.

The faunal assemblages from the castle and the largest tenant's house have been analyzed. The faunal analyst, however, warned that the bones from the excavations could have been deposited after the end of the occupation of the site; however, both series of ruins are so distant from more recent ruins and modern occupations that this possibility is very improbable. Mammalian species from the castle include horse, cow, possibly domestic sheep, cottontail rabbit and woodchuck. These probably represent subsistence remains except for the remains from the horse, this mammalian being represented by teeth only. The mol-

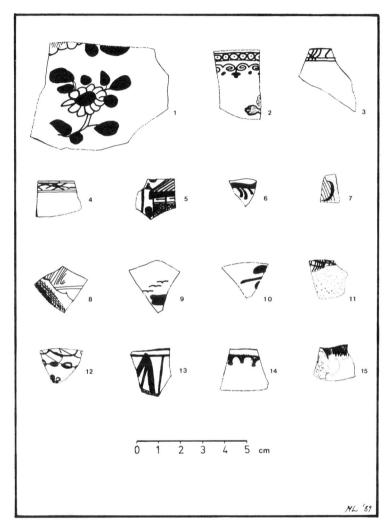

0   1   2   3   4   5   cm

ML '89

7. Ceramics from the mansion at Castle Frederick. Nos. 1 and 2 are Batavian porcelains. Nos. 3 to 5 are rim sherds from Oriental or Chinese Export porcelains, representing bowls, saucers or small plates. No. 6 is a rim sherd from a small porcelain bowl; it could be Oriental in origin, but the decorations are those of European craftsmen. Often, decorations were added to imported Oriental porcelains stored in European warehouses before they were exported overseas to the New World. No. 7 is a fragment from a small bowl in English White Salt-Glazed Stoneware with scratch-blue decorations. Nos. 8-15 are early English pearlwares; some of the designs illustrated are "chinoiseries" or pseudo-Chinese motifs, copies of decorations found on Oriental porcelains.

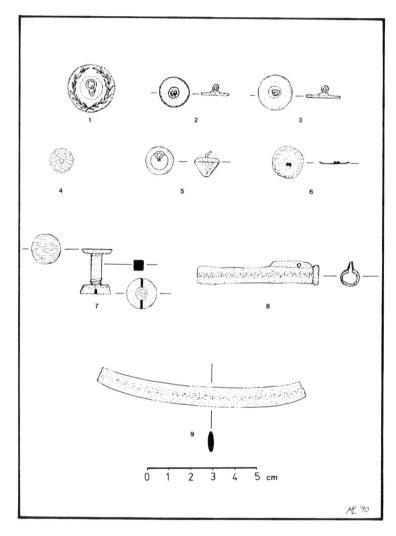

8. Some metal and bone finds from the mansion at Castle Frederick. Nos. 1 to 6 are copper alloy, iron and bone buttons used on clothing; no. 4 is a bone-backing for a button, while No. 6 appears to have been larger at one time and was reworked to its present size. No. 7 is a hand-made cooper-alloy precision screw, the work of a craftsman. It could be part of a tripod for some sort of survey instrument. No. 8 is a ramrod guide for a flintlock gun, also of copper alloy; it would have been attached to a gun's stock, below the barrel. No. 9 is part of a handle or drawer-pull of copper alloy for a commode or a desk.

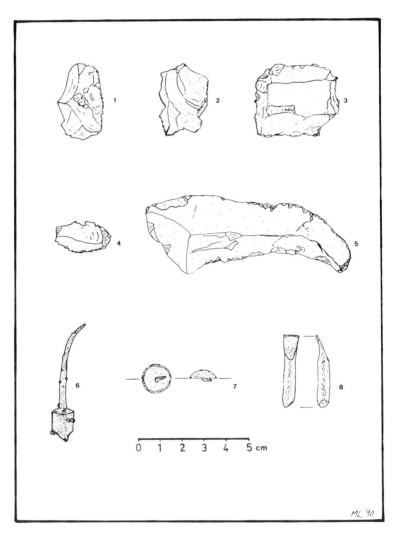

9. Artifacts from the mansion at Castle Frederick. Nos. 1 to 3 are gunflints; nos. 1 and 2 show extensive usage, while no. 3 still informs us on its initial shape, representing an English, prismatic type of gunflint. No. 4 is a glass scraper made from green bottle glass; scrapers were used for precision woodworking in the absence of fine tools or sandpaper. No. 5 is a uniface, a prehistoric tool; its presence at the mansion might indicate that Native Peoples visited the site, or simply represent a collectible or curio brought back to the house by one of its residents. No. 6 is an iron drill bit. No. 7 is a furniture tack. No. 8 is a fragment of a pewter or lead spoon displaying a segment of the spatulate stem-end.

luscan species are represented by scallops and probably hard-shelled clams. Seventy-three bone fragments from the tenant's house were submitted for analysis. Only a small number of bones were identifiable; they represent the remains of relatively young cattle. In comparison, very little can or should be said about the food bones retrieved from these excavations. To date, we are left with an impression of the type of mammals and molluscs possibly consumed at the site.[17] We have only identified one site with which to compare the collection from Des-Barres' castle: John Wentworth's mansion in New Hampshire, occupied from 1768 to 1775. The range of artifacts from Governor Wentworth's mansion appears to duplicate the finds from Castle Frederick, indicating that DesBarres was indeed an affluent member of society and had access to a great variety of objects with which he furnished his house and table.[18] Similar, large dwellings in Granville Ferry and at Pré Rond in Nova Scotia will add to our understanding of the range of finds, the daily life and activities of both affluent and non-affluent members of Planter society.[19] However, excavations at these sites have not yet been completed. Also, contemporary finds from the City of Halifax could inform us further on the potential range of objects imported and used in the city during the Planter Period.[20]

In conclusion it must be emphasized that our work on Planter period sites is preliminary in nature. However, archaeologists will continue to examine Planter ruins recovering and interpreting a different type of information — artifacts in archaeological context research. By working together, archaeologists, material culture analysts, historians and geographers could produce a multi-facetted look at these people, the best kind of historical analysis. The research to date can be summarized in four series of statements and questions:

1) A limited number of Planter sites are located in the general vicinity of older Acadian ruins. Is this the result of the availability of cleared land, dyked marshes or a combination of the two, or the result of our search for Acadian sites? Archaeologists must look into other kinds of Planter settlements, as the sites identified thus far, represent essentially only two types of occupations, those of farm-

---

17 See D.W. Black, "Report on Faunal Remains from the Castle Frederick Sites (BfDb-4, BfDb-5 and BfDb-6), Nova Scotia," m.s., 1990, on file, History Section, Nova Scotia Museum, Halifax.

18 D.R. Starbuck *et al.*, "America's first Summer Resort: John Wentworth's 18th Century Plantation in Wolfeboro, New Hampshire," *The New Hampshire Archaeologist*, XXX, 1 (1989).

19 These sites were registered by Dr. Brian Preston over the past 20 years. In the fall of 1990, Dr. Preston and Mr. M.C. Lavoie shovel-tested the sites, but it will be some time before they are excavated.

20 Excavations at the Sellon Site at the corner of Barrington and Cornwallis streets, and the collection of finds from the Central Trust site between Hollis Street and Bedford Row, at Duke Street, constitute collections for comparative purposes; they inform us about the range of objects which were brought and used in the capital, and plausibly available and sold to visiting individuals from the countryside. See P. Erickson *et al.*, "Sellon Site (BdCv-7)," Davis *et al.*, Archaeology in Nova Scotia, 1985 and 1986, 9-76; and S.A. Davis *et al.*, *Artifacts from Eighteenth-Century Halifax* (Halifax, 1987).

ers and traders. Both fishing and urban communities must be examined to fully realize the range of Planter Period sites in the Maritimes. Furthermore, since the Planters migrated from New England (and overseas), we must also attempt to compare what their material culture was like before they came to Nova Scotia and New Brunswick and compare these findings with research on New England (and European) communities from ca. 1765 to 1830, to gain a full understanding of Planter life in the Maritimes. How cohesive and homogeneous is the Planter tradition?

2) The range of houses attributed to the Planter period is varied. There are small, perhaps temporary, shanties or flimsy structures along with larger, more permanent houses and mansions attributed to this period. The shanties dating to the 1760s duplicate those from the 1780s. Is there a basic type of shelter that is standard for settlers establishing themselves in an area, dwellings which have perhaps survived as sheds, dependencies or cottages in later years and perhaps to the present day?

3) The age of every structure described above is directly related to the age of the objects recovered from excavations. This should make the study of artifacts very interesting, if only to verify and support chronologies obtained from other sources.[21]

4) The very nature of the artifacts recovered from archaeological excavations at Planter sites informs us on the everyday life of their occupants, and on their social status, the trading networks and markets. The origins of most of these finds can be traced back to their factories; this should inform us about regional, national and international markets. Furthermore, these artifacts are more informative than museum collections in that the range of objects is greater and the finds are recovered in context, whereas heirlooms and collectibles are represented in museum collections.[22]

---

21 This is based on the idea that in eighteenth-century Anglo-American sites there is a high correlation between the dates of ceramics manufacture and the period of site occupation. See South, *Method and Theory in Historical Archaeology*, 210.

22 Here, I do not mean to diminish the value of museum collections; they are indeed extremely valuable for comparative studies and the identification of problematic finds from excavations. However, large quantities of artifacts are recovered from the excavations of domestic sites, and it has been shown that the study of museum collections to interpret daily life in the past is suspect when archaeological collections are not used as complementary and supplementary evidence. See L. Sussman, ''Comparing Museum Collections with Archaeological Collections: an example using a class of ceramic items,'' *Northeast Historical Archaeology*, XIV (1985), 50-54.

The Image and Function of Women
in the Poetry of Affection
in Eighteenth-Century Maritime Canada

Thomas Vincent
Department of English
Royal Military College

This paper focuses on a selection of literary documents from late eighteenth-century Maritime Canada, documents which are generally ignored or, at best, viewed as superficial and unimportant. Part of the reason for that neglect stems from the subject matter that forms the common denominator of the group: the poetry of affection deals with the broad and varied circumstances surrounding the emotion of love. Given such a large and complex subject, most scholars would question whether amateur colonial poets tucked away in Maritime Canada could ever have had anything to say about love worth remembering. But our concern is not so much with the subject itself as with the cultural sensibilities of the poets who wrote about it. What do the efforts of these colonial poets, as they struggle to deal with such a complex subject, tell us about the emotional and imaginative worlds of experience they aspired to create and explore, even if only for brief moments and in the artificial context of literary convention?

What this poetry reveals is something of the character and range of the emotional condition into which the poet imaginatively presumes to enter and, through the use of affective language, attempts to share with the reader. This kind of insight is important because the emotional and imaginative dimensions of human experience are perhaps the most difficult to study historically. Our analyses and descriptions of human history tend to concentrate on the evolution of ideas and institutions, events and lives, because we can approach them as objectively structured phenomena. But the history of emotional and imaginative experience is by nature subjective and is embodied in imaginative documents that demand a sympathetic appreciation of their subjective intentions. In earlier papers, dealing with other types of eighteenth-century Maritime poetry, I have attempted to bridge the objective and subjective insights offered by that poetry by focusing first on thematic concerns, then on the emotive implications of patterns of imagery and their affects.[1] Early Maritime satire, for example, quite naturally springs from political, social and moral issues which are also of interest to the historian. But in addition, the patterns of imagery of which the poetry is composed provide special insight into prevailing casts of mind embodied in unique sets of emotional conditions. The early religious poetry allows for much the same approach. It is

---

1   See "Alline and Bailey," *Canadian Literature,* 68-69 (1976), 124-133; *Narrative Verse Satire in Maritime Canada, 1779-1814* (Ottawa, 1978); "Eighteenth-Century Maritime Verse," *ECW,* 31 (1985), 23-34; and "Henry Alline: Problems of Approach and Reading the *Hymns* as Poetry," in Margaret Conrad, ed., *They Planted Well* (Fredericton, 1988), 201-10.

rooted in objective doctrinal concerns but its imaginative intention has more to do with the subjective quality and character of faith than with the tenets of theology.

Early Maritime love poetry, however, does not provide this convenient bridge. The basic object of its thematic concern (the emotion of affection) is not an area of historical human experience in which Canadian scholars have shown much interest. To the best of my knowledge, no historian has attempted to write the history of love in Canada, let alone in Maritime Canada. Such neglect may be a sad comment on historical scholarship in this country and may even point to a fundamental deficiency in Canadian national character, but in the context of this paper, it simply means there is no shared starting point. The poetry of affection must be approached directly as a set of imaginative documents whose concern is a subjective expression of the emotion of love within the socio-cultural context of late eighteenth-century Maritime Canada.

There is a second point that should be made at the outset of this paper: it is impossible to link these poems specifically to a uniquely Planter literary culture. The paper deals with an aspect of the broad cultural milieu of early Maritime Canada in which Planter experience unfolded. The reason we cannot identify the specific responses of the Planters in this regard is because there is not a sufficient body of imaginative literature exclusively associated with the Planter community from which to draw such conclusions. That deficiency, however, does not imply that the Planters were culturally or imaginatively ignorant or that they deliberately shut themselves off from all aspects of prevailing literary culture. Limitations in access and formal education may well have had some bearing on the range and sophistication of their cultural sensibility, but an awareness of the broad features of seventeenth- and eighteenth-century English literary modes and poetic conventions would have formed the foundation of their general literary knowledge. There is no question that they would have recognized the sentiments reflected in these poems as part of a spectrum of emotive response that had cultural and literary legitimacy even if for some reason they did not agree with all of them. In other words, the materials discussed here would not have been viewed as being culturally alien.

This paper proceeds, then, in the light of two assumptions: first, that imaginative forms of literature (particularly poetry) provide insights into how the mind of an author operates imaginatively to project an intimate awareness of some dimension of the world shared with the intended reader; and second, that the early Planter community did not consciously isolate itself from the cultural contexts of its time and at the very least would have recognized and understood the attitudes of mind reflected in the poetry under discussion.[2] It seems fitting therefore

---

2 I offer this second point without benefit of clear documentation, but base it on two observations. One, there is no evidence that the Planter community consciously or unconsciously pursued a policy of cultural conservatism (xenophobic or otherwise) as a means of articulating or defending a perceived cultural identity. The fact that there is no significant body of uniquely Planter

that most of the poetry in question is anonymous or written by occasional poets about whom we know little or nothing. We are forced to approach the poetry in terms of its broad collective characteristics.

Technically, we find a wide spectrum of eighteenth-century poetic forms and conventions, which are for the most part competently rendered. The influence of neo-classical and pastoral verse forms that dominated English verse in the earlier part of the eighteenth century is unmistakably present and shapes the structural framework of much of the verse. But also present are the more contemporary conventions of sentimental verse, which emerged in the latter part of the century. Maritime poets (and their readers) appear to have been quite aware of current poetic modes and perspectives, but also felt free to employ forms and patterns of an earlier period. The breadth of this technical spectrum does not reflect a problem of cultural lag so much as it reflects a fluid and open cultural environment in which a broad variety of poetic forms speaks to a wide range of poetic sensibilities. Older forms are still pertinent and have a useful place in this cultural environment. They are not viewed as being in conflict with newer poetic forms. The need for cultural richness and variety is greater than the need to feel fashionably current. We should not interpret this variety of techniques and conventions as a poetical hodge-podge indicative of cultural confusion, but as a reflection of the fluidity, openness and vitality of cultural concerns within the community at large.

But the substantive insights that flow from the poems under discussion are not derived from analyses of technique. They come from recognizing that literature (poetry in particular) is an integral part of the process of articulating acceptable social, moral, and spiritual standards in an emerging community. From this point of view, the poetry of affection functions to project models of acceptable patterns of emotional response relating to human love. These models are focused around three common types of emotional circumstances in which love and affection play a significant role. First, there is the love eulogy, poetry in praise of love itself and the charming beauty of the loved one. Second, there is the love lament, poetry regretting the loss of love and/or separation from a loved one. Third, there is the love elegy, poetry lamenting the death of a loved one, which not only involves the loss of love but also casts doubt on the efficacy of the power of love. For the eighteenth century, all of these emotional situations lay potentially within the range of ordinary human life, be it in England or colonial America, and all were viewed as part of universal human experience in the past as well as the present. Not surprisingly, then, there are conventional and traditional ways of express-

---

imaginative literature suggests that they did not feel compelled to employ literature as a means of cultural defense. In the literate world, such a strategy is virtually unknown in the cultural histories of communities which attempt to develop and sustain a unique cultural identity. Culturally, the Planter community appears to have been more open than closed. Second, subsequent writers whose genealogical and social roots lie in that early Planter community readily absorb the broad literary stances and forms of their time and do not, even as a nostalgic act, nurture a sense of unique literary tradition.

ing them in literature, and again not surprisingly, Maritime poets drew upon these traditions and conventions.

The integration of literary convention and historical reality, however, is not always an easy one. In the context of eighteenth-century Maritime Canada, some of the established conventions of the love eulogy present certain problems of credibility. On the face of it, it seems ludicrous that a colonial poet in a somewhat rustic environment should be depicting refined forms of love and romance in terms that often appear to be inappropriate to the social and even the geo-physical circumstances in which his readers exist. Perhaps the most striking example is a short lyric entitled "The Nosegay. Verses addressed to Miss Mary P---e with a nosegay, on her arrival in St. John, New-Brunswick." It appeared in the *Royal Gazette and New Brunswick Advertiser* on Tuesday, 15 August 1786, above the pseudonym Zephyrus. One can imagine how raw and unfinished the physical environs of Saint John would have been at this time, scarcely two years after the arrival of the Loyalist refugee fleets. Yet, the language and tone of this poem, turning as it does on a balance of charming urbanity, gentle sentimentality and philosophic didacticism, projects an image of a cultivated, polished, sunlit world in which there is both the time and the desire to nurture the nuances of genteel human experience.

THE NOSEGAY

> Ruddy youth's, the gay season, and made for delight
> To our senses how charming, how fair to the sight
> In the heart of my Flora this lesson instill
> How obdurate old time is, relentless his will
> That to merit he's careless to beauty less kind,
> To your graces and charms unimpassioned and blind:
> To her bosom when plac'd, seated next to her heart,
> I to you happy flowers this maxim impart,
> To her soul gently steal, softly whisper her ear
> Like the morning of life is the spring of the year.
> At the dawn of the day, by the side of each bush
> How sweet sings the Linnet, sweet carols of Truth;
> How fragrant the flowers, see how verdant the mead
> In a bosom so tender in vain do they plead,
> 'Tis my passion they plead and united thy prove,
> The sweet morning of life, is the season of love.

What is entirely missing here is any mention of the pragmatic imperatives of life that would ultimately make Saint John the "city of shopkeepers." Rather, the poet's imagination presents us with a sophisticated vision of an emotional circumstance working itself out in a setting which is implicitly cultivated if not urban, social in character, and consciously literary by design. Moreover, the whole effect is held together by a sense of gentility and aristocratic exclusivity that belies historical reality. The world of the poem is an imaginative, literary world, and the poet's imagination here draws its poetic tone and imagery from both classical and renaissance sources. The proper nouns, the pastoral depiction of nature, and the rational sensibility are classical characteristics. The sentimental sensibility and the idealized treatment of the woman flow from renaissance literature.

What are we to make of a poem like this one? Is it simply a case of provincial literary pretentiousness or is there a legitimate cultural dynamic at work here? I would argue that, by employing forms and conventions which draw on the recognized literary and cultural traditions of Europe, the colonial poet is consciously or unconsciously attempting to project particular, personal experience against the broad universal realities of the civilized world (at large). This aspect of local literature gives a sense of immediacy and pertinence to the greater world of European culture, while at the same time ameliorating the sense of cultural isolation in geographically distant communities.[3] From this point of view, one cannot afford to ignore or denigrate the constructive contributions that imitative literature makes to the development of a sense of cultural integrity in emerging societies.

But in the case of eighteenth-century love poetry, we are not only put off by the apparent superficialities of the conventions but also by the sociological implications of the relationship between the male speaker and the female subject. In these poems, images of women are projected as cultural and emotional points of reference, a function which implicitly depersonalizes the subject. It means that, if we are going to understand anything of the constructive role this poetry played in Maritime cultural development, we must separate the sociological implications from the cultural. When we look at the depiction of women in the poetry of affection, we find that these images are shaped by two central characteristics defining the function of "the woman" within the poetic context. The first is the relative passivity of the woman's role in the emotional dynamics of the love relationship. The second is the idealization of female beauty as an aesthetic, and frequently as a moral phenomenon, a process which essentially fosters a symbolic role for women. In the late twentieth century, we generally find these images disturbing because of the artificiality and depersonalization of the woman as an individual and because of the apparent superficiality of consciousness that these idealized women seem to represent. Moreover, we know from the recent work of Jane Errington, Margaret Conrad, and others that women in early colonial Canada played an active and integral role in a wide range of communal concerns and were at times engaged in some of the same familial and social responsibilities as men.[4]

---

3   This important function of a local literature is a significant aspect of the satiric and topographical verse produced during the period.

4   See particularly Jane Errington, "Pioneers and Suffragists," in Sandra Burt *et al.,* eds., *Changing Patterns: Women in Canada* (Toronto, 1988), 51-78, and " 'Woman . . . Is a Very Interesting Creature': Some Women's Experiences in Early Upper Canada," *Historic Kingston,* 38 (1990), 16-35; Margaret Conrad, "Recording Angels: The Private Chronicles of Women from the Mar-

Nor did they bury themselves in hidden personal lives, symptomatic of restricted opportunities for emotional interaction. They appear to have been no more neurotic than the men who lived in the same socio-economic and geo-physical circumstances. Why then this peculiarly unrepresentative role for women in literature?

To argue that, consciously or unconsciously, it is the product of a male conspiracy amounts to reverse sexism and gets us no where. To point out that male roles in early literature are generally as unrealistic as female roles begs the question: why is there a difference between literary depictions and historical realities? Clearly, the purposes and intentions of imaginative literature are quite different from those of history. In the case of eighteenth-century literature, we must first recognize that there the function of literature is not psychological and analytical but is rhetorical and demonstrative. Poetry is not an instrument to explore the emotions and the psyche but a means of articulating acceptable patterns of emotional and intellectual conduct and recognized levels of human understanding. When we apply this observation to the depiction of women in the poetry of affection, we begin to see that the focus of the poetry is not so much on women or even on love but on emotional sensibility, the capacity to feel. The poetry does not set out to prescribe roles for women any more than it intends to describe women's roles in the historical context. The poem is an imaginative construct which nurtures degrees of emotive response and solicits levels of aesthetic consciousness through conventional images of idealized love and female beauty. The roots of these conventions lie in the Renaissance in the poetry of Petrarch and the neo-platonism of Plotinus and Ficino, filtered through the love poets of the sixteenth and seventeenth centuries, poets such as Sidney, Spenser, Shakespeare, Jonson and Herrick. In imaginative terms, they present a spectrum of emotional stances which act as models, not of psychological conditions per se, but of levels of emotional awareness and aesthetic consciousness. The idealized woman is the focus but the real subject of this poetry is the dynamics of feeling.

For example, the following love lament, published in the *Nova-Scotia Magazine* of February 1790 by Pollio, turns on the evocation of a sense of nostalgic melancholy, precipitated by the neglect and indifference of the poet's lady for his love. But the poem keeps shifting the reader's attention. As a narrative, it is ostensibly focused on describing a series of evocative pastoral images, but in the end that narrative turns out to be anchored in the poet's unrequited love for a hidden focus, the idealized mistress of his heart. When viewed as a lyric, however, the real power and focus of the poem lies in another level of consciousness; it lies in the emotional condition of melancholy reflected in the tone of the poem, flowing from a fusion of pastoral description and love lament. The complex conjunction of tone and mood that evolves here is like the interaction of color and light in pictorial art.

STANZAS

How sweet! at early dawn, to stray
  Along the wild sequester'd vale,
To dash the dew-drop from the spray
  And taste the balmy breathing gale.
From sunny hills, and mossy seats,
  To view the lovely landscape round;
To hear amid the green retreats,
  The music of the woods resound.
How sweet! when noon embrowns the glade,
  To linger in the woodbine bower;
Or by some babbling streamlet laid,
  To listen to the summer shower.
Or when the rainbow decks the sky,
  To wander thro' the woodland scene,
Mark in each flower a brighter dye,
  In every mead a deeper green.
How sweet! when on the mountain's head,
  The sun displays his latest ray;
The western skies are lively red
  And Zephyr fans the parting day.
No more alas! the morning breeze
  Awakes to joy my anxious breast —
The soothing songsters of the trees
  No more can charm my soul to rest.
The fragrance of a summer shower,
  The sweetly pensive walk at eve,
The varied brightness of a flower,
  No more my gloomy cares relieve.
O thou! dear author of my pain,
  Return — restore my wonted ease —
Indulgent hear thy faithful swain,
  And nature's charms again shall please.

The emotive power of the shadowy, idealized woman overrides the potential effects of the sharply drawn, if conventional, pastoral landscape, creating a stronger impression of the nuances of melancholy than a clear impression of the poet's love. The message of the lyric rests in its mood and tone which is articulated in the voice of the poet and invested impressionistically in the descriptive imagery.

Even when the woman is more directly the focus of the poem, the real subject of the lyric is generally the pattern of emotion that unfolds in the context of imagined circumstance. It would be a mistake to consider these pieces in any way autobiographical. They are carefully crafted models of complex emotional conditions, delicately balancing affection, melancholy, reason and a sense of human dignity. The intention is to present cultivated emotion, civilized emotion. One of the finest is the lyric "To a Lady" by G.T., published in the *Halifax Gazette* of 30 October 1792.

TO A LADY

As from your presence sadly I withdrew
To ev'ry happiness I bade adieu!
To every joy which FANCY could inspire,
To every tender hope and fond desire!
Farewel! — and oh! where'er thou dost remain,
Pride of the town, or envy of the plain!
Whether in WEDLOCK'S happy union join'd,
Or in the silken snares of LOVE entwin'd,
To thy fond breast may sorrow never steal,
Nor any care, but such as lovers feel!

How oft, *****, didst thou, smiling, say,
Absence wou'd wear my love for thee away,
And oh! how often have I vainly strove
To check that passion thou wou'dst disapprove;
But, ah! those charms where Beauty, void of Art,
Sports unconfin'd, and captivates each heart;
Those fatal charms, whence all my sorrows rose,
Serve still to wake the Genius of my woes;
For now, alas! where'er I turn my view,
IMAGINATION fondly figures you;
Views, in idea, all the worth you boast,
While in the lover all the man is lost:
Ev'n from the circle of the belles I see,
My heart, still constant turn to thee;
Turn to *****, where the gods have joined
The gentlest manners with the noblest mind!
For know, fair MAID, tho' prostrate at your shrine,
Admiring vot'ries hail your charms divine;
To act the hero's or the lover's part,
None bears a nobler, few a truer heart,
Than he who pays your worth the tribute due,
And only asks — to live or die with you!

What is striking here is the emotional control of the poetic voice as it struggles with resignation, if not despair. The woman functions as an unwitting agent of an unfeeling world which drains the passion of life without renewing its vitality, and in the end offers only indifference to individual worth. For the poet, this indifference reflects the nature of the world at large, the nature of the human condition. His relationship to the woman of the poem simple crystalizes this perception in literary form.

This rather bleak picture, however, should be balanced by Benjamin Marston's more positive and optimistic tribute in his poem "To Eliza" dated June 1776.[5]

TO ELIZA

Accept dear Maid in friendly part
This artless lay, from one whose heart
Forever yet has constant prov'd
And faithful to the Fair he lov'd.
To you at W-----r's happy place,
The Seat of plenty, joy and Peace,
Where oft Apollo does resort
And with the Muses keeps his Court.
'Tis sent, in hopes it may amuse you
When the writer's present state it shews you.
Quite chang'd from that he enjoy'd of late
At Winkworth's hospitable Seat,
Where with the wise, the good, and young
A hundred years he'd scarce think long,
While every day new objects brought
To please the Sense or engage the Tho't.
   * * * * *
But very different is the Scene
In which I ever since have been.
Apollo's nor one Muse's face
I've ne'er yet seen in all this place;
No genial souls with whom to sit
And gravely talk or gayly chat;
No little Will with whom to play;
No Rebuses, no Bouts rimez;
Nor no Eliza who with ease
Made every Scene and Object please.
But Mars and Neptune's boisterous Sons

---

5 The original is found in Benjamin Marston's diary, which is part of the Winslow Papers at the University of New Brunswick.

With pipes and fifes and swords and guns,
With rattle, driving, firing, tearing
Bawling, thumping, scolding, swearing,
Present mine eyes a different view
From that I late enjoy'd with you.
But let me hope, these storms o'erblown,
And smiling Peace again return'd,
In some secure retreat I prove
The happy Object of your love.
This irksome scene I then would pass
With heart resolv'd and steady face;
Nor mind the waves that should roll o'er me
So fain a haven lying before me.

The object of the poet's affection here would appear to be the historical Eliza, but as the poem ends, she becomes part of a greater vision of life, one characterized by peace, plenty and emotional contentment. The Eliza of the poem becomes the key to a literary vision in which an infelt satisfaction and a sense of the fullness of life are the dominant characteristics.

Finally, I would like to draw attention to a love elegy in which the poet consciously casts his lyric in the traditional pastoral mode of the shepherd's song. Pastoral conventions are among the most artificial and deliberately literary of English poetic traditions. There is no question that the pastoral world is a world of the imagination and one not intended to be taken literally. Thus, the focus of the poem is centered quite clearly on the dynamic complexity of the speaker's emotional state. Even though the poet approaches his subject indirectly as a third-person narrator, the poem nonetheless becomes an expression of the shepherd's complaint, his emotional condition, in the form of an apparently simple song by a simple rustic. That simplicity, however, is deceptive; the poem turns out to be strikingly complex both structurally and emotionally.[6] The piece I have selected was published anonymously in the *Nova-Scotia Magazine* of August 1790 and is titled "Delia: An Elegy."

DELIA: AN ELEGY

E'er I awoke, rouz'd by the neighb'ring herds,
Blythe Morn had spread around her rosy veil,
When charming was the song of earliest birds,
And sweetly breath'd the aromatic gale.

---

6   In the poem selected, there is a further distancing effect in having the narrator as a third-person commentator on a lost love-relationship, rather than as a primary participant. But the emotional relationship of the poet to his subject remains the same, as does the consolation at the end of the poem. Damon suffers the loss of Delia, while the poet's sensibility is affronted by the inexplicable destruction of this idyllic relationship, signalling the vulnerability of love to death. The pattern of emotional melancholy and philosophic resolution for the two males is much the same.

The solar God advancing on his way
    Forth lur'd me, and my wonted tour I took;
All Nature round seem'd lively, young and gay,
    Save where I stray'd without or friend or book.
Along the path and o'er the well-known style,
    Where trav'lers pass to their long dreary rest,
To read each tearful tomb I stray'd awhile,
    And with vain pity heav'd my throbbing breast.
The once-loved Delia, fair as is the morn,
    (Which now directs me to her clay-cold bed)
Whose cheeks unconscious blushes did adorn,
    Lies here a guest among the awful dead.
Her fate was like the rose not fully blown,
    Cut by the barb'rous and untimely steel,
Who, (e'er her odorif'rous sweets were known)
    Was taught the bitter pangs of death to feel.
Time was when with that flower she might contend
    Both for its sweetness and its ruddy hue,
While yet those genial charms together blend,
    Her lovely person and her virtues too.
Now she, alas! nor charms th'enamour'd youth
    Nor bounds his heart to meet her in the grove;
No more to her he vows eternal truth
    Nor tells the faithfulness of his pure love.
Ah! I have seen them, but no more shall see,
    When lover-like they hail'd the blissful hour,
And innocently she upon his knee,
    Conversant sat within the fragrant bower.
Oft as those lovers met, so oft they told
    The secrets of each others fond desire,
No virtuous wish did ever they withhold;
    So equal love augments the mutual fire.
But ah! Death's cruel unrelenting stroke,
    Forc'd from his wish'd embrace the charming fair
The strongest ties of love and friendship broke,
    That might subsist between the happiest pair.
The youth no sordid interest ever knew,
    Nor aught what might his Delia disapprove,
Her lovely self was all he had in view,
    But she with angels slew a mortal love.
Well, Damon, soon the hours shall fly away,
    When thou (if virtue fills thy humble breast)
Shalt with thy Delia spend eternal day,
    In the bright mansions of immortal rest.

The theme of death here exonerates the woman from charges of callous indifference resulting in unresolved love. She is as much a victim of fate as the complaining lover. She has lost out to physical death, he, to an emotional death at her passing. For both, death has betrayed the power of love and the lovers have fallen into a kind of spiritual and emotional wasteland in spite of the vitality of the pastoral world around them. But there the similarity ends; Delia is as passive and idealized as her sisters in the poems discussed earlier. Indeed, there appears to be little difference in the poetic function of these women, whether they are dead or alive.

The reason that these women do not intrude into the active world of the poem is because they function as sounding boards for more central issues which involve neither women nor love. At the heart of the poem lies a vision of the condition of life emotionally and imaginatively perceived and an assumption that emotional and imaginative perceptions are fundamental to a profound appreciation of human experience and human reality. Sentimental poetry, therefore, becomes an opportunity to exercise refined feeling and to nurture a perceptive sensibility. The degree to which individuals are capable of exercising refined sensibility is a measure of the civility of the society. This capacity is an essential component of a civilized society and especially of an emerging society. There the opportunity for cultural and aesthetic experience is limited while the pragmatic imperatives of the prevailing social, economic and geo-physical conditions work to blunt and make irrelevant the values which support the significance of aesthetic sensitivity. No wonder these verses often seem so out of place in the historical reality of eighteenth-century Nova Scotia and New Brunswick. But the refinement of sensibility and the degree of civility it represents was desperately yearned for by those who did not wish to see the darkness of ignorance and the crudeness of pragmatism set the tone of the socio-cultural reality that was gradually being built in colonial Maritime Canada.

In this effort, the idealized woman of love poetry played and continued to play an important role as a catalyst to gentle emotions. But there was a related cultural development involving women which was perhaps even more far reaching in its sociological effects. By the late eighteenth century, the symbolic function of women in literature as focuses of emotional and aesthetic response contributed significantly to the historic transfer of social responsibility for emotional and aesthetic values to the stewardship of women. With it came responsibility for moral, spiritual, and educational matters. Women became idealized purveyors of these values to the culture at large. Ann Douglas's study, *The Feminization of American Culture* (New York, 1977) explores this process in considerable detail. Also valuable are the works of Barbara Welter and Nancy Cott.[7] For our purposes, however, the transfer of aesthetic and moral authority to women simply provides some interesting observations on local cultural history. The evolving relationship

---

7   See, among others, Barbara Welter, "The Cult of True Womanhood," *American Quarterly,* 18 (1968), 151-74; Nancy Cott, *The Bonds of Womanhood* (New Haven, 1979); also Joan Burstyn, *Victorian Education and the Ideal of Womanhood* (London, 1980).

between women and literature, for example, helps explain the emergence of
Grizelda Tonge, Sarah Herbert and Margaret Desbrisay (all young women poets
who died early) as cultural icons in the literature of nineteenth-century Maritime
Canada. It also helps explain the inclination that women poets show for religious
and moralistic verse, and it provides an interesting slant on Joseph Howe's
unwittingly sexist remark on the progression of his career from poet to politician:
"Politics was the termagant matron to whom we were married — Poetry was our
first love for whom we have ever since kept a corner of our heart."[8] And yet,
although Howe went on to pursue his political/masculine destiny logically and
single-mindedly, he recognized the importance of imaginative literature in the
evolution of his society. In a telling statement he notes: "But for the poetic spirit,
pervading and permeating through our very existence, by this time we should have
been a savage — or a dead, dull clod of the political valley, without as much
vitality as a turnip."[9] The early poets of Maritime Canada, particularly those that
dealt with the sentiments of affection, worked to insure that the history of Maritime Canada would turn out to be something more than a history of turnips.

---

8   Joseph Howe, "[Editorial:] Night Thoughts with the Muses, No. 1," *Novascotian* (Halifax),
     26 May 1845.

9   *Ibid.*

The Musical Traditions of the Planters
and
"Mary Miller Her Book"

Nancy F. Vogan
Department of Music
Mount Allison University

(The presentation of this topic at the conference included a live performance by Mount Allison University students dressed in period costume. They performed the following selections: *Public Worship* from *Urania*, James Lyon, (Philadelphia, 1761); Southwell, two versions lined out in "the old way of singing"; *Singing School* from Stephen Humbert, ed., *Union Harmony* (Saint John, 1816); *French* and *Hundred Psalm Tune* from "Mary Miller Her Book." Colored slides of "Mary Miller Her Book" were also shown.)

Singing schools represent one of the earliest musical activities of the Planter settlers. Many of these settlers were familiar with the singing school movement in New England and brought this tradition with them to their new home. Helmut Kallmann maintains that in the area that is now Canada, "singing schools appear to have flourished most strongly in the Maritimes."[1] In speaking of the work of the early singing school teachers, or singing masters as they were then known, Margaret Filshie states: "As a result of their work an Anglo-American music culture developed in British North America" which "would play an important role in religious worship in the Maritimes and in the Canadas during the pre-Confederation period."[2] Several sources provide accounts of these schools prior to 1800. In addition to work by Kallmann and Filshie, articles by the late Phyllis Blakeley,[3] and Dorothy Farquharson's[4] study of the singing school movement in Canada are noteworthy. The diary of Simeon Perkins is an especially rich primary source documenting the Planter experience of singing schools.[5] The tradition of holding singing schools continued throughout the nineteenth century and into the early twentieth century in many part of the Maritime region, primarily in rural areas.

---

1   Helmut Kallmann, *A History of Music in Canada 1534-1914* (Toronto, 1960), 53.

2   Margaret A. Filshie, "Sacred Harmonies: the Congregational Voice in Canadian Protestant Worship, 1750-1850," *Religion/Culture: Comparative Canadian Studies*, *Canadian Issues*, VII (Ottawa, 1985), 288. See also Margaret A. Filshie, " 'Redeeming Love Shall Be Our Song': Hymns of the First Great Awakening in Nova Scotia," MA thesis, Queen's University 1983.

3   Phyllis Blakeley, "Music in Nova Scotia, 1605-1867," *Dalhousie Review*, 31 (Summer and Autumn 1951), 94-103.

4   Dorothy H. Farquharson, *O For a Thousand Tongues to Sing: A History of Singing Schools in Early Canada* (Waterdown, Ont. 1983).

5   *The Diary of Simeon Perkins*, Harold Adams Innis *et al.*, eds., 5 Vols. (Toronto, 1948-78).

From "Mary Miller Her Book," Courtesy of the Colchester Historical Museum, Truro, Nova Scotia.

Singing schools were traditionally held in the fall and winter months for two or three nights per week from five or six o'clock to eight o'clock in the evening. They usually lasted for about three months and at the end of that period a special presentation was made by the pupils under the guidance of the singing master. It seems that most, if not all, of these singing teachers were male and little information is known about most of them. As Dorothy Farquharson states: "These men are hard to trace because in most cases they wandered from place to place, and in county directories or assessment rolls were never listed as singing school teachers because this was a wintertime sideline to some other seasonal occupation."[6] The theory of itinerancy in New England has been challenged more recently by Nym Cooke who maintains: "It is now clear that scores — perhaps hundreds — of singing masters never left their home towns to teach."[7]

Initially a reform movement in both Britain and North America, singing schools began in the early 1700s as an attempt by the clergy to teach note reading to the members of their congregations. They represent an attempt to improve "the old way of singing," an ornamented folk style of singing which often bore little

---

6 Farquharson, *O For a Thousand Tongues*, 15.
7 Nym Cooke, "Itinerant Yankee Singing Masters in the Eighteenth Century," *Itinerancy in New England and New York*, Annual Proceedings of the Dublin Seminar for New England Folklife, 1984, 16.

From "Mary Miller Her Book," Courtesy of the Colchester Historical Museum, Truro, Nova Scotia.

resemblance to the original psalm tune.[8] Several reformed-minded members of the clergy were active in the singing school movement and published their own tunebooks. Such tunebooks began to appear in the American colonies around 1710. Examples include *The Grounds and Rules of Music Explained or An Introduction to the Singing of Music by Note* by the Reverend Thomas Walter and *A Very Plain and Easy Introduction to the Singing of Psalm Tunes* by the Reverend John Tufts, both published in Boston in 1721.

By the 1760s the singing school movement had expanded and become more diversified and the tunebooks began to carry more elaborate music than the rather stolid psalm tunes from the seventeenth-century British sources. One such volume was *Urania*, compiled by James Lyon and published in Philadelphia in 1761.[9] It is generally considered the first major tunebook collection published in the United States; many new works were included and most selections were arranged for four voices rather than two or three as had previously been the case.

James Lyon was born in Newark, New Jersey, in 1735. He received an AB degree from the College of New Jersey (Princeton) in 1759; a composition by Lyon was performed at his commencement; he also composed the music used at

8   For a detailed discussion of this topic see Nicholas Temperley, "The Old Way of Singing: Its Origins and Development," *Journal of the American Musicological Society*, XXXIV, 3 (Fall 1981), 511-44.

9   James Lyon, *Urania: A Choice Collection of Psalm-Tunes, Anthems and Hymns* (Philadelphia, 1761). Reprinted by Da Capo Press with a new preface by musicologist Richard Crawford, 1974.

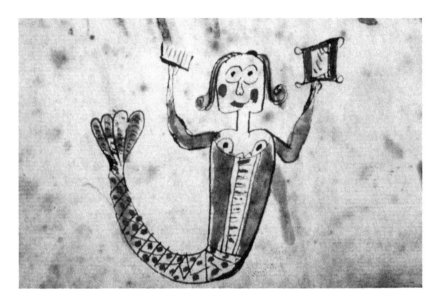

From "Mary Miller Her Book," Courtesy of the Colchester Historical Museum, Truro, Nova Scotia.

his MA commencement in 1762. While in Philadelphia he taught a singing school; presumably he used the material in *Urania*. After ordination as a Presbyterian minister he travelled to Nova Scotia where he spent a short time in Halifax and then accepted a charge in Onslow. He subsequently moved to Machias, Maine. Although it seems that Lyon was not involved in music as a professional after he left Philadelphia, he did maintain his interest in music. A visitor to Machias remarked: "I met with that great master of music, Mr. Lyon. — He sung at my request, & sings with his usual softness and accuracy — He is about publishing a new Book of Tunes which are to be chiefly of his own composition." [10] According to Crawford,[11] this book of tunes was not published. Lyon's experience with singing schools in Philadelphia suggests that he may have engaged in similar activities in Nova Scotia but we have no documentation of such activity, and no copies of *Urania* have, to date, been found in the province.

Singing schools gradually developed into social institutions at which secular as well as sacred music was taught and performed. They became an integral part of community life, especially as a place to meet members of the opposite sex, for as Farquharson notes, "Chaperones were not deemed necessary since after all

---

10 Quotation from the "Journals and Letters" of Philip Vickers Fithian (Princeton, N.J., 1900) quoted in Oscar G.T. Sonneck, *Francis Hopkinson and James Lyon* (New York, 1967), 186 and Crawford, Preface to *Urania*, ii.

11 Crawford, Preface to *Urania*, ii.

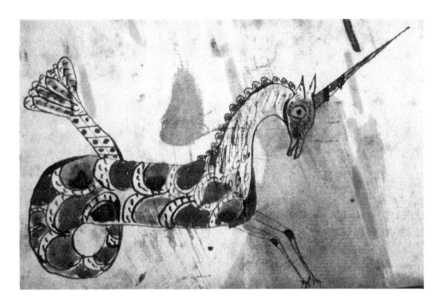

From "Mary Miller Her Book," Courtesy of the Colchester Historical Museum, Truro, Nova Scotia.

you were going to learn to sing sacred music!''[12] Many of the teachers compiled their own tunebooks which they then sold to their pupils. Such was the case with New Jersey Loyalist Stephen Humbert who opened a Sacred Vocal Music School in Saint John in 1791 and published Union Harmony a decade later. No copies of the 1801 edition have been found, but the 1816 and subsequent editions include secular as well as sacred works, including the more elaborate fuguing tunes which became popular in singing schools.

One of the earliest examples of music in the Maritime region and one which may be connected with a singing school and with the Planters is a small hand-copied music notebook located in the Colchester Historical Museum in Truro. "Mary Miller Her Book," is inscribed on the flyleaf corner as well as the date "1766." It contains thirteen psalm tunes. Nine of the tunes are in two parts (melody and bass); the other four have only the melody line. The titles of the tunes are included: *French, London, York, Dundee, Elgin, Martyrs, Dublin, Hundred Psalm Tune, Abbys, Davids, Newtown, Marys,* and *Southwell.* The tunes are written on five-line staves in fasola notation, a method of solmization used in England and later in North America. No texts are given for the psalm tunes but the titles are decorated and a number of child-like coloured drawings are included. This book is similar to those used for singing schools in that two pages at the front are devoted to theoretical aspects of music and the fasola notational system.

---

12   Farquharson, *O For a Thousand Tongues to Sing*, 15.

This four-note fasola notational system which uses mi for the seventh degree of the major scale is sometimes referred to as English, Lancashire, or four-note sol-fa. The letters f s l and m are placed on the appropriate lines and spaces of the staff. It later developed into the shaped-note system which is still used in some parts of the United States. This type of notation was used by the Reverend Tufts in *A Very Plain and Easy Introduction to the Singing of Psalm Tunes* (Boston 1721 and many later editions); another version of this notation system with the letters written below noteheads on the staff was used in the 1698 Bay Psalm Book supplement with tunes. Although each of these publications contains some of the items which appear in the Miller book, neither of these publications includes all thirteen tunes.

Musicologist Nicholas Temperley has checked the versions of the Miller book tunes in the Hymn Tune Index which he has developed at the University of Illinois. In this project, "all printed sources of tunes associated with English-language hymns, wherever published, from the Reformation to the year 1820"[13] have been indexed and entered into a computer program which then allows one to check the sources of these tunes by entering the melody in a special coded form. All the tunes in Mary Miller's book appear in this index; they are all Scottish in origin and all except *Southwell* are in common metre. However, as yet it has not been possible to identify a single publication containing these thirteen tunes, so it is assumed that they were copied from several different sources.

There is no acquisition history on this item at the Colchester Historical Museum and a search of files of the Colchester Historical Society and several items at the Public Archives of Nova Scotia has not revealed definitive information on this particular Mary Miller. There is a Mary Miller listed in Onslow in 1770, wife of Noah Miller, but further information of this family has not been found. It is possible that this is the Mary Miller who owned the book. The name Samuel Miller is written inside the book in two places, one with a verse of scripture and the date 1782 and the other as Samuel Miller, Halifax. This is the only indication found thus far that the book was actually in Nova Scotia during the eighteenth century and was not imported into the province at a later date. The names John Densmore and Mary Elsie Densmore are also written in the book. The title page includes the inscription: "per me John McCl???" (McClung, McClorg, McClary?). This name has not been identified as yet; it seems that it may be the name of the teacher, but the question remains as to who did the writing, music manuscript and drawings in the book. Much work remains to be done on this fascinating little volume and it is the writer's hope that more information can be found which will provide more concrete evidence of a Planter connection. Until such time, the mystery still remains unsolved: who was Mary Miller and what is the story of "Her Book"?

---

13   Nicholas Temperley, "Stephen Humbert's *Union Harmony*, 1816," *Sing Out Glad News: Hymn Tunes in Canada* (Toronto, 1987), 58.

Planter Elections:
The First One Hundred Years

B.C. Cuthbertson
Head, Heritage, Nova Scotia Department of
Tourism and Culture

In studies of contemporary elections, the use of statistical data has become almost mandatory. For the pre-Confederation period, however, historians of Nova Scotia politics have generally used the descriptive approach, relying for the most part on newspaper reports and private correspondence. Little attempt has been made to provide a statistical underpinning to analyses of elections from the first in 1758 through to that in 1847, which ushered in responsible government and party voting. In this paper I shall attempt to produce a statistical profile for that period for those constituencies which were unquestionably Planter in population — namely, those in Hants, Kings and Queens counties, and Barrington and Yarmouth townships. By "unquestionably Planter" I mean those townships where the sole or major settlement group was New England Planter and there was no later significant settlement by another group such as the Loyalists. I have, therefore, excluded Granville and Annapolis townships because so many Loyalists settled in them; in the case of the townships of Truro and Onslow, much of their settlement was Scotch-Irish and came either directly from northern Ireland or via New Hampshire. I have included as Planter the townships of Hants County because Falmouth and Newport, though to the lesser extent Windsor, remained "Planter" throughout the period; the Loyalists of Rawdon and Douglas could only vote in the county elections and they did not become an important factor in the voting until late in the period. The freeholders in all the townships classed as Planter in this paper could vote for a single member of the legislative assembly (MLA) in each of their respective townships, and also for two members for the county in which their township was located. The dual member constituencies of Hants, Kings and Queens counties have been classed as Planter, but not those of Yarmouth and Shelburne counties; in the latter two, only the townships of Yarmouth and Barrington are included as Planter constituencies.

I will begin by comparing statistically Planter and non-Planter (that is with the remainder of the province) by occupation, religion and origin of members of the House of Assembly.[1] The most striking statistic for occupations of MLA's

---

1   The data used for comparisons in this paper comes from research completed for a larger study on Nova Scotia electoral history from representative to responsible government, 1758 to 1847. The work is planned for publication in 1992 under the title of "Bluenose MLAs and their Elections: from Representative to Responsible Government."

    Among the 19 computer fields of biographical material, compiled for each of the 436 MLAs elected in this period, are those of occupation, origin, religion and whether or not the member was resident in his constituency. This information was gathered from various sources. The most comprehensive is, of course, Shirley Elliott's *The Legislative Assembly of Nova Scotia,*

elected in Planter constituencies is the high number of merchants. Even for the early period from 1759 to 1783, 31 per cent were merchants and another 14 per cent were office holders, who were generally closely allied with the mercantile class. From 1784 through to 1847, merchants accounted for around half the MLA's elected, well above the provincial average of generally less than a third. When it came to electing lawyers, Planters fell well below the provincial average; the percentage for the period 1830 to 1847, which was the highest for any, was 14 per

1758-1983: A Biographical Directory (Halifax, 1984). Other sources included: county histories, biographical files in the Public Archives of Nova Scotia (hereafter, PANS), denominational histories, newspapers and deed and probate records. For controverted elections; that is, those where a candidate petitioned the Assembly against the election of an opponent, the Journals of the House of Assembly (hereafter, JHA) and RG 5, Series E and P in PANS are the main sources. These sources, with newspapers and family histories, proved the best in determining those elections where there was contest (right up to 1847 many were not contested, with only one candidate coming forward); the incompleteness of the documentary evidence, however, makes it impossible to be certain about the number of contested and uncontested elections. These same sources also were most useful in compiling the names of defeated candidates by constituency and by election (including by-elections) with data on their occupations and religion, etc.

The above data was then put into tables by constituency and by election and then this material was further summarized in tabular form by constituency for four separate historical periods: 1758-84; 1785-1811; 1812-30 (Brandy Election); and 1831-47 (responsible government). A sample of the latter type of table, prepared for Kings County for the period 1831-47, is given below:

CONSTITUENCY	OCCUPATION		RELIGION		ORIGIN	
Kings County	merchant	3/7	Anglican	4/7	Planter	4/9*
	lawyer	1/2	Baptist	1/3	Loyalist	1/1
	postmaster	1/1				
Horton	merchant	1/1	Baptist	1/1	Planter	2/4
	farmer	1/1	Methodist	2/4	Other	2/2
	miller	1/3	not known	1/1		
	physician	1/1				
Cornwallis	merchant	1/2	Anglican	1/2	Planter	2/5
	farmer	1/3	Baptist	1/3		

* The figures refer to the number of MLAs who as merchants 3, Anglicans 4 and Planters 4 were elected, compared to the number of times merchants 7, Anglicans 7 and Planters 9 were elected. For example, Jonathan Crane was a merchant, Methodist and Planter who was elected 8 times.

By summarizing the data in these tables for each historical period, it is possible to compare by occupation etc., in percentage terms, within differing periods and overall, the selected Planter constituencies with those of the province as a whole; although the number of MLAs from the selected Planter constituencies remained the same at 12 members from 1785 to 1847, the provincial total in the period rose from 38 to 51 to provide representation for an increasing population, mainly caused by immigration to the eastern parts of the province. A sample table with percentages for occupations is given below, with the provincial percentages bracketed:

OCCUPATIONS	1758-84		1785-1811		1812-30		1831-47	
office holders	14	(23)%	8	(8)%	nil	(2)%	nil	(1)%
merchants	31	(35)%	50	(26)%	57	(31)%	47	(39)%
farmers	30	(20)%	19	(7)%	14	(12)%	21	(19)%
lawyers	3	(3)%	10	(13)%	8	(18)%	14	(26)%
others/n/k	21	(18)%	13	(19)%	16	(37)%	17	(16)%

cent, half that of the province as a whole. Although one would expect a high number of farmers for Hants and Kings counties, this was only true for the former, where electors sent to the assembly usually twice as many farmers as merchants. But in Kings County merchants elected greatly outnumbered farmers; from 1811 to 1830, for example, freeholders in county elections, and those for the two townships of Horton and Cornwallis, elected merchants 17 times and farmers but twice. As to be expected in the non-agricultural townships of Yarmouth and Barrington and in Queens County, farmers were elected only on three occasions for the entire period from 1758 to 1847. Merchants, except for a few mariners and lawyers, dominated the electoral field throughout.

When it came to religion of members, Planters in the early period chose Congregationalists half the time, with Anglicans close to a third. For 15 per cent of the representatives elected their religious affiliation is unknown, but the likelihood of them being Congregationalist is strong and so the percentage for that faith was probably 60 per cent or more. The near complete collapse of Congregationalism in Nova Scotia, caused by the Allinite Revival and the lack of a resident ministry, cannot be better illustrated than by the fact only five Congregationalists were elected from 1785 to 1811, which was about the same number as for Methodists, Baptists or New Lights. Anglicans, however, now accounted for half the members. This figure for Anglicans dropped somewhat from 1811 to 1830, but rose again to 45 per cent from 1830 to 1847. The Baptists were by far the largest denomination in Kings County and had a substantial following in Hants, but this was not reflected in the religion of those they sent to the assembly. Of all the constituencies in these two counties, only Falmouth Township consistently elected a Baptist. In the 1844 election, with J.W. Johnston leading an informal Baptist/Tory alliance, called into being by the feuding over financial support for Acadia College and other denominational colleges, these two counties sent to the assembly five Anglicans, three Baptists and one Methodist. Even in Horton Township the Baptist William Johnston was unable to unseat Perez Benjamin, a Methodist. Similarly, as Yarmouth Caleb Cook from the hustings stated, he had entered the township election from "the duty I owe to the denomination [Baptists] with which I am connected" and as a supporter of public funding for denominational colleges.[2] He stood no chance against the sitting member Reuben Clements, a Methodist, and withdrew from the contest when the poll stood 305 for his opponent and only 30 votes for himself.

If the religion of candidates seems not to have been a significant factor for Planter electors, neither was the origin of those who sought a seat in the assembly. Non-Planters were elected in Planter constituencies well over 50 per cent of the time from 1759 through to the end of the Napoleonic War. About half of these were non-residents who were elected in the years of initial settlement when the practice was to send to the assembly Halifax natives, mostly merchants or office holders. After the assembly decided to pay members and communications

2 *The Yarmouth Herald*, 29 November 1843.

improved somewhat, the non-residence percentage dropped dramatically below the prevailing provincial average. William Blowers Bliss, who took one of two Hants County seats in 1830, was the only non-resident elected in a Planter constituency from 1830 to 1847. Still, in this period freeholders sent non-Planters to the assembly in 40 per cent of the elections held. An important reason for this result was the number of Loyalists who settled in Planter townships and rose to political prominence; freeholders elected MLA's of Loyalists origin in about 25 per cent of the elections held between 1785 to 1847. Loyalist members were, however, concentrated in Hants County, with such notables as Henry Goudge, L.M. Wilkins and James D. Fraser, and in Barrington; in the latter the Sargent and Homer families between them completely controlled the township from 1793 through to 1847. For Kings County only two Loyalists, William Baxter and Samuel Leonard, ever found favour with the electorate, though Daniel Moore, a son of a Loyalist, born in Canning, won a seat in 1847.

How seriously did Planters take their politics? There are three interrelated types of statistical data that can assist us in arriving at some conclusions about this question: the number of elections that we know were contested, the number of disputed or controverted elections, and, the most tenuous of all, the percentage of eligible freeholders that voted. Any answers to these questions must be leavened by the knowledge of how elections were conducted. Open voting, the failure to move the poll so that more people could vote without having to travel great distances, and the drunkenness and riotous behaviour that increasingly accompanied voting, all greatly mitigated against contested elections and voter turnout. The effects of these factors varied considerably from constituency to constituency. The smaller the electorate, the more likely that only one candidate would be nominated by general agreement. In the case of Falmouth Township, whose electorate was never in this period to exceed 200 freeholders, Jeremiah Northrup was elected unopposed from 1785 to the 1806 election, which he won by four votes; there was not to be another contested election until 1826 when it was decided by 35 votes for William Henry Shey to 15 for John Manning. There was to be just one contested election for Queens county until 1820; then every election, except that of 1826, was to be contested until 1847. For Liverpool Township the reverse was nearly true; most elections were contested through to 1826 and after that only one candidate appeared for the succeeding elections until 1847 when, as for the county, it was a straight fight between reformer and tory. A 1790 contest in Barrington Township between two Halifax merchants resulted in such disturbance and drunkenness that the community resolved this should never happen again; only four of the next 12 elections were to be contested and even as late as 1847 John W. Homer went in unopposed. For Yarmouth Township Samuel Sheldon Poole was first elected in 1785 unopposed, again in 1793, lost in 1799, unopposed in 1806, did not run in 1811, then unopposed again for the 1818, 1820 and 1826 elections. When in 1830 he lost by 227 to 224 votes to Reuben Clements, he was able to retain his seat, though 79 years old, by convincing the assembly he had a right to it by long possession — Governor Sir James Kempt called him ''the Father of the House'' — and because Clements had been at sea and not taken the candidate's oath.[3] When Poole died five years later, Clements was elected in an unopposed by-election, and was the unanimous choice in both the 1836 and 1840 general elections; in 1844, as discussed above, he won over Caleb Cook in what was really no contest.

Poole was one of those Planters whose religious history marks them out from other Nova Scotians. A Harvard graduate, Poole failed to obtain a Congregational pulpit in New England, though after settling at Chebogue in 1774 he preached many times. In 1789 he purchased a pew in the First Baptist Church, but four years later he was listed as one of the proprietors for purchasing the first Anglican church. The 1827 census list him as a Presbyterian, but one year later the Methodist records show him as a subscriber. It is, however, certain that he withdrew from the Methodists in 1833 and went over to the Church of England in which faith he died two years later in full communion. Poole's life also mirrors the varied occupations undertaken by many of his contemporaries. Throughout he maintained a farm; at times he operated a store from which he exported moose skins to Boston, owned or was a partner in the ownership of several vessels, and in 1811 became the first principal of the Yarmouth Grammar School. His legendary performance as a justice of the peace is illustrated by the following story: ''Once when his house was broken into by a neighbour, as sole witness he lodged the information with himself, issued the warrant as Sheriff, returned it to himself, served it as constable, arrested the party, brought him to his house for examination, tried him before himself as Justice, found him guilty, convicted and sentenced him, and lodged him in his own cellar for lack of a jail.''[4]

It is perhaps no wonder that Poole was elected unopposed so many times. In Kings County there were no Pooles or Jeremiah Northrups. The county elections were lively contests from 1793 onwards; the same was largely true for both Cornwallis and Horton Townships. In all the constituencies, the preponderance as candidates of those engaged in some form of mercantile activity was certainly a major factor in the number of fiercely fought elections, and consequently disputed ones. What took place for electing the two county representatives exemplifies the mercantile influence. The Horton merchant and landowner Jonathan Crane was first elected in 1784 and again in the general election of 1785, apparently without opposition. But in 1793 five candidates — Crane, Elisha DeWolf, Benjamin Belcher, William Allen Chipman and John Allison, all merchants — battled it out, with Chipman and Allison resigning early in the face of the strength of the first three. John Allison was Crane's brother-in-law and likely ran in the hope that Crane's supporters would also vote for him; similarly with Chipman and Belcher who were natives of Cornwallis Township. Such temporary alliances or compacts, based on family connections and local loyalties, were a common feature through-

3   See G.S. Brown, *Yarmouth, Nova Scotia* (Boston, 1888), 50 and *Journals of the House of Assembly* (hereafter *JHA*), 15 November and 11 December 1830.

4   Clifford K. Shipton, *Sibley's Harvard Graduates 1768-1771*, Vol. XVII (Boston, 1975), 420.

out this period. Over 400 voted out of likely not many more than 500 eligible free-holders in the county which then included Parrsborough Township. Elisha DeWolf easily headed the poll at both Horton Courthouse and when it was moved to the Parrsborough Shore. At the final Parrsborough count for the second seat, Crane led by seven votes over Belcher and was declared elected. Belcher protested the result to the assembly, accusing Crane of splitting freeholds and making occasional voters. Crane freely admitted that he had, subsequent to the issuing of the writ, given 100-acre lots to 29 individuals who had then voted for him, but said this was legal.[5] The assembly disagreed and gave the election to Belcher.

In 1799 Crane and William Allen Chipman triumphed over Belcher, who also ran and was defeated for Cornwallis. During the 1806 election there was a spirited contest, with Crane and the merchant John Wells defeating Chipman and Joseph Allison; the latter another of Crane's brothers-in-law and one of the few farmers ever to run. Allison was the previous holder of the Horton Township seat, but, when faced with two opponents this time round, declined to be a candidate; he presumably hoped Crane's interest would be enough to give him one of the county seats. Chipman, determined to be back in the assembly, entered the 1808 Sydney County by-election and won, only to have the assembly overturn the result because the sheriff had so irregularly conducted the election. Chipman was successful in 1811 in winning Cornwallis, while his nephew Jared Chipman, a young barrister, took on Crane and Wells for the two county seats. Chipman and David Borden nearly defeated Crane and Wells, who had agreed to join their interest and act in concert. Only by Crane using his extensive land holdings to create voters was victory secured for the compact. In some cases the property descriptions were so deliberately confusing that no title was, in fact, likely transferred; in others the same premises were conveyed twice, or conditions of sale placed that meant Crane retained title.[6] The fraudulent purpose was blatantly exposed at the hustings, where Crane and his agents went about informing individuals that Crane had made over title so they could now vote. Chipman and Borden seem to have been guilty of the same practice, which is perhaps why the select committee investigating the election determined, as best it could, the number of invalid votes for each candidate and then deducted the figure from their total. This did not change the order of winning and so Crane and Wells retained their seats. About 650 freeholders voted.

For the 1818 general election, with the popular merchant Elisha DeWolf entering the race for the first time since 1793, Crane declined at the opening of the poll in favour of none other than William Allen Chipman, in the process deserting his former erstwhile colleague John Wells who, without Crane's interest, finished last.[7] Crane then turned around and won Horton Township with ease, building up such a lead initially that his two opponents resigned by the evening of the first

---

5   For petitions and declarations by the various parties, see RG 5, Series A, Vol. 4, No. 111, PANS.

6   Petition of Jared Chipman and David Brown, *JHA*, 12 February 1812.

7   *Acadian Recorder*, 4 July 1818.

day of polling. Chipman topped the poll in the 1820 election with 610 votes, by far the highest yet recorded for any one candidate. Crane threw his support to his son-in-law Sherman Denison, but still the merchant and a former member of Horton Township, Samuel Bishop, took the second seat for the county fairly easily. Crane again won Horton, with his one opponent William Hunt, a storekeeper in Kentville, declining on the second day of polling.

Hunt was the only candidate in Kings county for the whole period from 1758 through to 1847 known to have challenged the prevailing power brokers of the day. The deep depression after the Napoleonic War caused him much financial distress. His speech from the hustings in 1818 on his nomination created such a stir that it was carried in the Halifax newspapers. Hunt spoke for many when he declaimed that ''yet ... we live in this land of liberty, under a glorious constitution ... [but] we are oppressed, insulted, abused, we live in bondage.'' With peace, he said, had come no money and suits for debt: ''We see nothing, we hear nothing,'' he told the assembled freeholders, ''but LAW and LAWYERS in the House of Assembly and in the Country.''[8] By 1820 the poor man, weighed down by financial misfortune, was called a ''radical'' which he bitterly resented. He entered the county election solely as a means of once again speaking from the hustings against the evils of a system that failed to protect the virtuous in ''his sylvan labours'' from mortgages that deprived him and his offspring from the benefits of his labour.[9] In his letter to Gentlemen Freeholders he called on them to vote for those ''who are not under the controul of others, nor seeking after preferment from those in authority, Men who are not ashamed to stand for the cause of their constituents...'' and for them to make their own choice ''without being controuled by the rich and vain canvassers who are continually buzzing in our ears to their own disgrace.''[10]

No doubt Hunt had Crane foremost in his mind. Merchant, extensive land-owner, judge of the inferior court of pleas, colonel in the county militia, reputed to be the wealthiest man in the county and among the most distinguished in appearance in the province, Crane had been in the assembly since 1784, with the exception of the period of 1793 to 1799 when the house had voided his victory over Belcher. Beamish Murdoch remembered him as ''a tall, handsome man, with fluent speech and an amazing readiness of natural wit and illustrative power.''[11] Lord Dalhousie was less impressed, finding him ''a very harsh and illiberal landlord'' as well as ''one of the principal canting hypocrites'' in the assembly.[12] Crane's land holdings were certainly large, and almost entirely within Horton

8   *Ibid.*

9   *Halifax Journal*, 26 June 1820. Hunt's speech was taken down verbatim by a ''By-Stander'' on 22 June.

10 A transcript or copy, which I attribute to Hunt, is in the Chipman family papers, MG 1, Vol. 189, No. 138, PANS.

11 Beamish Murdoch, *History of Nova-Scotia or Acadia*, Vol. III (Halifax, 1867), 99.

12 Lord Dalhousie's Journal, 1817, 6 October, transcript, MG 1, Vol. 1776, PANS.

Township, and amassed in 570 different property transactions over his lifetime. Shortly after the 1830 election Crane died and his son-in-law Sherman Denison was unopposed in the resulting Horton by-election.

In 1826 the county contest again revolved around Chipman, Wells and Samuel Bishop, with the additional nomination of the highly successful Halifax merchant John Starr; Starr was in England and did not even take the candidate's oath. Initially, Wells had decided to run for Cornwallis but resigned when faced with certain defeat, blaming Chipman for not sufficiently coming to his support.[13] Wells then stood for the county; though placing last with 208 votes, he took enough away from Chipman so that Bishop won the second seat, with Starr easily leading the field with 563 votes. Chipman was not to enter the lists again, but his son Samuel, along with the son of Elisha DeWolf, also named Elisha and married to the daughter of John Starr, overwhelmed Samuel Bishop and two other candidates in the Brandy Election of 1830. When the poll opened for the 1836 election, Chipman re-offered, Thomas Andrew Strange DeWolf came forward in place of his brother Elisha, upon which Samuel Bishop withdrew and gave his support to young DeWolf; for the first time since 1820 two farmers, Augustus Tupper and Joseph Crane, grandson of Jonathan, stood as candidates. Chipman led the poll with 791 votes, followed by DeWolf with 545, while Crane managed 355 and Tupper a mere 116 votes before both resigned.

Crane then tried again in 1840, but was defeated once more by Chipman and DeWolf. A new entrant was the lawyer John Clarke Hall, who, when he stood again in the 1843 general election, was successful in dethroning Chipman, though DeWolf easily led the poll with 629 votes. Party lines were not yet so clearly drawn that those who voted for DeWolf would give their second vote to his fellow conservative Hall. Either many voted only for DeWolf — such votes were called "plumpers" — or divided their second vote on the basis of personal preference, for Hall obtained only 387 and Chipman 298 votes; the total of the two was just over DeWolf's count. One reason for Chipman's dramatic reversal of electoral fortunes seems to have been a feeling that "Sam must go" and with him the control the Chipman family held over numerous offices in the county.[14] As a merchant, with an expanding interest in shipping, Chipman had not been backward in the use of "ledger influence" to maintain his electoral ascendancy; during the election a supporter of his boasted that his "Ledger shall go the whole hog."[15] By the 1847 election Chipman's influence was further reduced by his father's death in 1845, leaving insufficient real and personal property to cover the liabilities on the estate. As a result there was a probate court order requiring the collection of debts owed to William Allen Chipman by 223 individuals whose indebtedness could no longer be used by the family to make votes, as the expression went.[16]

---

13 See William Allen Chipman to S.G.W. Archibald, 24 June 1826, MG 1, Vol. 89, No. 61, PANS.

14 "Nimrod," King's County, 13 November 1842 [*sic*], *The Times*, 15 December 1843, 374.

15 *Ibid.*

16 Kings County Probate Records, Estate of W.A. Chipman.

Chipman, with Edward Borden, led the reformers in 1847, only to go down to defeat again before the conservatives John Clarke Hall and Daniel Moore, a rising merchant of Kentville.

From 1784 through to 1847, a total of 63 years or 126 member-of-assembly years, Jonathan Crane, William Allen Chipman and son Samuel, with Elisha DeWolf and sons Elisha and Thomas Andrew combined, held seats for 86 of those member-years. Such an ascendancy in Planter townships was not unique to Kings County; in Queens County, except for the period 1820-26, there was always to be a member of the interconnected Collins, Barss and Taylor families elected for at least one of the three seats for the county and Liverpool Township. The other dominant family connection was that of the wealthy merchant Joseph Freeman — (at his death in 1837 he was worth £21,000, mostly in money owed him) — his son Snow Parker and son-in-law James R. Dewolf. Between them they won 13 of the 18 township and county elections held from 1811 to 1847. In the case of Barrington Township the merchant John Sargent held that seat through four elections and during which he was opposed only once; at his death he was owed £7000. In both Kings and Queens counties the wealth from mercantile pursuits was a critical factor in the ascendancy held by particular families; the expense entailed in county elections virtually precluded candidates, engaged in such other occupations as farming, from contesting these seats.

It is tempting to argue that nothing separated such political contemporaries as Jonathan Crane and William Allen Chipman than simple rivalry for the social and economic benefits of being a county MLA. An examination of their voting records in the assembly, however, suggests otherwise. Crane could always be relied upon to support governors and the council in their disputes with the House over money bills, the building of Government House and requests for pensions and special grants to officials. Not so Chipman, who never faltered in his advocacy of assembly rights and in his opposition to further funding of Government House, though he usually voted in favour of militia funding, as did of course Crane. He and Crane agreed on increased jurisdiction for justices of the peace at the expense of that for the inferior court of pleas, though both were judges of the latter, and also the need for treasury notes. On grants for the Halifax Grammar School, Crane was supportive while Chipman was not; the reverse was the case for Pictou Academy. Interestingly, Crane was for the freeing of slaves without compensation and Chipman against this measure. Chipman, an Anglican,[17] voted in 1803 with the majority in refusing to make a £100 grant to King's College to purchase a perma-

---

17 I have classed Chipman as an Anglican because of his association with the building of first the Church of England parsonage and then particularly St. John's Church, Cornwallis. I have not found evidence of him being associated with, or supporting any other denomination, except the Church of England. On the other hand, I have not found him owning a pew at St. John's, but a George Chipman did in 1811; it was common practice for a family to own a pew and list ownership under one name. There is no record of his burial in any denominational records and he died before the 1851 census. I believe that at least until the end of the first decade of the nineteenth century he was a member of St. John's, but he may well have left later in the century.

nent interest in Christ Church, Windsor. Crane, however, was the only non-Anglican to support the resolution. At the time he was probably at least nominally a Presbyterian. Because of his wife's, and her family the Allison's, strong adherence to Methodism, he contributed liberally to that denomination, though apparently he never united with them until he had a death bed conversion.[18] Although from 1800 to 1806 the court and country parties were never more than loose and shifting alliances, there was a semblance of party voting. William Cottham Tonge was the nominal leader of the country party and Chipman voted the same way as Tonge 34 times out of the 54 recorded votes in which Tonge participated; only George Oxley and S.B. Robie did so more than Chipman. In contrast, no member in those years voted opposite to that of Tonge on more occasions than did Crane.

The most distinctive characteristic of Planter electoral history is the extent that single individuals, generally merchants and often as members of local family compacts, were able to exert such a high degree of political influence and for such lengthy periods. This was especially true for Kings and Queens counties, Barrington and Yarmouth townships, but less so for Hants County. In the case of Hants County there was greater diversity in origin — Planters, Loyalists, Irish and Scottish — and this may have mitigated against particular families gaining an electoral ascendancy; an exception has to be Jeremish Northrup of Falmouth who was opposed just once in five elections during the 34 years he sat in the assembly. Moreover, only one merchant, Benjamin DeWolf, was able to exercise the same degree of ''ledger influence'' as Jonathan Crane or the Chipman family. At DeWolf's death in 1819 over 400 individuals owed him a total of £43,384; included among these debtors were such former and present MLA's as W.H.O. Haliburton for £1221, Shubael Dimock for £356, Jeremiah Northrup (his estate) for £576 and William Young of Falmouth for £150. The record for greatest longevity must go to S.S. Poole and his 41 year electoral reign over Yarmouth township; although Poole engaged in mercantile pursuits he was never a merchant of the Chipman or DeWolf class. Yarmouth was one of the very few constituencies, Planter or otherwise, where neither merchants nor lawyers played any significant political role.

Another distinguishing feature of Planter electoral history was the separation of religion from political life. Only in the 1844 election did religion become a factor and then it failed as an issue to result in any significant voting along religious lines. The reasons for this situation may lie partly in a more tolerant religious culture than elsewhere in the province, and where the very multiplicity of

---

18 Matthew Richey records in his *A Memoir of the late Rev. William Black...* (Halifax, 1839), 179: ''How deeply is it to be regretted, that characters so estimable ... should live short of the reception and profession of that faith which worketh by love and purifieth the heart. Short of it, however, through the mercy of God, Mr. Crane did not die. In his last affliction he was led to seek God with the whole heart.'' I have classed Crane as a Methodist, though he was apparently not a member until his death bed repentance; it is possible that earlier he was Presbyterian, as I suggest in the text, or possibly an Anglican, or of no denomination.

faiths worked against any special alliance between party and a denomination. The separation of religion from politics certainly was a major contributing factor in the general lack of violence accompanying Planter elections; the worst outbreaks of violence were in Pictou County and Cape Breton Island and can be directly related to religious divisions. Another important contribution was the high number of uncontested elections; itself a result of the desire to avoid the expense and disturbances of elections.

All these factors, taken together and when viewed over nearly one hundred years of Planter electoral history, strongly suggest a conservative, though tolerant political culture, open to arguments for reform, but completely closed to any suggestion of radicalism. In the election of 1847 on the issue of responsible government and reform, and the first clearly fought along party lines, Planters predictably elected eight conservatives and six reformers, with conservatives succeeding where merchants and local family compacts still exercised a pervasive control.

Future Directions in Planter Studies

James E. Candow
Project Historian
Canadian Parks Service

At the first Planter Studies Conference, Brian Cuthbertson urged us to leave the eighteenth century and the New Lights behind, and to carry Planter Studies forward into the nineteenth century. Brian has taken up his own gauntlet with his paper on the first one hundred years of elections in Planter townships. However, except for Brian's work, and that of a handful of others, this conference has largely maintained the eighteenth century focus of the first. I do not have any great problem with that, but I do feel that until Planter Studies are carried into the nineteenth century, and well in the nineteenth century, we will not be able to understand fully the Planter impact on Nova Scotian society.

Today I would like to suggest one possible framework for the study of Planter political culture in the nineteenth century. Thanks to the work of George Rawlyk, we are all by now familiar with the profound religious conversion which the Planters experienced during the Great Awakening. But it seems to me that by the mid-nineteenth century, the Planters had also undergone a profound political conversion.

In an important article written in 1933, D.C. Harvey traced the demise of the New England form of township government in Nova Scotia.[1] The Planters had arrived believing that township government, with its emphasis on local autonomy, would prevail in their new home. However, by the end of the 1760s, the central government at Halifax had thoroughly emaciated township power. This, of course, caused bitterness and resentment in the Planter townships.

After 1783 the Loyalists joined the struggle against Halifax since, as Neil MacKinnon has pointed out, Loyalists and Planters had a good deal in common.[2] But with the exception of Cottnam Tonge's short-lived "country party," the Halifax family compact, through the Governor's Council, remained firmly in control of Nova Scotian affairs.

A genuine reform party did not finally emerge until the 1830s. Joseph Howe, the son of a Loyalist, soon cornered the reform party's leadership. Surprisingly, political leadership of the Planters, or at least of Baptist Planters, fell not to one of their own, but to Halifax businessman J.W. Johnston, a Loyalist who had converted to the Baptist faith in the 1820s.

Unlike Howe, Johnston was politically conservative. When the reformers sought the withdrawal of provincial support for denominational colleges, John-

---

1 D.C. Harvey, "The Struggle for the New England Form of Township Government in Nova Scotia," *Canadian Historical Association Report* (1933), 15-22.

2 Neil MacKinnon, *This Unfriendly Soil: The Loyalist Experience in Nova Scotia 1783-1791* (Kingston, 1986), 105-106.

ston and Baptist religious leaders were galvanized into action against Howe. In so doing they allied themselves with the Halifax Tory establishment, with whom they eventually opposed the introduction of responsible government. All this was a long way from the democratic ideals that the Planters had brought to Nova Scotia in the 1760s. It appears, then, that the Planters had indeed undergone a political conversion. How had this come to pass?

I would like to suggest that the Planters' political conversion was influenced by the Great Awakening. One sees in the Baptist participation in politics a recurring theme: concern for the maintenance of moral and social order. Thus, for example, during the temperance debate of the 1830s and 1840s, the Baptists again allied themselves with conservative forces. This concern for moral and social order was a legacy of the Great Awakening.

During the 1790s, a rump of New Light preachers, notably Edward and James Manning and Harris Harding, championed the cause of new dispensationism, which held that the direct relationship between the convert and God took precedence over church rules, ministerial leadership and even the Scriptures. In the ensuing chaos, preachers lost control of their congregations. By this time Halifax-based civil authorities began to fear that the extreme levelling tendencies of the New Lights were threatening not only religious order in Nova Scotia, but civil order as well. New Light ministers began to realize the need for a formal church organization to impart doctrinal and social harmony to the movement, and to allay the suspicions of civil authorities. Thus in 1800 they merged with Baptists to form the Nova Scotia Baptist Association.

Fear of anarchy, which underlay the creation of the Nova Scotia Baptist Association, appears to have coloured the Baptist sensibility. It also appears to have spilled over into the political world, perhaps explaining the emergence of some very strange political bedfellows in the 1840s — strange given the Planters' pre-1760 political background.

Here, of course, we are on *terra incognita,* so we must tread carefully. Barry Moody claims that Johnston and a core group of other Anglican converts to the Baptist faith engineered the crisis atmosphere over education in order to derail Howe and to further their own political ambitions.[3] Although Baptist clerics certainly fell in behind Johnston, Moody concludes that the Johnston clique did not have the Baptist community's broad support. He cites the 1843 general election, in which Reform candidates defeated Baptists in some key Planter ridings. Thus the historian must treat cautiously the idea of a monolithic Planter viewpoint on the education issue and, by extension, other political and social issues of the day.

I would like to see Brian Cuthbertson's analysis of elections in Planter townships extended into the latter half of the nineteenth century to see if indeed the Planter townships became bastions of Toryism. I would point out that two of the greatest politicians of Planter descent, Sir Charles Tupper and Sir Robert Borden,

---

3   Barry M. Moody, ''Joseph Howe, the Baptists and the 'College Question,''' in Wayne A. Hunt, ed., *The Proceedings of the Joseph Howe Symposium* (Sackville, N.B., 1984), 53-70.

both of whom became Prime Minister of Canada, were Tories — perhaps a coincidence, but perhaps not.

Maybe I am too far out on a limb in seeing the influence of the Great Awakening here. Perhaps nineteenth-century Planter political culture owes more to Elizabeth Mancke's concept of extreme localism, or perhaps Planter conservatism was simply a function of the rural nature of Planter society. I do not have the answers to these questions, but then that is one of the advantages of being on a future directions panel.

One last point, completely unrelated to what I have just said. The Second Planter Studies Conference is now behind us, and we have yet to see a single paper on the role of women in Planter society. Hopefully, by the time of the next conference, somebody will have begun to do something about that.

Carman Carroll
Provincial Archivist
Public Archives of Nova Scotia

I appreciate the opportunity to say a few words at the close of this conference on "Future Directions." First, let me congratulate the organizing committee on this conference; it has been a marvellous conference all the way around. I am particularly impressed with the speakers that we have heard and we all should congratulate those who organized this conference for the work that they have done on our behalf. We have had an amazing number of people attend as we can see even on Sunday morning. My usual experience at conferences is that people tend to go away after a few sessions. That certainly has not happened at this one.

I am not going to talk about archival sources; Barry Cahill did that very adequately a few years ago. I am not going to talk about H.H. Stevens and the Reconstruction Party and try to relate them to Planters or discuss my experience with the Mackenzie King diaries and the Planters. Planters was probably the only topic that Mackenzie King did not talk about! But I will say a few words about Planters Conferences and things archival in the next few minutes.

My first recommendation is that we continue the current format of a multidisciplinary approach in the study of the Planters. In my estimation this is one of the strong points of this conference. We have heard people from so many disciplines — professional, amateur, probably paid and unpaid as well — covering so many occupational areas — university, government, private sector and the community at large — which again I think is a real plus for this conference and a measure of the success of the organization of the conference.

My second recommendation relates to the bibliographic work that is being done on the Planters by the Planter Studies Centre. The Centre has already published an excellent bibliography and we know the very fine work that Judith Norton is doing on archival primary sources. It is absolutely critical that after the current SSHRCC grant runs out at the end of this fiscal year that this work be continued in some manner and I would urge the Planter Committee to find whatever means and methods possible to continue this work. It is unfortunately quite clear that archives can no longer do this type of very detailed work. Brian Cuthbertson made an interesting comment three years ago about the work that the Public Archives of Nova Scotia used to do; for instance, in the publishing of Nova Scotia history. For a variety of reasons over the past decade or so priorities have had to change. So we must find ways to continue bibliographic efforts — whether it is through other funding bodies, the use of volunteers, or whatever — because we all know how unfortunate it is when a first class research tool is not kept up to date.

Mentioning SSHRCC brings up a third recommendation that I would like to make. Even as we speak the Canadian Studies Research Tools program within the Social Sciences and Humanities Research Council, the body that is funding this project, is currently under internal review by SSHRCC. I would urge the Planter group and everyone individually to lobby on behalf of this program. There are no sacred cows within SSHRCC as we all know — these programs come and go. This program has been in existence for ten years and I think it is a very important one, from the bibliographic and archival point of view. There are all too few funding opportunities and I would hope that those of us in this room will lobby to keep that program going. It is difficult for archives to get hold of this money; for instance, PANS is not eligible for the program. So we need researchers to take on the responsibility of detailed bibliographic activities using the new information technology.

Another point that I would like to make about this conference is how pleased I am to see the growing use of photographs, maps, architectural plans, paintings, drawings, prints and museum objects to enhance the quality of presentations. Both from an oral presentation and a publication point of view, the use of all of these artifacts is very important. Unfortunately, archives and archivists all too often separate maps, photographs, etc. from textual material and hide them away. Hopefully with the development of descriptive standards — work that is going on now in the archival community — we will be able to make those linkages and provide better tools for all of you in the years to come. It is through this work on descriptive standards that we will be able to use automation in a much better way. It is amazing to realize that it has been fourteen years since the Public Archives of Nova Scotia published an inventory of part of its holdings and yet we simply are not in a position at this time to do that again — which brings me to the next point while I am on a lobbying mode here.

I would urge everyone to support, in whatever way possible, local archives, museums and historical societies in their efforts to collect material. There are over 50 archives in Nova Scotia and we have seen from the presentations over the past several days the wide use of material found in many of them. Many of these institutions are a one person operation — the ''lone-arranger'' as my archival colleagues call them — and I think it is very important for us not to forget the valuable sources that are in these local archives. Whether it is Acadia University Archives, the Shelburne Genealogical Society, the Queens County Museum — all

over this province we have marvellous sources, which, alas, are not documented on a nice automated system. Perhaps this group can also lobby institutions like
the National Archives of Canada to resurrect the old *Union List of Manuscripts*
and similar tools to provide those linkages between archives. Your work frank-
ly is only as good as the archival sources and other sources that you have at your
disposal.

While I am passing archival work on to other shoulders, I should also suggest
that the Planter group consider establishing an acquisitions committee — I know
that within the mandate there is that wish to have funds available for purchasing
material but I would like more thought given to this matter. I know that Judy Norton has found sources in New England and elsewhere that are valuable for us to
have in the province. We must consider the prospects of doing cooperative acquisitions work to cut down costs and to spread around some of the work and
expertise.

When I reflect on the quality of the papers that we have heard over the past few
days, it really does make what we do in our various archives and museums all
worthwhile. I congratulate all of you who have given presentations and hope that
the comments that I have made on the archival side of things will help us to move
toward ''Planters III, the next generation.''

William Godfrey
Dean of Arts and Professor of History
Mount Allison University

Esther Clark Wright would probably give these proceedings a passing grade,
despite our failure at times to ''speak up.'' I note that at the first Planters Conference she urged the participants, while learning more about the Planters, also
to consider their contemporaries: the Germans, the English, the Irish and the
Scots. This conference has succeeded admirably in widening our consideration
of Planter societies but it also has considerably enriched our understanding of the
non-Planter dimensions of pre-and post-revolutionary Nova Scotia and New Brunswick. Indeed, as happens so often in historical research, we might already not
only be adding to the broader picture but fitting into place, however tentatively,
some of the missing pieces in the Planter puzzle — what might be termed the other
side of the Planter experience.

We have been offered a delightful picture of the trials and tribulations of one
Planter, Jonathan Seccombe, and his ''gay guests from the Baytown'' which
raised questions about the upward, or downward, mobility of these new arrivals
once settled into Nova Scotia. One also wonders about the level of disillusion-
ment and disenchantment which might precipitate a movement back to what eventually became the United States. In the Chignecto area we know that there was
a considerable exodus, fortunately balanced by the Yorkshire arrival, an exodus
which threatened to make the Yankee presence merely a temporary ''Footprint(s)

in the Marsh Mud.'' Just as the extent of the Loyalist exodus from Nova Scotia has been recently considered, the Planter arrival should be balanced by this other reality of an abrupt and disappointed departure by some.

Balance of a different sort was provided by the several papers underlining the cultural diversity, the vibrant mosaic, which marked the Nova Scotia of this period. The Scots/Irish community at Truro, the consideration of German grave-stones at Lunenburg, and the reminders of a Black presence and the existence of the institution of slavery, however limited or gradually restricted, provided signs of the complexity and diversity within and beyond Planter society. Obviously much more work needs to be done before the exploitation, of such groups as Blacks and Micmacs, can be completely understood and assessed. The spectre of the Acadians looms large in this area as well and, as Naomi Griffiths will undoubtedly point out, their perception of and adjustment to the Planter presence, as well as the Planter perception of Acadians and any sense of complicity in the Acadian tragedy, remain open to the aspiring cultural/intellectual historian.

Women in history, to steal another potential Griffiths point, have only recent-ly appeared and it is interesting how several papers addressed this reality. The stimulating presentation on literacy in New England not only established the importance of this issue but underlined the emasculated position of women both within the educational sphere and the broader world. As the *Dictionary of Cana-dian Biography* biographer of Joshua Winslow, I was fascinated to see Anna Green Winslow become a centre-piece rather than a young girl used merely to explain the career and progress of her father, Joshua. Likewise in the examina-tion of land, kinship and inheritance in Granville township, it was refreshing, although somewhat disconcerting at times, to hear hints concerning the situation of widows, mothers and daughters, and the arrangements, or non-arrangements, made on their behalf.

Property, politics and prosperity, or non-prosperity, were other questions addressed in a good number of papers. The extensive land-selling and trading activities in Granville provided intriguing insights about the possible breakdown of the closed corporate community and the existence or non-existence of gener-ational controls. The presence of ''ledger management'' as a factor in political success, in even the purest of Planter constituencies, struck home. My own recent examination of the 1870s and 1880s political and economic career of a prominent Yorkshire descendant in Westmorland County graphically revealed the way in which outstanding and substantial mortgages, loans and other debts were the real key to his continuing political success. The impact of war and British military spending on the Maritime economy through this entire period and into the nineteenth century was dissected for our benefit. One would like to hear more about the Acadian expulsion as an act of economic suicide if the economic after-effects were still being felt as late as 1815. As well, the Halifax mercantile com-munity's takeover of the Bay of Fundy hinterland from the former Boston masters, during the Revolutionary War, has now been well documented. But would this change of masters be a factor worthy of separate consideration when prices, wages and other measurements are manipulated? Finally, the always difficult question of political culture reared its head all too frequently. Were the Loyalists absorbed into the existing Planter culture in Nova Scotia? Were the Planters absorbed into the Loyalist elite culture in New Brunswick? Were Planters, pioneers, Loyalists, new arrivals and original residents all both absorbed into and reshaping a North Atlantic/North American political culture?

A final balance that must be noted is that provided by the disciplines involved and the audience reached. As we listened to lectures on Planter genealogy, archaeology, literature, religion, map-making, architecture, and a particularly enjoyable and praiseworthy music presentation, the inter-disciplinary and multi-disciplinary nature of the enterprise is apparent. At the same time as we reach beyond the tools available in any single discipline, and we must continue to do so, we also reach beyond the traditional academic audience. Taking a lesson from the realization that Planter Nova Scotia can only be understood in the context of its place within and interaction with non-Planter Nova Scotia, there appears to be a real desire to present research results to an interested and very much involved non-academic community as well as to the academics. This cross-fertilization, if preserved in future programmes and guaranteed a continuing place in the future Planter Studies agenda, will further stimulate and enhance both the research underway and the impact it has on a broader society's comprehension of itself.

In conclusion, one expects a keynoter to capture the essential issues and approaches about to be discussed and this was our fortunate situation. There must be a calibration of the environmental and societal within the broader perspective, in a continental and even imperial context, if we are to understand Florida, the Lower Mississippi and even Nova Scotia. In the latter colony new strategies of survival were being devised and executed by a wide variety of individuals and groups which can be better understood by further research on promoters and people, natives, Acadians and newcomers, and a balanced, comparative, multi-disciplinary thrust could prove to be the most successful approach.

Esther Clark Wright might be pleased but John Bartlett Brebner might be turning uneasily. It could be more than an escape from his long shadow that this renaissance in Planter and Maritime Studies has unleashed. At the very least a substantial revision, at its fullest a substantial rewriting, of the Neutral Yankees may be imminent.

Naomi Griffiths
Professor of History
Carleton University

One of the things that matters a great deal to all of us is the question of craft because, while I think that most of us would wonder whether or not we know anything about truth, none of us really want to teach error and it is extraordinarily important that we get the data clear, the facts out into the open. One of the interesting things in the Planters Conferences or in conferences on the Acadians which I have attended, is that there is a great deal of presentation of what, for a better word, we can call grist. The part of these conferences where grist is brought forward is enormously important. After that we must move from the particular to the general, which is the reason we all work, whether we are amateurs or professionals (and as a woman I find that kind of distinction just about as difficult to deal with as a distinction of work which is valued as volunteer as opposed to paid labour).

The reason why we look at the individual is to find the place on which to stand. But it is a very lonely business if that is where we remain and do not find somebody who wants to talk to us about their perception of that place or our perception of the universe from that place. It seems to me that one of the things we are dealing with as historians (having got our facts straight with the help of an enormous amount of individual work) is trying to find something which can move the Braudel School — which is really very static and looks at societies in photographic non-developmental patterns — forward by looking at individuals and seeing how the individual life-cycle and life-structure takes an area and pattern and moves it to the next stage. After all, individuals shape the processes which control their lives. And if that is a difficult sentence, I mean it to be difficult. Because it seems to me that this is the problem which we face as historians. At what point is it that you are not shaped, that you are not only a person that is predetermined by environment, by talent that God gave you, by organization, but instead say this is where I want to go whatever my world, my action, my imagination can take me.

I would like to see Barry Moody's ideas on Granville moved into a larger arena by looking at the extraordinary mobility of people in the eighteenth century — refugees moving from one background and intersecting with people of other cultures and becoming part of a community which makes the environment in which they are established. I would like to see more of the type of work that has been done in the papers which dealt with the Micmac and Blacks (and unfortunately to a very minor extent here, the Acadians). I would like to see these papers drawn together and I would like the topic brought forward so that persistence of minority identity is not merely seen as a decision to preserve something, but also analyzed as a defiance of the larger community. If you say that you will remain Welsh that is stating that you will not be English and, therefore, that being English is not the measure of all things. If you say that what you are about is being Catholic, you are saying that there is an interpretation of Christianity which is not contained within the views of the particular Protestant variations. And I would like to see centred upon the Planter experience but looking at these other groups within Nova Scotia some series of papers which deals with this question of the defiance which a minority has when it establishes itself as a continuance and refuses to be assimilated to what later ages consider to have been the dominant construct for the society.

This brings one to the two final points I would like to make. One of the most interesting topics which scholars deal with is the changing interpretation of the past. I remember that Stan Mealing once said to me, happily, ''We may run out of history by knowing everything. We will never run out of historians because there will be a series of new questions which each age demands of the past.'' I would like to take that one step forward and say we create what we need as a past in order to confront what we must live with in the present. And I think an examination of the importance given to particular parts of different people's history at different stages is of enormous value. I know for example the extraordinary shadow which the deportation has thrown backwards across the Acadian experience; that much of Acadian history is written as if everybody was sitting around waiting for the deportation to occur. And yet I would contend, at least for the majority of the Acadians until those hot days in the summer of 1755, the idea of deportation was not a reality within the Acadian communities and, therefore, if you consider that there is such a thing as an Acadian before 1755, that identity must be other than something which is founded upon the events of 1755 to 1763.

A marvellous conference could be held in which scholars explored different ways in which Planters, Loyalists, Scots-Irish and Acadians have looked at particular periods in the past. We could look at the eighteenth century from 1850, 1900, 1950 and analyze, for example, what the Acadians think was the essential interpretation of eighteenth-century history in 1884 when they are struggling against Quebec nationalism and in 1954 when they fear that Anglophone nationalism is of much greater importance, and so on for the other cultural groups.

George Rawlyk
Professor of History
Queen's University

I will be very brief since I had an opportunity to say a few words last night and rather than suggesting that we must work and move into the nineteenth and twentieth centuries, I would stress that we have to know a lot more about the eighteenth century. The time has come for a bold, if preliminary, attempt at synthesis of existing Planter literature, one that deals with the uprooting process, the crossing, the settling experience, adjustment or return and then revolution. I think the return is extremely important as Bill Godfrey has pointed out. We know hundreds returned: we do not know why. And I think that would be a very good topic for someone to pursue three years from now. Perhaps a Christopher Moore-like Planter Portraits study can be considered, as we search for a new bench mark work to wrench the topic free from the Brebnerian hammerlock. I think there is enough material out there now for this synthesis to take place.

This conference appeals to me because I learn a great deal about material culture here. I learn more about material culture here at this conference than any other conference I attend and I hope that this aspect of the conference remains. The comparative dimension, as I think Bill Godfrey and John Reid have pointed out, remains very, very important. We just cannot look at the Planters in splendid isolation. We have to fit them into a Nova Scotia context, a New England context, an American context, a North American context. We also have to take into account the British centre. I have some reservations with the Gibsonian/Andrews/Jack Greene approach which looks at the region as a kind of periphery. To my mind at this stage it is probably not very valid to compare the Florida/Louisiana experience with that of Nova Scotia. I still think that the Maine/Nova Scotia comparison makes the greatest sense. We have to link the Planter experience in the 1760s and 1770s to what is going on in the areas of New England from which these people emigrated. It is a dynamic, ongoing relationship that must be addressed. We can look at Louisiana and Western Florida as well but I think that New England, in the short run, is far more manageable and historically relevant.

I see from papers presented at this conference and the conference three years ago, two important book length studies dealing with important aspects of the Nova Scotia Planter experience. We have Elizabeth Mancke's study of Liverpool and Machias (soon to be published) using this comparative approach to raise very big issues like idiosyncratic localism, how the two communities respond to the revolution, the development of key institutions and collective mindsets. Once that study is published, we will be able to respond to it within a Planter context. But I think we need to have that kind of a major study in order to have a response. Is this the exception? Is it the rule? And then we have a very different kind of study: Ernie Clarke's work on the Chegnecto area. He covers a very short period of time in 1776 but it is the prism through which he sees the evolving tensions in that community, many of the tensions to which Jim Snowdon referred in his very fine MA thesis. Because of the rich texture of Clarke's study, it will throw a great deal of light on the tensions between Planters and Yorkshiremen and it will also tell us a great deal about some of the questions that we have raised here — the role of women in the society, the role of religion and so on. And I would hope that when these two studies are out that there can be some kind of serious response to both of them.

A number of us would like to have further studies on Micmacs and Acadians and other groups and how they respond to the Planters. I would also like to see someone at the next Planter conference really challenge Bernard Bailyn's thesis that at the periphery of empire you have all sorts of manifestations of violence with Indians, British troops and convicts. It seems to me this is not happening in this part of Nova Scotia, even near Machias. And we need to challenge that assumption because it is now becoming the standard interpretation and he is wrong, I am certain. And it would be a good idea to challenge Bailyn early rather than late because volume two of his four-volume series will be published soon. I think the thesis needs to be tested and I think the Planter experience is one way of doing it.

Reference has also been made to the role of ideology other than religious ideology and I think that is a very suggestive avenue to pursue. It is important to know what is going on in Halifax because of course Halifax attracts a number of Planters. They may not be the rural Planters but there are New England settlers there. Some are ordinary yeomen, others are leaders, and we need to know a little more about how these individuals view Halifax and Nova Scotia reality. In reacting to Brebner, we must not forget the ongoing importance of Halifax and Great Britain in the Planter experience. How did official Halifax view the Planters and why? I think we have to go beyond Brebner there. We must not take Brebner for granted and really look at how governmental attitudes evolved over time.

And, finally, I suppose I should say something about religion. I have been told over and over again, let us forget about the New Lights; let us forget about religion. Religion is far too important to ignore. It may not be as important as some people suggest that it is, but I would say that it is still very central and significant. I think that we must now look at mainstream religious groups. For example, somebody should do something on Congregationalism in the 1760s and early 1770s. I would like to see somebody at the next Planter conference do something on poor, maligned Jonathan Scott. A paper on the Church of England and its attitude towards the Planters would also be helpful. It is clear to me that a number of Anglican ministers in Planter areas have a lot to say about the Planters and the kind of stereotype that emerges raises important questions.

Those are some of the areas where I think the next conference might want to go and I am suggesting two important things in conclusion: first, that the time has come for a bold synthesis for a benchmark; second, we should continue as an important part of the conference, to stress the eighteenth century because we still need to know so much more about it, in its local context but also in its richly-textured comparative context.

Graeme Wynn
Professor of Geography
University of British Columbia

This has been an uncommonly varied, interesting and cohesive conference and like everyone else on the panel I would love to be here in three years time. Although this is a future directions discussion, it seems to me that it is worth while at the beginning to take stock.

Twenty years ago I came down here from Toronto to start my own work on the Maritime region, specifically to look at the New England migrants and their agriculture on the Bay of Fundy marshlands in the wake of the Acadian expulsion. I got hooked on the region, quite obviously, but as I look back on that early experience, it does seem to me that I began my studies here on a very lonely marsh dyke. There were few other people working in the field.

There *were* some other students doing theses but I neither met many people in the archives nor was I referred to others who were working on allied topics in the period that we have spent two days (and twenty Nova Scotia papers) considering. The new documentary discoveries revealed in this conference are enormously exciting. Nancy Vogan's little music book, some of the maps that Joan Dawson has turned up, David Bell's diary of Zeba Pope, Judith Norton's newly documented records in New England — all of these things really are testimony to the amount of new work that is being done, and from which so much more is becoming known.

I also feel, in company with other people on this panel, that one of the real attributes of work in this area is its interdisciplinary character. It makes for enormously stimulating conferences and it also means that we are continually revitalized by new people moving into the area, bringing their perspectives and their training from different disciplines. Consider, for instance, the range of topics covered by Bill Wicken, Don Desserud and Richard Field, each of whom has contributed a good deal to our developing understanding of Planter Nova Scotia. Moreover, it seems to me that there is a great deal of cumulative potential in this varied, multi-disciplinary work.

George Rawlyk has called for synthesis, and I certainly think that we should strive to achieve that. But as I listened to the papers over the last two days, it seemed to me that we still have some distance to go to reach that goal. One of the concerns that I had in the back of my mind when I first surveyed the program for this conference was that the very notion of "Planter Studies" might create a tendency to focus inquiry so narrowly, to blinker the view so, that people would hook on to the Planters and ignore other things that were developing in and around Nova Scotia at the same time. Almost inevitably the individual research projects of which we have heard in this conference are very tightly focused. Yet I think it is remarkable that we have not rarefied the Planters to the degree I feared. Quite clearly, this conference has dealt with people who fall beyond the traditional description of Planters but who were cohabitants of Nova Scotia with those people. I think, too, that we should remember the observation that some of us heard when we took tea with Mrs. Trask. In the view of Mrs. Trask and her neighbours, "Planter" was an unfamiliar word. Down in Yarmouth, "Yankees" was the term that people used to describe themselves. These little signs warn us against the dangers of thinking too monolithically about what I take to have been a very diverse group. As Naomi Griffith has suggested, we should not interpret the Planters as possessing a particular, uniform identity despite the fact we now look back at them as a group who were here before the Loyalists, who came in the wake of the Acadians, and who thus seem to fit together in a nice package.

Because I favour the quest for synthesis and because I see the work we have heard about in the last two days as potentially cumulative, I think that John Reid's suggestions on the opening day were very useful. He outlined some possibilities for designing and building a kind of "synthetic temple" from the bricks of individual studies. But I want to be a little more specific in suggesting some of the "future directions," and the type of work, that I would like to see in the next little while. Here I am going to talk unashamedly about building walls rather than designing temples.

If I had a willing student who was extremely able but had no idea about a thesis topic (an unlikely combination, admittedly), I would probably say to that student, "Take yourself off to New England and conduct a detailed study of one of the townships from which a large group of Planters came. It might be Lebanon, Connecticut, or any one of a number of places down there where the records are good — we stand a chance of identifying that place now through Judith's work — but it would have to be a place where we could begin to see who these "Planter" people were before they became Nova Scotian Planters, and where they stood in their New England communities. There was some discussion, earlier, about whether the Planters "came down" in social standing in terms of housing, in terms of economic well-being, when they came to Nova Scotia. But we do not really know. We can look at the big houses in Massachusetts and we can ascertain the evidence of small houses here, but we have not yet moved to the point of linking in clear and direct ways those who came — the Planters — to the settings and societies in which they grew up. Of course we could go beyond the big house/little house issue in many ways, and I think we should. Because I believe that by looking at the "hearth areas" of our Planters in more detail we could address a whole series of questions about what motivated them to come to Nova Scotia and thus understand them better when we examine them here.

My other suggestions about future directions are far less specific but I would identify three relatively broad issues that I think warrant some attention. I'll call these, in shorthand fashion, the question of competency, the issue of power and the matter of social order. Let me say something about each of them in turn.

Competency is a notion that has been receiving a fair amount of attention in literature from New England and elsewhere, and I use it as an umbrella term to suggest that we need to come to grips with the motivations, the world views and the aspirations of our Planters. It does seem clear to me that the people who formed this group were neither backward, blinkered peasants or latent John D. Rockefellers. They were not completely divorced and isolated from the market. Barry Moody showed us that they traded in land in Granville, a phenomenon that has been demonstrated in other townships. They clearly were connected into commercial activity. Yet I cannot conceive of them as thoroughly accumulative individuals in the nature of late twentieth-century capitalists.

I think it likely that the Planters came here with the aim of trying to establish independence; that they came to satisfy relatively limited human needs, the human needs of individual families; and that they were not endlessly acquisitive in the way in which they acted. Although they sought to satisfy such needs as independence by acquiring land, I think we need to sort out just what the purpose of that acquisition was, how far it went, whether the people who did accumulate enormous quantities of land perceived the possibilities of windfall profits from speculation, and whether they were unusual in their acquisitiveness. There is a big literature out there on this topic and some of its points can be brought to bear on the motivations of the Planters.

My second thematic point is this question of power. Again we have heard people talk around this issue at the conference. Their comments have indeed sharpened my sense that we need to address this issue a little more fully and in a variety of ways. Power, it seems to me, is exercised at all sorts of levels and impinges on the lives of individuals in thousands of ways. We can see the issue of political power, administrative power, Halifax vs. Liverpool, the metropolis vs. the outports, and we can, then, begin to suggest that power could be exercised in countless ways. For instance, Statutes were passed in Halifax, but how were they implemented locally? We need to pay a little more attention — and I know that the documentation to address this issue exists — to the ways in which local justices combined their theoretical responsibilities to the crown and allegiance to Halifax with the fact that they had to live in these small, tight communities, and administer law that was often unpopular.

Let me simply say a couple of things about the question of social order because I think it is related. Again in the wider literature of New England, there is some, emerging, discussion (picking up on British scholarship) about the moral economy. I wonder sometimes about the extent to which we can expect to find a moral economy in Nova Scotia, or indeed in New England, that is anything like as strongly developed as in tradition-bound England. A moral economy could emerge in Britain because practices had been followed, as it were, from time immemorial. But if we do not expect to find such a fully developed sense of what was appropriate and moral in the Nova Scotian context, it does seem to me that there must have been, at some lower level, an appreciation of the bounds that could not be transgressed. Clearly there were tensions within households and within communities, among people and among groups, and these were resolved somehow. And that is an area that I think we need to know a little more about.

By approaching these concepts it seems to me that we are likely to strip away some of the myths of wealth and harmony among the Planters. By doing that we might well reveal them as people who often had harsh lives, who struggled and who quarrelled but who were resilient and capable people who were able despite it all (as Nancy Vogan reminded us last afternoon) to lift their voices in song.

George Rawlyk:
Planter Scholar

This is a real honour for me. When I received a telephone call informing me about the award I thought somebody was joking. As many of you know I had a very high regard for Esther Clark Wright. I feel that she was a historian without honour in her own country, not necessarily without honour here at Acadia. It is a privilege to be a member of this exclusive club to which she belongs.

I have been fortunate in that I have received a number of rewards, most of them coming from a stable of first-rate graduate students, many of whom have in fact outdistanced their master and for this I am very, very proud. There are many dear friends here tonight, people I have known for a long time. I cannot single out all of you but if I did I would have a story about each of you. I think of Barry Moody here who for the first time yesterday complained to me in public that he had had difficulty with his comprehensives at Queen's, largely because I phoned him up the night before to baby-sit. I did not realize that he baby-sat that evening. But I thank him for it and I hope that he received the going wage — I think it was 75 cents an hour at that time, before the minimum wage was introduced in the Socialist Utopia ,now the new Jerusalem of Canada, Ontario. Some of us have been waiting in expectation for the millennium to come and, of course, it just came. Some of us did not expect the millennium to come in our lifetime but it has come and without a rapture!

I have been called many things in reviews. In one memorable review of two or three years ago I was called a fundamentalist, which surprised me and most of my friends. So be it. I remember once at Mt. Allison when I was Dean of a Residence, there was a phone call at three in the morning. I was only at the beginning of my teaching career. I was upstairs preparing lectures for the next day, of course, since I had four different preparations. My wife was teaching at Sackville High School but she got up to answer the phone. "Is Professor Rawlyk there?" "No." "Can you give him a message?" "Yes." "What's your name?" "No name." "What's the message?" "Your husband is a Republican Cromwellian bastard!" So my dear wife Mary said, "How do you spell Cromwellian?" That was my Mount Allison career. That is where I began to teach and that is where I began to think seriously about the Planters.

I look out at this gathering and I see Marie Elwood. Marie is responsible for the house we lived in in Halifax when we first moved to Dalhousie in 1963. We didn't know Marie at the time but mutual friends said that she would help us. We didn't realize at the time that she had, I think, two children, if not three, but she certainly helped us at the time and she now is part of my scholarly world because she now is in Planter Studies. I am delighted that she has joined the Planters' project in her own unique way. She has been a very, very dear friend for a long, long time. And of course there is Naomi Griffiths. We began to work in the Nova Scotia Archives together. I remember once looking out of a window at the Nova Scotia Archives with Naomi as she talked about her research on the Acadians.

George Rawlyk, Planter Scholar

I talked about my new work on Nova Scotia's Massachusetts, many, many years ago now, Naomi. I am so pleased that you are here and that you are part of the Planters project because I think you should be part of this project.

Some of us have worked hard together in the research vineyard. Often our work has not been appreciated for a variety of reasons but the Planters project shows me that serious work can indeed be done in a very, very important area of North American history. And I am honoured to be part of this project. And I'm sure that Esther Clark Wright would say the same thing; she said it, I think, three years ago. There is so much new work to be done and I see a number of young graduate students, young professors who are now in the field, working in Planter studies. For a period of two decades I tried to persuade my students at Queen's to do community studies. I said Yarmouth, Yarmouth. Do something on Yarmouth. No one was interested in Yarmouth — at Queen's. Then I said the same thing about Liverpool. I said the same thing about a variety of other communities. Eventually, of course, people would begin to work, sometimes in Baltimore, sometimes in British Columbia, sometimes at Dalhousie. And now the picture is starting to emerge and we are beginning to see the rich complexity of the Planter experience. It is so rewarding for me to see this emerging in this way in the last ten or so years.

Finally, I want to say something about another Planter scholar here, of course, who is Sam Nesdoly. Sam was part of my graduate seminar at Queen's. Margaret doesn't know anything about this, but she should know that Sam had a Planter background and he is an authority in the field and I think that perhaps three years from now he can present a paper. I am a strange kind of Planter but I, too, like many Planters, am part of the immigration process. My father was a Planter; he was a Ukrainian Planter who came to Canada in 1922 and I think I can understand something of the Planter experience in Nova Scotia in the 1760s. I assure you that I will maintain my interest in Planter Studies and I thank you very, very much for this honour which means so very much to me.